RANKING, RESOURCE AND EXCHANGE

T0370900

RANKING, RESOURCE AND EXCHANGE

ASPECTS OF THE ARCHAEOLOGY OF EARLY EUROPEAN SOCIETY

EDITED BY COLIN RENFREW
AND
STEPHEN SHENNAN

CAMBRIDGE UNIVERSITY PRESS
CAMBRIDGE
LONDON   NEW YORK   NEW ROCHELLE
MELBOURNE   SYDNEY

CAMBRIDGE UNIVERSITY PRESS
Cambridge, New York, Melbourne, Madrid, Cape Town, Singapore, São Paulo, Delhi

Cambridge University Press
The Edinburgh Building, Cambridge CB2 8RU, UK

Published in the United States of America by Cambridge University Press, New York

www.cambridge.org
Information on this title: www.cambridge.org/9780521105095

First published 1982
This digitally printed version 2009

A catalogue record for this publication is available from the British Library

Library of Congress Catalogue Card Number: 81–21611

ISBN 978-0-521-24282-0 hardback
ISBN 978-0-521-10509-5 paperback

To the memory of
David L. Clarke

CONTENTS

CONTRIBUTORS

C.J. Arnold, Department of Archaeology, University of Leeds.
Lewis R. Binford, Department of Anthropology, University of New
    Mexico, Albuquerque, New Mexico, USA.
John Bintliff, Undergraduate School of Archaeological Sciences,
    University of Bradford.
Sara Champion, Department of Archaeology, University of
    Southampton.
Timothy Champion, Department of Archaeology, University of
    Southampton.
Robert Chapman, Department of Archaeology, University of Reading.
John Collis, Department of Prehistory and Archaeology, University of
    Sheffield.
Andrew Fleming, Department of Prehistory and Archaeology,
    University of Sheffield.
Clive Gamble, Department of Archaeology, University of
    Southampton.
J. Gledhill, Department of Anthropology, University College, London.
Paul Halstead, Department of Archaeology, University of Cambridge.
Colin Haselgrove, Department of Archaeology, University of Durham.
Ian Hodder, Department of Archaeology, University of Cambridge.
Richard Hodges, Department of Prehistory and Archaeology,
    University of Sheffield.
John O'Shea, Department of Anthropology, University of Iowa, Iowa
    City, Iowa, USA.
Klavs Randsborg, Forshistorisk-Arkaeologisk Institut, University of
    Copenhagen, Denmark.
Colin Renfrew, Department of Archaeology, University of Cambridge.
M.J. Rowlands, Department of Anthropology, University College,
    London.
Stephen Shennan, Department of Archaeology, University of
    Southampton.

Susan Shennan, Department of Archaeology, University of
    Southampton.
Andrew Sherratt, Department of Antiquities, Ashmolean Museum,
    Oxford.
Robert Whallon, Department of Anthropology, University of
    Michigan, Ann Arbor, Michigan, USA.

PREFACE

Over the past fifteen years several processual studies in
the field of European archaeology have appeared. It is noteworthy however that this is the first substantial volume
taking such an approach which has set out to make Europe
the primary focus of all its contributions, and to embrace the
long time range from the period of the first farmers up to the
Middle Ages. There is a tendency, both in the United States
and in Europe, to regard processual archaeology as a purely
American invention — a view which offers a source of
chauvinistic self-congratulation to some, and a reason for
ignoring it to others. In fact Europe has enjoyed a long
tradition of ecologically based studies which has been
especially strong in Scandinavia, the Netherlands and Britain.
Many of the elements of contemporary processual archaeology can be recognised already in the writings of O.G.S.
Crawford and Gordon Childe in the 1920s, and in the subsequent development of the ecological approach. A distinctive
European tradition of 'new archaeology' has run parallel with
that in the United States from the start, most strongly in
those same three regions.

The rich archaeological data from early Europe indeed
offer potential insights into the workings of culture process
whose interest and relevance extend far beyond Europe. It
was in this belief that a symposium, focussing on the
European material and entitled 'Socio-economic change in
ranked societies', was offered to the Society for American

Archaeology, for its 45th Annual Meeting at Philadelphia. Some twenty participants crossed the Atlantic to take part in the all-day symposium, held on 1 May 1980.

The occasion proved a fruitful one, both in exposing the participants to Americanist archaeology, and in reminding the Americanists that the practice of processual archaeology is not restricted to those residing in the New World. It was decided to put together a volume, based on the theme of the symposium, with papers revised in the light of the discussions which took place both then and subsequently on much less formal occasions. All the speakers at the symposium, with the exception of Graeme Barker and Richard Bradley (whose papers were already committed for publication elsewhere) have contributed.

Robert K. Evans and Patricia Phillips respectively acted with Colin Renfrew as Chairman for the morning and afternoon sessions. Ian Hodder and Robert Whallon were discussants for the morning session and Ruth Tringham and Lewis Binford in the afternoon.

We hope that the studies presented in this volume will demonstrate to the American audience that there is indeed a distinctive European processual approach, perhaps rather more catholic in its outlook than the transatlantic version; and to the serried ranks of European traditionalists that processual archaeology can no longer be ignored.

Chapter 1

**Socio-economic change
in ranked societies**
Colin Renfrew

*The wide range of societies archaeologically docu-
mented in early Europe is first stressed, and the potential of
this rich data base for the understanding of social and economic processes of ranked societies in general is emphasised.
But what exactly is meant by 'ranking'? The limitations of
the so-called 'evolutionary' sequence of egalitarian, ranked
and stratified societies are reviewed. The available archaeological criteria which offer potential for the investigation of
different degrees of socio-economic complexity are then discussed in terms of the evidence offered by settlement studies,
by a consideration of monuments and mobilisation, and by
indications of individual status and property, notably from
funerary remains.*

*Socio-economic change and its causes are reviewed
under two broad headings: intensification of production,
whereby the potential resources of society are developed and
actualised, and interaction. It is stressed that interaction
between polities of approximately equal complexity (peer
polity interaction) is often as significant a factor in promoting change as are the more frequently discussed consequences of contacts with societies more developed economically. The significance of the societies of the early
historic period (e.g. the Anglo-Saxon kingdoms) for the
understanding of these processes, alongside the more commonly studied prehistoric cases, is underlined.*

Good archaeology, it would be agreed by all those who think of themselves as processual archaeologists, should be problem-oriented. And at first sight contemporary archaeology is just that. Many interdisciplinary expeditions have been mounted in different parts of the world to investigate for instance the origins and development of food production, and it can reasonably be claimed that the 'neolithic revolution' has been a well-defined subject of research. Much the same may be asserted for the question of the origins of the state, and the often concomitant issue of the development of urbanism. This too has given rise to well-conceived field projects in many areas.

But if 'agriculture' and 'civilisation' are both relatively well-defined concepts (at any rate until they are examined more closely), the same can scarcely be asserted for the study of those food-producing yet non-urban societies which, on any simplistic evolutionary trajectory, are conceived as lying 'between' these two. The problems are often less clear-cut and the concepts less clearly formulated for egalitarian or ranked societies, to which the term 'the state' cannot properly be applied.

In fact students of such societies have not yet succeeded in defining the issues with any great clarity. Only recently have archaeologists squarely faced the difficulties of recognising ranking on the basis of the archaeological materials, or of establishing the archaeological correlates of ranked societies (Renfrew 1974; Peebles and Kus 1977). Attention has moreover focussed rather more on the problems of demonstrating the existence of ranking than on endeavouring to explain it.

These criticisms apply with equal force, I believe, to the practice of processual archaeology upon the ranked societies of any area: certainly they are true of North America and of Europe. The situation is yet worse in regions where fully fledged state societies developed relatively early – such as Mesopotamia and Mesoamerica. Interest in these lands has often, quite naturally, focussed upon the early states. The less complex societies which preceded them are often dismissed as 'Protoliterate', or 'Protodynastic', or 'Formative', and sometimes accorded less respect than the 'Classic' or 'Dynastic' phase which frequently follows. Only a few studies (e.g. Flannery 1976) deal with the formative stage in its own right, without regarding it as merely some muted prelude already overshadowed by the splendours yet to come.

Early Europe offers a vast scope for the consideration of ranked societies. When Julius Caesar described the customs of the native inhabitants of France in his account of *The Gallic War* he was writing of a land where agriculture had been practised for nearly five thousand years without the formation, until his own time, of anything approaching the societal organisation of the state. And in the Scandinavian lands to the north it was a further millennium before such an organisation finally emerged. Caesar and the other Roman commentators, notably Tacitus, have left ethnographic accounts which are as lucid and careful as the narratives of voyagers to North America, such as Thomas Harriot in the sixteenth century AD. There are thus ample opportunities here for the study of both egalitarian and ranked societies.

Many of the problems which emerge are, however, of a significance which goes far beyond Europe.

What is ranking?
The use of the term 'ranking' in the title of this volume, or of 'ranked society' at the head of this introductory chapter, should not be taken as asserting firm adherence to any preconceived evolutionary or other typological scheme of social organisation or social structure, such as those of Service (1962) or Fried (1967). The focus of our interest is in *change* in society and economy, and in its *explanation*.

But these terms do help to focus our attention upon the wide range of societies which do not have the well-differentiated institutions of the state. Anthropological theory was for too long content to retain the old dichotomy, set out by Plato and Aristotle and followed by Hobbes, between ordered government (the state) and primitive disorder ('warre'). So it is that what remains the best general book on African political systems (Fortes and Evans Pritchard 1940) employs the same simple dichotomy between 'primitive states' and 'stateless societies'.

Service (1962) set out clearly the useful distinction between 'tribe' and 'chiefdom', and the latter in many ways remains a valid term, albeit a rather general one. The tribe has, however, been shown to be a rather inadequate general category (Cohen and Schlegel 1968), since many food-producing societies do not in fact group themselves into tribes, or display what is normally regarded as 'tribal' behaviour. This realisation underlies the present scepticism surrounding the archaeological concept of the 'culture' as a socially meaningful category (Renfrew 1978, 94; S.J. Shennan 1978). While it may still be useful for some purposes to define archaeological cultures, they can no longer be assumed to represent the material remnant of ethnic groups or tribal units. The recognition in the material culture of features characteristic of specific ethnic groups remains an interesting problem which is now being examined afresh (e.g. Hodder 1978): it is an empirical matter and not one to be dismissed by a procedure of defining taxonomic units and then calling them 'cultures'.

The recognition of ranking from the archaeological record may be little easier than detecting ethnicity, and has certainly been less carefully thought out. The root of the matter may in fact be the absence of any very clear definition of exactly what is meant by ranking, in the living ethnographic present, even before its archaeological correlates are sought in material culture. Fried (1967, 109) certainly starts clearly enough: 'A rank society is one in which positions of valued status are somehow limited, so that not all those of sufficient talent to occupy such statuses actually achieve them.' He later (1967, 186) defines a stratified society as 'one in which members of the same sex and equivalent age status do not have equal access to the basic resources that sustain life', and asserts (1967, 109) that a rank society 'may or may not be stratified'.

There are clear risks of confusion here, for many archaeologists have tended to equate state societies with stratified societies, and chiefdom societies with ranked societies. The concept, which Fried clearly entertains as meaningful, of a stratified rank society cannot be reconciled with such simplistic notions. Fried adds to our perplexity by asserting (1967, 224): 'Societies that are stratified but lack state institutions are not known to the ethnographer.' Yet most ethnographers would regard the chiefdom societies of Polynesia, for instance, as lacking state institutions, but there àre many indications that the chiefs often enjoy privileged access to basic resources.

Rank is defined by the Shorter Oxford English Dictionary as 'A class in a scale of comparison; hence relative position or status.' But it is a task for the ethnographer or archaeologist to make clear exactly what is the nature of the *variable* in terms of which individuals are being ranked. Fried refers to 'valued status', but goes on to speak of 'sufficient talent to occupy such statuses', implying apparently that talent may be a relevant factor. Both prestige and status seem in reality rather vague concepts unless it is made clear precisely how they may be measured.

The fundamental confusion here, in my view, is to define or classify *societies* (as ranked, stratified etc.) on the basis of the differential *status* of *individuals* within those societies. For although differential status is indeed of the greatest interest, so too are the institutions of the society and the processes at work within them. Hierarchy of settlement, for instance, or of organisation, may be documented archaeologically in the absence of clear indications of personal ranking — and are indeed used by Wright and Johnson (1975) to define state organisation. And great numbers of people may be mobilised for monumental works — it has been estimated that eighteen million man-hours were expended upon the British neolithic monument of Silbury Hill within the space of two years — in circumstances where personal ranking may perhaps be inferred but not necessarily documented. Surely a more fundamental question is the degree to which a society was *centrally organised*? And is it not a matter for empirical investigation, by the ethnographer as much as by the archaeologist, to determine to what extent such organisation correlates with the presence of salient personal ranking and of stratification within the society? Clearly we shall expect that in general the correlation will be a strongly positive one, but the relationships have to be explored in detail. Contemporary archaeology has in fact taken three different routes to explore ranking within society: only one of them relates to personal ranking.

1. Settlement ranking and political structure
I take here as my text (while not specifically embracing

his concepts of tribe and chiefdom) the words of Service (1962, 142) about the chiefdom: 'the society is also more complex and more organised, being particularly distinguished from tribes by the presence of centers which coordinate economic, social and religious activities'. For it is the existence of the centre, and of the *central person* who generally goes with it arìd actually does much of the coordinating, which establishes the asymmetry which is surely the crucial element of ranked societies, distinguishing them from the essentially symmetrical, mechanical solidarity of egalitarian ones.

If we wish to study organisation and complexity, it is logical to look for a spatial representation of the undoubted asymmetry which these terms imply. The most welcome indications would testify directly to the nature of the organisation — for instance in the storehouses of goods, or the craft-specialist workshops, or the palace or residence of the chief — which we might hope to document. But these can in general only be revealed through excavation, and we cannot readily excavate an entire settlement pattern. I would claim, however, that there is a very general and strong positive correlation between size and centrality. The organising centre of a polity is nearly always (with the exception of some rather recent anomalies associated generally with federal government) the largest settlement or site of that polity. Geographers rightly caution us not to confuse organisational or urban or central place functions with size as such, but the correlation remains. It has moreover been shown to apply more strongly to less highly industrialised societies, with their primate cities, than to the industrialised and urbanised nations of the twentieth-century west (Berry 1961).

At the same time, simply to plot a frequency distribution of site size, and to seek to divide settlements into size classes (conceived as corresponding to first, second and third order centres of Central Place Theory), as Johnson has done (1975), is not appropriate. Within a given region, while it remains the case that the largest site of each polity is generally its centre, the centres of smaller polities will often be smaller not only than the centres of larger polities, but than those of other non-primate sites in those larger polities also. The frequency distribution approach makes assumptions about spatial behaviour and about conformity with classical Central Place Theory which are not appropriate to a region containing several independent polities, however these assumptions may work *within* a given nation.

The problem for the archaeologist seeking to identify a pattern of centres from the archaeological record becomes one of deciding which sites or settlements are large enough to dominate (in the political sense) their smaller neighbours. It also entails deciding which are sufficiently large, and sufficiently distant from larger sites, to be able to maintain their own autonomy.

A recent paper (Renfrew and Level 1979) sets out a procedure by which these questions may be investigated. The input consists simply of the locational coordinates of sites, and of some appropriate measure of their size or scale. This may be expressed in terms of settlement area or population, but other measures are possible (such as the number of coins struck by a mint). The output is then a series of maps, showing the hypothetical political configuration, making assumptions based on those indicated above. The most important variable is the 'slope' – which is a measure of the radius of influence of a site of given size. The XTENT model will produce a different map for each slope selected. The map indicates the independent centres of the hypothetical polities, the subordinate sites, and the notional boundaries of the polities.

Naturally no model is better than the assumptions which sustain it, and several here are open to question. Yet within these limitations the model allows a transition from archaeological data set to socio-political map. It has already been used to suggest possible chiefdom territories on the basis of the size and distribution of iron age hill-forts, and the extent of urban territories (the equivalent of early states) in Mesopotamia during the Uruk period, and in early Susiana. A test run with twentieth-century Europe, using the location and population of the hundred largest cities, yields a series of interesting political maps.

This approach is simply a tool, a means of investigation, but it makes more explicit some of the procedures which have led a number of archaeologists (notably Johnson 1975; Earle 1976; Blanton 1978; Sanders, Parsons and Santley 1979; Alden 1979) to seek to reconstruct political organisation from settlement data. Nor is it necessary for settlements and sites to be urban for such treatment to be applicable, as Cunliffe (1976) has shown, and as Bintliff (this volume) demonstrates.

The key notion underlying the XTENT approach is not simply that of ranking – i.e. of relative size – but of *dominance*. For it is dominance which establishes hierarchy, which generates the different levels or strata within a system of ranking, thereby establishing it as one of stratification. The assumptions underlying such approaches must be questioned at each stage, particularly when applied to non-state societies. Indeed they should not be accepted as assumptions, but as postulates which test some of the real issues which are validly in question.

2. Monuments, mobilisation and organisation
A second approach to the social organisation of ranked societies has been through the scale and distribution of non-residential sites. Although in some cases it may be possible to relate a given monument to an individual (for example, in the case of a burial within a funerary mound), the focus of interest here is in the first instance with the scale of communal endeavour seen as a product of the society, and as a measure of social integration, rather than of personal eminence.

Such matters have been considered in south Britain (Renfrew 1973), in Ireland (Darvill 1979), in Malta (Renfrew

1974), in Hawaii (Tainter 1973), for the Mississippian (Peebles and Kus 1977), and elsewhere. In some cases a hierarchy of monuments, in terms of scale (measured for instance, in man-hours of constructional labour) can be established. The relationship between an observed ranking or hierarchy in the monuments and any organisational aspects of the society itself is of course a matter for analysis (Renfrew 1981a). There can be little doubt, however, that aspects of social organisation are monitored and in some cases these are hierarchically structured. But it certainly does not follow that such structuring can be equated directly with a hierarchy of persons or of statuses within the society: some relationship may be inferred but not a direct equivalence.

In the case of funerary monuments, further inferences may be possible about the land rights of corporate descent groups (Saxe 1970; Chapman, this volume), since one purpose of monument building can be the establishment of territorial claims in visible and durable form. The monumental funerary and ritual constructions of Europe and elsewhere are currently undergoing reassessment from this perspective by a number of workers.

Monumental works can of course have a very much more direct bearing than do tombs upon land utilisation. This has long been perceived for the major irrigation projects of the Near East. And recently several land boundaries in the landscape of south Britain have been dated back to the bronze age (Bowen 1975; Fleming 1978). Such features constitute social statements about control of, and access to, land, as well as serving more utilitarian functions such as field clearance.

Further features in the organisation of non-state societies are reflected in other monumental works: the complex pattern of roads linking the various sites at Chaco Canyon in the American south-west give indication of aspects of organisation which cannot be inferred from the study of individual sites. And of course the scale and manner of construction of fortifications, from pre-pottery neolithic Jericho or the British iron age (Cunliffe 1976) to the *burhs* of Saxon England and the cities of the Middle Ages, offer data by means of which the sites and societies in question may be ranked.

3. The ranking of individuals
Ranking, in the sense which Fried, in common with most anthropologists, uses the word, relates to the status of individuals. The individual is, however, difficult to catch in archaeological terms: so far there are two major approaches. The first is in terms of his handiwork, where stylistic variation offers the opportunity of identifying individual hands (Hill and Gunn 1977). The second approach is the obvious one of locating the individual's mortal remains. Here the various practices associated with the disposal of the dead, including the deposition of artefacts, may allow the establishment of ranking (Renfrew 1974; S. Shennan 1975; Randsborg 1974; Peebles and Kus 1977; Tainter 1978;

Shephard 1979; Wells 1980; S. Shennan, this volume; Arnold, this volume). The extent to which this ordering, established by the archaeologist on the basis of the material remains, may be related to the ranking of statuses within the society in question is always a matter for careful consideration (O'Shea 1979).

These three very different approaches illustrate that there are indeed different ways of ranking societies, and of ranking individuals within societies, ways which have in the past been too readily lumped together. The term 'ranked society', like 'chiefdom', lacks precision and hence coherence, although it remains very useful for purposes of generalisation and description. But the analysis cannot be a dynamic or explanatory one until these aspects are clarified and linked with other variables and processes.

Socio-economic change

The explanation of change is not an easy undertaking. As Whallon (this volume) reminds us, it requires the construction of theory, rather than the mere suggestion or demonstration of a correlation of variables. I have come to feel that many of the most fruitful approaches hitherto can be reduced, in effect, to the study of the effect of two processes upon social structure and upon each other, and of the influence of social structure upon both. The processes in question are the intensification of production, and the interaction between polities. The papers for this volume (and for the symposium which gave rise to it) centred upon the consideration of these two processes.

1. Resource and intensification

A decade ago, under the influence of Boserup's book (1965) *The Conditions of Agricultural Growth*, population pressure came to be regarded widely as a possible 'prime mover' in the emergence of ranked and stratified societies. Some of the most persuasive explanations for the emergence of the state thus now use population growth as the initial driving mechanism, which is seen as giving rise to the other significant changes. (Many of these are reviewed in Spooner 1972). The possible effects of population growth upon prehistoric Europe were well outlined by Sherratt (1972).

Objections have emerged, however, to the notion of demographic pressure operating, in effect, as an independent variable (Cowgill 1975; Hassan 1978). So that while carrying capacity remains a useful concept in many ways (Glassow 1978; Bayliss-Smith 1978), social attitudes and relationships within the societies in question are seen as governing, or at least significantly influencing, the demographic variables.

Agricultural intensification remains, however, a major research focus, for it is widely felt to correlate closely with social complexity (Gilman 1981). The correlation is generally assumed rather than demonstrated, but seems logical in that only through intensification can the larger population density be supported that is necessary for urban life. Intensi-

fication of agriculture is necessary also to support the craft specialists and the non-productive elite required for the differentiation of roles indispensable to complex society. Recent work on such intensifying processes as irrigation (Oates and Oates 1976), plough agriculture (Fowler 1971), and Mediterranean polyculture (Halstead and O'Shea, this volume) has made some of the relevent events clearer.

It is only very recently, however, that the social correlates of these technological advances have been systematically considered, and the social and economic implications of intensification (Bradley 1978; Bradley and Hodder 1979; Renfrew 1981b) explored more fully in relation to other aspects of society. The most promising area of exploration at the moment seems to be land use. The study of ancient field systems, as our Scandinavian colleagues (Lindquist 1974; Widgren 1979) have long realised, offers the possibility of considering farming practice in its totality. This should allow an examination of the scale of the farming group, and of the relationships between groups. The work of Fleming (1971, 1978), Wainwright, Fleming and Smith (1979), Bowen (1975), Bowen and Fowler (1978), Fowler (1971) and Bradley (1978; n.d.) is now addressing itself profitably to the relationship between farming practice, as attested on the ground, and social structure, as inferred from these and other aspects of the archaeological record.

Already for the neolithic period of Britain, consideration of the distribution of the monuments allows the formulation of models of farming practice (Barker and Webley 1978). And with the developed bronze age, and the construction or formation at that time of field boundaries, including the so-called 'Celtic fields', a mass of new evidence is available about the organisation of the land.

Much of this work is at present at an exploratory phase, and Whallon's demand for theory has not yet been effectively met. But until a decade ago, the data was so limited and so little understood that there were in reality very few observations which theory could be called upon to elucidate or to relate to each other. Theories are not possible, or at least they are not useful, in the absence of data, and progress was not feasible. It may well turn out that the data relating to land use in north-western Europe will now offer scope for important theoretical developments which will succeed in relating intensification to social structure and to ranking.

2. Exchange and peer polity interaction

The second popular 'prime mover', to be set alongside population pressure as a favourite ingredient in many current theories about the growth of complex society, is trade. Internal trade and exchange have been used by several writers who, following Service (1962), see redistribution as a fundamentally important process in ranked societies. Although the 'functionalist' view of the chief as an altruistic redistribution agent has been criticised (Earle 1977) — not least by those wishing to emphasise the repressive and exploitative nature of some ranked societies (Gilman 1981), sometimes as an exemplification of a Marxist class-struggle — the role of redistribution in the emergence of some complex societies can hardly be doubted (Halstead and O'Shea, this volume).

External trade has at times been used by exponents of the diffusion of culture in so vague a way that the explanatory content of their arguments has seemed weak. For simply to demonstrate the existence of external trade at a period of rapid change is hardly to explain that change. More specific, and hence more interesting models (Webb 1974) have been formulated in recent years, and some of them are reviewed later in this volume. Some of them may be classed as dominance models (S.J. Shennan 1982), where the exchange relations of a ranked society with a more developed state society secure for the elite of the former a whole range of sophisticated prestige goods which they can use to consolidate their social position (Frankenstein and Rowlands 1978; Wells 1980; S. Champion, this volume; Haselgrove, this volume).

Other workers (e.g. Flannery 1968) lay stress on interregional trade, which can exploit the distinction between ecological zones. This need imply no 'secondary' relationship for the society in question, since no more complex social system need be involved.

Both these are perfectly acceptable models in themselves, but in many instances they are not in practice particularly appropriate, since no inter-regional exchanges need be involved, nor any contacts with more complex societies. Yet in many cases the archaeologist working with the materials in question nonetheless feels that one of the crucial processes leading to the development of ranking or of other indications of complexity has indeed been exchange. In my own work in the Aegean, as described in the introduction to Part III, I have been led by this feeling to put forward a peer polity interaction model, where the interactions in question operate within the region, and do not involve contact with more advanced societies (Renfrew 1981b). As Shennan (S.J. Shennan 1982) has pointed out, this view is close to the 'cluster interaction' model of Price (1977). Indeed it comes close to what he has himself been arguing as an explanation for the Beaker phenomenon (Burgess and Shennan 1976).

An important feature of these models is that they lay stress as much upon the information which flows along the network between the various nodes as upon the exchange of material goods (Renfrew 1975). The effects of the interaction are therefore seen as much in stylistic uniformities or resemblances (Wobst 1977). The implications of such models, as Hodder (this volume) implies, remain to be explored. There can be no doubt, however, that they will add a new dimension to the already illuminating and influential work on early exchange in Europe (e.g. Phillips, Aspinall and Feather 1977; Sherratt 1976) which has already contributed to our understanding of prehistoric social change.

The difficulty still remains, however, that it is the *specific* social structure in each case which participates in such processes, and the response of the society to this interaction will depend very much upon the nature of that structure and on its past history. Despite the efforts in this direction by Rowlands and his co-authors (e.g. Rowlands 1980), the archaeological evidence cannot often convincingly be deployed to document the details of such features of social structure as kinship organisation, in the manner of Ekholm (1978) in her anthropological study of exchange relations in the Kongo.

Notwithstanding these undoubted limitations, one may detect in much current literature a feeling of optimism that progress is being made, and that new concepts are now being developed which will permit more adequate interpretation of much of the evidence currently available. Some of that progress will come about in Europe. For one important asset of the European case is the great time depth which it offers in the study of ranked societies.

In Britain, farming (which is, of course, the defining feature of what we still like to call the 'neolithic') begins around 4300 BC on a calibrated timescale. Evidence of ranked society, in the form of major monuments requiring a labour investment of around one million man hours (the large 'henges'), is seen around 2500 BC. Large stone or 'megalithic' tombs, which need not be interpreted as indicative of ranked society, occur at least one thousand years earlier. A widespread metal industry (defining the 'bronze age') begins by 2000 BC, and it is from this time that individual burials with distinctive prestige goods are found. The British 'iron age', which is associated with the development of a more highly ranked society, and of the hill-forts, may be said to begin around 800 or 700 BC.

The story does not end with the Roman invasion in the first century BC, consolidated in the next century with the effective imposition of a state society within the Roman empire. For Roman rule in Britain collapsed around AD 400, and the emergence and subsequent development of Anglo-Saxon society is highly relevant to our theme. That episode ends with the appearance of the later Saxon state, which is often equated (for south Britain) with the reign of King Alfred at the end of the ninth century AD. We thus have some five millennia of non-state agricultural societies to discuss. There is plenty of scope.

References

Alden, J.R. 1979. A reconstruction of Toltec period political units in the Valley of Mexico, in C. Renfrew and K.L. Cooke (eds.), *Transformations, Mathematical Approaches to Culture Change.* New York, Academic Press, 169–200.

Barker, G., and Webley D. 1978. Causewayed camps and early neolithic economies in central southern England. *Proceedings of the Prehistoric Society* 44: 161–86.

Bayliss-Smith, T.P. 1978. Maximum populations and standard populations: the carrying capacity question, in D. Green, C. Haselgrove and M. Spriggs (eds.), *Social Organisation and Settlement*. Oxford, British Archaeological Reports, 129–52.

Berry, B. 1961. City size distribution and economic development. *Economic Development and Cultural Change* 9: 573–88.

Blanton, R.E. 1978. *Monte Alban, Settlement Patterns at the Ancient Zapotec Capital*. New York, Academic Press.

Boserup, E. 1965. *The Conditions of Agricultural Growth*. Chicago, Aldine.

Bowen, H.C. 1975. Pattern and interpretation, a view of the Wessex landscape from neolithic to Roman times, in P.J. Fowler (ed.), *Recent Work in Rural Archaeology*. Bradford-on-Avon, Moonraker Press, 44–56.

Bowen, H.C., and Fowler, P.J. (eds.) 1978. *Early Land Allotment*. Oxford, British Archaeological Reports.

Bradley, R. 1978. *The Prehistoric Settlement of Britain*. London, Routledge and Kegan Paul.

Bradley, R., n.d. Prestige trade, agriculture and social change, some European examples. Paper presented at the 45th Annual Meeting of the Society for American Archaeology, Philadelphia, 1980.

Bradley, R., and Hodder, I. 1979. British prehistory, an integrated view. *Man* 14: 93–104.

Burgess, C. and Shennan, S. 1976. The beaker phenomenon, some suggestions, in C. Burgess and R. Miket (eds.), *Settlement and Economy in the Third and Second Millennia B.C.* Oxford, British Archaeological Reports, 309–31.

Cohen, R. and Schlegel, A. 1968. The tribe as a socio-political unit, a cross-cultural examination, in J. Helm (ed.), *Essays on the Problem of the Tribe*. Seattle, University of Washington Press, 120–49.

Cowgill, G.L. 1975. Population pressure as a non-explanation, in A. Swedlund (ed.), *Population Studies in Archaeology and Biological Anthropology, A Symposium* (Society for American Archaeology Memoirs 30), 127–31.

Cunliffe, B. 1976. Hill-forts and oppida in Britain, in G. Sieveking, I.H. Longworth and K.E. Wilson (eds.), *Papers in Economic and Social Archaeology*. London, Duckworth, 343–58.

Darvill, T.C. 1979. Court cairns, passage graves and social change in Ireland. *Man* 14: 311–27.

Earle, T.K. 1976. A nearest-neighbour analysis of two formative settlement systems, in K.V. Flannery (ed.), *The Early Mesoamerican Village*. New York, Academic Press, 196–223.

Earle, T.K. 1977. A reappraisal of redistribution: complex Hawaiian chiefdoms, in T.K. Earle and J.E. Ericson (eds.), *Exchange Systems in Prehistory*. New York, Academic Press, 213–32.

Ekholm, K. 1978. External exchange and the transformation of Central African social systems, in J. Friedman and M.J. Rowlands (eds.), *The Evolution of Social Systems*. London, Duckworth, 115–36.

Flannery, K.V. 1968. The Olmec and the valley of Oaxaca: a model for interregional interaction in formative times, in E.P. Benson (ed.), *Dumbarton Oaks Conference on the Olmec*. Washington, D.C., Dumbarton Oaks, 79–110.

Flannery, K.V. (ed.) 1976. *The Early Mesoamerican Village*. New York, Academic Press.

Fleming, A. 1971. Bronze age agriculture on the marginal lands of north-east Yorkshire. *Agricultural History Review* 19: 1–24.

Fleming, A. 1978. The prehistoric landscape of Dartmoor, Part I. *Proceedings of the Prehistoric Society* 44: 97–124.

Fortes, M. and Evans-Pritchard, E.E. (eds.) 1940. *African Political Systems*. Oxford, University Press.

Fowler, P.J. 1971. Early prehistoric agriculture in western Europe, some archaeological evidence, in D.D.A. Simpson (ed.), *Economy and Settlement in Neolithic and Early Bronze Age Europe*. Leicester, University Press, 153–82.

Frankenstein, S. and Rowlands, M. 1978. The internal structure and regional context of early Iron Age society in south-western Germany. *Bulletin of the Institute of Archaeology of London* 15: 73–112.

Fried, M.H. 1967. *The Evolution of Political Society*. New York, Random House.

Gilman, A. 1981. The development of social stratification in bronze age Europe. *Current Anthropology* 22: 1–8.

Glassow, M.A. 1978. The concept of carrying capacity in the study of culture process, in M.B. Schiffer (ed.), *Advances in Archaeological Method and Theory* 1. New York, Academic Press, 32–48.

Hassan, F.A. 1978. Demographic archaeology, in M.B. Schiffer (ed.), *Advances in Archaeological Method and Theory* 1. New York, Academic Press, 49–105.

Hill, J.N. and Gunn, J. (eds.) 1977. *The Individual in Prehistory*. New York, Academic Press.

Hodder, I. 1978. The maintenance of group identities in the Baringo district, western Kenya, in D. Green, C. Haselgrove and M. Spriggs (eds.), *Social Organisation and Settlement*. Oxford, British Archaeological Reports, 47–74.

Johnson, G.A. 1975. Locational analysis and the investigation of Uru Uruk local exchange systems, in J.A. Sabloff and C.C. Lamberg-Karlovsky (eds.), *Ancient Civilisation and Trade*. Albuquerque, University of New Mexico Press, 285–339.

Lindquist, S.-O. 1974. The development of the agrarian landscape in Gotland during the early iron age. *Norwegian Archaeological Review* 7: 6–32.

Oates, D. and J. 1976. Early irrigation agriculture in Mesopotamia, in G. Sieveking, I.H. Longworth and K.E. Wilson (eds.), *Problems in Economic and Social Archaeology*. London, Duckworth, 109–36.

O'Shea, J. 1978. Mortuary variability: an archaeological investigation. Ph.D. dissertation, University of Cambridge.

Peebles, C.S. and Kus, S.M. 1977. Some archaeological correlates of ranked societies. *American Antiquity* 42: 421–48.

Phillips, P., Aspinall, A. and Feather, S. 1977. Stages of neolithisation in southern France: supply and exchange of raw materials. *Proceedings of the Prehistoric Society* 43: 303–16.

Price, B.J. 1977. Shifts in production and organisation, a cluster interaction model. *Current Anthropology* 18: 209–34.

Randsborg, K. 1974. Social stratification in early bronze age Denmark, a study in the regulation of cultural systems. *Praehistorische Zeitschrift* 49: 38–61.

Renfrew, C. 1973. Monuments, mobilisation and social organisation in neolithic Wessex, in C. Renfrew (ed.), *The Explanation of Culture Change*. London, Duckworth, 539–58.

Renfrew, C. 1974. Beyond a subsistence economy, the evolution of social organisation in prehistoric Europe, in C.B. Moore (ed.), *Reconstructing Complex Societies* (Bulletin of the American Schools of Oriental Research 20 (Supplement)), 69–95.

Renfrew, C. 1975. Trade as action at a distance, in J.A. Sabloff and C.C. Lamberg-Karlovsky (eds.), *Ancient Civilisation and Trade*. Albuquerque, University of New Mexico Press, 3–59.

Renfrew, C. 1978. Space, time and polity, in J. Friedman and M.J. Rowlands (eds.), *The Evolution of Social Systems*. London, Duckworth, 89–114.

Renfrew, C. 1981a. The megalith builders of western Europe, in J.D. Evans, B.W. Cunliffe and C. Renfrew (eds.), *Antiquity and Man, Essays in Honour of Glyn Daniel*. London, Thames and Hudson, 72–81.

Renfrew, C. 1981b. Polity and power: interaction, intensification and exploitation, in C. Renfrew and J.M. Wagstaff (eds.), *An Island Polity, the Archaeology of Exploitation in Melos*. Cambridge, University Press.

Renfrew, C. and Level, E.V. 1979. Exploring dominance, predicting polities from centers, in C. Renfrew and K.L. Cooke (eds.), *Transformations, Mathematical Approaches to Culture Change.* New York, Academic Press, 145–68.

Rowlands, M.J. 1980. Kinship, alliance and exchange in the European bronze age, in J. Barrett and R. Bradley (eds.), *Settlement and Society in the British Later Bronze Age.* Oxford, British Archaeological Reports, 15–55.

Sanders, W.T., Parsons, J.R. and Santley, R.S. 1979. *The Basin of Mexico, Ecological Processes in the Evolution of a Civilization.* New York, Academic Press.

Saxe, A.A. 1970. Social dimensions of mortuary practice. Ph.D. dissertation, University of Michigan, Ann Arbor. Ann Arbor, University Microfilms.

Service, E.R. 1962. *Primitive Social Organisation.* New York, Random House.

Service, E.R. 1971. *Cultural Evolutionism, Theory in Practice.* New York, Holt, Rinehart and Winston.

Shennan, S. 1975. The social organisation at Branč. *Antiquity* 49: 279–88.

Shennan, S.J. 1978. Archaeological 'cultures', an empirical investigation, in I. Hodder (ed.), *The Spatial Organisation of Culture.* London, Duckworth, 113–40.

Shennan, S.J. 1982. Ideology, change and the European early bronze age, in I. Hodder (ed.), *Symbolic and Structural Archaeology.* Cambridge, University Press, 155–61.

Shephard, J.F. 1979. The social identity of the individual in isolated barrows and barrow cemeteries in Anglo-Saxon England, in B.C. Burnham and J. Kingsbury (eds.), *Space, Hierarchy and Society.* Oxford, British Archaeological Reports, 47–80.

Sherratt, A.G. 1972. Socio-economic and demographic models for the neolithic and bronze age of Europe, in D.L. Clarke (ed.), *Models in Archaeology.* London, Methuen, 477–542.

Sherratt, A.G. 1976. Resources, technology and trade, an essay in early European metallurgy, in G. Sieveking, I.J. Longworth and K.E. Wilson (eds.), *Problems in Economic and Social Archaeology.* London, Duckworth, 557–81.

Spooner, B. (ed.) 1972. *Population Growth, Anthropological Implications.* Cambridge, Mass., M.I.T. Press.

Tainter, J. 1973. Social correlates of mortuary patterning at Kaloko, North Kona, Hawaii. *Archaeology and Physical Anthropology in Oceania* 8: 1–11.

Tainter, J.A. 1978. Mortuary practices and the study of prehistoric social systems, in M.B. Schiffer (ed.), *Advances in Archaeological Method and Theory* 1. New York, Academic Press, 106–43.

Wainwright, G.J., Fleming, A. and Smith, K. 1979. The Shaugh Moor project, first report. *Proceedings of the Prehistoric Society* 45: 1–34.

Webb, M.C. 1974. Exchange networks: prehistory. *Annual Review of Anthropology* 3: 357–84.

Wells, P.S. 1980. *Culture Contact and Culture Change: Early Iron Age Central Europe and the Mediterranean World.* Cambridge, University Press.

Widgren, M. 1979. A simulation model of farming systems and land use in Sweden during the early iron age c. 500 BC to AD 550. *Journal of Historical Geography* 5: 21–32.

Wobst, H.M. 1977. Stylistic behaviour and information exchange, in C.E. Cleland (ed.), *For the Director, Research Essays in Honor or James B. Griffin* (Anthropological Papers of the Museum of Anthropology 61). Ann Arbor, University of Michigan.

Wright, H. and Johnson, G.A. 1975. Population exchange and early state formation in south-western Iran. *American Anthropologist* 79: 267–89.

PART I

The emergence of
hierarchical structure

Until recently archaeologists concerned with the neo-lithic and bronze age of prehistoric Europe have devoted most of their time to the ever-increasing refinement of space–time systematics in their area of interest. This work was carried out within the theoretical context developed by two key figures, Childe and Kossinna. It was Kossinna who developed the idea of archaeological cultures as the frame-work for the understanding of European prehistory, and who by his identification of cultures with peoples presented the replacement of one people by another as the explanation for the cultural changes observed in the archaeological record (Neustupný 1976). These cultural changes, however, were essentially static and repetitive, and it was Childe who devel-oped the framework for understanding the technological, economic and social trends which also seemed to characterise the European past, with his clearly formulated processual thesis of the irradiation of European barbarism by oriental civilisation (for example, Childe 1958).

In those parts of Europe dominated by the German archaeological tradition this traditional framework still remains largely intact, but elsewhere both its fundamental theses have been rejected in the last fifteen years (Clark 1966; Renfrew 1973a; Neustupný 1976) and since then the attempt has begun to develop an adequate replacement. This endeavour has been heavily influenced by the neo-evolutionary framework of Service (1962) and Fried (1967),

and the problems on which it has focussed have been Childe's legacy rather than Kossinna's: the processes of tech-nological innovation and adoption, subsistence change and social evolution (cf. Childe 1951). Inasmuch as a great deal of the work in European prehistory has been carried out within the Kossinna paradigm, one result of this reorien-tation is that much of the material collected by European archaeologists in the past has come to be regarded as irre-levant, of no help to the solution of current problems (cf. Bradley and Hodder 1979). It still remains unclear how use-ful it will be in the future, as orientations change once more (cf. Hodder 1982), but what is certain is that data collection in response to current questions has barely begun.

The importance of the influence of neo-evolutionary theory in redirecting the attention of European archae-ologists to general questions cannot be overemphasised (see Renfrew 1973a, 1974) but the narrowness and rigidity of its framework are now being found restrictive, since it follows from it that the only changes of importance are those organ-isational ones involved in the sequence from band to tribe to chiefdom to state. In certain areas and periods, particularly those in which early states were developing, this sequence plausibly represents the critical dimension of change. In pre-historic Europe outside the Mediterranean this seems not to be the case, especially prior to the later iron age: over a period of about six thousand years the sole change which occurred in terms of Service's evolutionary typology was that from tribe to chiefdom. This realisation has led on the one hand to the feeling that European prehistory must inevitably be on the sidelines when the major prehistoric transitions in human socio-economic organisation are being investigated, and on the other to the more positive, and in a sense Childean, reaction that the processes of change, and particularly hierarchisation, in European prehistory must be investigated in their own terms, although it is necessary to make use of a wide comparative framework. The papers in this section are examples of such investigations, all concerned with the emergence of hierarchies, whether from the point of view of describing the process, examining its effects, or attempting to explain the reasons for it.

One of the major problems remains the archaeological documentation of hierarchical organisation. This is so for several reasons. Much of the European evidence is very poor, especially when the attempt is made to draw comparisons between different regions and periods; settlement data in particular, so successfully exploited in the Near East (e.g. Wright and Johnson 1975), are very often lacking. The theoretical basis for comparative studies using burial data is not as secure as it might be. Furthermore, it is increasingly clear that to adopt a unitary concept of hierarchy is not entirely helpful: the way in which different hierarchies maintain and legitimate themselves varies, and this variation has a considerable effect on the way in which they operate and on the social trajectories which result (cf. S.J. Shennan 1982).

Despite the difficulties, certain broad socio-economic trends are apparent. The first agricultural economies of temperate Europe do not seem to have been based on slash-and-burn agriculture but on the small-scale static hoe cultivation of a restricted number of zones of high productivity (Kruk 1973; Willerding 1980). Gradual expansion of the cultivated zone occurred, on to soils less able to sustain continued cultivation, so that in some areas at least fairly large areas had been cleared by the later fourth millennium, and settlement was becoming less permanent. It seems to be in this context that what Sherratt (1981) calls the 'Secondary Products Revolution' occurred, involving the first use of animal traction for pulling ploughs and carts, as well as exploitation of cattle and sheep for milk and wool. In the Mediterranean parts of Europe this mode of intensification may be paralleled by the introduction of Mediterranean polyculture at around the same time (Renfrew 1972; Gilman 1981). There is much to be said for the argument that it was in the context of this changing subsistence economy and the continuing expansion of settlement that a major change in social relations began to occur which had important repercussions in the succeeding bronze age (Gilman 1981; Sherratt 1981).

In the early neolithic there is no evidence for other than egalitarian social relations, whether one looks at the Bandkeramik of central Europe (Sherratt 1976) or the early megalith building societies of the west (Renfrew 1973a). By the later fourth millennium BC, however, there are indications that this situation had changed, in some places at least, and that hierarchies had begun to develop. Milisauskas (1978) has suggested that settlement hierarchies were present in Poland at this time, while Renfrew (1973b) has based an argument for the presence of hierarchies in Britain on developments in monument building (see also Randsborg 1975; Shennan 1977); this is the period when the regular use of secondary products seems to have begun. Prior to this it is likely that the societies of prehistoric Europe were little different from those of hoe agriculturalists elsewhere in the world, many of whom have a relatively accessible source of animal protein. The use of secondary products, however, led to the development of an integrated and expansive subsistence economy in which the plant and animal elements were complementary to one another, and which did not occur outside the Old World.

Subsequently to these developments, much of central, northern and north-western Europe underwent profound changes, with the disappearance of monuments and settlement hierarchies and the emergence of a dispersed settlement pattern with small-scale settlement units, associated with cemeteries which include graves containing male status items such as battle-axes. This system formed the basis out of which the ranked societies of the early bronze age developed, except in parts of western Europe, where hierarchies and monumental traditions had continued and developed, until the latter disappeared and the hierarchies changed in nature, converging in form with those of central Europe (S.J. Shennan 1982). Gilman (1981) has argued for a direct link between the processes of agricultural intensification and the development of what he regards as stratified societies, as a result of the new potential for exploitation of producers created by the fact that the capital investment now required for agriculture meant that it was no longer so easy for groups to split up in response to attempts at domination by powerful individuals (cf. Neustupný 1967 for a similar argument from the new importance of 'capital investment' in agriculture). It seems likely that there is indeed a link but it is regarded here as more probable that it is indirect and relates to processes of competition between the new household units which had formed (cf. Rowlands 1980), competition which depended heavily on the maintenance of distant contacts for the obtaining of prestige goods. At all events, it seems difficult to escape the conclusion that in general hierarchies became far more prevalent in Europe in the aftermath of this subsistence intensification phase than they had been earlier, and particularly in the full bronze age, which developed at the end of the third millennium BC.

The papers in this section constitute specific case studies within the general framework of social and economic development just outlined. Most of them are concerned largely with the developments of the late fourth millennium BC and later, but Sherratt's paper, which begins the section, is an examination of the earlier cycle of hierarchisation in the Hungarian plain, from the sixth to the fourth millennia BC. He presents a dynamic picture of the relations between the central area of the plain and its surrounding margins in which an initially complementary relationship between the two, involving extensive exchanges of cattle and inorganic materials in an egalitarian context, gave way to a situation in which contrasts began to emerge between different parts of the regional system, and ranking began to develop.

Susan Shennan advocates a similar model based on locational advantage (cf. Johnson 1977) for the changes she describes in the early bronze age of south-west Slovakia during the third millennium BC. Her study is mainly concerned with the micro-level analysis of a group of cemeteries in order to provide the documentation necessary for reliable statements about the degree of hierarchy in this area, but her detailed examination also leads her to suggest that she has evidence for the process of emulation in the grave goods, an aspect of the social competition on which all the contributions to this section lay considerable emphasis.

The succeeding paper, by Stephen Shennan, takes a very different approach, with its study of a single exchanged material, amber, on a large scale, rather than the detailed analysis of a particular situation. After the presentation of an outline of the spatial and chronological distribution of amber, an attempt is made to show how that distribution reflects the growth of a certain kind of hierarchy in early bronze age Europe, whose maintenance was connected with the consumption of prestige valuables which were a source of intra-elite competition. The acquisition of these items depended on wide-ranging inter-regional contacts which resulted in the absorption of a number of initially peripheral areas, particularly southern Scandinavia, into a large-scale exchange system.

Chapman's study of the development of ranking in Iberia follows Gilman (1976) in ascribing the initial development of social ranking in Iberia during the late fourth and early third millennia BC to subsistence-related factors, particularly water control, and in regarding an emphasis on the importance of controlling prestige goods and materials, particularly metal, as characteristic of the beginning of the bronze age, at the end of the third millennium BC. On the whole the Iberian situation fits in very well with the general European trends, outlined earlier, of intensification, growth of ranking and increased emphasis on prestige goods; although the association between monumental burial and the consumption of large quantities of prestige items as grave goods which characterises parts of Iberia in the third millennium BC copper age (cf. Harrison and Gilman 1977) is not matched elsewhere.

Finally, Fleming also takes a diachronic view of the period from the beginning of the fourth to the middle of the second millennium BC, this time for southern Britain, where the trajectory seems to have many similarities to Iberia (Shennan 1981). Fleming, however, is sceptical of the inferences which have been made on the basis of the monuments

about the increasing scale of socio-political units through time (Renfrew 1973b) and emphasises the importance of using the available evidence for land boundaries to test such inferences. He argues convincingly that a study of land-use units provides critical evidence concerning the basic building blocks of social organisation and their integration with one another. Of particular interest, in relation to the growing debate on the significance for social evolution of land ownership as a basis of power (see Bintliff, this volume, *contra*, for example, Rowlands 1980, 49–50) is Fleming's argument that the Dartmoor field systems he has studied do not indicate individual ownership of land, as tends to be assumed, but its collective use and organisation.

These questions of the nature of the power base and of socio-political integration in the European neolithic and bronze age are clearly extremely important ones for the future study of these periods, as they are likely to have a considerable bearing on the reasons for the limits which characterised European society at this time, and which meant that the trends towards social complexity which are clearly apparent stopped short of statehood. If the later prehistory of Europe outside the east Mediterranean zone is to have a significance at the world scale rather than a historical pre-eminence by virtue of its seniority, then it may well lie in providing a negative test case.

S.J.S.

References

Bradley, R. and Hodder, I. 1979. British prehistory, an integrated view. *Man* 14: 93–104.

Childe, V.G. 1951. *Social Evolution*. London, Watts.

Childe, V.G. 1958. *The Prehistory of European Society*. Harmondsworth, Penguin.

Clark, J.G.D. 1966. The invasion hypothesis in British prehistory. *Antiquity* 40: 172–89.

Fried, M.H. 1967. *The Evolution of Political Society*. New York, Random House.

Gilman, A. 1976. Bronze Age dynamics in southeast Spain. *Dialectical Anthropology* 1: 307–19.

Gilman, A. 1981. The development of social stratification in bronze age Europe. *Current Anthropology* 22: 1–8.

Harrison, R.J. and Gilman, A. 1977. Trade in the second and third millennia BC between the Maghreb and Iberia, in V. Markotic (ed.), *Ancient Europe and the Mediterranean*. Warminster, Aris and Phillips, 90–104.

Hodder, I. (ed.) 1982. *Symbolic and Structural Archaeology*. Cambridge, University Press.

Johnson, G.A. 1977. Aspects of regional analysis in archaeology. *Annual Review of Anthropology* 6: 479–508.

Kruk, J. 1973. *Studia Osadnicze nad Neolitem Wyzyn Lessowych*. Warsaw, Ossolineum.

Milisauskas, S. 1978. *European Prehistory*. New York, Academic Press.

Neustupný, E.F. 1967. K. počatkům patriarchátu ve střední Evropé. *Rozpravy Československé Akademie Věd, Řada Společenských Ved* 77 (2).

Neustupný, E.F. 1976. Paradigm lost, in J.N. Lanting and J.D. van der Waals (eds.), *Glockenbecher Symposion Oberried 1974*. Bussum, Fibula–van Dishoeck, 241–7.

Randsborg, K. 1975. Social dimensions of early neolithic Denmark. *Proceedings of the Prehistoric Society* 41: 105–17.

Renfrew, C. 1972. *The Emergence of Civilisation.* London, Methuen.

Renfrew, C. 1973a. *Before Civilisation: the Radiocarbon Revolution and Prehistoric Europe.* London, Jonathan Cape.

Renfrew, C. 1973b. Monuments, mobilisation and social organisation in neolithic Wessex, in C. Renfrew (ed.), *The Explanation of Culture Change.* London, Duckworth, 539–58.

Renfrew, C. 1974. Beyond a subsistence economy: the evolution of social organisation in prehistoric Europe, in C.B. Moore (ed.), *Reconstructing Complex Societies* (Bulletin of the American Schools of Oriental Research 20 (Supplement)), 69–95.

Rowlands, M.J. 1980. Kinship, alliance and exchange in the European Bronze Age, in J. Barrett and R. Bradley (eds.), *Settlement and Society in the British Later Bronze Age.* Oxford, British Archaeological Reports, 15–55.

Service, E.R. 1962. *Primitive Social Organisation.* New York, Random House.

Shennan, S.J. 1977. Bell beakers and their context in central Europe: a new approach. Ph.D. dissertation, University of Cambridge.

Shennan, S.J. 1982. Ideology, change and the European early bronze age, in I. Hodder (ed.), *Symbolic and Structural Archaeology.* Cambridge, University Press, 155–61.

Sherratt, A.G. 1976. Resources, technology and trade, an essay in early European metallurgy, in G. Sieveking, I.H. Longworth and K.E. Wilson (eds.), *Problems in Economic and Social Archaeology.* London, Duckworth, 557–81.

Sherratt, A.G. 1981. Plough and pastoralism: aspects of the secondary products revolution, in I. Hodder, G. Isaac and N. Hammond (eds.), *Pattern of the Past: Studies in honour of David Clarke.* Cambridge, University Press.

Willerding, V. 1980. *Zum Ackerbau der Bandkeramiker* (Beiträge zur Archäologie Nordwestdeutschlands und Mitteleuropas, Materialhefte zur Ur-und Frühgeschichte Niedersachsens 16).

Wright, H. and Johnson, G.A. 1975. Population exchange and early state formation in south-western Iran. *American Anthropologist* 79: 267–89.

Chapter 2

**Mobile resources:
settlement and exchange
in early agricultural
Europe**
Andrew Sherratt

*This paper discusses the economic and social basis of a
phase of intensified exchange that took place in central
Europe within the Carpathian Basin during the fifth millennium BC. It suggests that certain features of the settlement
pattern and the occurrence of traded items can be related to
a temporary opportunity offered during agricultural expansion by the supply of domestic livestock from lowland plains.
This phenomenon may be of general significance in similar
circumstances in Europe and the Near East. Domestic livestock should thus be considered not only as elements of the
subsistence economy but also as significant items of trade.
The paper also discusses the social context of such transactions, and draws a contrast between these early systems
and those of later prehistoric Europe.*

Interpretations of the archaeological record in social
terms have usually been undertaken within an implicit evolutionary framework. The most successful of these studies
have been those concerned with the Near East and Mesoamerica. In these areas the rapid onset of social inequality
following the adoption of agriculture has suggested that
stages of increasing social complexity are a normal succession
in agricultural communities. In Europe, however, this
approach has been less fruitful. One of the notable features
of the European prehistoric sequence is the relatively late
appearance of complex societies associated with an urban

base. Even the appearance of societies as organised as the chiefdoms of Polynesia is closely associated with the effects of expanding Mediterranean trading networks in the first millennium BC.

Yet the first farming communities appeared in Europe in the seventh millennium BC, and the long intervening period cannot be adequately described by a simple evolutionary succession of increasingly ranked societies. Archaeologists have used technological criteria to divide this time into neolithic, copper and bronze ages on the basis of surviving artefacts; but although the use of metal is clearly relevant to the question of social change, the dynamics of such a process cannot be inferred from the artefacts alone. It is necessary to try and reconstruct the total flow of produce between different areas, since it is this pattern that determines how particular areas develop in terms of the opportunities open to them at different times.

Gordon Childe attributed the egalitarian nature of early farming communities to the primitive character of agriculture and the lack of a surplus for trade (1951). This view can be criticised on several grounds, not least the clear evidence that neolithic groups were capable of acquiring substantial quantities of materials from considerable distances (Sherratt 1976). Because of the importance of regional interaction in determining the course of economic and social development, it is worthwhile to examine the nature of such neolithic exchange networks and their social contexts. This paper proposes a fundamental reason for large-scale regional exchange in Early Old World agricultural societies, and investigates the social structures in which it was embedded. It uses detailed evidence from an area of central Europe to explore the usefulness of this model in explaining a wide range of archaeological observations.

The potential for exchange in early agricultural societies

In discussions of exchange in simple agricultural societies, attention has usually focussed on the movement of hard stones for axes and cutting tools (Sherratt 1976; cf. Hughes 1973). In a stimulating article in 1965, however, Kent Flannery discussed the development of early agricultural communities in the Zagros in terms of inter-zonal exchanges both of mineral resources and of new domesticates. The movement of domesticated species was seen as an aspect of social contact and trade rather than just a biogeographic dispersal. That domestic livestock were an important item of trade among early agriculturalists should not be surprising in view of their prominence in New Guinea exchange cycles (Rappaport 1968, 105); but archaeologists have usually considered them under the heading of 'subsistence' rather than of 'exchange'. While the role of horses as trade items (by analogy with their spread in North America) has recently been raised in unpublished work by Stephen Shennan and John O'Shea in connection with Beaker and early bronze age trade networks in Europe (cf. Schüle 1969), the significance

of livestock as an item of neolithic trade has not been systematically explored.

The role of cattle in this context is likely to have been particularly important. The earliest neolithic economies were based on sheep, which spread as part of the primary agricultural complex from a restricted mountain habitat. Cattle, on the other hand, were a widespread native animal in the areas to which agriculture was introduced, and were probably domesticated independently in a number of lowland foci (Herre and Röhrs 1977). These included northern Mesopotamia, central Anatolia, and parts of southern Europe. Domesticated cattle were supplied from these areas to surrounding regions. The continuing significance of lowland cattle-breeding centres is well known from the historical period: Thessaly and Boeotia exported animals in Homeric times, while classical Attica brought cattle by ship from as far away as Macedonia, North Africa and Scythia (Semple 1932, 318). The movement of livestock is thus likely to be of major importance in explaining regional exchange systems in prehistory.

One site which may be illuminated by being considered in this light is Çatal Hüyük in central Anatolia (Mellaart 1967; Todd 1976). Large herds of wild cattle (aurochsen) flourished in the seventh millennium in this well-watered part of the alluvial Konya Plain, and their skulls are a prominent feature of the numerous shrines found at the site. The capture or handling of an aurochs bull is actually shown in wall paintings. Cattle formed over ninety per cent of the faunal remains recovered from the site, and the stature of the animals decreased in the upper levels. Since domestic cattle arguably appeared in this region for the first time at Çatal Hüyük, it is likely that the site had a major role in the domestication of these animals (Perkins 1969).

The site also had a key role in relation to its surrounding region, since it is notable for the extraordinary quantity and variety of imported materials: some thirty-five different foreign minerals have been identified, including rocks for axes, grinding stones, pigments and beads, as well as several varieties of flint and very large quantities of obsidian (Todd 1976, 126; cf. Jacobs 1969, 27–54). The last is particularly notable, as it was obtained from the Acigöl source, which is 200 km away to the north-east. This trading florescence was a temporary one, however, as the site had no immediate successor of comparable size or importance – James Mellaart has called it a 'supernova'. A possible explanation for this brief concentration of wealth is the role of the site as a source of domestic cattle during the phase of agricultural expansion, when it supplied sites proliferating in the nearby upland basins and was thus able to acquire abundant supplies of highland resources.

Despite the flow of traded items at Çatal Hüyük, it did not form part of a site hierarchy in the same way as (for instance) the Protoliterate communities of the Mesopotamian Plain (Adams and Nissen 1972). Although only a fraction of the site has been excavated, the buildings are remarkably uniform and there is no differentiation of large elite or public buildings: the numerous shrines form part of domestic complexes. Whatever the precise social organisation of the site or the character of the trade that supported it, there is little indication of ranking of the kind discussed elsewhere in this volume. The site thus raises in acute form the question of the nature of exchange in neolithic communities and the social structures associated with it. It suggests that early agricultural communities were on occasion capable of operating large-scale exchanges in the absence of developed hierarchies, and that such societies may have undergone cycles of increasing complexity and devolution that defy characterisation as stages in a unilinear progression.

Another area where a phenomenon of this kind may have taken place is the Great Hungarian Plain. Its marshy depressions and open, steppe character provided a similar habitat for numerous herds of cattle in the postglacial period. Early farming groups (as in Thessaly) concentrated chiefly on raising sheep, though domestic cattle were known and aurochsen occasionally hunted. During the fifth millennium BC,[1] however, cattle became the principal form of domestic livestock, and there is evidence in one area for interbreeding

with wild herds and probably an intake of the latter for domestication. What is particularly interesting is that this period saw a notable increase in 'wealth' (in terms of both imported materials and local craft products), an elaboration of ritual, and a significant change in the character of settlements, with the emergence of large aggregated sites in between phases of dispersed settlement.

The rest of this paper consists of an examination of the relationships between these changes, at both a local and a regional level. It uses some of the preliminary results of intensive survey work around Szeghalom in the Körös depression[2] to describe patterns of settlement and material culture in the centre of the Plain. It then uses a colonisation model to examine changes in the role of this area within the larger regional system of the Carpathian Basin.

Settlement and economy in the central part of the Great Hungarian Plain

The Great Hungarian Plain is an alluvial basin with extensive areas of fertile land along its broad floodplains (fig. 2.2). Although it has a steppe climate, irrigation was not necessary in preindustrial times, and there are no sharp con-

Fig. 2.1. The Carpathian Basin and the Great Hungarian Plain (Nagy Alföld).

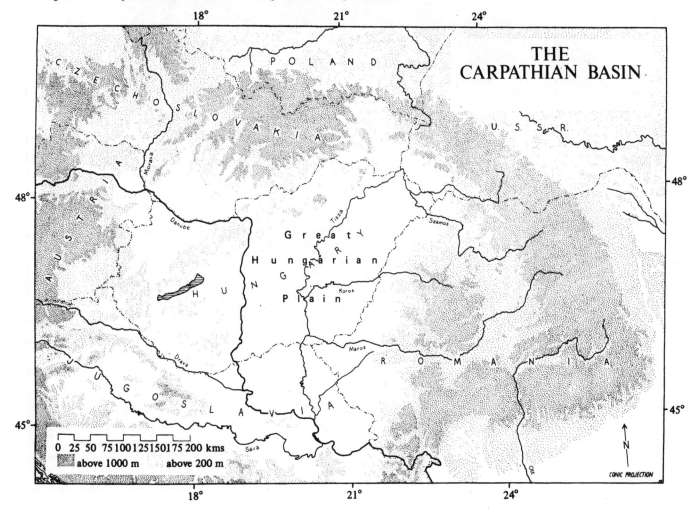

trasts in productive potential as in the Mesopotamian Plain. The landscape was undegraded at the time under discussion, and cultivation systems based on the hoe or digging stick can be inferred for the whole of the period before c. 3000 BC. The contrasts discussed here thus emerged from a relatively uniform environmental and technological base.

The earliest agrarian communities of the Körös culture,[3] spreading into the Carpathian Basin from the south along the major rivers, took the form of linear settlements up to a kilometre or more in length, along the levees of old watercourses. Such sites were composed of individual household clusters – consisting of postbuilt rectangular houses with their associated pits – arranged at intervals of 50 metres or so along the riverbank. They yield evidence of cereal cultivation, the keeping of domestic livestock (mainly sheep), hunting of deer and wild cattle (Bökönyi 1974), and plentiful indications of fishing in the form of fish remains and netsinkers. Large quantities of locally produced coarse pottery

Fig. 2.2. Landscape units of the Great Hungarian Plain and the location of the Szeghalom survey area, showing area of intensive survey in the Körös depression around Szeghalom.

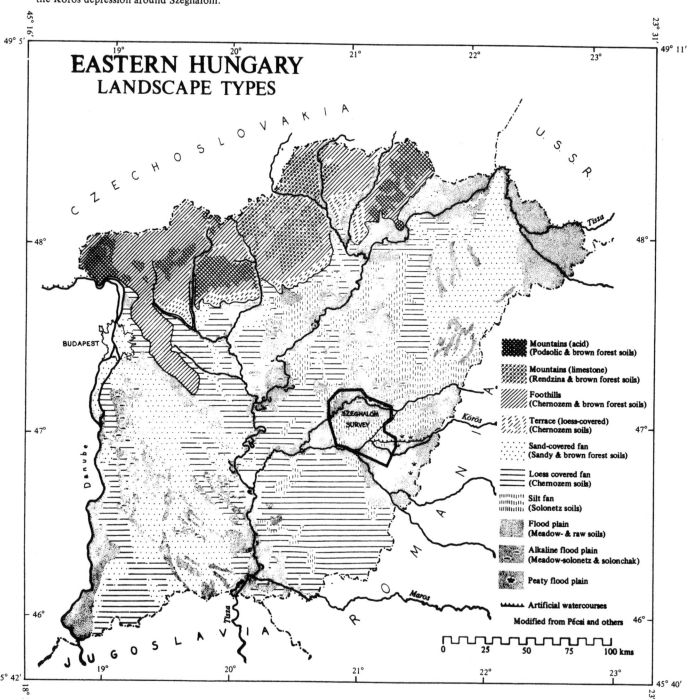

are present. The finer pottery is undecorated, and there are no marked local stylistic groupings. There are some clay figurines, but they are not elaborate. By the end of this period obsidian was reaching the area from the edge of the Plain to the north (Tokaj), though the chipped stone industry lacks the variety of materials used in later periods, and stone axes are rare. Burials were placed within the settlements, not unusually in rubbish pits with other animal bone, and no formal cemetery areas have been recognised.

The linear arrangement of settlement and the very large number of sites probably indicate frequent minor shifts of individual household clusters within the general area of exploitation over a relatively long span of time, rather than a high density of large contemporary settlements. The absence of cemeteries may imply that descent was not important in defining group membership. This pattern suggests considerable fluidity of pioneer settlement, freely growing and proliferating without constraint. Such adventitious colonisation at a low overall population density in a productive environment would not have created competition and would have made unnecessary the development of wider networks of alliance.

This pattern persisted with only minor modifications throughout the sixth millennium, during which the wave of population advance passed on through the Carpathian Basin to the other parts of the central European loess belt. Broad cultural affinities were maintained between these proliferating Bandkeramik populations further north and their contemporaries in eastern Hungary, who are distinguished as the Alföld variant (AVK).

A major change occurred in the Great Hungarian Plain around the beginning of the fifth millennium BC, affecting both settlement patterns and material culture. This corresponds to the beginning of the Szakálhát and Tisza cultures.[4] Although the same parts of the Plain continued to be occupied, settlement became increasingly aggregated. Far fewer sites are known, but on further investigation these turn out to be very large (of the order of 500 m × 500 m) and to consist of parallel lines of household-clusters, often centred on a slight prominence with natural defences or suggestions of artificial ditches.[5] True tells first appeared at this time. All sites have substantial accumulations of settlement debris consisting of several layers of mud-walled buildings, sometimes simultaneously burnt over large parts of the site. The subsistence base of these settlements contained no new species, but cattle now predominated heavily over sheep among the domestic livestock, while the hunting of aurochsen made a substantial contribution in the eastern part of the area. Fishing was now with harpoon rather than net, perhaps indicating that animal protein came mainly from meat.

The pottery includes a high proportion of elaborately decorated wares with painted and incised ornament often imitating textile patterns. These divide clearly into specific local styles in different parts of the Plain and surrounding areas.[6] Figurines and anthropomorphic vessels are similarly elaborate, as are decorated household fittings. Equally striking are the quantity and variety of imported materials. Many new types of flint make their appearance, along with large quantities of obsidian. Massive fragments of tabular

Table 2.1. *Summary of evidence for settlement and exchange in the central part of the Great Hungarian Plain, 6000–3500 BC.*

	Settlement	Subsistence	Material culture	Exchange	Cemeteries	Calibrated dates BC (non-linear scale)
Tiszapolgár/ Bodrogkeresztúr	Dispersed; small coherent settlements (not ditched); stable pattern	Domestic cattle predominate; cereals etc.	Plain pottery, without local styles; no figurines; 'battle axes'; (copper axes and daggers + gold ornaments on edge of Plain	Some obsidian, greenstone, etc.; occasional extra-Carpathian imports (esp. on edge of Plain)	Large formal cemeteries (for whole community or several sites)	4000
Szakálhát/ Tisza	Large aggregated settlements (defence ?); often burnt; stable pattern	Domestic cattle predominate; wild cattle locally important; cereals etc.	Elaborately decorated pottery and cult objects; in local styles; textiles	Large quantity and variety of imported materials – obsidian, flint, greenstone, grinders, etc.; imported fine pottery	Small formal groups of graves (households or lineages)	
						5000
Körös/AVK	Dispersed; linear shoreline settlements; fluid pattern	Domestic sheep predominate; fishing important; cereals etc.	Basic craft skills; decoration not regionally specific	Obsidian becoming important; some greenstone and grinders	No formal cemeteries	
						6000

flint up to 20 cm long show the size of the raw materials that were acquired. Saddle querns and grindstones are frequent finds, while greenstone axes occur in very large numbers. All these materials were imported from beyond the alluvial plain. Finely decorated pottery was also widely traded. Although burials occur in small formal groups within the settlement area, and male and female graves were differentiated by their orientation, large quantities of objects were not deposited with the dead.

The emergence of large, rich 'supersites' some 10 km or so apart indicates a greater stability and constraint on settlement coincident with the expansion of trading activity. The overall density of settlement was still relatively low, since there are few smaller settlements between the 'supersites'. Such sites, therefore, do not appear to form the upper level of a hierarchy, but rather a general tendency to aggregation

of settlement. The two factors most likely to have promoted aggregation are an enlargement of the resident cooperative (e.g. animal-breeding) unit, or more likely the need for defence — though the threat was not sufficiently severe to require enclosing earthworks (as in the bronze age). The sites probably consisted of an aggregation of compounds with livestock enclosures and kitchen gardens in between (cf. Brookfield and Hart 1971, fig. 9.1. A4). The burials, which seem to have taken place in the context of the domestic or lineage group rather than of the whole community, also suggest a loose aggregation of lineage groups rather than fusion into a single integrated unit. The evidence of ritual activities in the form of figurines and cult fittings also has a domestic context.

The pattern which succeeded this one in the later fifth millennium (Tiszapolgár culture) reversed many aspects of

Fig. 2.3. Idealised settlement patterns representing the three main successive types from 6000–3500 BC in the central part of the Great Hungarian Plain.

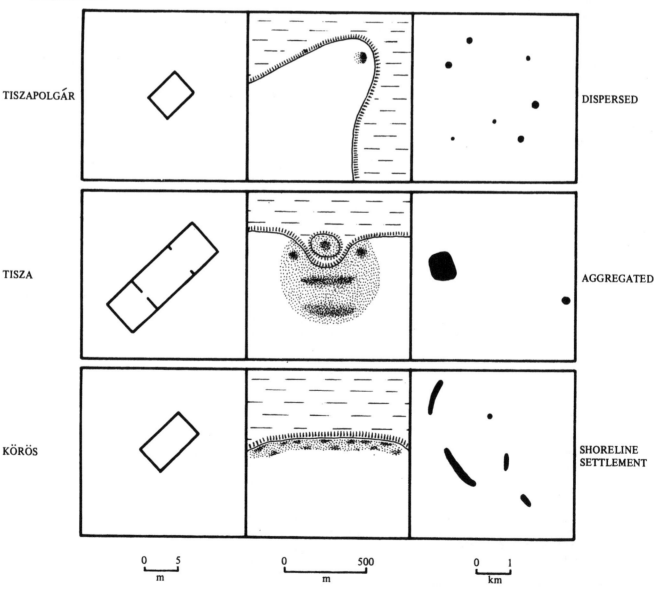

the picture, at least in the central area of the Plain. While the same parts of the area continued to be occupied, settlement reverted to a dispersed pattern. The sites themselves were more integrated than before, however, and consist of a concentration of huts and other facilities within a more or less circular area having a modal diameter of 50–100 m. They do not appear to have been ditched. Many tells continued to be occupied, though the layers are thinner and rarely burnt (Bognár-Kutzián 1972). The domesticates included no new species (with the exception of occasional bones of horse, which appeared in appreciable numbers only in the third millennium), and domestic cattle remained the most common animal. By the beginning of the fourth millennium cattle remains are almost entirely from domestic stock (Bökönyi 1974). The pottery is predominantly plain, with decoration consisting for the most part of knobs and perforations rather than elaborate patterns. Figurines are absent. The pottery is remarkably uniform over the whole of the Plain and does not divide into clear regional styles as in the preceding periods. Larger formal cemetery areas outside the settlements appear for the first time in this period, with graves arranged in rows and differentiated both by sex and by relative quantities of grave goods. The larger and richer excavated examples, however, come from outside the central area of the Plain. Stone continued to be imported for tools, but not in the quantity and variety of the preceding phase. New materials and products – long flint blades, and axes and simple ornaments of copper – are known from this period, but few seem to have reached the centre of the Plain.

The large number of substantial sites indicates that this period was stable and prosperous, and there is no evidence for declining fertility, even though materials from outside the Plain were not imported in such quantity. Conditions seem to have been more peaceful than in the preceding phase, since settlement was able to disperse and there is less evidence of destruction. Both the layout of Tiszapolgár sites and the existence of community cemeteries indicate a more organised composition of local groups, probably structured by descent.

The early fourth millennium BC (Bodrogkeresztúr culture) saw for the first time a major shift in the area under occupation in the central part of the Plain, with relative depopulation (or less visible settlement) in the parts previously settled most intensively. A truly radical break occurred in the later fourth millennium (Baden culture), with the settlement of new micro-areas and the construction of large burial mounds in the previously inhabited ones. Faunal remains show a shift to sheep (now probably for secondary products), while other parts of central Europe provide evidence for the use of paired draught animals and the plough (Sherratt 1981). This major transformation is beyond the scope of the present essay.

The Carpathian Basin as a regional system

These developments can only be understood in a regional setting (fig. 2.4). The earliest settlers in the sixth millennium formed part of a river-based network, spreading from the south and largely confined to the Plain itself. Contemporary settlements in adjacent areas occupied similar environments, and there was little penetration of surrounding uplands. Small quantities of necessary materials were imported, but early populations had a high degree of self-sufficiency.

The changes of the early fifth millennium coincided

Fig. 2.4. Agrarian colonisation and patterns of exchange in the east Carpathian Basin, 6000–3500 BC.

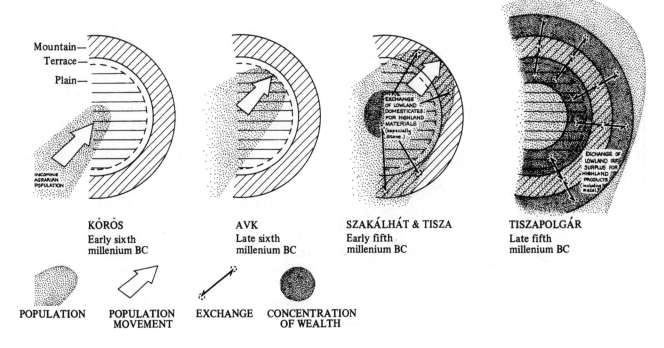

with the first major penetration of the uplands (Kalicz and Makkay 1977). Sites with clear cultural affinities to those on the Hungarian Plain are known not only from the valleys reaching up into the mountains but also up to 900 m in the limestone caves of the Bükk mountains themselves. The existence of groups with direct access to highland materials and the resources on the edge of the Plain[7] opened new possibilities for the supply of desirable materials to lowland areas. The appearance of large quantities of imported materials there suggests that contemporary alterations in settlement and material culture may be a part of a change in organisation to take advantage of these opportunities. The new pattern of relationships was a relatively short-lived episode, however, for many of its elements disappeared in the succeeding phase; though even so it lasted for several hundred years.

The sources of imported materials on one lowland site are shown in fig. 2.5, and can be seen to lie in a broad arc some 100 to 150 km away in the surrounding uplands to the north and east (cf. Comşa 1967). Such resources could only have been mobilised if the intensification of lowland production were articulated within a regional system of exchange. The first requirement of such a system would have

Fig. 2.5. Schematic summary of the range of selected imported items at the Szakálhát/Tisza site of Dévaványa-Sártó in the central part of the Great Hungarian Plain. (Other items from the same radius include greenstone axes and grinding stones.)

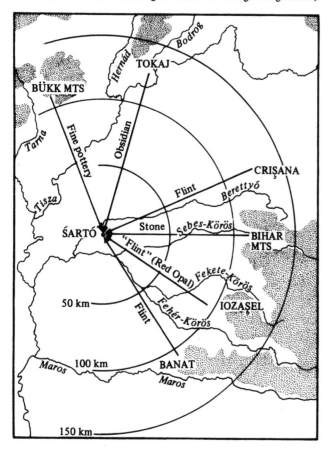

been the existence of an exportable lowland resource (cf. Godelier 1977, 141–5). While the archaeological record gives no direct evidence of what this was, it can be argued that cattle were the most important lowland product. The movement of surplus grain over such distances is unlikely in primitive conditions of transport, and in any case would give the central area no advantage over the peripheries. Textiles of plant fibres are a possibility, especially in view of the characteristic geometrical designs on pottery, though as flax grows well in surrounding areas (Illés and Halász 1926) its production is unlikely to have been a monopoly of the lowlands. Similar considerations apply to salt, which is known to have played an important role in the acquisition of stone resources by groups in alluvial lowlands in New Guinea (Godelier 1977). Fine pottery was manufactured both in the lowlands and in the area of the Bükk mountains, and traded in both directions.

The most likely commodities for specialised production in the Plain, therefore, are cattle and cattle products. The well-watered, open plains were a natural breeding-ground for cattle, both wild and domestic. Faunal remains from the Plain show a predominance (50%–75%) of cattle at this period, with very high proportions of wild forms especially in the eastern part. In this area (around Berettyóújfalu) the intergradation of sizes and mixture of morphological characteristics between domestic and wild forms is taken by Bökönyi (1962) as evidence of local domestication. The open character of the Plain environment (Kosse 1979) would have provided a valuable reservoir of livestock as population moved into the wooded areas on the fringes of the Carpathian Basin. The demand for cattle among these expanding populations could have been met by breeding cattle for export in much of the central Plain, and by actually domesticating new stock in the eastern part, where wild herds were extensive. If the practice of milking was a later introduction, as has been suggested (Sherratt 1981, 280), then it is the animals themselves rather than their secondary products that are likely to have been of importance. Such an export could literally move itself over the required distances. Since the initial clearings in forested areas would have been small,[8] herds in the wooded fringes and uplands would have taken some time to become self-sustaining. As it would in any case have been difficult to maintain large herds (which would only be able to expand after several generations of forest clearances), there was probably a continuing dependence on lowland supplies, both as breeding stock and as meat on the hoof.

If this interpretation is correct, then it suggests that the changes in settlement pattern and material culture in the Great Hungarian Plain in the early fifth millennium represented the intensification of one aspect of local production and the consumption of a wider range of goods through participation in regional exchange. The use of livestock as a commodity moved it from the subsistence sphere into that of negotiable wealth. The effect on settlement patterns was to concentrate population into larger and more permanent social units that could handle and protect a valuable and mobile resource.

The trade in livestock was the main means of acquiring necessary materials from the surrounding highland zone. These complementary exchanges also provided the opportunity for the distribution of other goods based on craft skills at a village level, such as fine pottery and textiles (cf. Jacobs 1969). The increase in the volume of traded goods thus coincided with the greatest diversity of local pottery styles and most elaborate types of decoration: it was advantageous to make local products sufficiently distinctive to · break into the flourishing regional exchange system. (This is equally true of highland areas: it is the limestone mountains of the Bükk — without volcanic rocks for axes etc. — that are most notable for their fine pottery.) Such local specialisation disappeared in the following period.

One feature that was characteristic of the whole region during the early fifth millennium, and disappeared in the following phase, was the production of elaborate cult items, especially figurines. These include some of the finest examples of neolithic art (e.g. Gimbutas 1974, figs. 102–9). Ritual activity was clearly an important feature of the social

system, and its significance in this context is considered in the next section.

In the later fifth millennium, a somewhat different pattern can be discerned. Some measure of local devolution (reflected in the dispersion of settlement and decline in imports) seems to have taken place within the central area of the Plain, but this was balanced by the rising wealth of areas nearer to the edge of the Plain (fig. 2.4). Metal objects (copper shafthole axes and daggers, gold ornaments) now supplemented those of stone as status items (Bognár-Kutzián 1972), and their distribution in the late fifth millennium is clearly restricted to sites immediately adjacent to the highlands or within 100 km along the major rivers (Tisza and Maros).[9] This most probably reflects the decline in importance of the central region as a cattle-breeding area and supplier of a major commodity. Groups on the Plain margins, however, were able to acquire objects such as fine flint blades (and perhaps also the first horses) from expanding populations on the other side of the Carpathians; and some of these objects travelled over longer distances than the commodities used in earlier intra-Carpathian exchanges (Sherratt 1976, 577).

Fig. 2.6. The succession of settlement and exchange systems in the central part of the Great Hungarian Plain, 6000–3500 BC (ellipses — external factors; rectangles — local elements). Similar models would apply for instance to central Turkey 7000–5000 BC, or northern Europe 4000–2000 BC.

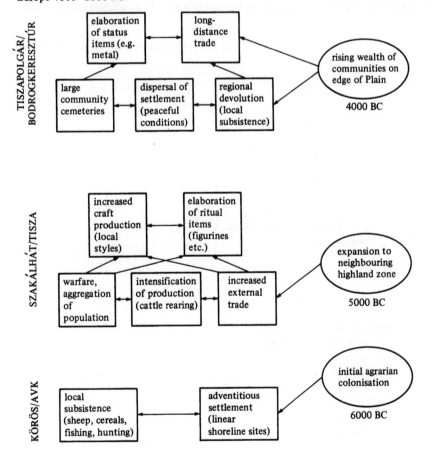

The social context of exchange

Discussion of the archaeological evidence for fifth-millennium exchange has emphasised the lack of discernible hierarchies, the general conditions of insecurity, and the increasing concern with ritual. A model of this exchange must encompass these three interdependent elements. Dalton (1977) has characterised exchange in acephalous (egalitarian)[10] societies as one aspect of alliance. Since the largest political unit was the local descent group, relations were horizontal — fluctuating coalitions and enmities between a multitude of similar small groups. Alliance allowed peace and therefore social and economic relationships. Such alliances were both initiated and maintained by exchanges of women, valuables and trade items; relations outside this network took the form of raiding, abduction and capture. Power within the group consisted in control over marriageable women, both directly and through valuables used as bridewealth and exchange items, and through access to ritual formulae for ceremonial.

Where relations between neighbouring groups were minimal, as in the phase of early settlement in the sixth millennium, such networks of alliance were little developed. The intensification of economic activity in the fifth millennium, however, was accompanied by increased competition between groups and a strengthening of control within them. Since alliances would have taken the form of chains linking different resource areas, rather than clusters in a coherent block of territory, individual settlements or groups are likely to have had potentially hostile relations with at least some of their neighbours. Defensive aggregation was the logical settlement pattern for an open plain. Control within the community, however, was a problem common to all. This control may have been accomplished by ritual and ideological means rather than by more overt expressions of power. The elaboration of cult objects at this period indicates the existence of ritual codes shared by all the communities of the area. Relations within groups could thus have been regulated by ritual; those between groups by selective alliance.

The pivotal points in both of these sets of relationships are likely to have been the men, especially senior males and lineage heads. The evidence for this comes from grave associations of goods which are likely to have played the role of primitive valuables. The late Bandkeramik cemetery at Nitra in Slovakia (Pavúk 1972) exhibits a striking pattern in which both stone axes and ornaments of imported *Spondylus* shell occur in all but one case in the graves of older males (fig. 2.7). Some 40% of men over twenty years old were buried with such items, and they occur in increasing proportion to age. Moreover, the greater longevity of males makes it likely that the age of marriage for men was high, so that powerful seniors could monopolise the women of marriageable age, probably by control of bridewealth valuables. Such valuables, which would have included the main prestige items of inter-group exchange like axes, obsidian blades, ornaments, fine pottery and cattle, are likely to have circulated in their own economic sphere and to have been exchanged only between

Fig. 2.7. The association of grave-goods by age and sex; a comparison of early fifth and fourth millennium examples. (From Sherratt 1976: data from Pavúk and Bognár-Kutzián.)

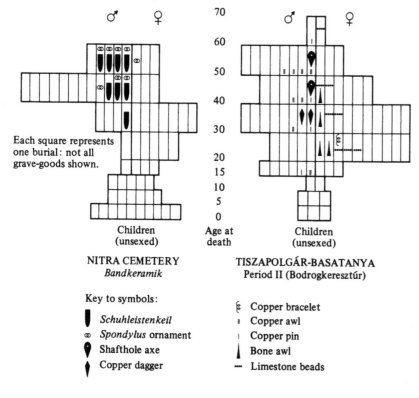

NITRA CEMETERY
Bandkeramik

TISZAPOLGÁR-BASATANYA
Period II (Bodrogkeresztúr)

Key to symbols:

Schuhleistenkeil

Spondylus ornament

Shafthole axe

Copper dagger

Copper bracelet

Copper awl

Copper pin

Bone awl

-- Limestone beads

eligible males (cf. Godelier 1977, 231 n. 29). The social system of these later neolithic groups can thus be reconstructed as one dominated by senior men, who controlled both the movement of goods and the formation of alliances through the exchange of marriage partners.

This picture of autonomous communities linked only by alliance and the attendant circulation of valuables, with ritual as an important medium of internal control, does not fit the pattern of the following Tiszapolgár and Bodrogkeresztúr periods. The evidence of insecurity diminishes, the volume of traded valuables declines, and the evidence of cult activity disappears. The large number of distinctive pottery types gives way to uniformity, suggesting that the pottery was no longer a competitive prestige item. At the same time, specific status-linked items appear, like shafthole axes and daggers of stone and copper, and ornaments of gold.[11] These are less common than the stone axes and shell ornaments at Nitra (occurring only in 15% of adult male graves at Tiszapolgár II (fig. 2.7)), and arguably indicate a new level of status differentiation. These items may also occur with younger adult men, especially the daggers. The cemeteries are larger, representing whole communities rather than household or lineage groups, and contain greater quantities of grave goods. (The cemeteries themselves may now have served as foci for groups of scattered settlements.) Family authority and ritual regulation seem to be giving way to wider structures in which a greater element of relative ranking and hierarchisation was possible. In regional terms, wealth was being spatially concentrated, with communities on the edge of the Plain or on main waterways becoming conspicuously richer than those in the centre. These communities had access for the first time to items of extra-regional trade.

The contrast with the preceding period should not be overdrawn: an ethnographic equivalent might be the difference between highland New Guinea and the more advanced parts of coastal and island Melanesia — both within the ethos of the Big Man rather than the Polynesian chief (Sahlins 1963). Nevertheless, European societies had entered the era of inequality.

Conclusions

The model presented here has important implications for the interpretation of early agricultural societies in many parts of the Old World. Although Çatal Hüyük is probably unique in that the whole region seems to have been focussed on a single site, the early spread of domestic cattle is likely to have had a similar effect in promoting regional exchange systems linking nodal lowland areas and their hinterlands, for instance during the Halaf period in northern Mesopotamia, and somewhat later in highland Iran. Such nodes may also have existed in south-east Europe, for instance in Thessaly, the Marica Basin and the lower Danube.[12]

A comparable, though attenuated, process may also have occurred even where initial agricultural occupation took

place in forested areas, as in much of central and northern Europe. In these areas there is a clear distinction between primary settlement, usually on loess, and secondary expansion, which occurred up to 1,000 years later. By this time there would have been a marked contrast between the already cleared and partly exhausted landscapes of initial settlement (where animals could be reared in quantity), and the small clearings round newly founded sites (cf. Kruk 1980). It is thus significant that enclosures often interpreted as cattle-pounds should appear by late Bandkeramik times, for example in the Rhineland; and that larger, centrally placed enclosures of a more elaborate kind should be associated with expanding settlement in the subsequent Michelsberg period (Boelicke 1976/7). Such enclosures are increasingly being recognised as characteristic elements of the late fourth- and third-millennium settlement patterns in northwest Europe, as forest cover was being opened up, and have analogies in many parts of the continent, from Les Matignons in the Charente to Dölauer Heide in central Germany.[13] They are likely to have served as centres for the concentration of surplus animals from the surrounding area, and their dispersal to outlying communities. These seasonal cattle fairs would have been occasions for general trade, as well as the observance of ritual. Such sites are of particular significance in northern Europe (including Britain), where expansion into forested environments was a large-scale process that continued into the period when animals were used for traction and secondary products.

The model is equally significant for understanding the social structure of early agricultural groups. The idea of self-sufficient groups 'budding off' and immediately achieving independence is probably true only in large uniform areas. In many cases there was probably an initial phase of continuing dependence and linkage. Where colonisation linked zones with complementary resources, regional exchange systems could develop that were capable of handling impressive quantities of goods. Such exchanges could be handled by transactions between acephalous groups linked only by alliance in conditions of general insecurity. A characteristic of such systems was the elaboration of many kinds of competing prestige items within the range of utilitarian artefacts. Since objects such as stone axes were used as social tokens (for example as bridewealth), they were probably produced in quantities beyond practical necessity. Although the importation of stone axes no doubt raised the productivity of the Hungarian Plain, demand was stimulated by social rather than technological factors. These societies appear 'wealthy' to the archaeologist in the sense that many sites produce quantities of stone tools, decorated pottery, ritual items, etc.

As regional differences in animal-raising potential became evened out with continuing forest clearance, the former structure, based on complementary exchanges in a regional system, began to break down. Contrasts emerged between areas whose wealth was purely agricultural and those which had both agricultural and mineral wealth. In the latter, competition was increasingly focussed on rarer and rarer prestige goods, especially metal objects. These usually take the form of prestige symbols (for example battle axes and sceptres) rather than commonly used items (for example work axes). Exchanges between these richer nuclei brought exotic materials over longer distances than before, and greater inequalities in access to imported materials are evident within the richer areas. These are well exemplified in the contemporary cemeteries of Tibava and Lučky (Bognár-Kutzián 1972) in the north-east of the Carpathian Basin (with both local stone and metal artefacts and imported materials from across the Carpathians) and at Varna (Todorova 1978) on the Black Sea coast of Bulgaria (with local copper and ?Anatolian gold).[14] Both areas have relatively undeveloped hinterlands where such prestige items are not found. These societies appear 'wealthy' to the archaeologist in the sense that a few sites produce spectacular quantities of specifically status items. Although many of these items are weapons, conditions appear to have been more peaceful than in the previous phase of acephalous communities linked by alliance.

A very similar succession seems to be behind later neolithic developments in north-west Europe. The communities of 'middle neolithic' megalith-builders, with their emphasis on ritual rather than rank, have many of the attributes of central European egalitarian communities in the period of intensive regional trade. The main difference lay in the availability of draught animals for tillage and construction. The significance of middle neolithic defended enclosures has already been noted. Ritual played a prominent part in social control, and burial took place in communal lineage ossuaries. Explicit symbols of rank are absent, but there was an elaboration of everyday items — decorated pottery, stone axes, flint leaf-points — for use as valuables. The succeeding 'late neolithic' pattern of Corded Ware and Bell Beakers was characterised by dispersed settlement without defensive and ritual elements, at the same time as the emergence of status-linked weaponry — battle axes, daggers and archery equipment, and rare ornaments. Long-distance trade (as opposed to the regional axe trade) brought increasingly rare materials into circulation, especially metals. This fits the pattern of rank competition. The last area to adopt the new pattern was the British Isles, where archaic structures (with a strongly ritual aspect) continued to be elaborated, producing sites like Avebury and Stonehenge long after comparable forms had disappeared from continental settlement patterns.

The element that transformed European economies in the early bronze age was the arrival (along with the horse) of woolly sheep (Sherratt 1981), that first provided a cash crop and the basis for a larger scale of textile production.[15] In this way, well-populated areas with extensive grazing were able to enrich themselves despite the lack of local metal sources. The chalklands and sands of Wessex and Jutland were able to

develop a complementary relationship with the Irish/Welsh and Harz metal sources respectively, and to intensify regional differences in wealth. Bronze (and textiles?) became a 'fetishised commodity' (Godelier 1977, 152) that could now be accumulated, with some of the characteristics of primitive *money* (cf. Douglas 1958, Dalton 1977) as opposed to primitive *valuables*. Competition was still largely for goods, and not linked to ownership of land. The rapid expansion of this extensive, land-hungry economy reached its ecological limits in the later second millennium, when land became a scarce good. Laid-out fields mark the beginning of formal landholding systems in which true social stratification could occur (Bradley 1980), creating the preconditions for interaction with the expanding Mediterranean world.[16]

The contrast between European and Near Eastern developmental trajectories from the fifth millennium onwards thus lay in the way such landholding inequalities were linked to the operation of regional exchange systems from an early date in areas like the Mesopotamian Plain. The conjunction of increasingly large-scale exchange with competition for access to high-yielding irrigated land caused inequalities between descent groups to build up into a truly stratified pattern from the fourth millennium onwards. The greater uniformity of the temperate European landscape deferred the emergence of such rigid forms of inequality for another 3,000 years.[17]

Notes

1 Dates are quoted in dendro-calibrated radiocarbon years.
2 Systematic surveys have been carried out by the Archaeological Institute of the Hungarian Academy of Sciences as part of the Archaeological Topography programme in Co. Békés (*Békés Megye Régészeti Topográfiája: A Szeghalmi Járás*, forthcoming). This is the basis for further fieldwork by a joint Hungarian–British team directed by Dr I. Torma and the author (Sherratt, forthcoming), with financial support from the British Academy, the University of Oxford, the Leverhulme Trust and the National Geographic Society.
3 For a general archaeological background see Kalicz (1970) and Tringham (1971).
4 Szakálhát and Tisza are successive phases, closely related in both material culture and settlement pattern. For other contemporary groups in the Great Hungarian Plain see n. 6.
5 Many examples are well known in the archaeological literature: Hódmezóvásárhely-Kökénydomb, H.-Gorzsa, Szegvár-Tüzköves, Battonya-Gödrösök, Szeghalom-Kovacshalom, Dévaványa-Sártó.
6 E.g. Szilmeg, Esztár and Bükk in the Szakálhát phase; Herpály and Csöszhalom in the Tisza phase.
7 Well exemplified in the settlement of Boldogkőváralya-Tekeres Patak (Co. Abaúj-Borsod-Zemplén), a site of the Bükk culture which included several workshops for flint and obsidian, including a cache of 567 blades as well as cores and lumps of raw material (Kalicz and Makkay 1977, 68–9).
8 It is likely that many animals were partly stall-fed on leaf-fodder in the early stages of settlement in forested areas, as suggested for neolithic Denmark and Switzerland on the basis of pollen diagrams and finds of excrement and leaf-fodder in settlements (see Guyan 1971, 151–4). If early neolithic

animals were not kept for milk, this would involve the fatten-
ing of individuals for slaughter, like the 'family pig' of recent
times.

9 Access to rivers for canoe transport became an important
element in determining settlement patterns from this time
onwards, and is especially notable in the Bodrogkeresztúr and
EBA periods.

10 Dalton's term is 'stateless': but this is too inclusive since it is
not intended to describe the various kinds of ranked society
(best attested by archaeology) that preceded the state.

11 A similar contrast may be observed at this time further north,
in Czechoslovakia and Poland, between the earlier and later
phases of the 'Lengyel culture'. The early phase has many local
styles of painted pottery, figurines, intensive use of local
resources (salt pans), regional exchange (obsidian) and
defended or enclosed sites (Kyjovice-Těšetice, Hluboke
Mašůvsky, Křepice); the later phase has plain pottery, no
figurines, long-distance contacts (metal, flint, pottery types)
and 'rich' graves (Jordanów, Brześć Kujawski).

12 For the west Mediterranean, Jim Lewthwaite has discussed the
importance of sheep as traded items in the Cardial interaction
area. As in central Europe, cattle seem to have increased in
importance in the fifth and fourth millennia, and the large
enclosed site of Passo di Corvo in Apulia − contemporary with
the Tisza sites discussed above − is likely to have had an
important role in this respect. The expansion of sheep-herding
(for secondary products) in the third millennium is again
associated with large defended sites, especially on limestone
plateaux.

13 The existence of earthworks and earth or stone monuments is
sometimes taken as evidence of the central direction of labour:
but this is to underestimate the capacity of egalitarian societies
to mobilise labour for communal projects (L. Groube, pers.
comm.). The existence of settlement networks with enclosed,
centrally placed sites is not evidence for social hierarchisation,
but is often characteristic of developed egalitarian societies
with a strongly ritual focus (cf. the fifth-millennium Moravian
Painted Ware sites in n. 11).

14 The importance of Varna is closely linked to its potential for
coastal trade. The composition of the goldwork, with its high
values for platinum, is almost unparalleled in Europe (Hartmann 1978). Although little is known of late chalcolithic
northern Anatolia, this source seems very likely. The objects
were *manufactured* locally, however, in the Balkan copper age
tradition.

15 In the east Mediterranean this was combined with another cash
crop, the olive, to produce high-quality manufactured commodities for the international maritime trade. This was the
economic basis of the Aegean palace system.

16 In sub-Saharan Africa, complex societies developed in the
absence of intensive agriculture and its attendant landholding
systems: hence the critical role played by competition for
prestige goods at the time of the early states (Goody 1969,
25ff.). Such systems are thus only partly analogous to those
of first-millennium Europe.

17 For discussions of the Hungarian evidence I must thank
especially my colleagues Nándor Kalicz, István Torma and
György Goldman. For general comments I am grateful to Steve
Shennan, Sue Sherratt and Henry Wright. The drawings are by
Nick Griffiths.

References

Adams, R.M. and Nissen, J. 1972. *The Uruk Countryside: the Natural Setting of Urban Societies.* Chicago, University Press.

Bökönyi, S. 1962. Zur Naturgeschichte des Ures in Ungarn und das Problem der Domestikation des Hausrindes. *Acta Archae-ologica Hungarica* 14: 175−214.

Bökönyi, S. 1974. *History of Domestic Mammals in Central and Eastern Europe.* Budapest, Akadémiai Kiadó.

Boelicke, U. 1976/7. Das Neolitische Erdwerk Urmitz. *Acta Prae-historica et Archaeologica* (Berlin) 7/8: 73−121.

Bognár-Kutzián, I. 1972. *The Early Copper Age Tiszapolgár Culture in the Carpathian Basin.* Budapest, Akadémiai Kiadó.

Bradley, R. 1980. Subsistence, exchange and technology − a social framework for the Bronze Age in southern England c. 1400−700 BC., in J. Barrett and R. Bradley (eds.), *Settlement and Society in the British Later Bronze Age.* Oxford, British Archaeological Reports, 57−75.

Brookfield, H.C. and Hart, D. 1971. *Melanesia: a geographical interpretation of an island world.* London, Methuen.

Childe, V.G. 1951. *Social Evolution.* London, Fontana.

Comşa, E. 1967. Über die Verbreitung und Herkunft einiger von den jungsteinzeitliche Menschen auf dem Gebiete Rumäniens verwendeten Werkstoffe. *A Móra Ferenc Múzeum Évkönyve,* Szeged (1967), 26−8.

Dalton, G. 1977. Aboriginal economies in stateless societies, in T.K. Earle and J. Ericson (eds.), *Exchange Systems in Prehistory,* New York, Academic Press, 191−209.

Douglas, M. 1958. Raffia cloth in the Lele economy. *Africa* 28: 109−22.

Flannery, K.V. 1965. The ecology of early food production in Meso-potamia. *Science* 147: 1246−56.

Gimbutas, M. 1974. *The Gods and Goddesses of Old Europe 7000−3500 BC.* London, Thames and Hudson.

Godelier, M. 1977. *Perspectives in Marxist Anthropology.* Cambridge, University Press.

Goody, J. 1969. *Technology, Tradition and the State in Africa.* Oxford, University Press.

Guyan, M.U. 1971. *Erforschte Vergangenheit* (Band 1), Schaffhausen.

Hartmann, A. 1978. Ergebnisse der spektralanalytischen Unter-suchung äneolithischer Goldfunde aus Bulgarien. *Studia Prae-historica* (Sofia) 1/2: 27−45.

Herre, W. and Röhrs, M. 1977. Zoological considerations on the origins of farming and domestication, in C. Reed (ed.), *Origins of Agriculture.* The Hague/Paris, Mouton, 263−7.

Hughes, I.A. 1973. Stone-age trade in the New Guinea inland, in H.C. Brookfield (ed.), *The Pacific in Transition.* London, E. Arnold, 97−126.

Illés, A.E. and Halász, A. 1926. *La Hongrie avant et après la Guerre.* Budapest, Société Hongroise de Statistique.

Jacobs, J. 1969. *The Economy of Cities.* Harmondsworth, Penguin.

Kalicz, N. 1970. *Clay Gods: The Neolithic Period and Copper Age in Hungary.* Budapest, Corvina Press.

Kalicz, N. and Makkay, J. 1977. *Die Linienbandkeramik in der Grossen Ungarischen Tiefebene.* Budapest, Akadémiai Kiadó.

Kosse, K. 1979. *Settlement Ecology of the Körös and Linear Pottery Cultures in Hungary.* Oxford, British Archaeological Reports.

Kruk, J. 1980. *Gospodarka w Polsce Południowo-wschodniej w V−III Tysiącleciu P.N.E.* Warsaw, Polish Academy of Sciences.

Mellaart, J. 1967. *Çatal Hüyük, a Neolithic Town in Anatolia.* London, Thames and Hudson.

Pavúk, J. 1972. Neolithisches Gräberfeld in Nitra. *Slovenská Archeologia* 20: 5−105.

Perkins, D. 1969. Fauna of Çatal Hüyük: evidence for early cattle domestication in Anatolia. *Science* 164: 177−9.

Rappaport, R.A. 1968. *Pigs for the Ancestors.* New Haven, Yale University Press.

Sahlins, M.D. 1963. Poor man, rich man, big man, chief: political types in Melanesia and Polynesia. *Comparative Studies in Society and History* 5: 285−303.

Schüle, W. 1969. Glockenbecher und Hauspferde, in J. Boessneck (ed.), *Archaeologie und Biologie.* Wiesbaden, 100–11.

Semple, E.C. 1932. *The Geography of the Mediterranean Region: its relation to ancient history.* London, Constable.

Sherratt, A.G. 1976. Resources, technology and trade, in G. Sieveking, I.H. Longworth and K. Wilson (eds.), *Problems in Economic and Social Archaeology.* London, Duckworth, 557–81.

Sherratt, A.G. 1981. Plough and pastoralism: aspects of the secondary products revolution, in I. Hodder, G. Isaac and N. Hammond (eds.), *Pattern of the Past: Studies in honour of David Clarke.* Cambridge, University Press, 261–305.

Sherratt, A.G. 1982. The development of Neolithic and Copper Age settlement in the Great Hungarian Plain. *Oxford Journal of Archaeology* 1.

Sherratt, A.G., forthcoming. Early agrarian settlement in the Körös region of the Great Hungarian Plain. *Acta Archaeologica Hungarica.*

Todd, I.A. 1978. *Çatal Hüyük in Perspective.* Menlo Park, Cummings.

Todorova, H. 1978. Die Nekropole bei Varna. *Zeitschrift für Archäologie* 12: 87–97.

Tringham, R. 1971. *Hunters, Fishers and Farmers of Eastern Europe 6000–3000 BC.* London, Hutchinson.

Chapter 3

**From minimal to
moderate ranking**
Susan Shennan

*This paper is a study of social change in one area of
central Europe during the early bronze age. Using the data
from several recently excavated cemeteries, it documents a
trend from a minimal to a more marked degree of ranking in
the early part of the period. However, this differentiation
remains at the intra-community level; there is no evidence of
regionally centralised organisation. This situation changes
abruptly in the late phase of the early bronze age in the area,
and the changes are linked to processes of social competition
for which there is evidence in the earlier period cemeteries.*

In virtually the whole 5,000 years of the post-
mesolithic prehistory of Europe north of the Mediterranean
the only change apparent in terms of the standard evolutionary typologies is that from egalitarian to ranked or perhaps
stratified society. In order to document and understand the
extensive changes which undoubtedly did occur in the period
from the neolithic to the iron age it is necessary to put aside
these gross evolutionary stages and define much more
sensitive scales of change.

This is likely to be particularly productive in those
periods and areas in which major socio-economic changes
have always been assumed to have occurred. One such period
is the early bronze age and one of the areas always assumed
to be at the centre of these developments is central Europe.
These beliefs have depended in the main on a superficial

inspection of the evidence rather than detailed analysis. Determination of the correctness of the assumptions and of the rate at which change occurred requires good data with tight chronological control.

A series of excavations of inhumation cemeteries carried out in the 1950s and 1960s, mainly in south-west Slovakia (fig. 3.1), provided the data necessary for carrying out such an investigation. (Točik 1963, n.d.; Vladár 1973; Ondráček n.d.; Budinský-Kricka 1965; Pichlerová 1966). These cemeteries cover the period from the very beginning of the early bronze age in the area to the end of its earlier phase, about 200–300 years. A later early bronze age phase lasts perhaps another 150 years. This later phase will be considered briefly at the end, but this paper will be mainly concerned with the cemeteries of the earlier period.

Before examining these in detail it is worth making a general point about the social organisation of this earlier period as a whole in the area. Earle (1978) has noted succinctly that chiefdoms are based on two organisational principles: the ranking of individual statuses within the local community and the regionally centralised organisation of local communities. No non-cemetery sites are known from this period in Slovakia to test directly for regionally centralised organisation, but there is no suggestion that there is any hierarchy among the cemeteries themselves. If this negative evidence is accepted it means that the degree of ranking present must be strictly limited: to talk about elites, and stratified societies with warrior aristocracies, as people have done, is to overstate the case.

A second general point concerns the size of the communities which were burying their dead in these cemeteries. It is essential to obtain an order of magnitude estimate of community size as an indication of the scale of organisation at the individual community level, but to make inferences concerning this requires a number of assumptions. First, it is necessary to assume that everyone was buried in the cemeteries. Some assessment of this in relation to age groups may be obtained — it suggests, predictably, that some of the youngest children are missing, but it is straightforward to make allowances for this. If some segment of the community representative as regards sex and age distribution were missing this could not be detected, but in the present case at least we have a number of different cemeteries all showing the same pattern, with no suggestion that any were restricted to

Fig. 3.1. (a) Location of study area.

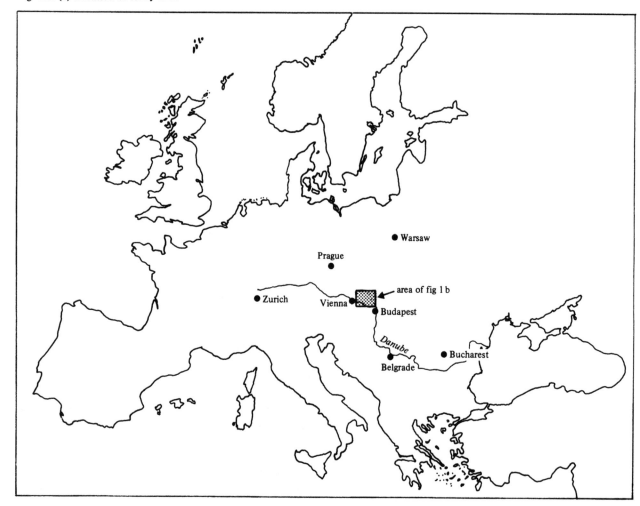

a specific section of society. We can add that the density of large cemeteries in the small area concerned over a comparatively short time indicates that the cemeteries might well represent fairly complete populations of particular communities. A second assumption is that of stationary populations. This is harder to check, but in the larger cemeteries at least it seems that graves were being fairly continuously deposited from the beginning of the period to the end without any major concentration at one particular time. On this basis it would appear that community size at all the sites at any given time was small. In no case were there more than one hundred individuals, of whom probably fifty per cent would be children.

It is the degree to which Earle's first principle — the ranking of individual statuses within these local communities — operates here, and its changes through time, which are the main subject of this paper.

One of the greatest problems in using cemetery data for the study of change through time is the fact that we have to group a large number of successive burials together and treat them as a cross-section of the community at any one time. This creates difficulties if change in our variables of interest (for example, the degree of ranking) has in fact taken place in the burials which make up our cross-section. In the present study this problem could be overcome, to some extent at least, by the use of typological information independently attested as having chronological significance; this could be used to distinguish some of the cemeteries from each other chronologically, and also to define the spatial growth of certain individual cemeteries. Assigning graves to phases within individual cemeteries in this way is clearly somewhat arbitrary but nevertheless means that through-time change can be studied. In the case of the cemeteries investigated here, the fact that the spatial position of the grave in the cemetery mainly relates to the growth of the cemetery through time is confirmed by the fact that tests did not reveal any spatial differentiation of age, sex or rank groups, and that the age/sex distributions of the hypothesised phases were not significantly different from one another.

It is worth noting here that in the same way that there appears to be no spatial dimension to the social variation exhibited in the burials, there are also virtually no differences in the degree of elaboration of the burial facility (i.e. the grave), either within or between cemeteries. This study is restricted to a consideration of the grave goods and certain aspects of the position of the skeleton in the grave, not out of narrow-mindedness but simply because these are the only aspects of the burials which actually vary!

Fig. 3.1. (b) The distribution of early bronze age sites in south-west Slovakia (after Točik 1964).

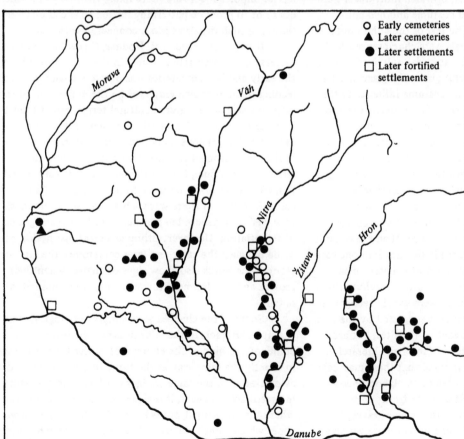

The very earliest cemetery, that of Veselé, is distinguished from those that come later by a number of features. The graves are, in general, far more similar to one another in their contents, and while it appears that certain artefacts are restricted to one or other sex, neither sex predominated in any of the groupings produced by cluster analysis, in which respect they differ clearly from those which come later. The standard female costume of the later cemeteries was also lacking, nor was there any real difference between male and female graves in the quantity of the grave goods present. On all the one-dimensional scales used to measure quantity of goods — variety of types, number of items, number of units in a wealth scale — the range of variation from top to bottom is very narrow.

The second cemetery in the sequence, Ivanka pri Dunaji, is also characterised by a narrow range of variation from top to bottom of these scales, but exhibits some new features which become characteristic of the later cemeteries — a more marked distinction between the sexes, as part of which, among other things, women have more grave goods than men, and the standardised female ornaments of necklaces and ear-rings appear. In both these early cemeteries, however, the quantity of metal deposited is very small.

In the cemeteries of the two succeeding phases, the patterns distinguished at the earlier sites are continued and become more clear-cut. A group of burials could be clearly distinguished at each of these sites, in which individuals were wearing an elaborate standardised costume and had consistently more grave goods than the rest of the community. In fact virtually all 'rich' individuals were characterised by the special standard costume worn at burial only by females, including elaborate necklaces, metal pins and leg garters. This clearly suggests that it is the female costume rather than the 'richness' as such which is the relevant factor here. It is also noteworthy that female subadults do not have such elaborate ornaments as some of the female adults. Those burials with elaborate ornaments also possessed idiosyncratic items of no intrinsic worth in terms of the 'wealth' criteria adopted but clearly of symbolic significance, which suggests that status corresponded with the right to a more impressive display at burial. There are a number of hints of an emphasis on display: if more ear-rings were worn on one ear than the other it was on the side which faced upwards in the grave; in one case a 'rich' grave contained a bone necklace which was a clear imitation of a type made of the more exotic *Dentalium* shell.

That the distinctions described were widely recognised and have more than local significance is suggested by the fact that the same pattern is found at each of the sites, but again it is important to emphasise the lack of inter-site hierarchy. Furthermore, it should be borne in mind that there may have been only one or two females entitled to an elaborate costume present in the community at any one time.

If one compares the male with the female graves, the goods are obviously very different and in fact more variable: some male graves are markedly 'richer' than others, but the differences between adult and subadult graves in this respect are far smaller than for females. This suggests a difference in attitude to the deaths of male and female subadults, and may indeed indicate that female status was in some way achieved, possibly on marriage; but to argue for inherited male wealth on the basis of the 'rich' male infant burials is to press the evidence too far. For one thing it suggests a more complex and sophisticated type of organisation than the rest of the evidence can really support. It should be noted that there would probably have been only one man who would eventually receive a 'rich' burial alive in the community at any one time.

We should perhaps be thinking in terms of a headman who focussed and coordinated community activities and whose position was achieved. Although wealth and status would not be ascribed, any sons of such a man who died young might receive a more elaborate burial than other boys because the big man wished to display his position at the occasion of their burial, because they had a certain position by virtue of their relationship to him, or simply because he had more resources available. The system would then be of a type well documented ethnographically in which rank and wealth were achieved competitively by males, but some males had a greater chance of achieving than others by virtue of their descent and differential opportunity from birth. It may be suggested that societies in which competitive display has an important role are more likely than those in which it does not to produce patterning related to social differentiation in such rituals as those connected with death.

It might be argued (cf. Hodder, this volume) that the increase in differentiation visible in the grave goods between the early and late cemeteries was due to a change in ideology leading to an increased emphasis on the expression of social differences in such material cultural terms, rather than an increase in social differentiation as such. In this case, however, the changes are simply a matter of degree in a system of burial symbolism which shows an essential continuity of structure from one phase to the next, and it is suggested here that such a pattern is unlikely to be the result of an ideological shift; rather, if there was such an increasing emphasis, it may well have proceeded *pari passu* with increasing social differentiation. However, although a clear distinction can be made between the early and later cemeteries, the later cemeteries themselves also show signs of change when their growth and development through time are examined in detail.

Some of the changes were simply typological: for example, artefacts in the later phase of the cemeteries which come into fashion at the expense of earlier types were used in exactly the same way as the types they replaced, and were associated with the same categories of age and sex. More interestingly, however, it is clear from those cemeteries where the growth pattern is known in detail, that certain types which came into general currency in the later period were on their first appearance restricted to the 'rich' graves.

This is an example of the widely prevalent innovation adoption pattern for prestige goods in which they are initially taken up by higher status groups within a community; it is interesting to see evidence for such a process of emulation in this early context.

Changes in other spheres were also apparent: there were more 'rich' graves in the late phase, indicating a slight increase in the deposition of 'wealth' through time. This point was examined in detail with special regard for the distinctions between the sexes. A Kolmogorov–Smirnov test on the proportions of females in the different wealth categories in the two phases revealed a significant difference between them. The maximum difference between the two groups was at the lowest 'wealth' category, showing that a larger proportion of the female graves were 'poor' in the earlier than the later phase, although it is worth noticing that the average 'wealth' of the 'rich' female graves is the same in each phase. The difference seems to be in the increased deposition of metal ornaments in the graves and may be related to a general increase in the availability of metal in the later phase, with the result that it lost some of its value and became more generally accessible. The same test carried out on male graves with their very different inventory of goods, involving less metal, did not produce a significant result.

It is interesting to note that the differences just described in the female graves do not represent an increase in differentiation but simply a general increase in the amount of 'wealth' that was deposited; nor do the males show increased differentiation. This situation may be contrasted with the distinction between the two very earliest cemeteries – Veselé and Ivanka – and the rest, where, as we have noted, such increased differentiation in the grave goods is clearly to be seen.

The results just described indicate that the degree of ranking prevalent in this area in the earlier period of the early bronze age was distinctly limited, although it seems to have increased during the period. They certainly do not prepare us for the developments of the final phase of the EBA in this area. Here the detailed work remains to be done, but in broad outline it appears that in a relatively short period some form of regionally centralised organisation became established, with one or two fortified sites appearing in each of the river valleys of the area, as well as a large number of other settlements (see fig. 3.1). This is a dramatic development, as settlements of any kind are unknown from the earlier phases of the early bronze age discussed above.

In these fortified sites (Točik 1964), have been found craft products, including metalwork, of a sophistication not found in earlier phases. There is also evidence of craft production, including moulds for metal ornaments as well as elaborate bone carving. New long-distance contacts are also apparent – for example, in the appearance of amber, likewise not found earlier.

The cemeteries of this later phase, however (Ondráček 1962; Dušek 1969; Chropovský *et al.* 1960), seem remarkably similar to those that went before. Although the settlements suggest increased social differentiation at this time, it does not appear to be reflected in the funerary evidence, which suggests a similar degree of differentiation between individuals as existed earlier, although without detailed analysis it is very difficult to be certain of this. Nevertheless, it seems that apart from typological changes in the grave inventory (as the more elaborate metal types mentioned above found their way into the graves), and perhaps a slight increase in the amount of metal deposited, the burials remain surprisingly unaltered. However, the pattern may be more apparent than real, especially the continuing lack of hierarchy between the cemeteries, as we do not as yet have those associated with the fortified sites. This can be appreciated from fig. 3.1, which shows the distribution of known settlement and cemetery sites from this later phase of the early bronze age.

One new development in the cemeteries of this phase has not yet been mentioned. Although more metal may have been deposited in an individual burial, there was a much greater prevalence of grave 'robbing' in this phase. 'Robbing' is an emotive term and probably inappropriate; nevertheless, it is clear that metal, once deposited in the grave, was frequently removed fairly soon after the individual was buried. It is tempting to suggest that this could relate to problems with the metal supply which made it necessary to bring the metal back into circulation.

The appearance of the impressive fortified sites must indicate a period of fairly rapid social change, which demands further investigation. Changes in subsistence production and its organisation may well have played an important role in this, but unfortunately very little is currently known about them. On the other hand, we have already seen evidence for the increasing significance of metal. The very fact that we see it having an obvious social role in the graves suggests that it had an importance in which lay a potential for competition and manipulation. The cemeteries which have been discussed above provide strong evidence for processes of emulation and competitive display in which this potential was being realised. The development of a settlement hierarchy may have been the end result of such competition as the location of communities in the distribution system of metal and other commodities became increasingly important. Any problems in supply, suggested by the grave robbing, would only have increased the competitive pressures, and the potential benefits to certain communities or sections of them.[1]

Note

1 I would like to thank not only the British Academy for its financial support which made my attendance at the 45th S.A.A. meeting possible, but also my mother, Mrs F.N. Lathbury, and my mother-in-law, Mrs J.F. Shennan, whose practical support in looking after Sophie and Henry while I was away made the visit possible.

References

Budinský-Krička, V. 1965. Gräberfeld der späten schnurkeramischen Kultur in Veselé. *Slovenská Archeologia* 13: 1–106.

Chropovský, B., Dušek, M. and Polla, B. 1960. *Gräberfelder aus der älteren Bronzezeit in der Slowakei* I. Bratislava, Vydavateľ'stvo Slovenskej Akadémie Vied.

Dušek, M. 1969. *Bronzezeitliche Gräberfelder in der Südwestslowakei.* Bratislava, Vydavateľ'stvo Slovenskej Akadémie Vied.

Earle, T.K. 1978. *Economic and social organisation of a complex chiefdom: the Halelea district, Kaua'i, Hawaii* (Anthropological Papers of the Museum of Anthropology 63). Ann Arbor, University of Michigan.

Ondráček, J. 1962. Únětické pohřebiště u Rebešovic na Moravě. *Sborník Československé Společnosti Archeologické* 2: 5–100.

Ondráček, J. n.d. Unpublished excavation report of the Nitra Group site of Holešov. The Archaeological Institute, Brno.

Pichlerová, M. 1966. Pohrebisko s neskorou šnúrovou keramikou typu Veselé u Ivanka pri Dunaji. *Sborník Slovenského Národného múzea* 60: 25–56.

Točik, A. 1963. Die Nitra Gruppe. *Archeologické rozhledy* 15: 716–74.

Točik, A. 1964. *Opevnené osada z doby bronzovej vo Veselom.* Bratislava, Vydavateľ'stvo Slovenskej Akadémie Vied.

Točik, A. n.d. Unpublished manuscript on the cemeteries of the Nitra Group. The Archaeological Institute, Nitra.

Vladár, J. 1973. *Pohrebiská zo Staršej Doby Bronzovej v Branči.* Bratislava, Vydavateľ'stvo Slovenskej Akadémie Vied.

Chapter 4

**Exchange and ranking:
the role of amber in
the earlier bronze age
of Europe**
Stephen Shennan

An outline is given of the changes in the spatial distribution of amber in central and western Europe during the neolithic and earlier bronze age. Its distribution in neolithic Denmark is then examined more closely and some reasons are suggested why it was largely restricted to Denmark in this period. This leads on to an investigation of the reasons for its subsequent expansion, which, it is argued, relate to major changes in European social organisation at this time. The implications of the new situation are looked at in detail for two areas, Denmark and Wessex.

In the last fifteen years exchange studies have played a major role in attempts to realise the aim of making inferences about past social organisation on the basis of archaeological evidence. The twin bases of this approach have been theoretical and methodological introductions to archaeology from other areas of study. On the theoretical side Polanyi's (1957) distinctions between reciprocity, redistribution and market exchange have been adopted and, on the assumption that they are associated with specific kinds of societies, have been used to construct social typologies. Methodologically, the basis for using exchange as a major index on which to base inferences about past societies has been the application of quantitative methods of spatial analysis to the study of distributions of archaeological data, on the assumption that differences in spatial patterns result from differing processes which produced them. More recently, the optimism which gave rise to the use of exchange studies to achieve such aims has given way to a much less sanguine view, as the association of types of exchange and types of society has been criticised (e.g. Yoffee 1979), the concept of redistribution has been reviewed (Earle 1977) and the relationship between spatial pattern and spatial process has been shown to be an indeterminate one (e.g. Renfrew 1977, Clark 1979).

These criticisms have diminished the role that large-scale spatial studies of the distributions of particular types of archaeological material of known source were once thought capable of playing, but not the importance of including exchange in the study of past social processes. Rather, they have emphasised the need for us to develop more adequate theory concerning the relation between exchange and society, at the general level, and to devote more attention to analysing the intra-societal roles of objects in the archaeological context.

In the light of these considerations this paper explores the case of amber exchange in the neolithic and earlier bronze age of Europe and attempts to explain why the chronological and spatial distribution of this material took the form which is evidenced in the archaeological record. It will be suggested that the explanation lies in wider changes which were affecting the societies of western and central Europe at this time, and which involved a change in the internal role of exchange within those societies.

The chronological and spatial distribution of amber

Amber is, of course, a fossil resin, and numerous sources of such resins are known throughout the world. Even within Europe itself a considerable number of different sources is known, from virtually all parts of the continent, including the British Isles. In recent years, however, the analytical work of Prof. C.W. Beck and his associates (Beck *et al.* 1964; 1965), has shown that virtually all amber examined from neolithic and bronze age contexts in Europe comes from the major Baltic source (fig. 4.1),[1] and at the European scale a general pattern in its chronological and spatial distribution may now be discerned.

In the early neolithic[2] and the first part of the middle neolithic (c. 3500–2500 bc) amber is confined to the Baltic zone. In the later middle and late neolithic (c. 2500–1900 bc) it spreads further south, although only in very small quantities, and is found, for example, in northern France and western Czechoslovakia. Up to and including this phase the distribution of amber is characterised by a general fall-off in quantity from the Baltic zone, but in the succeeding early bronze age phase (c. 1900–1600 bc) there is a change. Amber reaches the more southerly areas in far greater quantity than was the case earlier, and the boundary of the distribution extends further south, as well as west into Britain. In its Danish zone of origin, however, the quantity of amber in archaeological contexts decreases very markedly, so that there are now greater quantities further away from

the source than there are close to it. In the following middle bronze age phase (c. 1600–1300 bc), the last with which I am concerned in this paper, the lack of amber in the source area continues. To the south the quantities of amber are probably even greater, while the distribution expands yet further in a southerly direction, into southern France, northern Jugoslavia, and also into Mycenaean Greece.[3]

The patterns observed in this chronological development raise two major questions. Why did the distribution of amber expand in this way, which is not paralleled by any other contemporary exchanged materials? What was the relationship between the circulation of amber and its deposition?

These questions are, of course, closely interlinked; indeed, an adequate answer to the first is dependent on a valid model of the second. To suggest an answer to them demands a more detailed consideration of the evidence; in particular, it requires considerable care in the construction of a meaningful picture of the spatial and chronological distribution of amber at any level more detailed that the broad sketch just given. Amber is a fragile material which will oxidise and disintegrate in many archaeological contexts,

Fig. 4.1. Generalised distribution of amber in western and central Europe during the neolithic and bronze age.
The heavy line along the west coast of Jutland indicates the main amber source area in the western Baltic.

  ....   Approximate southern boundary of amber distribution c. 2500 bc.
  -------   Approximate southern boundary of amber distribution c. 1900 bc.
  -·-·-·-   Approximate southern boundary of amber distribution c. 1300 bc.
Triangle marks position of Mycenae.

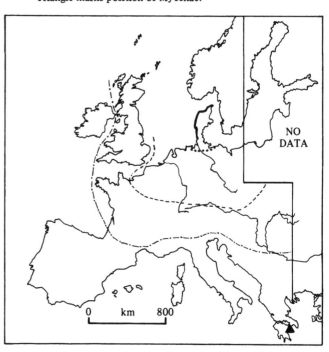

while the bulk of these contexts are graves, and to a lesser extent hoards, whose contents will have been the result of a variety of different factors. These considerations mean that the presence or absence of amber in a particular context at a particular time or place cannot necessarily be taken at its face value, but needs to be carefully evaluated.

In view of these points it has to be asked whether the expansion of the distribution of amber through time just described represents an extension of the area in which amber was circulating, so that circulation was spatially at least more or less coterminous with deposition, or whether it was an expansion of the practice of depositing amber in areas where it had been circulating from an early date. The latter seems highly unlikely but its rejection ultimately depends on negative evidence. In particular, the burial record of central Europe suggests that from the beginning of the late neolithic through into the early bronze age and beyond sociotechnic artefacts were deposited with individuals on burial. Occurrences of amber are extremely rare in the early period (Buchvaldek 1967, Hájek 1968) but increase through time; all the contexts are earth-pit graves from the same area with the same preservation conditions. It thus appears likely that in at least one of the areas away from the amber sources the deposition of amber was in a direct relation to the amount in circulation, so that, where no archaeologically visible deposition of amber occurs in a given period, amber was either not circulating at all or only present in very small quantities.

Amber in neolithic Denmark

Assuming then that the generalised distribution picture described is a valid one, it is necessary to focus on specific parts of the picture in order to understand it, beginning with the important source area of Denmark. Figures 4.2–4.6 present a diachronic view of the deposition of amber[4] in relation to distance from its source.[5] In demonstrating for most periods the general fall-off in quantity of amber deposited with distance from the west Jutland coast, the scatter plots bring out all the more the anomalous position of the Funnel Beaker (TRB) middle neolithic period, when the pattern was reversed and large quantities of amber were deposited in the Danish islands, particularly Zealand. In considering the significance of this it is first necessary to ask why the quantity of amber deposited does decrease with distance in the other periods. That it simply relates to some cultural norm concerning the quantity of amber to be deposited in graves seems highly implausible since there is no reason why such a hypothetical norm should show a gradient of the kind which is apparent; the same applies for recovery and preservation factors. The variation in deposition must relate to variation in the supply of amber: supply was affected by distance. Distance itself, of course, is only a measurable proxy for a variety of different processes affected in some way by spatial factors. It may be suggested that since amber is an extremely light material and was never used in bulk for

any purpose of which we have evidence, energy costs in transport are not the relevant aspect of distance here. More likely to be relevant is the number of intervening consumers taking their share of the available material before passing on a residue.

Randsborg (1975) has suggested that the relatively egalitarian societies of the Danish early neolithic gave way to more hierarchical forms of organisation in the middle neolithic, and it is at this time that the major deviation from a monotonic fall-off pattern is observed, with large concentrations of amber well away from the source area. Although the work remains to be done to test in detail the reasons for this, I would suggest that the monotonic fall-off within Jutland combined with the evidence for a much greater range of variation in quantity in the Danish islands is indicative of the expression of a greater degree of ranking in the latter area. The consumption of amber was sufficiently important, and certain individuals or groups sufficiently powerful, for large quantities of amber either to be obtained directly from west Jutland or, perhaps more likely, to go

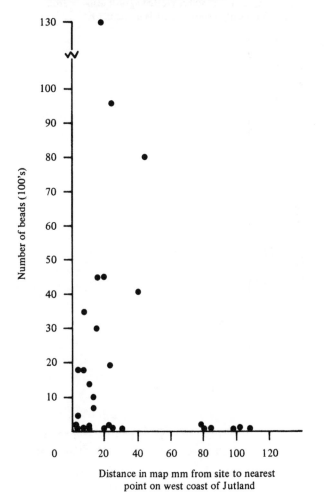

Fig. 4.2. Quantity of amber plotted against distance from source: TRB amber hoards in Denmark.

through the down-the-line system without being consumed and to accumulate in the islands, Zealand in particular.

The two succeeding periods revert to a monotonic fall-off pattern (cf. Mahler 1978), but it should be noted that the second of these, the earlier bronze age, was undoubtedly characterised by strongly ranked societies (Randsborg 1974, Kristiansen 1978), and that the eastern Islands seem to have been one of the richest zones. The sharp contrast in the pattern of amber distribution between this period and the middle neolithic, together with the generally small quantities deposited (compare the amber quantity scale of the early bronze age figure with that of the three earlier periods) suggests that amber was no longer being used in the same way as a rank indicator in Denmark; a reason for this will be proposed below.

The expansion of the amber distribution
As we have already seen, during the period of the Danish early and middle neolithic amber was very little used outside the Baltic zone. In view of the fact that demand for amber for consumption within that zone was high and that

the amber sources were obviously being exploited, it may be considered curious that an expansion of its area of distribution did not take place earlier (for the reasons discussed above it seems very unlikely that amber circulated extensively outside the Baltic zone without finding its way into the archaeological record).

To understand this anomaly it is necessary to suggest why its distribution did eventually expand at the end of the neolithic and the beginning of the bronze age. As I will argue more fully below, the reasons are the need of the Scandinavian area to obtain metal supplies from the areas to the south and west, and the appearance in these areas of a new form of hierarchical society in which social position depended on the consumption of prestige goods.

Neither of these conditions obtained prior to this time. West of the Carpathian Basin, metal objects occurred only extremely sporadically prior to the end of the neolithic, and both utilitarian and ornamental/prestige items were made of stone and bone. Denmark is extremely rich in high quality flint, including supplies appropriate for the manufacture of large stone artefacts such as axes, and did not have to import

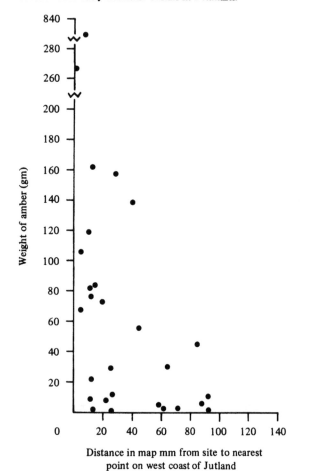

Fig. 4.3. Quantity of amber plotted against distance from source: TRB early neolithic burials in Denmark.

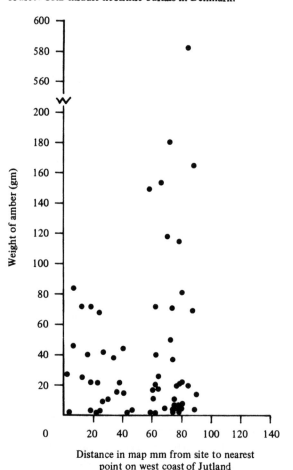

Fig. 4.4. Quantity of amber plotted against distance from source: TRB middle neolithic burials in Denmark.

it as other areas had to do.[6] This removed one reason for the Danish area to be involved in long-distance exchanges for which a reciprocal commodity was required.

Secondly, the case can be made (see Shennan 1982) that the areas immediately to the south and west of Denmark into which the amber distribution could theoretically have expanded were characterised by forms of society in which valuables of any kind, amber or otherwise, played little role. In particular, where hierarchies already existed, their existence was legitimised by means of monuments involving the collective labour of the community, rather than by the consumption of prestige items, while areas which do not show any monumental or other evidence of centralisation are also lacking in any evidence for such consumption.

In the period from c. 2200 to 1700 bc there was a major change in these basic conditions. A copper and bronze industry became established in parts of central and western Europe, producing weapons, ornaments, and flat axes which may have served as tools (cf. Harding 1976). The products of these industries began to be imported into Denmark (see below), which had no metal resources of its own and there-

fore depended on the areas to the south not just for the initial introduction of the innovations but for its continuing supplies of metal. It may be suggested then that one reason for the expansion of the amber distribution far beyond the south Scandinavian area was the need of that region to establish a commodity which could be exchanged in order to obtain the metal which is so abundantly evident in the archaeological record of the Danish bronze age.

However, the situation is certainly not as straightforward as this might imply. Amber does occur in those areas with which south Scandinavian metalwork has typological similarities, and also in the areas of the metal sources, but it occurs extensively too in areas which cannot possibly have been involved in the supply of metal to south Scandinavia. While this was the ultimate source of the amber, it seems certain that it became incorporated into other exchange networks which included various parts of central, southern and western Europe.

The obtaining of metal supplies is a clear enough reason why the Danish area should have been interested in establishing contacts with the south, but why there should

Fig. 4.5. Quantity of amber plotted against distance from source: Single Grave burials in Denmark. Large symbols represent mean values for successive distance bands away from source.

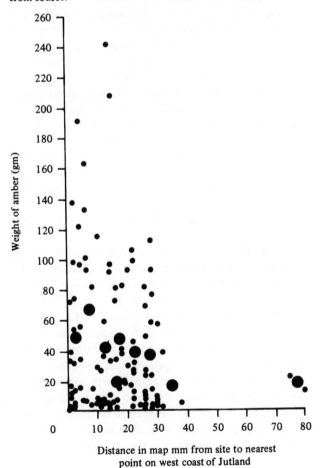

Distance in map mm from site to nearest point on west coast of Jutland

Fig. 4.6. Quantity of amber plotted against distance from source: earlier bronze age burials in Denmark.

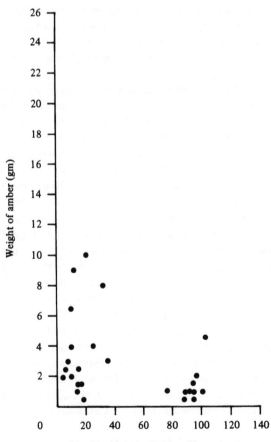

Distance in map mm from site to nearest point on west coast of Jutland

have been a demand for amber which led to its wider-ranging exchange is a matter that now needs to be considered.

As I have argued elsewhere (Shennan 1982), the other major change which occurred at this time was a social one. There was a shift in the ideology of those hierarchical societies which already existed in certain parts of western Europe, while in central Europe hierarchies actually appeared where they had not previously existed. In both cases a situation developed in which the maintenance of these hierarchies was closely bound up with the consumption of prestige valuables.

This was the result of an ideology involving legitimating rituals which emphasised the consumption of prestige items obtained through contact with elite groups elsewhere, and which came to characterise both western and central Europe. One consequence of the fact that prestige and rank were now represented in terms of objects was that those objects acquired an intrinsic value, and could actually be used to create a position. A medium for competition was thus created which had not previously existed and which greatly extended the possibilities of intra-elite rivalry. Such competition led to an emphasis on the active seeking out of distant contacts, amply documented in the archaeological record. These were a more or less inevitable corollary of the situation which has been postulated, since so long as a number of areas had social systems which depended on the supply and consumption of prestige goods which could only be obtained by contacts with elites elsewhere, a network of reciprocal demand was automatically created which would have a tendency to incorporate areas which has not initially been part of it.

That the expansion of the distribution of amber into large parts of central and western Europe correlated chronologically with the changes which have just been briefly outlined is clear, but it might be suggested that the correlation is a spurious one and that amber did not necessarily function as a prestige item in such a system. This seems unlikely for a number of reasons. First, amber is not a utilitarian material but was used almost exclusively for making ornaments, especially necklaces and pendants. Secondly, the very fact of its deposition as grave goods betokens some social significance. Thirdly, there is a strong correlation between the presence of amber in graves (and the quantity in which it occurs), and the presence of other objects and materials which would generally be considered as of an elite nature. Finally, there is evidence from some parts of the distribution zone that the exchange of amber was directed towards those areas with the most marked social differentiation.

This is clearest in the case of Mycenaean Greece. South-central Greece was a considerable distance to the south of the main southern frontier of the amber distribution in the middle bronze age, but all the evidence suggests that this area, and particularly Mycenae itself, was the part of Europe with the most developed hierarchies at this time. The demand created by the Mycenaean elite was such as to pro-

duce a very clear example of 'directional trade' (Renfrew 1977), whether as a result of entrepreneurial activity or inter-elite gift exchange. The connection of amber with the elite is amply confirmed by its restriction, when it first appeared, to only three centres, in particular Mycenae itself, where over 1,200 of the more than 1,500 beads known from Greece in this period were found in one of the Shaft Graves (Harding and Hughes-Brock 1974),[7] the most spectacular concentrations of grave wealth in the prehistoric Aegean.

Amber in the Danish earlier bronze age

More light can be thrown on the processes already discussed by returning to the question of the relationship between the circulation of amber and its deposition, specifically the apparent anomaly that far less amber has been recovered from bronze age contexts in Denmark than in some areas to the south and west. As virtually all our evidence for amber in the European bronze age stems from the consumption of objects by their deposition in graves and hoards, usually together with other items such as metalwork, the conclusion must be that the consumption of amber was occurring in large parts of Europe but to a much smaller extent in Scandinavia. It is now necessary to consider why this might have been the case.

It has already been suggested that the rich burials which characterise the earlier bronze age of so much of Europe are the result of the consumption of prestige items by members of the elites in the course of validating their status. Possible explanations of the lack of amber deposition in Denmark might then be that there were no elites in Denmark at this time, or that they did not consume prestige items in the same way. Neither of these seems to be the case. Randsborg (1974) has shown that there were strongly ranked societies in Denmark from Period II of the local bronze age onwards. Consumption of wealth in the form of graves and hoards was also widely practised (Kristiansen 1978; Levy 1977); however, in Denmark it was largely metalwork which was deposited. Amber was only rarely consumed in this way and it may be suggested that normally it remained in circulation and was moved out of the Danish system.

In order to account for this it is necessary to consider how the exchange system might have worked. Harrison and Gilman (1977) have suggested that the trade in ivory and ostrich egg shell between Iberia and North Africa in the late neolithic and early bronze age was conducted between groups of marked socio-economic inequality and was 'exploitative' in nature, in the sense that ivory and ostrich egg shell, important prestige commodities in Iberia, were obtained for next-to-nothing from North African tribes unaware of their 'value'. They also suggest that through time the situation changed and that some members of North African groups were able to achieve a superordinate status by virtue of their involvement in the exchange.

It seems probable that the second stage of the process

Fig. 4.7. Generalised distribution of amber in the British earlier bronze age. Quantity of amber in graves with amber; residuals from first-order trend surface.

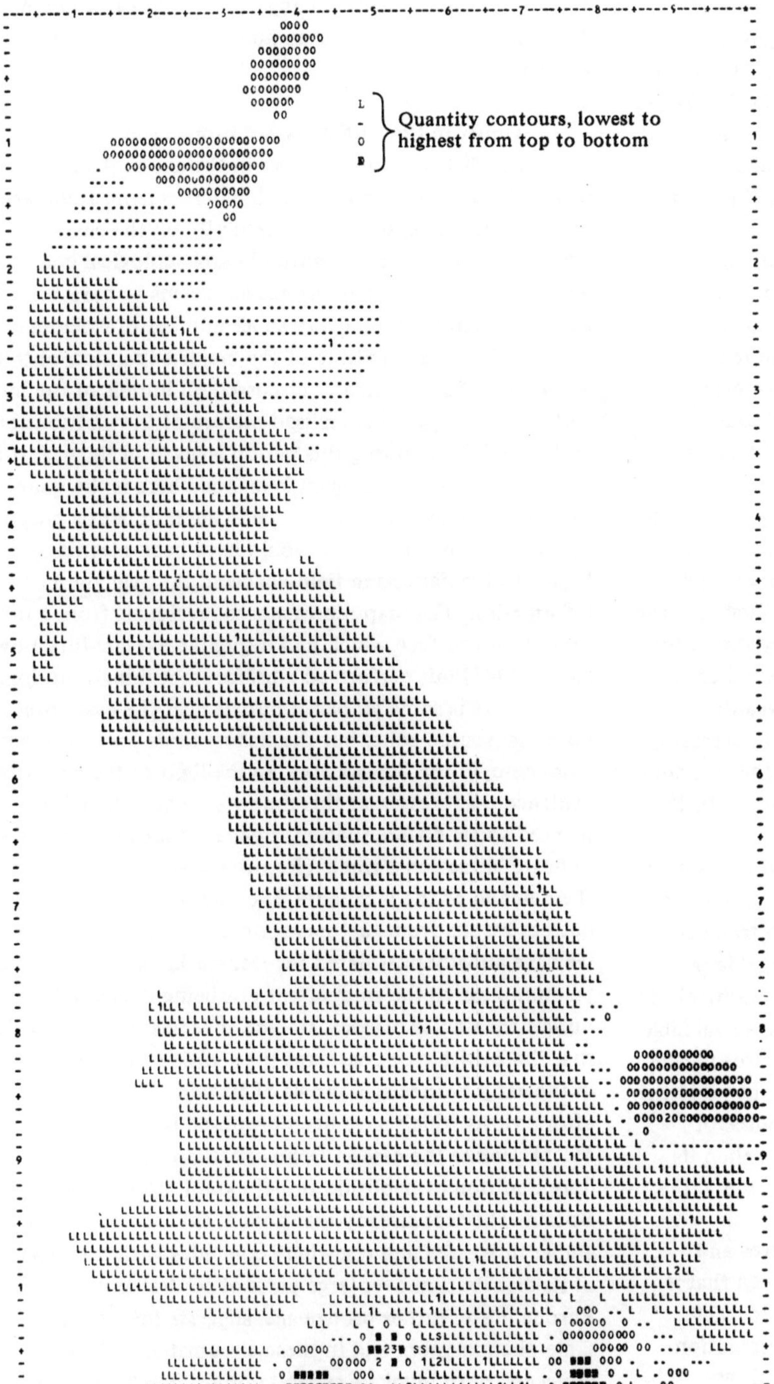

suggested by Harrison and Gilman is more relevant than the first in the case of the exchange relations between Denmark and the south. Metal objects of central European origin appear in Denmark at least as early as amber begins to be deposited widely in central Europe (Lomborg 1973). At this time only very small quantities of metal appear in the Danish archaeological record compared with later periods, no doubt as a result of its initial rarity, but the evidence such as it is does not fit the type of asymmetry discussed by Harrison and Gilman.

It is suggested here that a concern with individual male prestige items, albeit in an egalitarian context, is already visible in the later neolithic Single Grave phase. Subsequently, over large parts of central Europe where the battle-axe had been the main male prestige item it was replaced by the copper dagger (Shennan 1976). In metal-less southern Scandinavia the response to this was the production of a remarkable series of flint daggers (Lomborg 1973), which themselves came to have a wide distribution. A concern with prestige items then existed prior to the appearance of early bronze age metal items from central and western Europe, and these were accepted into Scandinavia as prestige items, in the form both of ornaments and weapons and of flat axes. Both Randsborg (1974) and Kristiansen (1978) have emphasised the association between land productivity and wealth deposition in bronze-age Denmark but this is not necessarily inconsistent with the possibility that control of the incoming metal supplies gave certain groups and their leaders a further source of power and prestige.

It is in this context that a reason for the lack of amber deposition in bronze age Denmark can now be suggested. It is not simply that it was all being exported south to meet demand elsewhere. Rather, it was no use as a valuable in Denmark because it could be obtained too easily; control of its distribution, an important criterion for a prestige valuable, was not possible. The exchange of amber southwards meant that it was funnelled into the control of those involved in the metal exchange, who thereby gained a further source of influence.[8] The circulation of amber, then, rather than its deposition, was of considerable importance. With metal the reverse was the case.

The quantity of metal deposited in the graves and hoards of the Danish bronze age is remarkable given that it all had to be obtained from sources at some considerable distance. Instead of this metal accumulating in circulation and Denmark becoming relatively self-sufficient, it was removed from circulation by prestige consumption, and new supplies were constantly needed. This in turn ensured a continuing basis for power, in the control of a resource which, it may be suggested, became more important as time went on and metal became increasingly significant for both tools and weapons. This control was bought at the price of a continuing vulnerability to fluctuations in the supply of metal from the south, as Kristiansen (1978) has shown very clearly. Indeed, it may be argued that the Scandinavian groups were

always the weaker partners in exchanges with groups nearer to the metal sources, since metal was probably more important to them than their exchange commodities, which no doubt included far more than amber, were to their southern neighbours.

Amber in the British earlier bronze age

The distribution of amber in Britain contrasts markedly with the picture which emerges from Denmark.

Although amber occurs naturally on the east coast of Britain (see n. 1), its deposition in archaeological contexts in Britain prior to the early bronze age seems to have been negligible. Apart from a very small number of isolated cases, it is first found at the time of the major expansion of the amber distribution already discussed, in burials of the local early bronze age. A generalised picture of the distribution of amber in Britain during this period is given in fig. 4.7. It is important to note that what is mapped here is the quantity of amber in graves with amber, not the number or proportion of burials with amber; this would have been meaningless because of variations in fieldwork and the availability of information. The map represents the residuals from a first-order trend surface which had negligible explanatory power ($R^2 = 2.6\%$) but performed a useful smoothing function.[9]

There is some amber in burials near the east coast potential source zone, but the richest finds are well away from here, in the Wessex area. In the light of the extensive evidence that Wessex at this time was characterised by marked social differentiation, I believe that these rich finds indicate 'directional trade' (Renfrew 1977), resulting from the demand of the local elite. It could be argued that the pattern results from the operation of a system similar to that we have already postulated for Denmark, with amber in circulation near to the source, but not being deposited in burials for similar reasons. In fact, it seems to me unlikely that the British east coast was the source of the amber found in the early bronze age burials of Britain, despite the 'least effort' views which have been proposed (Coles and Taylor 1971). Unlike the case in Denmark, there is no evidence of a long tradition of neolithic amber exploitation in eastern Britain. The fact already mentioned, that the appearance of amber in Wessex and elsewhere coincides with the expansion of its distribution over large parts of central and western Europe in the earlier bronze age, suggests that it is part of the same phenomenon, and in these circumstances it seems unnecessary to invoke a separate origin for the Wessex amber. Finally, the few finds of amber from relatively near the east coast include elaborate necklaces, while one of them is from the richest early bronze age grave in the area,[10] both facts suggesting that here too amber was a prized material used in elite contexts, again in contrast to the situation in Denmark. On the basis of these arguments, then, it seems reasonable to maintain the view that the rich amber finds of the Wessex area most probably do indicate directed exchange.

Within Wessex itself an attempt was made to see if

Fig. 4.8. Generalised distribution of amber from earlier bronze age burials in Wessex. Quantity of amber in graves with amber; contour map.

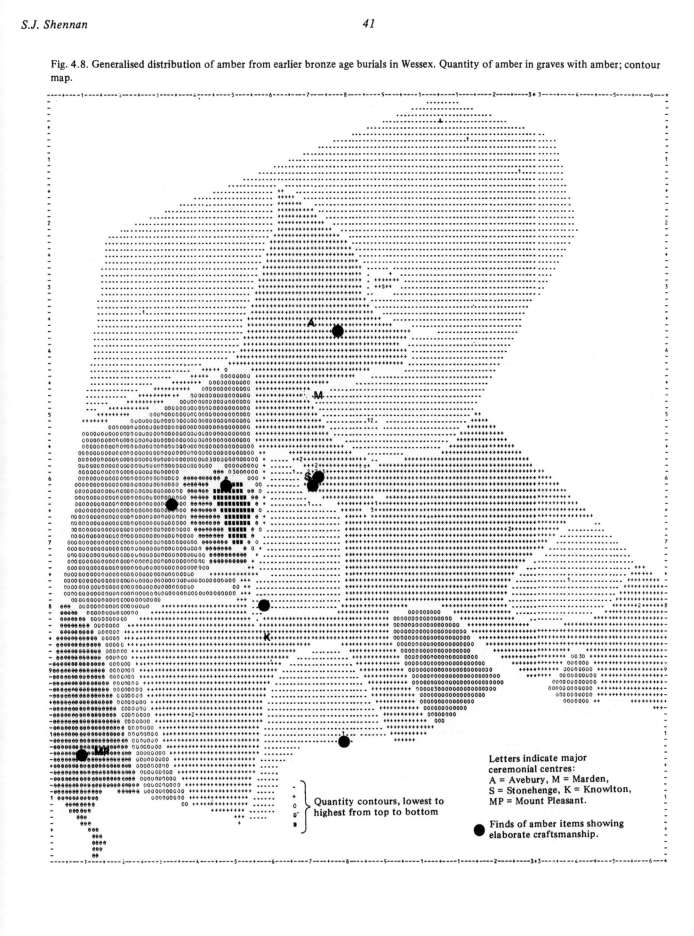

Letters indicate major
ceremonial centres:
A = Avebury, M = Marden,
S = Stonehenge, K = Knowlton,
MP = Mount Pleasant.

Quantity contours, lowest to
highest from top to bottom

● Finds of amber items showing
elaborate craftsmanship.

Fig. 4.9. Generalised distribution of amber from earlier bronze age barrows in Wiltshire and Dorset. Percentage of excavated barrows with amber by parish: contour map.

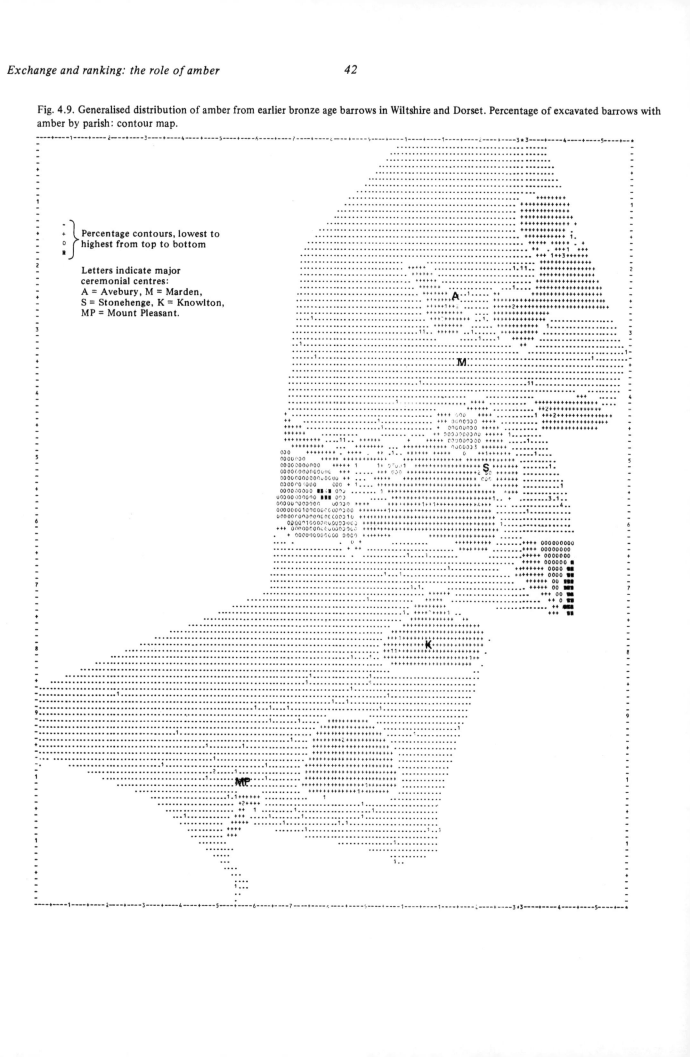

there was any overall regional patterning in the distribution of amber which might give an indication of the processes producing it. It was hypothesised that there might be a general fall-off in amber quantity away from a centre or centres which might be indicated by a good fit for a second- or third-order trend surface; or conceivably a first-order trend relating to distance of sites from the south coast, if amber was being transported directly to Wessex by sea. These ideas were tested with data from Wessex on the quantity of amber in graves with amber, and on the proportion of excavated burial mounds which contained amber in each parish.[11] In neither case did any overall patterning emerge from the trend surface analysis; the data are admittedly fairly poor but the lack of trend seems conclusive.

Quantity of amber: first-order trend $R^2 = 2.6\%$
second-order trend $R^2 = 5.7\%$
third-order trend $R^2 = 7.0\%$

Proportion of barrows with amber:
first-order trend $R^2 = 2.9\%$
second-order trend $R^2 = 6.4\%$
third-order trend $R^2 = 8.0\%$

If we look at the patterning (figs. 4.8–4.9), what we see is a series of localised concentrations, the majority corresponding to the locations of preexisting ceremonial centres. This pattern is amplified if we distinguish in the amber objects between simple rounded biconical beads and those items which show more complex craftsmanship — for example, necklace spacer beads with complex perforations; the latter are even more restricted in their distribution (fig. 4.8).

Renfrew (1973; 1974) has argued persuasively that the scale of organisation involved in the construction of the major late neolithic ceremonial centres of Wessex was such that they must have depended on a centralised chiefdom form of organisation, and that a similar inference may be made from the rich early bronze age burials in the area. It is clear that they represent different kinds of hierarchical society, and Renfrew (1974) has referred to the first as 'group-oriented' and to the second as 'individualising'. In both cases a socially generated surplus was being consumed, but the mode of consumption in the two cases was very different. It may be suggested that what we are seeing is a specific version of the general change which I have suggested above as characterising much of the European early bronze age, in this case the replacement of an ideology in which the existence of hierarchy was legitimised by the provision of monuments and ritual involving the whole community, by one in which inequality was more openly expressed and presented as natural by means of the consumption of prestige items and ritual symbols by powerful individuals. One can think of a variety of reasons for the clustering of rich graves in the vicinity of ceremonial centres in such a situation, whether because these areas remained centres of power or because of the ideological importance for the later elites of establishing a link with these centres.

Amber fits into this picture as one of the many different commodities in the prestige system. In this system the obtaining and maintenance of power would have depended on the ability to maintain supplies of the critical valuables, and on the active seeking out of distant contacts which had something new to offer (cf. Helms 1979). It follows from this relationship that there should be a correlation between the strongest positions in the most developed hierarchies and the best contacts for obtaining exotic goods, and it may be suggested that it is this which accounts for the 'directional trade' in amber which the British evidence indicates.

Conclusion

It has been suggested that much of earlier bronze age Europe, including Denmark and Wessex, was characterised by a prestige good ranking system. However, these two areas differed in their use of amber as part of this system because of their different spatial relationship to the sources.

It remains an open question to what extent amber itself was of any substantive significance, whether it was a major or only a minor element in inter-regional exchange. It was not a necessity; locally available shale was regularly substituted for it in parts of Britain; but this may be seen as a further indication that amber was rare and difficult to obtain. In fact, even if it had a very minor role compared with such archaeologically invisible commodities as textiles, the visibility of amber, together with the fact that its source is broadly known, gives it considerable importance as an index of the processes which were operating. This is not to say that the large-scale study of this or any other material will give us an archaeological key to making inferences about past societies. Rather, an attempt at accounting for the changes in the distributions of exchanged materials through time directs us to the comparative examination of local situations and also enables us to see the links between them.[12]

Notes

1   The major sources of Baltic amber are the eastern Baltic coast and the north and west coasts of Jutland. However, a large part of the amber-bearing beds is underwater, and amber, with its low specific gravity, is washed ashore, especially after storms, and collected. It is by means of such marine activity that amber from the Jutland source reaches the east coast of England. Glacial action has also had its effect on the distribution of amber, accounting for its presence in the Netherlands and also in Russia, south and east of the east Baltic source area. The infra-red spectroscopy simply enables a distinction to be made in samples of amber between Baltic and non-Baltic; further distinctions within the broad Baltic area cannot be made. Nevertheless, this basic characterisation is sufficient to make considerable progress.

2   The dates of the phases described as 'early neolithic', 'middle neolithic', etc., vary very considerably from area to area within Europe. These differences are particularly great in the earlier periods and by the time of the early bronze age are much less marked. In this paper the dates given for the phases are those current in north-west Europe.

3   The generalised picture of the changing distribution of amber

through time presented in this paragraph is based on a variety of different sources. For Britain and Denmark data were collected directly by the author. Other sources include Coles and Harding (1979), Bóna (1975), Trogmayer (1975), Buchvaldek (1967), Hájek (1968) and Čujanová-Jílková (1970).

4   Measuring the quantity of amber presents problems. A variety of measures of material quantity have been used in similar studies in the past, often some form of proportion; for example, the percentage of sites at a given distance from the source containing the material in question; or the percentage of, say, pottery of a specific type in the total pottery assemblage of a site. Such measures could not be used here owing to lack of information. To express amber quantity in terms of the percentage of all find contexts at a particular distance from the source which contained amber would have required, for each period, a complete list of all find contexts; such lists were not available. For this reason only those find contexts containing amber were considered and the absolute quantity of amber in each context was noted. With the exception of the information on the sizes of TRB early neolithic amber hoards, which was obtained from Rech (1979) and given in that source in terms of numbers of beads, all the data on amber quantity in Denmark were obtained by the author, by weighing the amber finds in the Danish National Museum, Copenhagen. For the Single Grave and TRB middle neolithic burials a 25% sample was taken; for the TRB early neolithic burials 50%, and for the earlier bronze age burials 100%.

5   Distance from the source was based on straight line measurements from the findspots to the nearest point on the west coast of Jutland, the main source area in southern Scandinavia. No more specific assumption about source could be made and it was felt that by this means a picture would be obtained which was meaningful at a generalised level. Examination of the scattergrams suggests that the assumption was justified, in that for three periods of the four considered quantities of amber deposited some distance from the west coast of Jutland were smaller than those deposited close to it. In general, the pattern is not one of simple fall-off but rather of great variability close to the west coast which decreases with distance, as the maximum quantities deposited in particular contexts become increasingly small.

6   See for example the complex exchange networks mainly involving different types of flint presented by Sherratt (1976).

7   As Harding and Hughes-Brock show, the situation in the late bronze age, at the end of the Mycenaean period, was very different. By this time amber was widely available in the northern Adriatic area, and in Greece it appears scattered in smaller quantities at a much larger number of sites.

8   It is interesting to note that in the earlier bronze age western Jutland appears anomalously rich in terms of its wealth:land productivity ratio in both Randsborg's (1974) and Kristiansen's (1978) studies. This may well relate to its position adjacent to the major amber sources, although Gilman (1981) presents an alternative view.

9   The trend surface analysis was carried out by means of the SYMAP computer mapping package on the ICL 2970 computer of the University of Southampton. Details of the technique are given in Davis 1973, Hodder and Orton 1976, and Bove 1981.

10 These are the necklaces from the rich barrow at Little Cressingham, Norfolk (Gerloff 1975, 75), and that from Rochford, Essex (Piggott 1938).

11 The data on quantities of amber were obtained by the author directly from the relevant museums; information on the proportion of excavated barrows which contained amber in each parish was obtained for the counties of Wiltshire and Dorset from Grinsell's catalogues (Grinsell 1957, 1959).

12 Work on the British amber was financed by a grant from the National Geographic Society of America; collection of the Danish data was made possible by a grant from the British Academy's Small Grants Fund for the Humanities. I would like to thank the curators of the numerous British museums who gave me facilities to examine their material, and also the staff of the Moesgard museum, Aarhus, and the Danish National Museum, Copenhagen, who gave me all possible assistance; Poul-Otto Nielsen was especially helpful. Virginia Allon made critical comments on an earlier draft. Finally, attendance at the 45th S.A.A. meeting in Philadelphia, where the first version of this paper was given, was made possible by grants from the British Academy's Overseas Conference Fund and the University of Southampton Conference Fund.

References

Beck, C.W., Wilbur, E. and Meret, S. 1964. Infra-red spectra and the origin of amber. *Nature* 201: 256–7.

Beck, C.W., Wilbur, E., Meret, S., Kosove, M. and Kermani, K. 1965. The infra-red spectra of amber and the identification of Baltic amber. *Archaeometry* 8: 96–109.

Bóna, I. 1975. *Die mittlere Bronzezeit Ungarns und ihre südöstlichen Beziehungen*. Budapest, Akadémiai Kiadó.

Bove, F.J. 1981. Trend surface analysis and the lowland classic Maya collapse. *American Antiquity* 46: 93–112.

Buchvaldek, M. 1967. *Die Schnurkeramik in Böhmen*. Praha, Universita Karlová.

Clark, J.R. 1979. Modelling trade in non-literate archaeological contexts. *Journal of Anthropological Research* 35: 170–90.

Coles, J.M. and Harding, A.F. 1979. *The Bronze Age in Europe*. London, Methuen.

Coles, J.M. and Taylor, J.J. 1971. The Wessex culture: a minimal view. *Antiquity* 45: 6–14.

Čujanová-Jílková, E. 1970. Mittelbronzezeitliche Hügelgräberfelder in Westböhmen. *Archeologické Studijní Materiály* 8. Praha, Archeologický Ústav ČSAV.

Davis, J.C. 1973. *Statistics and Data Analysis in Geology*. New York, John Wiley.

Earle, T.K. 1977. A reappraisal of redistribution: complex Hawaiian chiefdoms, in T.K. Earle and J.E. Ericson (eds.), *Exchange Systems in Prehistory*. New York, Academic Press, 213–29.

Ehrich, R.W. and Plestová-Štiková, E. 1968. *Homolka: an eneolithic site in Bohemia*. Praha, Academia.

Gerloff, S. 1975. *The Early Bronze Age Daggers in Great Britain* (Prähistorische Bronzefunde VI, 2). Munich, C.H. Beck.

Gilman, A. 1981. The development of social stratification in bronze age Europe. *Current Anthropology* 22: 1–8.

Grinsell, L.V. 1957. List of Wiltshire barrows, in R.B. Pugh and E. Crittall (eds.), *A History of Wiltshire* (*VCH*), vol. 1, part 1. Oxford, University Press, 134–246.

Grinsell, L.V. 1959. *Dorset Barrows*. Dorchester, Dorset Natural History and Archaeological Society.

Hájek, L. 1968. Kultura zvoncovitých Pohárů v Čzechach. *Archeologické Studijní Materiály* 5. Praha, Archeologický Ústav, ČSAV.

Harding, A.F. 1976. Bronze agricultural implements in bronze age Europe, in G. Sieveking, I.H. Longworth and K.E. Wilson (eds.), *Problems in Economic and Social Archaeology*. London, Duckworth, 513–22.

Harding, A.F. and Hughes-Brock, H. 1974. Amber in the Mycenaean world. *The Annual of the British School at Athens* 69: 145–72.

Harrison, R.J. and Gilman, A. 1977. Trade in the second and third millennia B.C. between the Maghreb and Iberia, in V. Markotic (ed.), *Ancient Europe and the Mediterranean*. Warminster, Aris and Phillips, 90–104.

Helms, M.W. 1979. *Ancient Panama*. Austin, University of Texas Press.

Hodder, I. and Orton, C. 1976. *Spatial Analysis in Archaeology*. Cambridge, University Press.

Kristiansen, K. 1978. The consumption of wealth in bronze-age Denmark: a study in the dynamics of economic processes in tribal societies, in K. Kristiansen and C. Paludan-Müller (eds.), *New Directions in Scandinavian Archaeology*. Copenhagen, National Museum of Denmark, 158–90.

Levy, J.E. 1977. Social and religious change in bronze age Denmark. Ph.D. dissertation, Washington University, St Louis. Ann Arbor, University Microfilms.

Lomborg, E. 1973. *Die Flintdolche Dänemarks*. Copenhagen.

Mahler, D. 1978. Den jyske enkeltsgravkultur. *Kontaktstencil* 15: 15–44.

Piggott, S. 1938. The early bronze age in Wessex. *Proceedings of the Prehistoric Society* 4: 52–106.

Polanyi, K. 1957. The economy as instituted process, in K. Polanyi, M. Arensberg and H. Pearson (eds.), *Trade and Market in the Early Empires*. Glencoe, Free Press, 243–70.

Randsborg, K. 1974. Social stratification in early bronze age Denmark: a study in the regulation of cultural systems. *Prähistorische Zeitschrift* 49: 38–61.

Randsborg, K. 1975. Social dimensions of early neolithic Denmark. *Proceedings of the Prehistoric Society* 41: 105–18.

Rech, M. 1979. Studien zu Depotfunden der Trichterbecher- und Einzelgrabkultur des Nordens, *Offa-Bücher* 39. Neumünster, Karl Wachholtz.

Renfrew, C. 1973. Monuments, mobilisation and social organisation in neolithic Wessex, in C. Renfrew (ed.), *The Explanation of Culture Change*. London, Duckworth, 539–58.

Renfrew, C. 1974. Beyond a subsistence economy: the evolution of social organisation in prehistoric Europe, in C.B. Moore (ed.), *Reconstructing Complex Societies* (Bulletin of the American Schools of Oriental Research 20 (Supplement)), 69–95.

Renfrew, C. 1977. Alternative models for exchange and spatial distribution, in T.K. Earle and J.E. Ericson (eds.), *Exchange Systems in Prehistory*. New York, Academic Press, 71–90.

Schrickel, W. 1966. *Westeuropäische Elemente im Neolithischen Grabbau Mitteldeutschlands und die Galeriegräber Westdeutschlands und ihre Inventare*. Bonn, Habelt.

Shennan, S.J. 1976. Bell beakers and their context in central Europe, in J.N. Lanting and J.D. van der Waals (eds.), *Glockenbecher Symposion Oberried 1974*: Bussum, Fibula-van Dishoeck, 231–9.

Shennan, S.J. 1982. Ideology, change and the European early bronze age, in I. Hodder (ed.), *Symbolic and Structural Archaeology*. Cambridge, University Press, 155–61.

Sherratt, A.G. 1976. Resources, technology and trade, in G. Sieveking, I.H. Longworth and K.E. Wilson (eds.), *Problems in Economic and Social Archaeology*. London, Duckworth, 557–81.

Trogmayer, O. 1975. *Das Bronzezeitliche Gräberfelt bei Tápé*. Budapest, Akadémiai Kiadó.

Yoffee, N. 1979. The decline and rise of Mesopotamian civilisation: an ethnoarchaeological perspective on the evolution of social complexity. *American Antiquity* 44: 5–35.

Chapter 5

**Autonomy, ranking
and resources in
Iberian prehistory**
Robert Chapman

*The development of social ranking is examined for
south-east Spain and southern Portugal c. 4000–1000 bc. It
is argued that dependency models of long-distance trade or
core-periphery type, linking southern Iberia with the east
Mediterranean basin, are irrelevant to this particular problem.
Instead an autonomy model is preferred, with special attention focussed upon the changing relationship between ranking and critical resources (e.g. water supply, copper and other
inter-regionally traded items) on a regional scale of analysis.
This approach is based upon recent theoretical discussions
linking the control or management of critical, restricted
resources to the origins of ranking. Water supply is found to
have been critical to the societies of south-east Spain, while
land and the objects of inter-regional trade are suggested to
have fulfilled this function in southern Portugal. As ranking
increases, the control of copper extraction and production
becomes of increasing concern to local elites and the consequent reorientation of society is most visible in southern
Portugal. In conclusion the need for further testing of this
autonomy model is stressed.*

Christopher Hawkes once expressed the opinion that
the analysis of past social organisation occupied a high and
precarious rung on the ladder of archaeological inference
(1954). Such pessimism is now reserved for those who feel
that the major result of the New Archaeology has been the
sight of so many optimistic young men falling off so many
wobbly ladders. For the archaeologists who have attempted
to climb these ladders, one of the major avenues of research
has involved the use of social types, derived from evolutionary anthropology (e.g. Service 1962; Fried 1967). Particular
attention has been focussed upon ranked societies, which
have been defined by Fried as those 'in which positions of
valued status are somehow limited so that not all those of
sufficient talent to occupy such statuses actually achieve
them' (1967, 109). According to Fried the defining characteristics of such societies include a generally agricultural subsistence, redistributive mechanisms (though note now
Peebles and Kus 1977) and, relative to egalitarian societies,
larger population densities, an increased size in the residential
community and more formalised kinship networks. Under
the guise of chiefdoms, to use Service's terminology (1962),
specific traits were elaborated and the archaeological record
inspected to detect their presence (e.g. Renfrew 1973; 1974).
While such an approach had an initial value in refocussing
attention upon society, and while it can still be argued that
there are 'major discontinuities' (Peebles and Kus 1977)
between egalitarian and ranked societies, an over-emphasis on
social types may preclude a productive analysis of societal
change. Certainly within European prehistory we have a rich
record of societies which could be included within the
ranked category, but the variability within and between these

societies over a period of four thousand years defies their simple inclusion within an all-embracing type. If we wish to pursue 'social archaeology', then we must utilise the time-depth that is archaeology's domain, analyse socio-economic change and its reflection in material culture and not reduce change to the interface between successive social types.

The development of social ranking has raised at least two important questions which have been posed in recent archaeological publications. First there is the question of autonomous as opposed to dependent development, which has been a prevalent theme within European prehistory for many decades (Renfrew 1979). Associated with this are the problems caused by the projection back in time of models of cultural change. Secondly there is the question of the part played in the emergence of social ranking by resource control. Differential access to critical resources has, of course, been discussed within the context of territorially defined groups in egalitarian societies, especially in relation to mortuary practices (e.g. Saxe 1970; Goldstein 1976; Chapman 1981). But here we are concerned with the emergence of vertical social divisions. James Brown (1981) has summarised two important arguments used to explain the origins of social ranking, stratification and central leadership. On the one side is the acquisition of power through the control of critical, restricted resources (e.g. Carneiro 1970) and on the other is the emergence of ranking and leadership as a response to problems encountered in the allocation of critical resources (e.g. Service 1975; Wright 1977). Given the focus of both arguments, it is not surprising, perhaps, that Binford has stated recently that 'power is always related to differential access or control of critical resources' (Hill 1977, 309). In this paper I will consider autonomy, ranking and critical resources in one area of Europe, the Iberian peninsula, during the period from c. 4000—1000 bc.

The archaeological context

Two areas are of importance in what follows: these are south-east Spain (the modern provinces of Almería and Murcia) and southern Portugal (fig. 5.1). In south-east Spain, settlement in the fourth millennium bc is represented by few habitation sites, communal burials in small megalithic tombs and a material culture of restricted range, with no copper metallurgy. In the third millennium bc larger, more complex tombs were constructed, enclosed settlements (e.g. Los Millares, Cerro de la Virgen) developed, copper metallurgy was introduced, a wider range of raw materials was in use (e.g. prestigious ivory, ostrich egg shell, amber and callaïs) and the distribution of these materials among the grave assemblages suggests a measure of social ranking (Chapman 1977; 1981). The existence of a social hierarchy may be inferred on the basis of the regional distribution of prestige grave goods, in the absence of sufficient settlement data (Chapman 1975). Intra-regional trade distributed supplies of copper and gold, while interregional trade provided the emerging elite group with ivory and ostrich egg shell from a

north African source (Harrison and Gilman 1977). Following Evans' criteria (1978) craft specialisation may be detected in the production of copper and gold objects, fine bifacial flint weapons and shell bracelets, and in the existence on one site of stone and bone workshops. In the second millennium, during the local bronze age, there is evidence for increased social ranking, as witnessed by the mortuary practices, with the change from communal to individual burial and the consumption of sometimes large amounts of copper, gold and silver, along with objects of ivory and faience in the graves. With regard to metallurgy there is the appearance of tin-

Fig. 5.1. (a) Third millennium bc 'copper age cultures' in Iberia discussed in this paper. 1. Vila Nova de São Pedro culture; 2. Millaran culture.
　　　(b) Second millennium bc 'bronze age cultures' in Iberia discussed in this paper. 1. South-West bronze age; 2. Argaric culture.

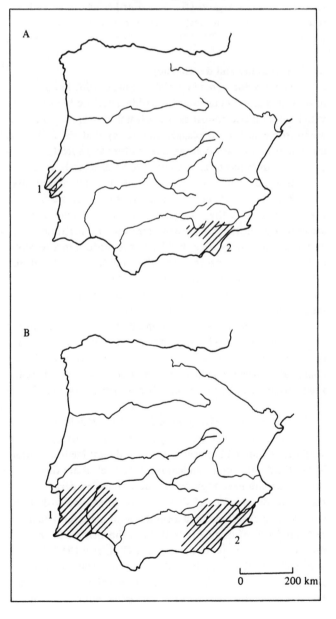

bronze and silver working, and an increase in the range and frequency of objects produced. Enclosed settlements occupy prominent, easily defensible locations.

In southern Portugal the third millennium witnesses a similar emergence of enclosed settlements (e.g. Zambujal, Vila Nova de São Pedro), copper metallurgy, a whole range of prestigious and ritual items and evidence for the existence of intra- and inter-regional trade mechanisms for the movement of copper, callaïs and ivory (the latter again from north Africa). The main concentration of such copper age sites and materials centres on the Tagus estuary and the area of Estremadura immediately to the north. In the second millennium an increase in social ranking is again evident in the presence of individual burial, but the amount of wealth deposited in the graves is not as great as in south-east Spain. Furthermore the distribution of these burials is different from that of the third-millennium sites, occurring in the Alentejo and the Algarve (fig. 5.1). Further details of and references to these cultural sequences can be found in n. 1, p. 50.

Autonomy and dependency

The developments in social ranking outlined above have been analysed consistently within a culture theory which views Iberia almost as the cultural 'dustbin' of the Mediterranean. It is no exaggeration to say that virtually every major innovation in material culture and society in these two areas has been attributed to an ultimately east Mediterranean source. The mechanisms by which these traits were carried to their Iberian destinations have ranged from the very general to the very specific. At one extreme there are nebulous 'influences', usually discussed in maritime metaphors and aptly described by Lewis Binford in a totally different context as representing the 'aquatic view of culture' (1965). At the other extreme there has been the more explicit dependency model involving colonies of east Mediterranean metal prospectors. As Gordon Childe put it, 'the urbanisation of Almerian economy seen at Los Millares . . . is presumably a reflection, however indirect, of Oriental cities' demands for metal . . . the townships thus created . . . constituted local secondary centres of demand and radiated their influence right across the (Iberian) peninsula' (1947, 267).

This interpretative framework can be criticised on two main counts. First one can analyse the detailed artefactual similarities claimed between the east and west Mediterranean in the third and second millennia bc. How clear are these similarities and need they reflect more than comparable functional developments? Can they be understood within the context of a clearly defined assemblage of material with a restricted area of origin? In both cases the answers to these questions are, I think, in the negative (Renfrew 1967; Chapman 1975; forthcoming b). Indeed, it is difficult to see any indisputable evidence for contact between the east and west Mediterranean basins before the first millennium bc. As is

also shown by the distribution of obsidian in the neolithic (Hallam, Warren & Renfrew 1976), there is no tangible evidence for contact even between Iberia and the central Mediterranean. This lack of concrete evidence for east–west contact can be contrasted with the middle of the first millennium bc, when Phoenician colonies were established in southern Iberia and left unambiguous archaeological evidence (references in Frankenstein 1979). This leads us to the second major criticism. The Phoenician colonies are not an apposite analogy which can be projected back into the third and second millennia, as archaeologists have attempted to do since the end of the last century. The Phoenician presence in the west Mediterranean must be understood within the context of the developing Western Asiatic trading system and the Assyrian state from the ninth to the seventh centuries bc and the specific demand for increasing quantities of silver (Frankenstein 1979). A comparable scale of trading and metallurgical activity in southern Iberia in the third millennium bc cannot be documented. The main indisputable trading network (albeit on a different scale of organisation) linked southern Iberia with the immediately adjacent areas of northern Africa (Harrison and Gilman 1977).

Thus I would argue that the emergence of social ranking in Iberia from c. 4000–1000 bc must be analysed as an autonomous development. Diffusionist or dependency models, whether in the context of Childe's formulation or the recent discussion of 'world systems' (e.g. Wallerstein 1974; Frankenstein and Rowlands 1978), lack conviction in relation to the available archaeological evidence and the development of cultural systems within the Mediterranean basin until the end of our period of interest.

Ranking and resources

Given the arguments presented above, the main challenge now is to propose mechanisms by which ranked societies emerged and developed in Iberia. As a contribution towards this aim, we must isolate critical resources in each area and search for correlation between their changing exploitation and the observed trends in social change.

Within south-east Spain water constitutes the most critical resource for human settlement (for a full discussion of water supply and its implications see Chapman 1978). To put it at its simplest, this area is the driest in the whole of Europe. The mean annual rainfall in the lowlands is low (c. 100–300 mm) and highly variable both seasonally and annually. Temperatures are high, reaching 26°C in summer. Evaporation rates may be up to four times the precipitation figures during the summer. Under modern dry farming both wheat and barley give low and irregular yields, with one good year being followed by three to five years of low yields. Undoubtedly there has been considerable vegetational clearance and erosion since prehistory, but available evidence suggests that there have been no major changes in climate since the third millennium bc. Pollen diagrams from both Iberia and north Africa could be employed to support the inference of periods of climatic oscillation, with consequent implications for cultural buffering during precipitation cycles (cf. Jorde 1977).

Archaeological evidence exists for methods of water conservation, by means of cisterns and pits, on both copper and bronze age sites, and water diversion, by the collection and distribution of water sources through the use of ditches (again for full details see Chapman 1978). The site of Cerro de la Virgen, which is enclosed by a bastioned wall and contains many prestigious materials (e.g. copper, ivory), has produced the first clear evidence for water diversion in Iberia before the Roman period. Examination of the location of known third- and second-millennium sites suggests also that water diversion could have occurred in the form of flood-water farming at the junctions of a major river and its tributaries. Given the problems encountered with the currently available data from this area, it remains possible to argue that social ranking could have emerged both as a result of existing resource control and as a response to problems posed by the management of the critical resources (in this case the variable water supply). The linkage between differential access to scarce water sources or problems in their allocation and the emergence of settlement and social hierarchies has also been made in other contexts (e.g. Downing and Gibson 1974).

How does another resource, copper, fit into this picture? Both native and arsenical copper were available and exploited in this area in the third millennium bc (e.g. Harrison 1974). The evidence of exploitation and production is visible on settlement sites (e.g. Siret and Siret 1887). However, the actual range and frequency of objects produced suggests that metal-working was not a continuous activity, but part-time in production and organisation. Inventories from settlements and tombs (e.g. Leisner and Leisner 1943) indicate that there were distinct variations in access to metal within the region. Certainly copper sources were not equally accessible throughout the south-east, with sites like Los Millares and Cerro de la Virgen being dependent upon intra-regional trade for supplies. I am inclined to argue that water supply was a far more critical resource than copper in the third millennium (cf. Gilman 1976). However, it can be argued that this situation changed in an interesting way during the second millennium bc, when social ranking became more marked. Metal production increased, in terms of the ranges and frequencies of objects, although it was in no way comparable to the central European bronze age. At the same time new sources of copper at higher altitudes in the Sierra Nevada were exploited (García Sánchez 1963). On the basis of current knowledge of the distribution of Bronze Age settlement and wealth (in the form of elite burials) it is arguable that, while water supply remained critical to human settlement, there was an increased concern with controlling access to metal sources and production.

In southern Portugal water supply was not such a critical resource, as the climate is most certainly not arid (e.g. Lautensach 1964). Hence the absence of any consideration of prehistoric water control in this area. The main concentration of third-millennium copper age settlements, metal, and other prestigious materials was in the area around Lisbon (fig. 5.1). To what extent this density of sites and finds is an artefact of modern destruction and the intensity of archaeological fieldwork is debatable. Discounting those areas with more recent alluvial soils, this area contains some of the more fertile soils in the whole of Portugal at the present day (Villar 1937; Naval Intelligence Division 1943). One can argue that there was a basis in land for the density of known copper age occupation. What is more interesting is the evidence for intra- and inter-regional trade. Ivory, callaïs, amber and jet were all exchanged into the area, and petrological analysis has shown that the clay used for one type of pottery (the so-called '*Importkeramik*') has a restricted source up to 100 km away from Vila Nova (do Paço and Sangmeister 1956). The source of the copper used on the settlement sites is a problem. When modern surveys do indicate any sources for this area, they are on its northern and southern boundaries: these are near Caldas da Reinha, some 80 km to the north of Lisbon, and near Grândola in the Setubal peninsula (sources cited in Harrison 1974, 104). If these sources were excluded, then the nearest copper would be south in the Alentejo (fig. 5.2). Whichever copper sources were exploited, it remains the case that the beginnings of social ranking occur in an area which depended fairly strongly upon inter-regional trade for access to prestigious materials and artefacts. What is interesting here is that in the succeeding bronze age the trend towards a further increase in social ranking is not visible in the same area, as has already been pointed out. Instead it can be seen further to the south, in the southern Alentejo and the Algarve, in what has been termed the south-west bronze age (fig. 5.1; Schubart 1975). Here are the individual burials with pottery and metal grave goods which form the counterpart of the bronze age burials in south-east Spain. On the other hand, the degree of ranking was less marked, as can be argued on the basis of the grave inventories and the continuation of a communal element in the mortuary practices. But not only is the development in social ranking in a different area to that of the preceding period, it is also the area which contains the main copper sources of southern Portugal (fig. 5.2). Taken at face value this would appear to represent an even more drastic reorientation of society towards the control of access to copper than in south-east Spain during the same period.

Discussion

In order to put this paper and the arguments presented so far in context, it is important to remember that the theory regarding the origins of ranking and resource control mentioned at the beginning of the paper is taken as the basis of my approach to the Iberian problems: I am taking this theoretical perspective and employing it to generate alternative views of these problems rather than seeking to build or improve theory itself.

Given the Iberian data with which I am working, the initial argument presented above is that dependency models, whether of the long-distance trade or 'core-periphery' type, are irrelevant to the emergence of social ranking. The interdependence of the cultural systems of the east, central and west Mediterranean, as well as those of Iberia and Atlantic Europe seen in the first millennium bc, is more appropriately analysed within the context of such models.

The approach to ranking in the Iberian copper and bronze ages which is adopted here is to focus on the relationship between emerging ranking and critical resources over a period of three millennia. This long time-depth is regarded as a suitable dimension against which to measure changes in this relationship. Of course it is also a selective approach, modelling only one relationship for a small number of resources at a regional scale of analysis. Both circumscription and management theories could be relevant to the origins of ranking in southern Iberia, and it has not been my aim to try and 'test' them. They have to be evaluated on different criteria. Referring to the symposium's contributors' use of their European data, Robert Whallon commented that 'you cannot build theory from the bottom up' and with this I would agree. Instead I have isolated three critical resources, water supply, copper, and other inter-regionally traded prestige materials. Through time and space, there is sufficient evidence for the proposition that the degree to which each resource or resource group is critical to local society varies. In the case of copper its social significance as a status indicator takes preference over any proposed technological advantages: as social ranking increases from the third to the second millennium, it becomes more important that the

social elite secure access to the primary sources of the metal. This is a feedback relationship relating increased social complexity to production and resource control.

The arguments presented above may prove useful only if they generate further questions and hypotheses for testing against Iberian data. In that context one would want to examine closely changes in the trading systems through time, as well as such factors as production, specialisation and changing settlement patterns. Currently available data are variable in scope and reliability; but this is not such a severe limitation, since data collection depends upon problem orientation and theoretical perspectives.[2]

Notes

1 I have decided to keep detailed referencing to Iberian cultures and sites to a minimum. Greater detail will be found in a future publication (Chapman, forthcoming b). However, a few points deserve additional substantiation and reference. First southeast Spain: the fourth-millennium neolithic culture may be termed 'Almerian', the third-millennium copper age 'Millaran' and the second millennium bronze age 'Argaric'. For all three millennia and 'cultures' the restrictions of the data base should be emphasised. Substantial fieldwork and excavation was undertaken in certain areas at the end of the last century and the results are contained in two particular monographs (Siret and Siret 1887; Leisner and Leisner 1943). Stratigraphic excavation was not practised until the last two decades, but although our knowledge of the detailed chronology of the second-millennium cultural sequence is now much improved (e.g. Schüle and Pellicer 1966; Arribas *et al.* 1975; Molina and Pareja 1976), we are still largely dependent upon seriation of grave assemblages for the preceding two thousand years (Almagro and Arribas 1963; Chapman, forthcoming a). Radiocarbon dating also remains skeletal for this long time span (Almagro Gorbea and Fernández-Miranda 1978). Many of the same problems recur in southern Portugal, where the best excavated of the third-millennium copper age ('Vila Nova culture') enclosed sites, Zambujal, has yet to be fully published (for interim reports see volumes of *Madrider Mitteilungen* from 1964 onwards). Many of the difficulties encountered in dealing with the local data are discussed by Harrison (1977), who also includes a substantial bibliography (see also Blance 1971). Our knowledge of settlement patterns, economic adaptations and socio-cultural development will be advanced considerably by the publication of Jose Arnaud's doctoral research (Cambridge University).

2 I would like to acknowledge the financial support of the Research Board of the University of Reading and the Overseas Conference Fund of the British Academy which enabled me to attend the symposium in Philadelphia. Jan Chapman typed the manuscript.

Fig. 5.2. Distribution of copper sources in Iberia.

References

Almagro, M. and Arribas, A. 1963. *El poblado y la necrópolis megalíticos de Los Millares.* Madrid, Institute Español de Prehistoria del C.S.I.C.

Almagro Gorbea, M. and Fernández-Miranda, M. (eds.) 1978. *C-14 y Prehistoria de la Península Ibérica.* Madrid, Fundación Juan March.

Arribas, A., Pareja, E., Molina, F., Arteaga, O. and Molina, F. 1975. *Excavaciones en el Poblado de la Edad del Bronce 'Cerro de la*

Encina' Monachil (Granada). Madrid, Ministerio de Educación y Ciencia.

Binford, L.R. 1965. Archaeological systematics and the study of culture process. *American Antiquity* 31: 203–10.

Blance, B. 1971. *Die Anfänge der Metallurgie auf der Iberischen Halbinsel*. Berlin, Gebr. Mann.

Brown, J.A. 1981. The search for rank in prehistoric burials, in R.W. Chapman, I.A. Kinnes and K. Randsborg (eds.), *The Archaeology of Death*. Cambridge, University Press, 25–37.

Carneiro, R.L. 1970. A theory of the origin of the state. *Science* 169: 733–8.

Chapman, R.W. 1975. *Economy and society within later prehistoric Iberia: a new framework*. Ph.D. dissertation, University of Cambridge.

Chapman, R.W. 1977. Burial practices – an area of mutual interest, in M. Spriggs (ed.), *Archaeology and Anthropology. Areas of Mutual Interest*. Oxford, British Archaeological Reports, 19–33.

Chapman, R.W. 1978. The evidence for prehistoric water control in south-east Spain. *Journal of Arid Environments* 1: 261–74.

Chapman, R.W. 1981. Archaeological theory and communal burial in prehistoric Europe, in I. Hodder, G. Isaac and N. Hammond (eds.), *Pattern of the Past: Studies in honour of David L. Clarke*. Cambridge, University Press, 387–411.

Chapman, R.W. 1981. The emergence of formal disposal areas and the 'problem' of megalithic tombs in prehistoric Europe, in R.W Chapman, I.A. Kinnes and K. Randsborg (eds.), *The Archaeology of Death*. Cambridge, University Press, 71–81.

Chapman, R.W. forthcoming a. Los Millares and the relative chronology of the Copper Age in south-east Spain. *Trabajos de Prehistoria* 37.

Chapman, R.W. forthcoming b. *Autonomy and Social Evolution: the later prehistory of the Iberian peninsula*. Cambridge, University Press.

Childe, V.G. 1947. *The Dawn of European Civilisation*. London, Routledge and Kegan Paul.

Downing, T.E. and Gibson, M. (eds.) 1974. *Irrigation's impact on Society* (Tucson, Anthropological Papers of the University of Arizona 25).

Evans, R.K. 1978. Early craft specialisation: an example from the Balkan Chalcolithic, in C.L. Redman, M.J. Berman, E.V. Curtis, W.T. Langhorn, N.M. Versaggi and J.C. Wanser (eds.), *Social Archeology. Beyond Subsistence and Dating*. New York, Academic Press, 113–29.

Frankenstein, S. 1979. The Phoenicians in the Far West: a function of Neo-Assyrian imperialism, in M.T. Larsen (ed.), *Power and Propaganda: a symposium on Ancient Empires*. Copenhagen, Akademisk Forlag, 263–94.

Frankenstein, S. and Rowlands, M.J. 1978. The internal structure and regional context of early Iron Age society in south-western Germany. *Bulletin of the Institute of Archaeology, University of London* 15: 73–112.

Fried, M.H. 1967. *The Evolution of Political Society*. New York, Random House.

García Sánchez, M. 1963. El poblado argárico del cerro del Culantrillo en Gorafe (Granada). *Archivo de Prehistoria Levantina* 10: 69–96.

Gilman, A. 1976. Bronze age dynamics in southeast Spain. *Dialectical Anthropology* 1: 307–19.

Goldstein, L.G. 1976. Spatial structure and social organisation: regional manifestations of Mississippian society. Ph.D. dissertation, Northwestern University.

Hallam, B.R., Warren, S.E. and Renfrew C. 1976. Obsidian in the western Mediterranean: characterization by neutron activation analysis and optical emission spectroscopy. *Proceedings of the Prehistoric Society* 42: 85–110.

Harrison, R.J. 1974. A reconsideration of the Iberian background to Beaker metallurgy. *Palaeohistoria* 16: 63–105.

Harrison, R.J. 1977. *The Bell Beaker Cultures of Spain and Portugal* (American School of Prehistoric Research, Bulletin 35). Cambridge, Massachusetts.

Harrison, R.J. and Gilman, A. 1977. Trade in the second and third millennia BC between the Maghreb and Iberia, in V. Markotic (ed.), *Ancient Europe and the Mediterranean*. Warminster, Aris and Phillips, 89–104.

Hawkes, C.F.C. 1954. Archaeological theory and method: some suggestions from the Old World. *American Anthropologist* 56: 155–68.

Hill, J.N. (ed.) 1977. *The Explanation of Prehistoric Change*. Albuquerque, University of New Mexico Press.

Jorde, L.B. 1977. Precipitation cycles and cultural buffering in the prehistoric Southwest, in L.R. Binford (ed.), *For Theory Building in Archaeology*. New York, Academic Press, 385–96.

Lautensach, H. 1964. *Iberische Halbinsel*. München, Keyserche Verlagsbuchhandlung.

Leisner, G. and Leisner, V. 1943. *Die Megalithgräber der Iberischen Halbinsel: Der Süden*. Berlin, de Gruyter.

Molina, F. and Pareja, E. 1976. *Excavaciones en la Cuesta del Negro (Purullena, Granada)*. Madrid, Ministerio de Educación y Ciencia.

Monteagudo, L. 1977. *Die Beile auf der Iberische Halbinsel* (Prähistorische Bronzefunde IX, 6). Munich, C.H. Beck.

Naval Intelligence Division 1943. *Spain and Portugal, volume II, Portugal*. London, British Admiralty.

Paço, A. do and Sangmeister, A. 1956. Vila Nova de São Pedro, eine befestigte siedlung der Kupferzeit in Portugal. *Germania* 34: 211–30.

Peebles, C.S. and Kus, S.M. 1977. Some archeological correlates of ranked societies. *American Antiquity* 42: 421–48.

Renfrew, C. 1967. Colonialism and megalithismus. *Antiquity* 41: 276–88.

Renfrew, C. 1973. Monuments, mobilisation and social organisation in prehistoric Wessex, in C. Renfrew (ed.), *The Explanation of Culture Change*. London, Duckworth, 539–58.

Renfrew, C. 1974. Beyond a subsistence economy: the evolution of social organisation in prehistoric Europe, in C.B. Moore (ed.), *Reconstructing Complex Societies* (Bulletin of American Schools of Prehistoric Research 20 (Supplement)), 69–95.

Renfrew, C. 1979. *Problems in European Prehistory*. Edinburgh, University Press.

Saxe, A.A. 1970. Social dimensions of mortuary practices. Ph.D. dissertation, University of Michigan.

Schubart, H. 1975. *Die Kultur de Bronzezeit im Sudwesten der Iberischen Halbinsel*. Berlin, de Gruyter.

Schüle, W. and Pellicer, M. 1966. *El Cerro de la Virgen, Orce (Granada)*. Madrid, Ministerio de Educación y Ciencia.

Service, E.R. 1962. *Primitive Social Organisation*. New York, Random House.

Service, E.R. 1975. *The Origins of the State and Civilisation*. New York, Norton.

Siret, H. and Siret, L. 1887. *Les Premiers Âges du Métal dans le Sud-Est de l'Espagne*. Anvers.

Villar, E.H. del 1937. *Soils of the Lusitano-Iberian peninsula* (abridged English text by G.W. Robinson), London, T. Murby and Co.

Wallerstein, I. 1974. *The Modern World System. Capitalist Agriculture and the Origins of the European World Economy in the Sixteenth Century*. New York, Academic Press.

Wright, H.T. 1977. Recent research on the origins of the State. *Annual Review of Anthropology* 1: 379–97.

Chapter 6

**Social boundaries
and land boundaries**
Andrew Fleming

*The paper discusses the extent to which the stages of
Service's evolutionary typology of social organisation can be
monitored by modelling 'territoriality' in the later prehistory
of north-west Europe. The dangers of adopting an over-
normative approach to territoriality and social-political
entities in segmentary societies are emphasised. Stress is laid
on the essential fluidity and flexibility of these societies,
first with reference to our perception of ceremonial monuments in prehistoric Europe, and then with regard to land
boundaries. It is suggested that the boundary patterns on
Dartmoor (south-west England) in the second millennium BC
reflect a range of different social entities which relate well to
segmentary principles. It is concluded that ancient land
boundaries provide a rich testing-ground for theories about
this stage of socio-political development.*

The socio-political understanding of the later prehistoric societies of north-west Europe has always presented
a challenge. Between 4000 and 1000 BC these farming communities were responsible for the building of major
ceremonial monuments like Stonehenge, Avebury, New
Grange, Maes Howe and the Carnac alignments, as well as
thousands of smaller chamber tombs, burial mounds and
ceremonial enclosures. We know that these societies included
skilled craftsmen and that raw materials and finished articles
could be circulated over distances of several hundred kilometres. Halfway through this period, around 2500 BC,
copper-working and then the use of bronze developed (for
general accounts see Burgess 1980; Megaw and Simpson
1979; Phillips 1980).

It seems probable that, in terms of Service's evolutionary typology (1962: for present purposes I do not consider
his later modification (Service 1975, 304)), the organisational
level of these societies lay somewhere between the band and
the state levels of complexity, and Renfrew specifically
suggested (1973) that what is known of the southern English
neolithic allows the postulation of the chiefdom level of
organisation here. This approach is potentially interesting.
Unfortunately, at present the apparent identification of
chiefdoms in neolithic Wessex, and the use of Thiessen poly-
gons to suggest that ceremonial monuments somehow indicate central places of some kind, along with the habit of
'systems thinking', have encouraged the development of
holistic, normative models of the societies in question. I
would argue that the definition of socio-political entities
must be balanced by the modelling of relationships between
and within these entities, and processual change through
time, and that the essential fluidity and flexibility of social
forms and arrangements at this level of social organisation
must be taken into account at the outset. Furthermore, it
can be argued that, in the broad spectrum presented by tribal
societies with greater or lesser degrees of ranking, the basic

ingredients of integration and conflict are at their most visible. The whole situation is of considerable sociological interest, perhaps more than is the case with band societies, where natural brakes on development occur, and with state societies, where a greater degree of organisational rigidity may be apparent and the prominence of the organisational core and its associated validation mechanisms may obscure the social parameters which operate for the bulk of the population.

The fluidity of entities and relationships within restricted geographical areas has been frequently stressed in recent years; see for example Edgerton (1971, 6) ('at that time anthropologists were still unquestioningly speaking of tribes as social entities, assuming the homogeneity of tribal cultures . . . ') or Boissevain (1974, chapter 1) comparing the structural–functional or normative model of society with the real world, or Macfarlane (1977, 10–22) pointing out the difficulties of modelling historical communities as if they were essentially monothetic entities, and the advantages of using an approach dealing with action sets and involving network analysis. These attitudes provide a neat counterpart to David Clarke's insistence on the polythetic nature of archaeological cultures, and they complement his investigations into the relationship between artefactual similarities and ethnic units in North America (Clarke 1968). They also allow the prehistorian to understand the real context in which increasingly sophisticated kinds of spatial analysis are being applied to archaeological data. Finally, their acceptance is an essential preliminary to the prehistorian's ability to make a real contribution to debates about socio-political evolution (the approach seems to have been accepted by Bradley and Hodder (1979)).

In band society, the fluidity and flexibility of social arrangements, at any rate by comparison with more evolved types of society, are well known; group membership is more flexible, territoriality less pronounced, leadership less institutionalised, and so on. But some predictions seem possible (e.g. Birdsell 1968; Wilmsen 1973): band size tends to fluctuate within a reasonably well-defined range, determined mainly by demographic considerations, the resources of the local environment, and the logistics of exploiting that environment in the most effective way (according to the perception of the group, not of the prehistorian). The presence of locally or seasonally abundant resources, coupled with the need for a biologically viable breeding population, will often imply the occurrence of periodic aggregations of people. Membership of bands and periodic agglomerations will fluctuate for well-known reasons, and artefacts and knowledge will spread accordingly. Relating artefact patterning to social structure will be correspondingly difficult.

It does seem probable, then, that the household, the group of linked households (the band) and the multiband aggregation, along with concepts of home range/territory and the structure of symbolism and ritual linking a band with its land, would have been present in late prehistoric hunter/

gatherer societies. To what extent did this pattern survive among the denser populations and larger, more permanent residential units of neolithic Europe? An initial guess would be that the unit of territory of maximum inclusiveness, corresponding to that of the band, would now have been both smaller and more clearly defined; smaller, as a function of the greater productivity of agriculture, and more clearly defined because greater population densities increased both the level of external threat and the ability of the community to maintain the integrity of its territory.

As the polity increased in size and complexity, concomitant increases in the quality and quantity of information exchange must have occurred. This and related issues have been rigorously treated elsewhere (Segraves 1974). A few years ago, I suggested implicitly that the development of the north-west European chamber tombs might be seen in terms of a quantum jump in information exchange which occurred in the primary neolithic (Fleming 1973), and the idea was later expanded by Klaus Randsborg. He suggested (1975) that in the Danish neolithic there were four idealised kinds of population distribution (dense and clustered, dense and dispersed, thin and clustered, thin and dispersed) and that these were reflected in variability in the monumentality of funerary structures and the number of grave goods in the tombs. Now whether the need for increasing social signalling related to the socio-political integration of dispersed residence units or to more intense social interactions in the more densely populated nucleated settlements is not a question that can be easily answered in terms of European archaeological data at present. But we certainly need to understand more about information flow and conformity behaviour at different levels of socio-political integration, and ceremonial monuments may be expected to help in this task.

At present, techniques of study for understanding ceremonial monuments in the role of attention-focussing devices are still in the process of development. It seems that in the early British neolithic (c. 4000–3000 BC) chamber tombs and related monuments in areas where they are well preserved were usually spaced at intervals of 2–5 km (Renfrew 1973; Darvill 1979). It looks as if the postulated territorial 'shrinkage' associated with farming may be supported empirically here. The rather similar spacing shown in many parts of England by mediaeval parish churches suggests that further work could be done on the relationship between agricultural productivity, biological viability and distance-decay factors in agriculture and socio-political integration to see whether 'natural' territorial units with fairly closely defined parameters could be predicted. Whether prehistoric ceremonial monuments were centrally located in their 'territories' remains to be determined; we also need a more rigorous way of determining the time-period over which they were still active in their original integrative and epideictic roles. Evidence for later burials and ritual deposits and changes of use needs more careful consideration than it has so far received. Furthermore, evidence for divisions and contradictions in monument-building communities needs more analysis; this is because of the need to assess the degree of internal stability and coherence of these communities, which is a matter relevant to their potential for further socio-political evolution (Segraves 1974, 541). In terms of the monuments, the implications of segmentary design (reflecting segmentary societies?), gang labour, abrupt changes in layout, destruction, contradictions in design, continued aggrandisement or reduplication of monuments, and various other categories of evidence, are all relevant to our assessment of social stability in space and time. There is no space to elaborate here; suffice it to say that in these probably segmentary societies, the suspicion must be that any integrative mechanisms were operating in an essentially unstable socio-political context, and would have been short-lived and episodic in time and loosely bounded in space.

In later prehistoric Britain (c. 3500–1500 BC) there were ceremonial centres, including stone circles, 'causewayed enclosures' and the earthworks known as henges. In some cases their spacing of 15–30 km (Smith 1971; Drewett 1977; Palmer 1976; Burl 1976) suggests a scale of socio-political activity altogether different from that associated with chamber tombs. Present evidence suggests that they arose several centuries after the onset of farming in Britain, which might suggest that they are the product of socio-political evolution. On the other hand, units of this size, perhaps without well-marked central places, could have existed much earlier. One could easily imagine a short early period of rapid population growth producing clusters of closely related communities. These could have cohered into larger political entities, based on natural geographical regions and attracted to central places discharging a range of functions easier to imagine than to establish archaeologically. At present the extent of our knowledge makes it very difficult to examine the different hypotheses which could explain how these centres arose.

One category of data which may be important in dealing with these issues is the ancient land boundaries of the area. It has become clear (Bowen and Fowler 1978), particularly in the British Isles, that large areas of land were being carefully subdivided in the second millennium BC, and in some cases even earlier. Although a unit of land use is not automatically the same as the activity sphere of a socio-political group, it is probable that such units, when analysed fully, will give us the best guide to the general scale of different levels of socio-political integration and to the articulation between different levels; in so doing, they will reveal the limitations of the site catchment analysis/Thiessen polygon approach.

Here I can only briefly indicate the kind of evidence available in the best cases, and some of its potential. My own study area is Dartmoor, an upland granite massif in south-west England. In the zone above the present-day fields there are ancient walls known as reaves, which date from around 1600 BC, in the later part of the bronze age. On the southern

part of the moor (Fleming 1978) it is possible to identify a clear pattern of boundaries, in which there are territories based on the valleys of the major rivers, which rise here. The valleys are separated by reaves running along the watersheds. Each valley has circular stone-walled houses usually grouped within, or immediately outside, walled enclosures. These were bases for exploitation of the moorland grazing and perhaps also of the tin ores which occur here. It can be argued (Fleming 1979) that the upper moorland was common land, shared by these communities, and certainly there is evidence for a 'contour reave' separating the upper moorland area from the grazing land lower down. From earliest times the upper moorland would have been a reserve of grazing and hunting land, with a perimeter much too long to have been defended by any group of village size even if it had needed such a large area, and the casual development of this land as a common may have had to be superseded by the careful arrangements shown by the reaves, where the agreement between several communities on an amicable shareout is symbolised by the long 'Great Western' reave, over twelve kilometres long on the western side of the moor. There is no evidence for a central place, or even that the arrangements fostered an enduring advance to a new level of social organisation. Similar models of communities clustered radially around extensive grazing resources have been suggested for fenland areas of England too, in Somerset and East Anglia (Coles 1978; Pryor 1976).

So here, at the regional level, is an instance of the fission and fusion principle, communities drawn together to share common land and perhaps limit the inroads of outsiders, but recognising their own separate identity with clearly drawn boundaries. This is illustrated more dramatically when we descent to the next level. Each of the communities mentioned also owned a block of parallel reaves, in which there are 'fields' of various sizes, some of which were used for cereal crops and legumes. These systems appear to have been laid out *en bloc*, although sometimes there is evidence that they have been extended, also *en bloc*. When one sees their extent and the way in which the boundaries conform to one major axis even when major landscape features make this a seemingly illogical thing to do, one is impressed by the evidence for apparent socio-political integration. Here, one feels, is a society of conformists, whether one sees them as bending to the will of one of Colin Renfrew's chieftains, or hammering out an obsessively egalitarian system after some interminable meeting of fellow commoners. Yet it is not as simple as that. All the groups using Dartmoor did the same thing; indeed many groups in other parts of southern England did the same thing, since Richard Bradley's Cohesive systems (Bradley 1978) appear to be similar in character. There seems to be widespread agreement about the general organisational principles of land division, and it can be argued that these related to traditions of collectively held land dating back to early neolithic times.

When we look within one parallel system, we start to

find further evidence for the fission and fusion principle. The houses here occur in clusters, typically of between five and ten houses, and it may be suggested that these were 'natural' units, residential groups of some thirty or forty people, perhaps half a dozen nuclear families. Within these groups the houses are often quite widely dispersed, separated sometimes by distances of over 200 m. There is no evidence that the individual houses were surrounded by coherent units of 'their own' land, and not very much evidence that the clusters of houses had their own allocations of land either; fieldwork suggests that each house (or pair of houses) had a domestic enclosure, and that the rest of the land was owned by the group which laid out the parallel system. Detailed studies of the number of houses per block of land, and the position of the houses within the boundaries, have demonstrated this. It seems that the parallel system is over-printed on groups of houses, that despite their close physical connection the houses and the boundaries form different kinds of networks. The essential homogeneity of the parallel system contrasts with the individuality of the domestic enclosures; no two farmers, it seems, required the same set of domestic arrangements. What is more, even within the same field, styles of reave-building can differ quite markedly. When one gets down to detail, it seems that there were rugged individualists, living in quite small face-to-face groups little bigger than hunting bands, arranging their own affairs according to their needs. Yet they also lived within large socio-political groups which laid out large blocks of land and negotiated the division of common pasture with their neighbours. Somehow we have always known that this hierarchy of different organisational levels was inherently likely among these early farming communities; the physical presence of land boundaries allows us to monitor it in some degree. It is against this background, against empirical evidence of the size of face-to-face communities and of the collective use of land, that we must discuss the boundaries of socio-political evolution and the growth of differential wealth, status and power. The 'interpretation' of ancient boundaries is, of course, no more straightforward than that of other artefacts. However, this may be a case, rarer in the modern practice of archaeology than many realise, where the variety and potential of the data have a real chance of matching the rigour and elegance which we rightly demand from theory.

References

Birdsell, J.B. 1968. Some predictions for the Pleistocene based on equilibrium systems among recent hunter–gatherers, in R.B. Lee and I. DeVore (eds.), *Man the Hunter*. Chicago, Aldine, 229–40.

Boissevain, J. 1974. *Friends of Friends: networks, manipulators and coalitions*. Oxford, Blackwell.

Bowen, H.C. and Fowler, P.J. (eds.) 1978. *Early Land Allotment in the British Isles – a survey of recent work*. Oxford, British Archaeological Reports.

Bradley, R. 1978. Prehistoric field systems in Britain and north-west Europe. *World Archaeology* 9: 265–80.

Bradley, R. and Hodder, I. 1979. British prehistory: an integrated view. *Man* 14: 93–104.

Burgess, C. 1980. *The Age of Stonehenge*. London, Dent.

Burl, A. 1976. *The Stone Circles of the British Isles*. New Haven, Yale University Press.

Clarke, D. 1968. *Analytical Archaeology*. London, Methuen.

Coles, J.M. 1978. The Somerset levels: a concave landscape, in H.C. Bowen and P.J. Fowler (eds.), *Early Land Allotment in the British Isles – a survey of recent work*. Oxford, British Archaeological Reports, 147–8.

Darvill, T.C. 1979. Court cairns, passage graves and social change in Ireland. *Man* 14: 311–27.

Drewett, P. 1977. The excavation of a Neolithic causewayed enclosure on Offham Hill, East Sussex. *Proceedings of the Prehistoric Society* 43: 201–41.

Edgerton, R.B. 1971. *The Individual in Cultural Adaptation: a study of four East African peoples*. Los Angeles, University of California Press.

Fleming, A. 1973. Tombs for the living. *Man* 8: 177–92.

Fleming, A. 1978. The prehistoric landscape of Dartmoor. Part 1: South Dartmoor. *Proceedings of the Prehistoric Society* 44: 97–123.

Fleming, A. 1979. The Dartmoor reaves: boundary patterns and behaviour patterns in the second millennium bc. *Proceedings of the Devon Archaeological Society* 37: 115–30.

Macfarlane, A. 1977. *Reconstructing Historical Communities*. Cambridge, University Press.

Megaw, J.V.S. and Simpson, D.D.A. 1979. *Introduction to British Prehistory from the Arrival of Homo sapiens to the Claudian Invasion*. Leicester, University Press.

Palmer, R. 1976. Interrupted ditch enclosures in Britain: the use of aerial photography for comparative studies. *Proceedings of the Prehistoric Society* 42: 161–78.

Phillips, P. 1980. *The Prehistory of Europe*. London, Allen Lane.

Pryor, F. 1976. Fen-edge land management in the Bronze Age: an interim report on excavations at Fengate, Peterborough, 1971–5, in C. Burgess and R. Miket (eds.), *Settlement and Economy in the Third and Second Millennia B.C.* Oxford, British Archaeological Reports, 29–47.

Randsborg, K. 1975. Social dimensions of early neolithic Denmark. *Proceedings of the Prehistoric Society* 41: 105–17.

Renfrew, C. 1973. Social organisation in neolithic Wessex, in C. Renfrew (ed.), *The Explanation of Culture Change*. London, Duckworth, 539–57.

Segraves, B. 1974. Ecological generalisation and structural transformation of sociocultural systems. *American Anthropologist* 76: 530–49.

Service, E.R. 1962. *Primitive Social Organisation: an evolutionary perspective*. New York, Random House.

Service, E.R. 1975. *Origins of the State and Civilization*. New York, Norton.

Smith, I.F. 1971. Causewayed enclosures, in D.D.A. Simpson (ed.), *Economy and Settlement in Neolithic and Bronze Age Britain and Europe*. Leicester, University Press, 89–105.

Wilmsen, E.N. 1973. Interaction, spacing behaviour and the organisation of hunting bands. *Journal of Anthropological Research* 29: 1–27.

57

PART II

**The development of
salient ranking**

A number of significant changes can be picked out as characterising the period from the end of the second millennium BC to the extension of Roman domination in temperate Europe, with which all the papers in this section are concerned. Obviously, one to which importance is always attached is the transition from the bronze age to the iron age. Nevertheless, it is worth noting that when the archaeological material of the bronze and iron ages in central Europe (always the key area for the establishment of chronological sequences) was first being systematised at the end of the nineteenth century, the major division drawn was not that between the bronze age and the iron age, but that between the end of the middle and the beginning of the late bronze age, on the one hand, and between the earlier and later iron age on the other (Reinecke 1903). The intervening period was named the Hallstatt period and was divided into four phases, two late bronze age and two early iron age.

With the new emphasis in recent years on socio-economic processes, it has become more important than ever that the old technological divisions of European prehistory should give way to a classification based on socio-economic criteria. In terms of such criteria it is becoming ever more clear that Reinecke's subdivisions are more relevant than the technological ones. There is an increasing amount of evidence to the effect not only that large parts of Europe underwent significant changes towards the end of the second millennium

BC (for example, Bradley 1981; Burgess 1980), but also that the developments of the later Hallstatt iron age, in the sixth century BC, were in large measure the outcome of processes which had begun half a millennium earlier (Rowlands 1980, 28–30; T. Champion, this volume). The developments of the later iron age, on the other hand, particularly from the second century BC onwards, seem to represent a very different phenomenon (Collis 1975; Cunliffe and Rowley 1976).

A clear implication of the title of this section of the volume is that the period under discussion saw the attainment of a previously unknown level of social differentiation, and for parts of Europe in the later iron age this seems undoubtedly to be the case. The *oppida* which developed in the first and second centuries BC are the earliest settlements in temperate Europe for which we can suggest an urban status. Nash lists a number of features which distinguish the *oppida* of France as a qualitatively new phenomenon:

> the wealthy residential areas, the permanent artisan quarters, the production and use of 'town' money, the new complexity of administration associated with coinage changes and an increase and concentration of imports from Italy, and the production and use in *oppida*, major *vici* and the scattered residences of the nobility, of mass-produced ceramic and household goods which constitute a material culture apart from that still normal in the countryside. (1976, 118)

Associated with these centres, it has been suggested, were the beginnings of a territorially organised administrative system, no longer based on kinship (Nash 1976, 112).

But if the later iron age in certain parts of Europe north of the Alps has indications of the beginnings of state organisation (Nash 1978), the same is not true of the preceding period, when everything suggests that we are still dealing with chiefdoms, as defined by Earle (1978) in terms of the ranking of statuses within the community and the regionally centralised organisation of communities. Most of Europe in the first millennium BC shows evidence of settlement hierarchies in the form of defended hill-top enclosures which seem to have evidence of elite associations (for example Petres 1976, referring to the early phases of occupation of later *oppida* in western Hungary; T. Champion, this volume), while certain areas show a clearly differentiated pattern in the distribution of rich burials. Nevertheless, such phenomena are also present earlier in the bronze age (see, for example, Susan Shennan, this volume) and it might be argued that the belief that the chiefdoms of the first millennium BC were more highly ranked than those of earlier periods is in fact simply an assumption, based on the further assumption that later societies are likely to be more highly evolved than earlier ones. Demonstration of such an increase is by no means easy; Tainter's attempts to develop an index of structure and organisation based on burial data (for example, Tainter 1977) have been strongly criticised (for example, O'Shea 1978). There may be indications of such a trend in the apparently growing scale of industrial production, the increasing elaboration of prestige bronze working, particularly vessels and weapons, or the wider scale of long-distance contacts. However, even if it proves to be the case that the maximum degree of ranking in the first millennium BC prior to the last two centuries did indeed exceed anything achieved earlier, this is probably less important than the wide extent of temporal and spatial variation in ranking which is also apparent. Many areas have evidence of cyclical processes of evolution and devolution, as expressed in the presence/absence of rich burials and settlement hierarchies. Moreover, from area to area these cycles were not in phase; some regions show such phenomena as rich burials at a time when in others centres seem to have failed and rich burials to have ceased (S. Champion, this volume).

The processes involved in these developments remain to be elucidated, and indeed it is the aim of the contributions to this section to investigate them with respect to particular case-studies. They differ in their emphasis but the main themes which emerge are those of agricultural intensification, warfare, and relations with the Mediterranean world.

Timothy Champion's paper is concerned with the first two of these, in the earlier part of the period, and examines the effect of agricultural intensification in response to the late second millennium BC abandonment of marginal land as a result of over-exploitation, a process which seems to have occurred in many parts of Europe at this time (cf. Bradley 1981). One effect of this was an increase in competition and warfare. Champion argues for the rise of competitive elites, involved in warfare and exchange and dependent on a progressive intensification of the agricultural base for their support, and it is politico-economic conditions of the kind he describes which Rowlands (1980) has suggested made the penetration of temperate Europe by exchange systems originating in the classical world very straightforward: any new basis for power in the continuing flux of inter-group competition, such as the control of a new source of prestige items, would have been instantly grasped.

From the sixth century BC onwards, if not earlier, it seems difficult to escape the view that the relations between temperate Europe and the Mediterranean had a major role. The assertion that civilisations have a dominating effect on the cultures on their peripheries is, of course, nothing new in archaeology, least of all in that of prehistoric Europe. Nonetheless, in recent years such arguments have been given a processual basis, in contrast to earlier discussions which simply revolved around the documentation of lists of imports and their typology and provenance. One of the main themes here has been provided by the theory of the 'world system' (see especially Wallerstein 1974), a large-scale spatial system having a core and a periphery, in which there is an interregional division of labour, and peripheral areas act as suppliers of various resources and raw materials, their socioeconomic development being strongly constrained by their position in the system. In the archaeological context this idea has been applied to the relations between Mesoamerica and the North American South-West (Gledhill 1978), between Mesopotamia and highland Iran (Kohl 1978) and Europe and the Mediterranean in the first millennium BC (Frankenstein and Rowlands 1978; Frankenstein 1979; Rowlands 1980). It is worth pointing out that Wallerstein's model, as applied to Europe, is exactly the same as Childe's was, as set out, for example, in *The Prehistory of European Society*. The difference is that it actually works far better for the first millennium BC than for the second millennium, to which Childe was applying it.

The impact of the Mediterranean world is clear, and indeed is instrumental in defining their character, in both the most spectacular phases of the temperate European iron age – the Hallstatt D period of the sixth century BC (see S. Champion, this volume) and the developments of the later iron age *oppida* – but the contexts are very different. In the first case we see a situation in which one or two strategically located chiefdoms were able temporarily to monopolise access to luxury items obtained from Mediterranean, particularly Greek and Etruscan, sources, which were still relatively distant and powerless, despite the foundation of the Greek colony of Massilia on the southern French coast. In the subsequent centuries the boundaries of the Mediterranean world moved northwards with the expansion of the Roman empire, and in the course of this process the potential for monopolisation of exchange decreased, or rather moved away northwards. Even more important according to Nash (1978), at least for the Gaulish case, was the expanding Roman demand for slaves, which had an effect similar to that of the same process in Africa over eighteen hundred years later (see, for example, Ekholm 1977). In the course of a continuing process of warfare and trade certain successful groups emerged with a structure and organisation of state-type, whereas others were reduced to a position of dependence made relatively permanent by the export of many of their members as slaves (Nash 1978, 470–2).

Sara Champion's paper in this section examines the changing distribution through time of one specific Mediterranean import, coral. She is able to show very clearly that initially the material was restricted to elite contexts and was used in the manufacture of special individual items such as inlaid brooches, but subsequently became far more widely available and was used in mass-produced items. The changeover from the special production of a small number of elite craft objects to the mass-production of much less elaborate ones has also been noted elsewhere, for example in the Maya area (Rathje 1975), and in both cases has been seen in the past as evidence for cultural decline; however, both Champion and Rathje are surely correct in their conclusion that the change is to be seen as one aspect of 'the transformation of society from one essentially simple, if stratified, to one much more complex' (S. Champion, this volume).

Collis's theme is very different. He is concerned with the processes which might have given rise to the *oppida* and their consequences. In particular he points out that in different areas they seem to have arisen from a variety of different initial conditions which need further investigation. He further notes that the pattern of continuing occupaticn of *oppida* after their initial construction is also very variable. In accounting for both their origin and their continuation, he argues, it is necessary to take into account local conditions and to define social and economic changes of which we are as yet little aware but which were certainly taking place.

After this emphasis on the local situation, Haselgrove, in what is chronologically the latest paper, once again returns us to the specific question of the effect of the expanding Roman empire on its peripheries, in this case southern Britain immediately prior to its conquest. He presents us with a clearly argued model similar to that already posited by Frankenstein and Rowlands (1978) for the central European late Hallstatt phase of contact, in which success in gaining control of imports from outside the system gave certain groups an advantage and enabled them to establish a position of paramountcy in relation to their neighbours.

Whether or not one accepts Wallerstein's 'world system' model, it is clear from the studies in this volume, and many others, that there are general processes which characterise the effects of expanding dominant powers on their neighbours, and that iron age Europe provides an excellent basis for examining these. There are many other parts of the world where such processes are likely to be relevant but

where they have barely begun to be studied, since scholarly concern remains centred on the rise and decline of the major polities. The long history of first-millennium BC researches in Europe north of the Alps provides a special reason for regarding this as a valuable case to study, despite the inaccessibility of much of the literature. Nonetheless, in carrying out this endeavour the lessons of recent years must not be forgotten: even if autonomy is rejected, local situations and locally operating processes remain vital to an understanding of the effects of external influences, and it is in the study of these that the greatest amount of work remains to be done.

S.J.S.

References

Bradley, R. 1981. Economic growth and social change: two examples from prehistoric Europe, in A. Sheridan and G. Bailey (eds.), *Economic Archaeology*. Oxford, British Archaeological Reports, 231–7.

Burgess, C. 1980. *The Age of Stonehenge*. London, Dent.

Collis, J.R. 1975. *Defended Sites of the Late La Tène in Central and Western Europe*. Oxford, British Archaeological Reports.

Cunliffe, B.W. and Rowley, T. 1976. *Oppida: the beginnings of urbanisation in Barbarian Europe*. Oxford, British Archaeological Reports.

Earle, T.K. 1978. *Economic and Social Organisation of a Complex Chiefdom: the Halelea district, Kaua'i, Hawaii* (Anthropological Papers of the Museum of Anthropology 63). Ann Arbor, University of Michigan.

Ekholm, K. 1977. External exchange and the transformation of central African social systems, in J. Friedman and M.J. Rowlands (eds.), *The Evolution of Social Systems*. London, Duckworth, 115–36.

Frankenstein, S. 1979. The Phoenicians in the far west: a function of Assyrian imperialism, in M.T. Larsen (ed.), *Power and Propaganda*. Copenhagen, 263–94.

Frankenstein, S. and Rowlands, M.J. 1978. The internal structure and regional context of early iron age society in south-western Germany. *Bulletin of the Institute of Archaeology, University of London* 15: 73–112.

Gledhill, J. 1978. Formative development in the North American South West, in D. Green, C. Haselgrove and M. Spriggs (eds.), *Social Organisation and Settlement*. Oxford, British Archaeological Reports, 241–90.

Kohl, P.L. 1978. The balance of trade in southwestern Asia in the mid-third millennium B.C. *Current Anthropology* 19: 463–92.

Nash, D. 1976. The growth of urban society in France, in B.W. Cunliffe and T. Rowley (eds.), *Oppida: the beginnings of urbanisation in Barbarian Europe*. Oxford, British Archaeological Reports, 95–133.

Nash, D. 1978. Territory and state formation in central Gaul, in D. Green, C. Haselgrove and M. Spriggs (eds.), *Social Organisation and Settlement*. Oxford, British Archaeological Reports, 455–75.

O'Shea, J. 1978. Mortuary variability: an archaeological investigation. Ph.D. dissertation, University of Cambridge.

Petres, E. 1976. The late pre-Roman age in Hungary with special reference to *oppida*, in B.W. Cunliffe and T. Rowley (eds.), *Oppida: the beginnings of urbanisation in Europe*. Oxford, British Archaeological Reports, 51–80.

Rathje, W.L. 1975. The last tango in Mayapan: a tentative trajectory of production–distribution systems, in J.A. Sabloff and C.C.

Lamberg-Karlovsky (eds.), *Ancient Civilisation and Trade.* Albuquerque, University of New Mexico Press, 409–48.

Reinecke, P. 1903. Zur Chronologie der zweiten Hälfte des Bronzealters in Süd- und Norddeutschland. *Korrespondenzblatt der Deutschen Gesellschaft für Anthropologie, Ethnologie und Urgeschichte* 33: 17–23 and 27–32.

Rowlands, M.J. 1980. Kinship, alliance and exchange in the European bronze age, in J. Barrett and R. Bradley (eds.), *Settlement and Society in the British Later Bronze Age.* Oxford, British Archaeological Reports, 15–55.

Tainter, J.A. 1977. Modeling change in prehistoric social systems, in L.R. Binford (ed.), *For Theory Building in Archaeology.* New York, Academic Press, 327–51.

Wallerstein, I. 1974. *The Modern World System.* New York, Academic Press.

Chapter 7

**Fortification, ranking
and subsistence**
Timothy Champion

*The relationship between social ranking, subsistence
economy and settlement hierarchy is examined, with reference to a specific area of West Germany in the first millennium BC. The long-term trajectories of temperate farming
systems are examined, and strategies for countering decline
and uncertainty in agricultural yields are suggested. A
strategy of intensification, technological investment, and
development of storage is demonstrated, and attention
focussed on land as the critical resource. The increase in
social ranking and the control of resources such as storage,
land and technological skills are related to readjustments of
the subsistence economy.*

Discussion of ranked societies has tended to concentrate largely on the recognition of such ranking by its archaeological correlates and on the circumstances of its first
emergence. Despite the wide variety of social organisation
subsumed in the term 'ranked society', changes within such
societies have not received the attention they deserve. Later
European prehistory offers a fruitful base for such studies,
but European archaeologists have largely failed to capitalise
on these opportunities, and have concentrated instead on the
pursuit of chronological and typological precision, while
archaeologists outside Europe have remained largely unaware
of this rich field of well-dated material. It is proposed to look
at the relationship between ranking, subsistence and settle-

ment hierarchy in one area over a period of approximately one thousand years from 1500–500 BC – that is, the later bronze age and the beginning of the iron age.[1]

The area to be examined is the Rhine–Main basin in central West Germany around modern Frankfurt. It consists of part of the valley of the middle Rhine, the lower Main valley and the Wetterau, a broad basin stretching away to the north. It is a rich agricultural area with good loess soils, constricted on the north, east and south by mountains. It forms one of the most fertile areas of Germany, and was heavily occupied from the neolithic onwards.[2]

Though the archaeology of this area in the earlier bronze age is not yet adequately known, there are similarities in funerary structures, funerary rituals and grave goods to contemporary early bronze age practices in north-western Europe. The area is, however, peripheral to both this north-western complex and the central European early bronze age groups, and does not share in their extreme wealth or their long-distance exchange relations. There are, however, signs of status differentiation in the mortuary data, especially in the deposition of bronze daggers and of distinct ornament sets. The nature of these differentiations is not yet well understood, since mortuary studies correlating grave structure,

grave assemblage and the evidence of physical anthropology are not well developed; but the degree of ranking is apparently slight. The distribution of these burials is widespread, and although settlement is predominantly limited to the valleys, the richer graves do not concentrate there.[3] There are indeed some signs of settlement expansion, since field systems probably related to burial monuments of this period have been recorded on the slopes of the mountainous regions of the Vogelsberg and the Rhön to the east of the Wetterau basin. This would accord well with the general pattern of agricultural expansion in the late neolithic and the early bronze age in northern and western Europe.

From about 1250 BC, however, this pattern is radically altered, with major changes in burial, technology and settlement distribution. The dominant burial rite changes from inhumation in a barrow to cemeteries of urned, flat-grave cremations – the so-called Urnfields – and there is also an increase in the number of burials. One class of grave is sharply differentiated by elaborate stone structure and markedly richer grave goods;[4] these are best interpreted in terms of what Peebles and Kus (1977) have called the super-ordinate dimension, though confirmation by correlation with anatomical data is difficult because of the cremation rite.

Fig. 7.1. Location of study area.

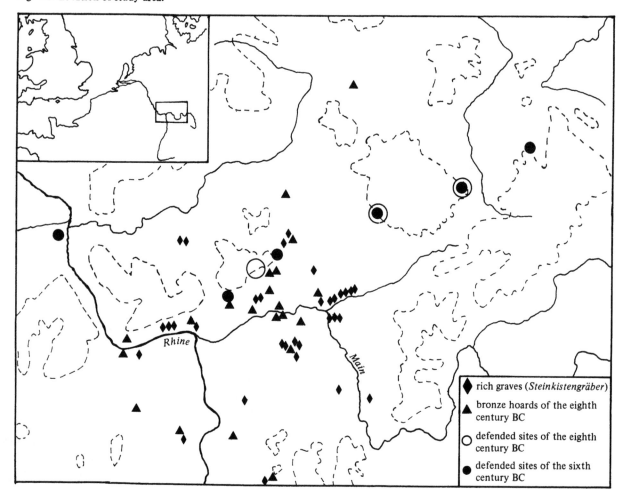

Rhine

Main

◆ rich graves (*Steinkistengräber*)

▲ bronze hoards of the eighth century BC

○ defended sites of the eighth century BC

● defended sites of the sixth century BC

These burials are concentrated on the richest loess soils of the valleys. There is also a great development in the bronze industry, with new technologies especially associated with sheet-metal working being used for the production of cauldrons, buckets, cups, weapons and armour. These objects are confined to the richest graves and to finds from rivers — apparently a new form of ritual activity.[5]

The settlement pattern of this phase contracts, and the high fields of the earlier period are abandoned. There are possible signs of agricultural intensification in the adoption of new crops such as spelt and millet, in the appearance of small pits on settlement sites, and in the sporadic occurrence of metal agricultural tools, although the evidence is slight in comparison to later developments.[6]

There is one further new element at this time, the development of the salt industry, which underwent a massive expansion, both inland and on the coast, from the middle bronze age onwards, though the salt deposits of this area are not known to have been exploited till later.[7] Little attention has been paid to use of the salt itself, and there is a variety of functions for this commodity observable in more recent farming economies. It could have been used for leather-processing or cheese-making, or as an additive to cattle diet for its mineral trace elements, but the most likely explanation is that it was needed for the preservation of meat, especially that of cattle and pig. Whichever of these explanations is adopted, however, the salt was used for the processing of animal products, and the increasing importance of salt manufacture demonstrates an increased reliance on the products of pastoral farming.

Perhaps naturally in view of the predominance of burials in the archaeological record, traditional explanations of this transformation have concentrated on the change to urned cremation and have relied heavily on the notion of the migration of Urnfield people. The actual form of the new burial rite is, however, less important than the reorganisation of ritual activity and the changed structure of society: enhanced differentiation of wealth distribution, concentration of wealth on better soils, growth of a specialised technology producing status-related objects, and a reorganised pattern of ritual activity in which these objects figure prominently.

These developments are, in fact, found widely through central and western Europe. The concentrations of artefactual wealth and technological skill tend to coincide with areas of maximum agricultural potential, especially in the river valleys of western Europe such as the Loire, Thames and Rhine. These areas were joined together by a network of exchange links manifested in the high-status objects, and such widespread ties established a considerable degree of homogeneity in the forms and fashions found throughout Europe, in contexts associated with high-status population groups. More generally, the pattern of settlement relocation, subsistence innovation, enhanced social ranking, technological development and new ritual activities is one that can

be seen in most of the established agricultural communities in temperate Europe, though the details of form and chronology vary from place to place. This phenomenon is of interest as a whole as a major readjustment in the long-term trajectory of temperate agricultural systems, but it also offers the opportunity for a study on a more local scale. The archaeological record in the Rhine—Main area is particularly good and can be used to examine some ideas concerning the emergence or growth of social ranking.

It is difficult to ascribe a major role to population growth. Precise estimates of population or population change are not yet possible, since such figures could only come from the burials, and the processes affecting burial mode and archaeological recovery are not yet well enough understood. Certainly, more burials have been discovered than of earlier periods, but this seems at present to be due more to factors of their location and modern disturbance than to a real increase in prehistoric population. An imbalance between population and subsistence resources could, however, have been produced by a decline in available resources, and it seems likely that the contraction in the settlement system was due to the abandonment of marginal areas whose agricultural potential had been reduced by over-exploitation in the late neolithic and early bronze age. Climatic deterioration may possibly have been an additional factor, with the beginning of the transition from Sub-Boreal to Sub-Atlantic perhaps producing more rainfall, lower mean summer temperatures and shorter growing seasons. It is necessary to ask, therefore, what the connection is between the emergence of enhanced social ranking and the observed readjustments in subsistence economy and settlement pattern.

Possible strategies to counter the effects of an imbalance between subsistence resources and population are numerous. Balance can be restored by reducing population: this may happen naturally through reduced fertility or increased mortality from diseases related to malnutrition, or may be deliberately imposed either through limitation of population or net emigration. Anthropological techniques have not yet been applied to examining any of the former possibilities in this specific case, but emigration was certainly a strategy adopted later in the first millennium BC (Champion 1980), though it may be doubted whether it would have been adopted as a first choice. Alternatively, resources could be increased, either through external appropriation through raiding or through internal development. In the specific case under discussion here, internal development could not take the form of extending the area under agriculture, since it was precisely the contraction of agriculturally usable land that caused the imbalance; the problem was therefore to utilize the same land resources, only part of which remained suitable for crop-production, at a time when the imbalance was compounded by a worsening climate. The introduction of new crop types, the adoption of winter sowing and the development of new tools and facilities would represent one response to the imbalance, but the experimentation with new crops, more intensive land use and shorter fallow seasons, and the climatic deterioration were all factors that led to variability in crop production and uncertainty in estimating yields.

In such circumstances, an alternative strategy would have been to guarantee a buffer against uncertainty by diverting more labour to products that could be stored and transported with comparative ease. In particular, this would have meant animal products. Meat and cheese can be preserved for considerable periods, and have a comparatively high ratio of food value to bulk compared to crop products. Pigs in any case would have been efficient producers of food from agriculturally useless land, while the comparative inefficiency of cattle in turning plants into consumable calories could have been outweighed by the utility of their products for storage and transport.

Some of the consequences of such a strategy could be predicted. Extension of the critical seasons of ploughing, sowing and harvesting would reduce the time available for other, non-agricultural activities: specialisation in agriculture would be accompanied by increasing specialisation in other forms of production. Specialisation in agriculture and intensification of labour input might lead to a demand for tools of a more specialised nature and of superior quality. Intensification of agriculture might also lead to a perceived advantage, at the level of the individual family, in population growth (at least in the short term) in order to increase available labour.

In such a system the critical resource is land as the basis of all agricultural production. The larger the territory controlled, the greater the chances of compensation for any variation in yield, but the greater the problems of internal organisation. At the same time, reliance on cattle would increase the opportunities for augmenting subsistence resources by external appropriation, that is through predation on neighbouring communities. Competition for land and protection of mobile resources would therefore be of extreme importance, and would give a particular advantage to expansion of community size, both territorially and demographically. It might further be expected that such competition would lead eventually to a stable state with communities of approximately equal size.

Internal and external pressures therefore would have demanded an increased level of organisation: externally to defend against or prey upon neighbouring communities, and internally to manage the increasingly complex land—crop—animal relationships. To meet this demand, a more marked degree of social ranking would have emerged. Centralised control may also have extended to specialised craft production, to the acquisition of an essential subsistence item such as salt, and to the management of food storage and distribution. It is possible also that the changing emphasis on land would lead to a more defined concept of ownership, and certainly land and cattle would have provided suitable means of measuring and storing wealth.

Such a system of social and economic readjustments offers a more suitable explanation for the emergence of enhanced social ranking in central Europe than other suggested theories. A role for the new elite in the redistribution of products from ecologically diverse zones within the region seems impossible, since the movement of the settlement pattern is towards a single ecological zone on the loess soils: diversity is, if anything, reduced. Nor are there any major agricultural facilities that demanded complex arrangements for their installation or maintenance, though successful exploitation of some new crops would have needed more rigorous control of agricultural operations, for instance to protect winter- and spring-sown crops from livestock in a more intensively farmed landscape.

The role of the new elite was to control and manage the exploitation of the land, to guarantee the food supply against uncertain production and to protect the community against possible attacks. It may be no coincidence that the two areas in which the status of this rank in society was displayed, in their burials at least, were closely related to these functions; buckets, cups and cauldrons were associated with the conspicuous consumption of food and drink, while arms and armour clearly indicate a military role.

These changes do not appear contemporaneously in the archaeological record. The new burial rites are seen first, and in them the status-related objects produced by the newly stimulated bronze technology. The salt industry also developed rapidly at the same period, but adequate empirical data are unfortunately lacking from settlement sites to document in detail the changes in subsistence economy. New crops were certainly introduced, as described above, and other neighbouring areas show a heavy reliance on cattle and cattle products at this period,[8] but the picture is far from clear.

The longer-term developments can also be observed, in population growth and in reorganisation of craft production. Population increase was not by itself either cause or effect of the expansion of production, but is best seen simply as part of that process. By the eighth century the effects of these changes can be seen. There are again changes in the burial rite, with the richest burials adopting a new symbolism with greater reliance on horse-gear, though the bronze vessels and armour continue. More importantly, bronze ornaments largely disappear from the graves and at the same time bronze hoards appear, associated with a new system of industrial organisation involving scrap-collection and the increased output of tools such as axes and sickles.[9] Bronze was increasingly diverted to the production of domestic and agricultural tools.

It is only now that defended hill-top enclosures are found in this area to demonstrate the existence of a settlement hierarchy. They have mostly been seen in a military light, as signs of disturbed times, sometimes specifically as refuge places — an idea based partly on an apparent lack of occupation which is more likely to result from a real lack of adequate excavation. Though precise definition of function is as yet impossible, they can clearly be regarded as a sign of the emergence of a settlement hierarchy and as the result of organised communal labour. Some have evidence of manufacture, especially of bronze, and there are occasional finds of objects otherwise associated only with the richest burials. Though physically separate from the location of the richest burials, they are thus linked to the elite and may have served as defended sites of centrally controlled production, and possibly also of storage.[10]

The development of this system in the seventh century is unclear, but the hillforts may have been abandoned, though the burial tradition certainly continued. The break in settlement pattern may, if real, be related to the transition from bronze to iron for many purposes at this time. This too is perhaps best regarded as a further stage in intensification and as a means of supplying a growing demand for tools. The breakdown of long-established exchange networks to supply bronze would then be the consequence, not the cause, of the technological change.

Whatever the seventh-century pattern may be, in the next century hillforts again appear, in a chain of large sites at approximately regular intervals dominating this zone. There is a considerable degree of similarity between these forts in size, location and construction, and this together with the regularity in spacing suggests that a position of equilibrium has been reached after a prolonged phase of expansion; this settlement pattern in fact now persists for some centuries. Once again the hillforts are not well documented by excavation, but finds from some suggest continued functions of storage and production, and further links to the richest graves.[11]

By 500 BC the agricultural basis of the society had been diversified still further by the introduction of new crops, rye and oats; and other local resources were beginning to be exploited, especially iron ore and salt. The pattern of settlement had begun to expand again, partly to gain access to the iron ores of the mountains but also for agricultural reasons. Here, as throughout central and western Europe, the earlier strain on subsistence resources had been successfully overcome by a combination of new crops, new tools, new facilities, new methods and a new level of organisation. The guaranteeing of subsistence was no longer a major aim of society, and with the establishment of an equilibrium, the overt signs of competition began to disappear from the graves.

Many of the features of technology, burial and settlement described here are common to many different areas of central and western Europe; it would, however, be wrong to assume that the same pattern of development had occurred everywhere. In this particular case, the initial condition which was necessary, but by no means sufficient, for the emergence of this enhanced ranking in society was the strain on subsistence resources in the late second millennium BC. The particular strategy adopted to meet this strain was to

minimise risk and provide a buffer against subsistence failure. This required increased levels of managerial control internally and of exchange relations externally, and had an inbuilt predisposition towards growth. Competitive elites thus arose, controlling new technologies and the exchange and deposition of their products. The existence of these elites was supported by progressive intensification of the agricultural basis of society, of which the transformation of the metal supply industry and the long-term growth in population were integral parts.

Notes

1 The chronology used is that established by Müller-Karpe (1959) and Kossack (1959): modifications have been proposed, e.g. by Sandars (1971), but these are not significant for the present argument.
2 The fundamental surveys of material in this area are by Herrmann (1966) for the later bronze age and by Schumacher (1972, 1974) for the earlier iron age.
3 For earlier bronze age burial data, see Richter (1970), Kubach (1977), Herrmann and Jockenhövel (1975); female ornament and possible interpretation are discussed by Wels-Weyrauth (1975).
4 The *Steinkistengräber* of Herrmann (1966, vol. I, 22–6).
5 For armour, see Schauer (1975), e.g. helmet and shields from the Rhine; for bronze vessels, e.g. cist graves at Eschborn containing bronze cups (Herrmann 1966, vol. II, plates 83–4).
6 The subsistence economy is little understood because of the comparative neglect of settlement excavation. The evidence for crop types cited by Körber-Grohne and Piening (1979, fig. 1) suggests the introduction of spelt and millet at this time and rye and oats in mid-first millennium BC. Millet and rye are better adapted to damper and colder climates than most wheat species, but spelt may have been winter-sown; this would have enabled larger areas to be cropped in any year by spreading the critical activities of ploughing and harvesting over a longer period.
7 For a general discussion of salt-working, see Coles and Harding (1979, 61–3 with further references). Several different technologies were involved, in particular extraction from sea-water, extraction from terrestrial saline deposits and deep mining.
8 Evidence of very high proportions of cattle at this period is given by Ostoja-Zagórski (1974). This is also the time at which the first identifiable specialist leather-working tools appear (Roth 1974).
9 The hoards, as elsewhere in western Europe, are concentrated on the richest agricultural lands (Herrmann 1966, 43–5 and fig. 11; Jockenhövel 1974, fig. 17). Many of them contain several examples of the same item, best interpreted as stock accumulated for distribution, while others contain predominantly old or broken items, representing scrap for reuse.
10 For hill-top enclosures generally, see Jockenhövel (1974). Three sites in this area, Bleibeskopf, Glauberg and Haimberg, show definite evidence of occupation and fortification in the eighth century, and all have produced remains of metal-working (Jockenhövel 1974, 52–3 and table 1; Müller-Karpe 1974). For the Dünsberg, a similar site immediately to the north, with evidence for craft-production in the form of specialist tools, see *Fundberichte aus Hessen* 15 (1979): 479. The links to the richest graves are found in the presence of fragments of bronze vessels, and of small rings, *Knebelringe*, otherwise only found in such contexts (Jockenhövel 1974, 58).

11 The later development of the settlement pattern is discussed by
    Härke (1979, 223–8).

References

Champion, T.C. 1980. Mass migration in later prehistoric Europe, in
    P. Sörbom (ed.), *Transport Technology and Social Change.*
    Stockholm, Tekniska Museet, 31–42.

Coles, J.M. and Harding, A.F. 1979. *The Bronze Age in Europe.*
    London, Methuen.

Härke, H.G.H. 1979. *Settlement Types and Settlement Patterns in the
    West Hallstatt Province.* Oxford, British Archaeological
    Reports.

Herrmann, F.-R. 1966. *Die Funde der Urnenfelderkultur in Mittel-
    und Südhessen* (Römisch-Germanische Forschungen 27).
    Berlin, de Gruyter.

Herrmann, F.-R. and Jockenhövel, A. 1975. Bronzezeitliche Grab-
    hügel mit Pfostenringen bei Edelsberg, Kreis Limburg-
    Weilburg. *Fundberichte aus Hessen* 15: 87–127.

Jockenhövel, A. 1974. Zu befestigten Siedlungen der Urnenfelderzeit
    aus Süddeutschland. *Fundberichte aus Hessen* 14: 19–62.

Körber-Grohne, U. and Piening, U. 1979. Verkohlte Nutz- und
    Wildpflanzenreste aus Bondorf, Kreis Böblingen. *Fund-
    berichte aus Baden-Württemberg* 4: 152–69.

Kossack, G. 1959. *Südbayern während der Hallstattzeit* (Römisch-
    Germanische Forschungen 24). Berlin, de Gruyter.

Kubach, W. 1977. *Die Nadeln in Hessen und Rheinhessen* (Prä-
    historische Bronzefunde XIII, 3). Munich, C.H. Beck.

Müller-Karpe, A. 1974. Neue Bronzefunde der späten Urnenfelderzeit
    vom Bleibeskopf im Taunus. *Fundberichte aus Hessen* 14:
    203–14.

Müller-Karpe, H. 1959. *Beiträge zur Chronologie der Urnenfelderzeit
    nördlich und südlich der Alpen* (Römisch-Germanische
    Forschungen 22). Berlin, de Gruyter.

Ostoja-Zagórski, J. 1974. From studies on the economic structure at
    the decline of the Bronze Age and the Hallstatt period in the
    north and west zone of the Odra and Vistula basins. *Przeglad
    Archeologiczny* 22: 123–49.

Peebles, C.S. and Kus, S.M. 1977. Some archaeological correlates of
    ranked societies. *American Antiquity* 42: 421–48.

Richter, I. 1970. *Der Arm- und Beinschmuck der Bronze- und Urnen-
    feldzeit in Hessen und Rheinhessen* (Prähistorische Bronze-
    funde X, 1). Munich, C.H. Beck.

Roth, H. 1974. Ein Ledermesser der atlantischen Bronzezeit aus
    Mittelfranken. *Archäologisches Korrespondenzblatt* 4: 37–47.

Sandars, N.K. 1971. From Bronze Age to Iron Age: a sequel to a
    sequel, in J. Boardman, M.A. Brown and T.G.E. Powell (eds.),
    The European Community in Later Prehistory. London,
    Routledge and Kegan Paul, 1–29.

Schauer, P. 1975. Die Bewaffnung der 'Adelskrieger' während der
    späten Bronze- und frühen Eisenzeit. *Ausgrabungen in
    Deutschland 1950–1975*, Bd 3. Mainz, Phillip von Zabern,
    305–11.

Schumacher, A. 1972 and 1974. *Die Hallstattzeit im südlichen
    Hessen*, I and II (Bonner Hefte zur Vorgeschichte 5 and 6).
    Bonn.

Wels-Weyrauth, U. 1975. Schmuckausstattungen aus Frauengräbern
    der jüngeren Hügelgräberbronzezeit in Deutschland (14. Jahr-
    hundert v. Christ). *Ausgrabungen in Deutschland 1950–1975*,
    Bd 3. Mainz, Phillip von Zabern, 300–4.

Chapter 8

**Exchange and ranking:
the case of coral**
Sara Champion

*The appearance of Mediterranean coral in graves of the
earlier iron age (750–250 BC) of central and western Europe
is studied, and is found to be of value both in defining
different levels of ranking, and in isolating groups of craft
products emanating from specialised, apparently patronised
workshops. Its presence assists in the recognition of both
internal and external exchange patterns, though the underlying mechanisms are not altogether clear. The continued
appearance of coral after the cessation of other prestige
imports from the Mediterranean world enables the identification of an alteration in exchange patterns which reflects
transformations in social organisation and parallel economic and industrial processes.*

In European iron age studies, the emergence of an elite
group in the early phases, as well as the transformation in
society evident in the middle of the period, have traditionally
been ascribed to invasions of people from the east; while the
phenomenon of the appearance of prestige imports from the
Mediterranean in Transalpine Europe has been simply
described as 'trade' undertaken by enterprising individuals,
with few attempts to explain how such trade between the
complex societies of the Mediterranean world and the essentially simpler ones of central Europe came about and was
maintained. This paper will show that there are two distinct
patterns for the social context of one particular import,

coral, which, in association with apparently contrasting mechanisms of production, serve to elucidate the evolution of iron age society as well as the relationship with the Mediterranean.

The iron age in central Europe (fig. 8.1) started around 800 BC, though there is evidence of actual iron-working before that time. The emergence of an elite class dignified by special burials and habitation sites occurred during the eighth and seventh centuries BC, reaching its apogee in the sixth. This first part of the iron age, named the Hallstatt period after a site in Austria, ended somewhere in the fifth century BC when the so-called La Tène period began; it is the sixth to third centuries BC that we are concerned with here. The sixth century saw the flowering of the well-known phenomenon of the *Fürstengräber*, or princely graves, along with the *Fürstensitze*, or princely seats or residences.[1] The occupants of the graves were buried under massive tumuli, normally in wooden mortuary chambers, with accompanying four-wheeled vehicles, goldwork, and lavishly produced local goods, as well as items imported from the Mediterranean world such as Greek pottery cups, wine-drinking vessels like

jugs, mixing bowls and cauldrons, furniture like the ivory-inlaid couch from the Grafenbühl near Stuttgart and the wheeled bronze day-bed from Hochdorf in the same area, and even more exotic goods like silk and chickens. The rich settlements, most of which have had the minimum of good excavation,[2] show similar links with the Mediterranean in their sherds of Phocaean and other Greek pottery and wine amphorae from Marseilles; while at the Heuneburg in southern Germany, a copying of southern architectural ideas resulted in a defensive wall being built with bastions unnecessarily close, suggesting a misunderstanding of their function, and constructed in sun-dried brick, a singularly inappropriate building material for the inclement climate of the Transalpine region. From these settlements comes evidence of industry — of pottery-making, metal-working, and the handling of other raw and sometimes imported materials like amber, lignite and jet. Coral from the Mediterranean coasts takes its place among the imports, being found both as ornaments in the graves and as a raw material in the settlements. These major settlements appear to be regularly spaced, though the reasons for the siting of

Fig. 8.1. Map of principal sites with imports in earlier iron age Europe.

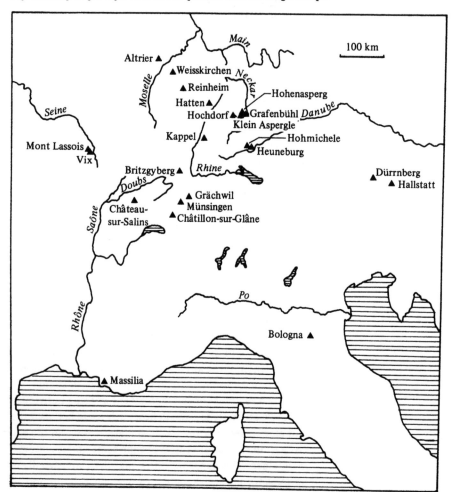

some of them are quite unclear, while others have direct access to raw materials such as salt or metal ores, or to routes of communication such as strategic water courses.

Two approaches have been combined in this analysis of the prestige import phenomenon as seen through coral. The first has involved the detailed examination of all finds of coral in an attempt to group them according to their processing centre. Though in most cases this proved impossible for simple beads and raw, unmodified corals, the results were more encouraging for inlaid objects, particularly the brooches worn as clothing fasteners.[3] It was found that while few objects were identical to each other, implying their manufacture to special order or at least in very small batches, individual tricks of construction or decoration could be isolated which allowed the supposition that many of the brooches found in one region were actually made in one workshop. Since some of the *Fürstensitze* produced evidence of metal-working and even unfinished brooches, it is hard not to conclude that the rich centres were the places of manufacture. The assumption that these central places were the only sites where the manufacture of the whole range of metal types took place cannot be upheld, however, for the lack of excavated settlement sites of types other than *Fürstensitze* is a serious problem in any analysis of industrial organisation in iron age Europe. Recent excavations at a rural settlement at Hascherkeller in Bavaria (Wells 1980) have produced a mould for rings which, though only the first piece of hard evidence, suggests that at least some types of object were made at lower-level sites; it is therefore possible to suggest only that the more prestigious items, along with some basic types, were likely to have been made at the major sites.

The second approach has been to analyse the cemeteries in which coral was found in an attempt to reconstruct social organisation, and to compare the contexts of coral with those of other imports.[4] The analyses of these mortuary data showed that there were many poorly endowed graves in each tumulus or cemetery, and proportionately few very rich graves. Imported goods were exclusively associated with graves already designated as rich because of the large number of artefact types they contained; in this and any other method of scoring graves for wealth, the same few graves came out on top. The only Mediterranean import to reach graves below this top level was coral, which, while occasionally absent from the richest graves (perhaps because these, usually central, had frequently been robbed in antiquity for their precious goods), was also found in burials with more than the normal number of local grave goods but no other imports. Coral perhaps helps to define a level of society below the so-called princes and above the remainder of the interred population. What emerged clearly from cemetery analyses in several different geographical areas was that coral was not available to the lower ranks of those buried (fig. 8.2, top).

Although quantification of the coral is difficult because inlays cannot be weighed or accurately measured,[5]

and the sources cannot be identified more closely than as the Mediterranean coasts in general, it is clear from a simple object count that there are concentrations of coral in and around the major centres and no smooth fall-off away from the notional source, which must suggest directional rather than down-the-line trade (Renfrew 1977).

The appearance of coral at the rich major settlements, the concentrations of material in their regions, the workshop groups tentatively identified, and the socially restricted availability of the material, all point to the conclusion that the coral was imported, along with other Mediterranean goods, directly to the central sites, where it was fashioned into beads or amulets, or was inlaid into specially made brooches or other artefacts, perhaps by a craftsman attached to the elite group.[6] It can be postulated that these prestige commodities were then redistributed in line with the social obligations of the elite group. Against this, it could be suggested that some kind of market exchange might be responsible for the distribution of goods away from the centres. In the absence of written records to substantiate the existence of such a mechanism in the early iron age, only the spatial pattern produced by the archaeological material can offer any evidence, and it is recognised that 'central place redistribution and central place market exchange are spatially identical' (Renfrew 1977, 88). It is possible to suggest only that the very narrow range of goods available from Mediterranean sources, prestigious though they were, together with the apparent absence of the complex bureaucratic structures (and certainly of recording devices) normally associated with market economies, would tend to argue in favour of a redistributive system.

At the beginning of the fifth century BC some of the rich centres ceased to exist. In particular, the strategically placed sites of the Heuneburg and Mont Lassois have no La Tène material, though the salt-based sites in Austria and eastern France continued to be occupied (the latter only for a short time), as well as the putative centre at the Hohenasperg. In those areas where the centres failed, rich burials ceased to appear, and with them the imports. Already by this time in other areas such as Switzerland, flat-grave cemeteries reflecting a different social organisation were using imported coral; but in the Heuneberg and Mont Lassois regions, though burials of less prestigious individuals still continued, coral is no longer found, emphasising the role which these settlements probably played in its distribution.

At the same time, new centres of elite society emerged, particularly in the Middle Rhine region, a phenomenon as short-lived as it was spectacular.[7] In an area rich in gold and iron ores which had, apparently, no elite group in the Hallstatt period, suddenly there appeared rich graves containing two-wheeled vehicles, Greek pottery, Etruscan wine flagons, and coral. Here too, analysis of the metalwork suggests manufacture in one or two centres (though these remain unidentified); here too, coral is available only to the richest members of society (fig. 8.2, centre).

By the end of the fifth century this phenomenon too is almost over; but it is not the end of the story. In all previous work in this field, the end of the spectacular imports and the associated monuments has been seen as the end of trade with the Mediterranean and all that it may be thought to have signified. However, the new flat cemeteries already being used by half-way through the century in Switzerland and north-eastern France demonstrate that coral, at least, continued to be imported, although its social context had changed. Analysis of the material on which it occurs shows that its uses were similar to those of the preceding period, although the groups of material are now much more hom-

Fig. 8.2. The percentage of graves containing coral plotted against the number of artefact types (NAT) in graves. Top: late Hallstatt period. Centre: early La Tène period, Middle Rhine. Bottom: early La Tène period, Switzerland.

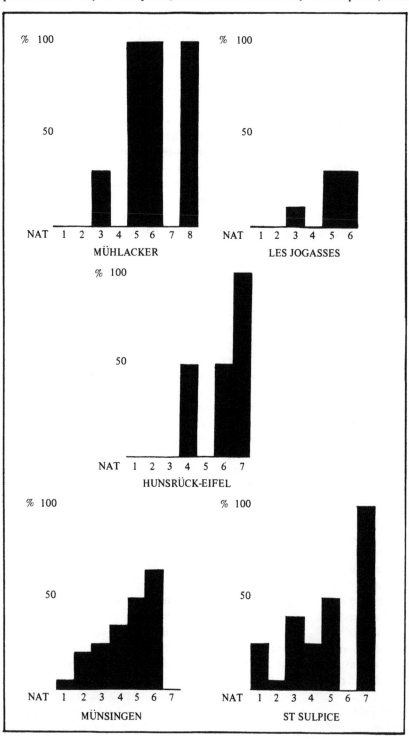

ogeneous internally, and it can be suggested that items were made in batches for stock, though special orders were still catered for. The most striking factor to emerge from the cemetery analyses, however, is that now coral was available to everyone who merited interment (fig. 8.2, bottom). The cemeteries still demonstrate degrees of ranking, but instead of the sharp distinctions between the large number of less well-endowed graves and the few very rich, the gradations form a smoother curve: and whether an individual was buried with one object or forty, he or she could have coral. One of the implications of an imported raw material is that it will be more expensive than one locally available because of transport costs, and yet in the social milieu just described no-one was excluded from acquiring it. From this must be inferred a change in the distributive mechanism since the previous period, a change which has already been reflected in a shift from small tumulus cemeteries to large flat-grave cemeteries, and from apparently ranked settlement types to something different, though our evidence for what that something different is in the relevant areas is minimal. Associated with all these changes is an apparent shift in production practices from the individually commissioned object to the manufacture of larger numbers of stock items, particularly with reference to decorative goods as opposed to everyday tools; however, the recognition of this change is based on a perhaps subjective analysis of the finished material, and only the location of actual workshops on sites of both periods could illuminate the problem.

   This combination of approaches to the material and the mortuary data has succeeded in distinguishing two patterns of social and industrial organisation which, for a short time in the fifth century, actually coexisted and interacted: there is some evidence that objects made in one workshop reached both vehicle burials in the Middle Rhine and burials in a Swiss flat cemetery.[8] Let us now examine the implications of the contrasting structures that have been identified.

   It has already become clear archaeologically that the emergence of a powerful elite in central Europe was not the result of an invasion and superimposition of an upper layer of society on the indigenous population. The material culture, burial rites and settlement patterns all had their roots in preceding traditions, trading links with southern neighbours had already been established before the emergence of the central places, and the growth of an elite group was already visible in earlier versions of the rich graves. What we are looking at is a sudden intensification of these processes; and to what extent the centres arose in response to the historically documented expansion of the commercial interests of Mediterranean groups, or as a result of developing internal mechanisms, remains as yet uncertain. While some centres, such as those with salt as their main natural resource, were in existence before the intensification of contacts, the foundation of the Greek colony at Massilia (Marseilles) around 600 BC must have played a major role in the rise of Mont

Lassois as a centre; indeed, its dependence on its link with Massilia appears crucial, since the decline in the commercial fortunes of Marseilles is contemporary with the failure of Mont Lassois. The southern German sites of the Heuneburg and the Hohenasperg may also have emerged as a result of increased Transalpine activity, but a clear explanation of why one should fail and the other continue in the fifth century is not yet available. For the complex societies of the Mediterranean world, raw materials such as ores, agricultural produce (grain, and probably salted meat) and possibly slaves, were clearly attractive; the prestigious goods which came in the other direction were doubtless controlled by the elite and were used to maintain their positions of strength as Frankenstein and Rowlands (1978) have suggested. In a situation balanced in this way, disruption in the less complex, and perhaps less stable society represented by the central European communities may be less likely to affect the activities of the dominant partner than is a change of circumstances at the Mediterranean end, since the power base of the European elite was presumably their ability to control access to the prestige goods, the outward signs of their authority. However, the regional shift from southern Germany to the Middle Rhine in the fifth century, and the contemporary development in Switzerland of new patterns of life and death suggests internal changes in European society that may have affected the relationship with the Mediterranean just as much as those events in the Mediterranean, underlined by Frankenstein and Rowlands, which may have caused a lessening of interest in Europe north of the Alps.

   Though changes in social and economic organisation coincide in some areas with the demise of the elites in southern Germany and eastern France, the analysis of these changes suggests that contacts with the south did not break down, but that materials previously available only to members of the elite group became available to a wider section of society. A continuity in manufacturing techniques in some areas, in contacts between different regions with different social organisations, and in extra-territorial relationships, suggests that invasion is not a satisfactory explanation for the changes in burial rite and settlement organisation. Clear evidence of products from north of the Alps reaching Italy and *vice versa*, together with the development of long-distance internal contacts,[9] demonstrate that the end of the elites cannot be viewed, as it has been in the past, as a complete breakdown in social organisation, but is rather to be seen as a stage in the transformation of society from one essentially simple, if stratified, to one much more complex.[10]

Notes

1 The *Fürstengräberkreis*, or area in which this type of site occurs, comprises southern Germany, Switzerland and eastern France, and specifically excludes, in this early period, the Middle Rhine. Frequently, rich graves and settlement sites are spatially related: for example, the Heuneburg in Württemberg,

one of the most important, and best and most extensively excavated, of the settlements, has nearby a large group of tumuli including the well-known Hohmichele; and Mont Lassois, Côte d'Or, near the head of the Seine, has the famous Vix and Ste Colombe graves close by. The Camp de Château at Salins, Jura, is also associated with a number of rich graves, while the exceptionally well-appointed burials in the Stuttgart area, which include the Grafenbühl and the newly discovered Hochdorf example, are linked with the suspected, though now seriously built-over, rich settlement on the Hohenasperg.

2 The concentration of Continental scholars on excavating burials has resulted in a serious neglect of contemporary settlement excavation. In general, even the examination of the wealthy settlements has been on a small scale, though the Heuneburg campaign is an exception. Excavation at Mont Lassois was very limited, and the Camp de Château was dug early this century, producing a stratigraphical sequence that may not be wholly reliable. Other apparent centres at Châtillon-sur-Glâne, Switzerland, Britzgyberg, Alsace, and Würzburg and the Hohenasperg in Germany have been the subjects of minimal excavation.

3 The raw corals were unmodified after their preliminary trimming from the parent stem, with the exception of a clearly recognisable group from the Champagne region (with exports) which were engraved with two or three lines around the main stem. Spherical or tubular beads were unyielding to further analysis: even size appeared not to have been a variable factor between production centres. Brooches, commonly known as fibulae, come in various general types in the whole period under discussion. They range from the plain arc and serpentiform types of Italian origin, through the kettledrum (*Pauken-fibel*) and decorated foot (*Fusszierfibel*) of the late Hallstatt period, and the various classes ornamented with bird, animal and human representations, to the long series of La Tène fibula types with decorated disc foot. For the La Tène period in particular, the number of types into which coral is inlaid increases, and includes decorative plaques and disc brooches, scabbards, spears and shield ornaments, helmets, horse-gear and vehicle mountings.

4 It has to be admitted that the data base for these analyses from the Hallstatt period is not ideal or even good. A tumulus, even if fully excavated, may contain a very small number of burials, and may have been excavated in the nineteenth century with lack of care or poor recording. The number of tumuli in any cemetery may be small, and frequently not all are excavated. A high percentage of tumuli have been robbed, particularly in the centre, where the principal burial may be expected to have been; there is evidence that some were robbed within thirty years of burial, so that decorative objects would still have been usable. The conclusions drawn here are therefore based on a small actual number of graves, and are thus subject to severe limitations.

5 Measurement of surface area is possible, but the depth of the inlays is almost impossible to estimate in cases where the setting goes into a solid area of metal. Understandably, museum curators do not allow the removal of inlays from their settings, and therefore quantification has to be extremely approximate.

6 There are ethnographic parallels for a 'skilled craftsman attached to a high-status group' (Rowlands 1972, 210), and this form of craft organisation seems to fit well the evidence that is at present available.

7 Sites are exclusively funerary in the Middle Rhine, there being no settlements as yet located with fifth-century Mediterranean imports. Rich burials such as those at Reinheim and Weiss-kirchen contain vehicles and spectacular equipment, much of

it with gold decoration. A contemporary phenomenon occurs in the Champagne region of France (sites such as La Gorge-Meillet and Somme-Bionne) and in Bavaria and Bohemia; and a settlement site with fifth-century imported Attic pottery has been located at Uetliberg in Switzerland which would clearly repay further investigation.

8 Objects made from iron or bronze clad with gold and decorated with coral and sometimes amber have decorative traits which can be recognised as virtually identical on material from Reinheim, Saarland, and St Sulpice, Ct. Vaud, among others.

9 There is clear evidence, too detailed to embark on here, for contacts between the Swiss plateau and Dürrnberg in Austria, the Marne region, the Rhineland and possibly southern France.

10 This paper could not have been delivered in Philadelphia without the generous assistance of the British Academy with travel funds, for which I am very grateful.

References

Frankenstein, S. and Rowlands, M.J. 1978. The internal structure and regional context of Early Iron Age society in south-western Germany. *Bulletin of the Institute of Archaeology, University of London* 15: 73–112.

Renfrew, C. 1977. Alternative models for exchange and spatial distribution, in T.K. Earle and J.E. Ericson (eds.), *Exchange Systems in Prehistory.* New York, Academic Press, 71–90.

Rowlands, M.J. 1972. The archaeological interpretation of prehistoric metalworking. *World Archaeology* 3: 210–44.

Wells, P. 1980. The early iron age settlement of Hascherkeller in Bavaria: preliminary report on the 1979 excavations. *Journal of Field Archaeology* 7 (3): 313–28.

Chapter 9

**Gradual growth and
sudden change —
urbanisation in
temperate Europe**
John Collis

*This paper presents a simple model for analysing the
impact of centralisation for defence which produced the
earliest fully urban settlements (*oppida*) in temperate Europe
north of the Alps in the second and first centuries BC. It
stresses the need to study the settlement patterns and social
structure in the period immediately preceding the foundation
of the* oppida *to understand the processes which produced a
society capable of establishing and supporting an urban
system.*

During the second and first centuries BC a number of
massive defended sites known in the archaeological literature
as *oppida* were established in the zone north of the Alps,
extending from Czechoslovakia, through southern Germany
to central and northern France (fig. 9.1). Almost all were
deliberate foundations constructed in defended situations,
and though many are situated on major trade routes, the
need for defence was a primary consideration. They range in
size from about 25 hectares to over 1500 hectares. Some
were quickly abandoned, but others developed into urban
settlements which survived into the Roman period if not to
the modern day — Avaricum/Bourges, Vesontio/Besançon,
Lutetia/Paris. I have discussed their nature, origins, industry
and trade elsewhere (Collis 1973; forthcoming), and here I
wish only to deal with the circumstances of their foundation.

A model for fieldwork

From the fifth century BC onwards we have increasing historical references to the areas north of the Alps in Greek and, later, Latin literature, with contact culminating in the Roman military conquest of much of the area where we find *oppida*, mainly in the first century BC. Inevitably the framework for studying this period has been dominated by historical models – the expansion of the Celts and their final disappearance squeezed between Roman expansion from the south and 'Germans' from the north. At its worst this has degenerated into simplistic questions – 'Are these Celts?', 'Did Caesar sleep here?' – at best it has been concerned only with establishing detailed chronologies, mainly from the extensive burial evidence.

The trade inter-relationship between the Mediterranean civilisations and central Europe has also been extensively studied, as has its impact on the material culture, especially art, so that the main outlines and developments of La Tène art, the central European response to artistic stimulus from the south, are now well documented. The result has been that excavation has concentrated on rich or major sites which can fit into these models – cemeteries with rich grave goods, major settlements – and little field survey has been done to place these in their regional and local contexts. Though we

know some of the main trends of the iron age,[1] there are obvious glaring gaps. One of these is the period La Tène C, where virtually no work has been done on settlements, and cemetery studies are limited to chronological and art-historical problems. But this is largely due to a lack of models of socio-economic development. In this paper I wish to put forward a simple model from which we can start, and from which it will emerge that this 'boring' period of La Tène C in fact holds the key for understanding the urban process in this area.

The 'crisis' model

A major characteristic of the European iron age is the appearance of defended sites of various sorts – the *oppida* of the late iron age, or the earlier 'hill-forts' which are generally smaller and more simple than the *oppida* in terms of their social and economic status. The outlay of time and resources in the construction of these sites, and their often inconvenient siting in relationship to access, agricultural land, water, etc., and the 'cost' of translating perhaps the whole population to within the defences is clearly not something that would be undertaken by choice. It may be forced by external pressures: 'historical' interpretations for the foundation of *oppida* point to attacks by Germanic tribes such as

Fig. 9.1. Distribution of defended oppida of over 25 ha in the first century BC; and other sites mentioned in the text.

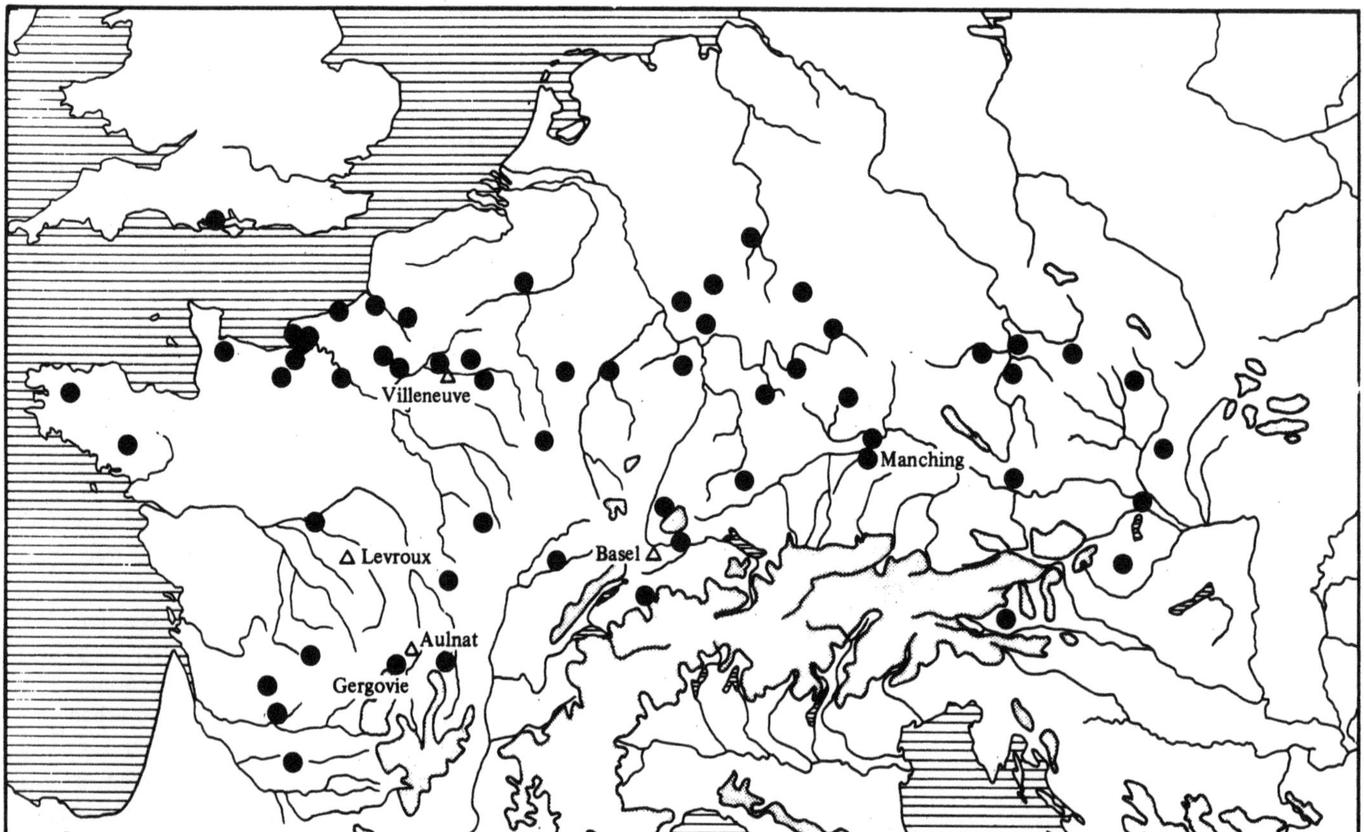

the Cimbri and Teutones, or Roman conquest. But equally it could be internal within the society: the inter-tribal conflict in Gaul in the first century BC apparently to control the Mediterranean trade and collect trade goods such as slaves; or personal conflict within the tribe between individuals aiming at supremacy.

This sudden change in settlement pattern I wish here to term 'crisis' – I avoid the term 'catastrophe' as my model is not intended to be mathematical, but is essentially descriptive. Likewise it is not to deny that a 'crisis' within a society might have a very different effect, such as the total abandonment of the territory. The model is more closely related to graph theory in that at each phase there are several possible variable states which can be reached from several, but not all the variable states of the preceding phase, and can lead on to some but not all the variable states in the succeeding phase. Thus the variable states act as nodes for the various trajectories of different societies. This will be clarified with an example.

On fig. 9.2 I have postulated a dispersed settlement pattern with a hierarchical society (the hexagon grid is merely to assist the eye and for aesthetics!). Specialists, part-time or full-time, are equally dispersed. Clearly, many other variable states could be postulated – I have elsewhere discussed this model in relationship to hill-forts (Collis 1981). Also for phase 2, the 'crisis' phase, I have postulated only one variable state – total nucleation, though non-nucleation and partial nucleation are other possibilities, dictated by such variables as the proximity of the crisis and the ability of the society to organise itself. A good historical example is the Danish invasion of Saxon England – of the Saxon kingdoms, only that of Wessex under Alfred was able to construct defensive 'burhs' to shelter the population from attack.

When the crisis disappears, we can postulate another series of potential reactions (fig. 9.3). These will be governed by factors such as the longevity of the crisis, the input of labour on the new site (houses, etc.), accessibility, centrality, exposure of the site to the elements, as well as social and political pressure. Some of the alternative possibilities are:

(a) everyone returns home leaving an empty site;

(b) everyone stays, in which case this is not a 'central place'[2] as there is no-one to be central to;

(c) all farmers return home, artisans stay because of the advantages of joint cooperation, and the elite remain to exploit the concentration of political, economic and social power, perhaps migrating seasonally to their country estates which are placed in the hands of bailiffs. This produces a true 'central place';

(d) most farmers and elite return home because of the distance to farms/territorial base, but those who live closest to the site remain. Again this is not a 'central place'.

This model, simple though it may be, does give us a framework of questions for investigating rural settlements. It also demonstrates the fallacy that major sites even with dense

occupation, need necessarily be 'central places'. At the time of 'crisis' and especially 'post-crisis' we should be able to identify cases of abandonment or 'downgrading' of sites in terms of social status or of economic functions (e.g. the disappearance of industry). The model does also stress the need to understand all three phases of the process, but at present we have virtually no data on the 'pre-crisis' stage or the 'crisis' stage, but more on the 'post-crisis', which has often been taken to be the 'typical' period of the *oppida* (e.g. Bibracte/Mount Beuvray). The plan of a deliberately founded settlement should give us a unique insight into how a particular society was organised, as social and economic relationships may be clearly translated into spatial terms.

Field data[3]

At present there are few basic field data available for even the most simple distinctions. Only from one site, Villeneuve-St-Germain, near Soissons on the River Aisne in northern France, do we have the beginnings of a plan of a

Fig. 9.2. (a) 'Pre-crisis' distribution. (b) 'Crisis' distribution.

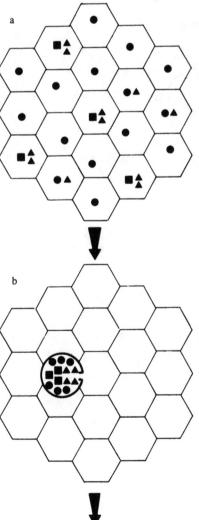

site at the 'crisis' stage, with courtyard houses laid out along a street. In the Auvergne near Clermont-Ferrand in central France, we can detect at least three main phases. In the first, we encounter open settlements, some, such as Aulnat, certainly semi-industrial villages, but possibly also sites of higher social status, such as the hill-top site of Corent. The second phase sees the establishment around 30 BC of a defended urban site at Gergovie, and the abandonment of Aulnat — indeed it is possible that we are dealing with a totally nucleated situation. In the third phase in the Augustan period the town of Augustonemetum on the site of modern Clermont-Ferrand is established, and possibly low-status farms reappear in the surrounding countryside. But surface survey has only just started, and these interpretations are tentative in the extreme.

At Levroux on the other side of the *Massif Central* the pattern is different. The open settlement of the first stage is already nucleated, and the *oppidum* which replaces it is of virtually the same size (about 12 ha). Field survey some 5–10 kms around the site has totally failed to produce any sites contemporary with either phase. A third situation is represented by Manching on the Danube in southern Germany. Here the open site starts probably early in the third century BC as a small farming site which gradually increased in size so that by the beginning of the first century BC there was a large nucleated open settlement of 80–120 ha. This growth is due to Manching's unique siting on the Danube: it controls the river route, and a river crossing, and also straddles the east–west route along the river, which is here forced into a narrow strip of dry ground only a few hundred yards across. The site was later given defences, but disappears in the mid-first century BC. It is unclear whether the apparent lack of contemporary sites around is due merely to the lack of field survey.

Fig. 9.3. Some possible variable states of the distribution in the 'post-crisis' situation.

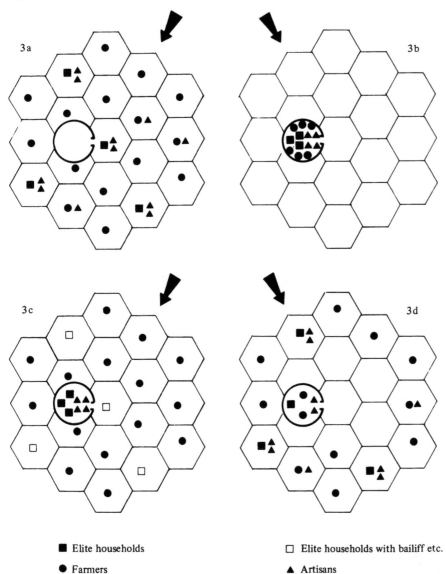

■ Elite households   □ Elite households with bailiff etc.

● Farmers   ▲ Artisans

Gradual growth

The examples that I have quoted above show that there was not in fact a single 'variable state' from which *oppida* developed – around Aulnat there would seem to be little nucleation, small villages at the most; at Levroux (and elsewhere, for example Basel in Switzerland) large nucleated villages; at Manching a preexisting urban complex. This was not due to certain areas being 'backward'. Aulnat lies at the heart of the tribe of the Arverni, according to classical authors the richest and most powerful tribe in Gaul in the second century BC. However, the changes of the first century BC resulted in a similar settlement pattern in these areas. But in others, though *oppida* were established, they were quickly abandoned. The pattern of occupied and abandoned sites has always been difficult to interpret in simple terms such as the degree of contact with the Mediterranean world: some sites on the northern fringe remained occupied while in some 'advanced' areas nearer the trade routes the *oppida* were abandoned. The model I have put forward here does contain a stochastic element which can allow for such variation.

The problems of the origin of the *oppida* lie in La Tène C. In earlier periods 'crises' had led to the construction of hill-forts which were in no way urban in character. Something happened in La Tène C which produced a society not merely capable of organising large defensive centres, but with the political, social and economic systems capable of maintaining an urban site. Only at Manching can we see this as a gradual process: elsewhere it is difficult to detect any changes in the archaeological record. Burial evidence in La Tène C shows little indication of a markedly differentiated society, indeed grave goods generally become rarer, but unfortunately burial data are largely lacking for La Tène D. La Tène C also sees the introduction of high-value coinage and the resurgence of trade with the Mediterranean world. Social and economic changes were clearly taking place which the archaeologist has so far hardly documented.

The implications of centralisation

These I can discuss only briefly here. The concentration of industry certainly allowed greater specialisation, and there seems to have been a great upsurge in industrial output. In political terms the concentration of the leading families could allow the development of the institutions which we associate with early states – Caesar several times mentions magistrates – and the changes hinted at in the classical sources from kingship to oligarchy may be one spin-off. Defences keep people out, but they also keep people in, allowing greater economic and social control over the population by the emerging state.

These changes in the late iron age are clearly going to be one of the major themes of prehistoric research in Europe in the next decade.[4]

Notes

1 The central European iron age, which starts towards the end of the eighth century, has been divided into two main phases named after Hallstatt, a salt-producing site in Austria, and La Tène, a cult site on Lake Neuchâtel in Switzerland, both of which have produced rich and diagnostic finds. The main simplified dates and characteristics of these phases are:

Period	Date BC	Social structure	Settlement structure	Foreign trade
Hallstatt C	700–600	hierarchical	decentralised	limited
Hallstatt D	600–500	extremely hierarchical	hierarchical, centralised	extensive
La Tène A	500/450–400	strongly hierarchical	partly centralised	extensive
La Tène B	400–250	relatively egalitarian	decentralised	very limited
La Tène C	250–100	becoming hierarchical	decentralised at first	reappears at the end of the period
La Tène D	100–20	hierarchical	highly centralised, hierarchical	very extensive

2 The term 'central place' is used to mean a concentration of population which offers services (administration, special cultural and religious facilities, redistribution/market centre), to a surrounding more rural population.

3 *Major sites mentioned in the text*
Further details can be found with descriptions of sites in Collis 1975. Otherwise I quote only the most recent publications, or major volumes of synthesis.
Aulnat, Clermont-Ferrand, France
A small village in an undefended situation in the rich agricultural plain of the Grande Limagne. Little can be said of the layout of the site, but it has produced traces of a range of industrial activity – the working of metals (iron, gold, silver, bronze), glass, coral, bone, and possibly pottery; and gold and silver coins were manufactured. In its later phases there was extensive trade with the Mediterranean, especially in Italian wine amphorae. The site starts perhaps in La Tène B, but was abandoned in about 40–30 BC, just after the Roman conquest (see Gergovie). Interim reports and full bibliography in Périchon 1975a; Collis 1975, 1980.
Basel, Switzerland
The earliest settlement of late La Tène C–La Tène D on a gravel terrace on the Rhine was a large village engaged in trade and some industry. It was abandoned in favour of a defended site of about 12 ha on the hill of the Münsterberg (Major 1940; Furger-Gunthi 1980).
Gergovie, Clermont-Ferrand, France
Identified by some with the Gergovia of Caesar, this site of c. 150 ha, high on a lava flow, included industrial zones, temple sites and courtyard houses. Archaeologically it starts in about 30 BC, but was abandoned within a generation (full bibliography in Périchon 1975b).
Levroux, Chateauroux, France
A large village of about 12 ha of La Tène C was replaced by a defended site of similar size on a nearby hill. This in turn was replaced by a small Roman town at the foot of the hill (Büchsenschütz 1978).

Manching Ldkr. Igolstadt, Bavaria, West Germany
The site controls the east—west land route along the Danube
at the point where it crosses a tributary, the River Paar. There
is a small cemetery of La Tène B—C, and excavations have
produced settlement evidence from La Tène C to the middle
of La Tène D. Its gradual expansion has been documented by
artefact distributions (Stöckli 1975), culminating in a dense
settlement 1 km X 0.5 km in size. Defences enclosing 330 ha
were constructed in La Tène D. It is published in a mono-
graph series (of which six have appeared), *Die Ausgrabungen
in Manching*, produced by the Römisch-Germanisches Kommission des deutschen archäologischen Instituts, Frankfurt-
am-Main.
Villeneuve-St-Germain, Soissons, France
A spur overlooking the River Aisne is cut off by a slight earth-
work. Within is a systematically laid out settlement, the
excavated area being of houses set within palisaded enclosures.
It dates to about 60—20 BC. Interim reports are published in
the annual publications of the Centre de Recherches Protohistoriques, Université de Paris I, *Les Fouilles Protohistoriques
dans la Vallée de l'Aisne.*

4   *Acknowledgements*. My thanks to Barbara Segraves-Whallon
who offered comments from an American viewpoint on an
earlier version of this paper; the British Academy who provided the bulk of the finance for my visit; and to many British
and American colleagues who provided advice, hospitality
and opportunities to lecture during my visit.

References

Büchsenschütz, O. 1978. *Levroux: Histoire et Archéologie d'un Pay-
sage.* Levroux, Association pour la défense et l'étude du
Canton de Levroux.

Collis, J. 1972. Oppida: the beginnings of urbanisation in temperate
Europe. Ph.D. dissertation, Cambridge University.

Collis, J. 1975. *Defended Sites of the Late La Tène in Central and
Western Europe.* Oxford, British Archaeological Reports.

Collis, J. 1980. Aulnat and urbanization: a second interim report.
Archaeological Journal 137: 40—9.

Collis, J. 1981. A theoretical study of hill-forts, in G. Guilbert (ed.),
Hill-fort Studies (Papers presented to A.H.A. Hogg). Leicester,
University Press, 66—76.

Collis, J. forthcoming. *Oppida: earliest towns of temperate Europe.*

Furger-Gunthi, A. 1980. Der Murus Gallicus von Basel. *Jahrbuch der
schweizerischen Gesellschaft für Ur- und Frühgeschichte* 63:
131—84.

Major, E. 1940. *Gallische Ansiedelung mit Gräberfeld bei Basel.* Basel.

Périchon, R. 1975a. Le site protohistorique d'Aulnat, Puy-de-Dôme:
premières observations. *Germania* 53: 85—100.

Périchon, R. 1975b. *Les Découvertes Archéologiques sur l'Oppidum
de Gergovie.* Clermont-Ferrand, privately published.

Stöckli, W.E. 1975. Bemerkungen zur räumlichen und zeitlichen
Gruppierung der Funde in Oppidum von Manching.
Germania 53: 368—85.

Chapter 10

Wealth, prestige and power: the dynamics of late iron age political centralisation in south-east England
Colin Haselgrove

The development of centralised polities in south-eastern England, during a period of intense trade with the Roman empire, is considered here as a possible instance of the elaboration of a prestige good system at the periphery of an expansive state society. The archaeological correlates of the model, and various methodological problems implicit in its testing, are discussed, and analyses of mortuary data, precious metal coinage and imported commodities, assessed in relation to environmental factors, are presented in an attempt to establish the existence of the ranking categories and phases of political expansion and contraction predicted by the model, and to relate these to changes in the production and circulation of prestige items and exportable materials.

From an archaeological perspective, the late pre-Roman iron age[1] witnessed a series of changes in south-east England[2] which are almost unparalleled in British prehistory in their rate and complexity. Among other developments may be cited the adoption of coinage and of an accompanied cremation rite, technological innovation in metal-working and pottery production, an increase in long-distance trading activity, particularly with the Roman world, and the growth of major nucleated settlements with an obvious productive and distributive function and well sited for communication. At a more inferential level, conditional literacy, the development of a limited market economy (Collis 1971) and markedly increased social stratification and political expansion (Allen 1944) have all been claimed.

The question to be addressed here is that of the role played by trade relations with the Roman empire in this latter process. The sheer diversity of overseas trade from the first century BC is amply attested by archaeological and textual evidence (fig. 10.1), although the real significance of many of these categories is less easy to assess,[3] only imported pottery featuring in deposits in any quantity. Given that the characteristics of existing structures must have shaped the course of these developments, it should be noted that neither cross-channel contact nor long-distance trade represent entirely new phenomena; the former is a feature, albeit fitful, of the whole millennium (cf. Bradley 1978), with particularly close links existing between south-east

England and north-east France from early in the first century BC, while a variety of traits[4] point to the existence of cross-cutting interaction spheres (Caldwell 1964) based on well-developed internal exchange networks. What *is* novel is the articulation of this region for the first time with an organised, commercial economy.

However, rather than focussing immediately, as many have done (e.g. Cunliffe 1978; Haselgrove 1976; Rodwell 1976), on the new material and information flows made possible by this trading relationship, it would perhaps be more profitable to begin by considering the social context of change, and specifically by asking what kind of system of social reproduction has properties which might give rise to marked hierarchisation, when it becomes linked to a more developed economy through the medium of external trade. For late iron age Britain, one possible answer is that develop-

Fig. 10.1. British imports and exports during the late pre-Roman iron age.

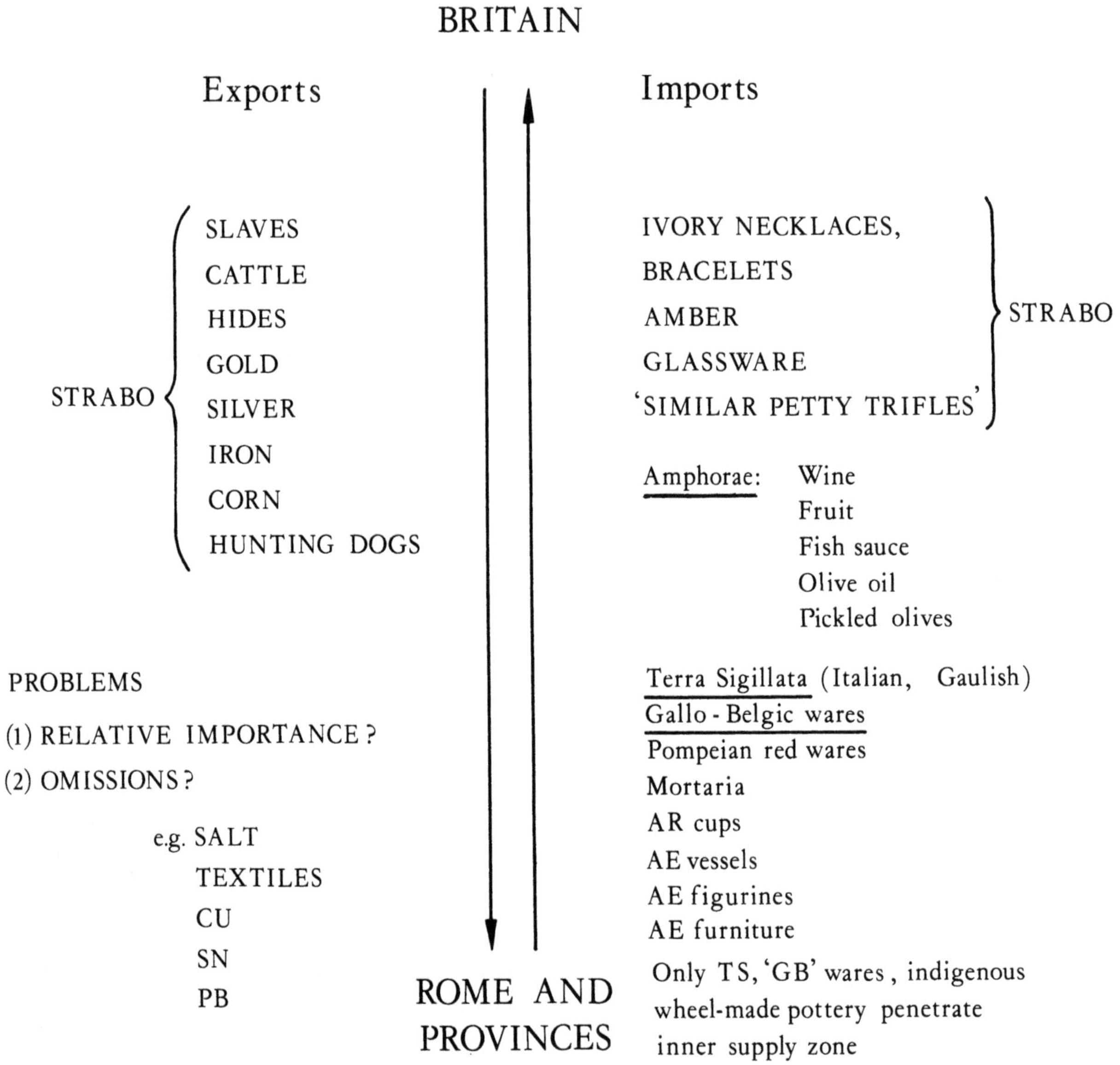

BRITAIN

Exports   Imports

STRABO { SLAVES
CATTLE
HIDES
GOLD
SILVER
IRON
CORN
HUNTING DOGS

IVORY NECKLACES,
BRACELETS
AMBER
GLASSWARE
'SIMILAR PETTY TRIFLES' } STRABO

Amphorae: Wine
Fruit
Fish sauce
Olive oil
Pickled olives

PROBLEMS

(1) RELATIVE IMPORTANCE ?

(2) OMISSIONS ?

e.g. SALT
TEXTILES
CU
SN
PB

Terra Sigillata (Italian, Gaulish)
Gallo - Belgic wares
Pompeian red wares
Mortaria
AR cups
AE vessels
AE figurines
AE furniture

Only TS, 'GB' wares, indigenous wheel-made pottery penetrate inner supply zone

ROME AND PROVINCES

ments represent a further instance of a generalised phenomenon which has been documented ethno-historically, for example in west Africa (e.g. Ekholm 1972) and claimed for other regions of temperate Europe during the first millennium BC (Frankenstein and Rowlands 1978); the rapid and often short-lived elaboration of a so-called prestige good system within the periphery of an expanding state society.

The prestige good system and its elaboration

The salient features of the prestige good system have already been discussed at length elsewhere (Friedman and Rowlands 1977; Frankenstein and Rowlands 1978) and need be no more than briefly reiterated here. Building on Marcel Mauss' discovery of the link that exists between the material transfer of objects and social hierarchy, 'to give is to show one's superiority; to accept without returning or repaying more is to face subordination' (Mauss 1954), a number of anthropologists (e.g. Meillassoux 1960; Dupré and Rey 1973) have shown how in lineage societies, where no privileged group has control over land or the means of production, the seniors exercise their control over the juniors by supplying the prestige items needed by the latter on critical occasions in their own advance to senior status — initiation, marriage, the payment of fines, or religious services — in return for which the juniors direct the produce to the elders.

Given a situation where local groups are linked within a wider regional sphere of generalised exchange and marriage alliance, it is quite possible under certain conditions for what is essentially the same system of control to be instituted as a feature of inter-lineage relations.[5] In particular, where one lineage either has the capacity to produce large quantities of prestige goods, through demographic strength or the localised distribution of appropriate resources, or alternatively has the opportunity to realise new sources of prestige goods through external exchange, it may be in a position to transform what was previously a relationship of competitive equality with other lineages into one of dominance and dependence, such that those at the apex of dependent groups will be encouraged to direct their produce towards the dominant partner in return for the prestige items they require to maintain their own status *vis à vis* their dependants. Moreover, what was formerly a symmetrical flow of women and debt slaves within the wider exchange sphere is then transformed into an asymmetrical one, where the conversion of prestige goods for women and slaves enables the dominant group to increase its own demographic strength and thus its productive capacity at the expense of the weaker groups (fig. 10.2).

Thus with the emergence of a dominant lineage, prestations to elders became tribute to a chief (MacCormack, n.d.), and a new condition of unstable equilibrium is reached. A further cycle in the hierarchisation process may occur, however, with any new input of foreign prestige goods to the system, and should one of the dominant chiefs be able to achieve an outright monopoly over these imports, this may

lead to his establishing a position of absolute paramountcy.

From this state, two lines of development may be predicted: devolution or continued expansion. Where the external connections are with a society organised on different economic principles, with the profit-margin and supply and demand as important variables, the paramount may experience considerable difficulty in maintaining his external trade monopoly. A fall in demand for his resources, attempts by specialist traders, unbound by social conventions as to with whom exchanges may be made, to maximise their outlets, or simple competition between different economic concerns may all lead to the undermining of an individual's monopoly and thus to the collapse of his authority.

Where the external monopoly is maintained, continued expansion is likely until checked by the rise of the tribute demands for export to a level exceeding the productive capacity of the local system, or the failure of other exchange networks to supply non-local resources and commodities needed for export. In such circumstances, the paramount may resort to alternative mechanisms to procure items for export, e.g. warfare for slaves; but while such strategies may alleviate the situation satisfactorily in the short term, they can hardly be other than extremely damaging to the long-term prospects of the system.

Archaeological manifestations of the system

From this general statement, one can make certain predictions as to the kind of archaeological data which should be recovered. The recognition of prestige goods is obviously highly subjective as we are dealing with a culturally specified dimension of an item's meaning, which may vary according to its context. Nevertheless, one would predict that prestige

Fig. 10.2. A model for the hierarchisation process in lineage society.

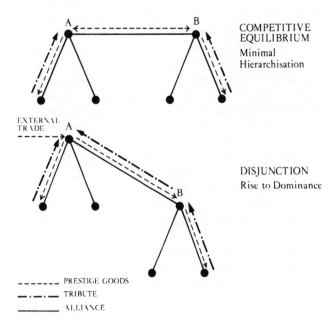

goods are likely to be artefacts which require rare materials, considerable technical skills or a high labour investment, or are only available from outside the local system e.g. foreign trade goods — all factors which are likely to have influenced a past group's own process of categorisation. With the emergence of a distinct hierarchy, it is obviously open to higher-ranked individuals to try and reinforce their power over dependants by manipulating the quantities or even by redefining the nature of the valuables acceptable in the discharge of social obligations. However, since the coherence of the system will continue to depend on group consensus,[6] the newly introduced prestige goods would have to conform to the same set of prerequisites as before and should still be archaeologically recognisable.

It may also be possible to recognise certain items used as material markers of status — commodities exchanged only as gifts between equals, or featuring in the acts of conspicuous consumption which may themselves be expressions of status, categories of imports retained by the individual controlling foreign trade to symbolise his own position, other imports or centrally produced items distributed to his immediate subordinates as their status insignia, and so on (cf. Frankenstein and Rowlands 1978). Compared with other prestige goods, these should have a restricted and non-random distribution in archaeological contexts such as burials, although, as Hodder has pointed out (this volume), to equate such differentiation with ranking entails certain assumptions about the kind of ideological system invoked to legitimate rank in a particular society, since the precise symbolism employed will be dependent on this.

Among the more obvious features of the system that one might anticipate in a determinate situation is the expansion and contraction of political domains, provided that suitable archaeological indicators for the territorial extent of political authority can be isolated, accompanied by increased social differentiation. Such developments should correlate with the chronological and geographical distribution of foreign imports. The demographic expansion of dominant lineages might be reflected by an increase in the size of their head's settlement, although a change in its anatomy would not occur other than perhaps in the provision of specialist workshop areas (such that the settlements would appear simply as scale transforms of their progenitors).[7] There should also be evidence for the intensification of production, both directly for export, and of items used to mobilise exportable resources not available within the domain, achieved by a greater investment of labour and technological innovation such as mass-production (often consequent on the information flow accompanying the foreign trade), linked to the distribution of such items over increasingly large territories.

For our knowledge of prestige circulation, particularly of non-breakable and recyclable items, we are at first sight largely dependent upon the specific depositional behaviour of a particular group, e.g. whether or not furnished burials

were made, or hoarding occurred. But is this entirely a culturally random phenomenon? In the context of a prestige good system, one suspects not. As Dupré and Rey (1973) point out, because the production of prestige goods is an integral part of the system, there will be a tendency for them to accumulate, leading to an 'inflationary spiral' and the collapse of the whole structure, unless some form of periodic readjustment is made. Such readjustments may be particularly vital where a major external input of prestige items is involved, and such behaviour patterns as burial, hoarding and votive deposition might well have a role in the overall regulation of the system.

Thus, although not susceptible of further proof, it is of interest that the late iron age in south-east England sees not only the appearance of an accompanied burial rite for the first time in several centuries, but also widespread hoarding and a marked increase in the deposition of probable prestige items in rivers and on temple sites: while certain features might be explicable in terms of particular historical events (Rodwell 1976), the overall trend is too emphatic to be disregarded lightly. Even so, many of the categories which we might envisage as objects of elite circulation, for example, weaponry, chariot fittings and horse harness, torcs etc., are poorly represented in deposits, and can only be inferred for the earlier period. Thus the present analysis has perforce to be restricted to those items and contexts available in some quantity: burials, coinage, and ceramics.

Ranking and chronological distribution of burials
Perhaps the best evidence for increased ranking linked to the acquisition of imports during this period is that afforded by burials, always allowing for the absence of an earlier burial population against which to compare the late iron age mortuary data. To avoid the danger of *a priori* definition of burials containing luxury articles as those of high-status individuals, a simple quantitative analysis of the number of artefact types (NAT) per grave has been carried out, based on Hedeager's method (1977).[8] From the histogram (fig. 10.3) it is seen that burials with a high NAT value invariably contain imports, while the distribution of imports is clearly non-random, and appears to reflect a real differentiation. Further analysis, in fact, suggests a more precise differentiation of the burials into four categories on the basis of items restricted to a particular set, mirrored at the higher level by distinctions in grave form (Stead 1967).

With one or two exceptions, the actual burial grounds are small, with individual cremations frequently grouped in relation to primary burials in arrangements referred to as 'family circles', sometimes in distinct enclosures, and compatible with the notion of lineage organisation.

In contrast to the generalised distribution of low-category burials throughout the south-east, it is clear, although the sample is small, that the highest-category burials are non-randomly distributed spatially and temporally, the earliest occurring in Hertfordshire, those of intermediate date in East Anglia and the latest, one of which is certainly post-Conquest, in the Fen margins (fig. 10.4).

Production and circulation of precious metal coinage

As an indicator of late iron age political relationships, we are fortunate to possess the information provided by inscribed coinage (Allen 1944). Certain fundamental assumptions must be made: that the striking of coinage was centrally controlled and reflects the political authority of named individuals; that precious metal coinage was not a generalised medium of exchange, but circulated along with other valuables in the prestige sphere, being used in the discharge of a variety of social obligations, and passed down the social hierarchy from the issuer to his subordinates; and thus that its distribution allows us to infer, within broad limits, the extent of contemporary political authority.

Fig. 10.4 shows a series of eight territorial domains which can be identified, sampling biases notwithstanding, from an analysis of the distribution of various precious metal coin types (Haselgrove, forthcoming), and the existence of

Fig. 10.3. Frequency distribution of NAT per grave for late pre-Roman iron age cremation burials in south-east England.

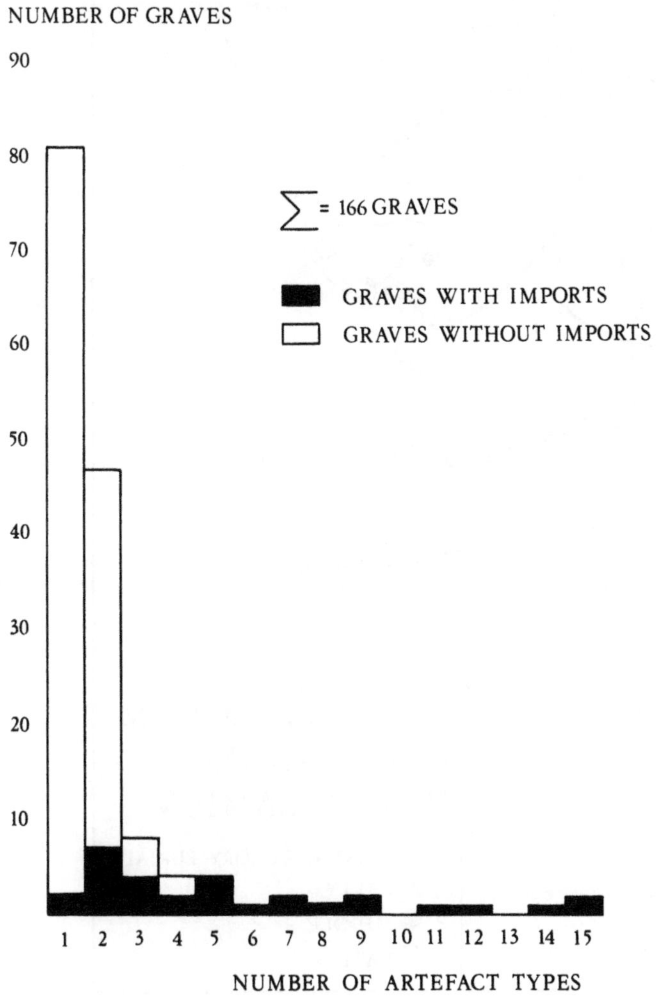

NUMBER OF GRAVES

$\sum$ = 166 GRAVES

■ GRAVES WITH IMPORTS
☐ GRAVES WITHOUT IMPORTS

NUMBER OF ARTEFACT TYPES

which receives support from Hodder's trend surface analysis of the find spot density of all inscribed coin types (Hodder and Orton 1976). The domains appear to persist through time, and where one domain becomes incorporated in a larger political entity, there is a distinct tendency for coins struck from particular dies within the overall sequence to cluster within that domain, suggesting that they were distributed in bulk by their issuer to the highest ranked individual in subordinate domains and passed down the hierarchy there (Haselgrove, forthcoming). There is no indication of an uninterrupted fall-off with distance from the place of minting, as has been reported in other studies (Hogg 1971); the pattern is one of positive residuals at various distances from the centre. In the final phase of the iron age, the coinage of Cunobelin, referred to by a Roman author, Suetonius, as '*Britannorum Rex*' (with his capital at Camulodunum, according to Dio), is found within all the domains which constitute the core area (fig. 10.6).

Distribution and chronology of Roman imports, etc.

The distribution, temporal and spatial, of imports from the Roman empire is also a non-random one. Many of the earliest imports (Dressel amphorae, silver cups, bronze vessels) are concentrated in Hertfordshire, whereas the distribution of later amphorae is clearly centred on Camulodunum (fig. 10.5).[9] If amphorae are to be regarded as evidence of their contents, then most of the perishable imports were restricted to Essex, with only wine being moved further afield in quantity. However, like coinage, fine imported pottery and mass-produced indigenous wares were distributed to the subordinate domains in some quantity and down the social hierarchy to relatively minor settlements.[10]

Relationships with peripheral areas and the Highland Zone (fig. 10.6)[11]

It is, however, the question of imports and exports which brings us up against the degree of our ignorance. It is not possible at present to test many of the predictions one might make as regards the mobilisation of tribute or the intensification of production for export. However, it does seem likely, both from the distribution of natural resources in Britain and from the distribution and density of settlement during the later iron age, that to maintain its trading relations with the Roman world, the south-east must have been partly dependent on commodities obtained from beyond its boundaries.

What one might term the inner periphery is characterised in the later iron age by the presence of four major coin-using groups (i.e. the Durotriges, Dobunni, Coritani and Iceni), which all have attributes of decentralised societies (cf. Hodder 1977). Penetrating this area from the Camulodunum core, three principal axes of procurement are perhaps discernible:

1. Across East Anglia into the East Midlands and beyond that area, into northern Britain and North

Wales. In the 'Coritanian' area there are a number of south-eastern imports, which were imitated in local ceramic production (Cunliffe 1978), while the intensive exploitation of surface iron ore deposits at this time is well attested in both Lincolnshire and Northamptonshire.

2. Up the Thames and Kennet valleys into the Cotswolds, and beyond into south Wales and the south-western peninsular. Again there is evidence of imports and acculturation, while agricultural intensification and increased animal husbandry have both been claimed in the Cotswolds for this period, albeit on extremely tenuous evidence (Clifford 1961; Marshall 1978). Among the mineral resources which were being

exploited one can probably list Forest of Dean iron, south-Welsh gold, Mendip lead (for desilverisation) and Cornish tin.

3. A third procurement axis is probably that crossing the Thames estuary and penetrating the Weald along the Medway. There is some evidence for intensification in the production of Wealden iron in the late pre-Conquest period, coupled with technological innovation in furnace construction, in the form of provision for the tapping of slag (Manning 1979).

It is noteworthy that it is those areas which lie outside these axes, for example, Dorset and Norfolk, which display the greatest degree of material culture homogeneity during the late iron age. If Hodder's notions on the relationship

Fig. 10.4. Major settlement sites, rich burials, and principal coin circulation areas, C 1st BC–AD.

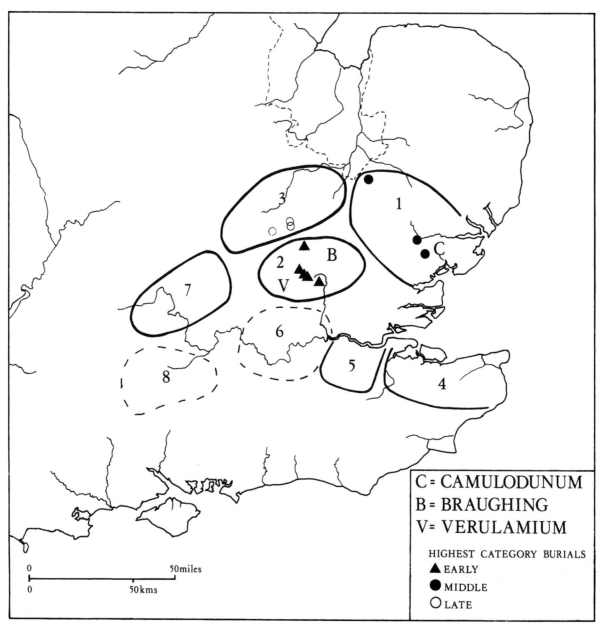

C = CAMULODUNUM
B = BRAUGHING
V = VERULAMIUM

HIGHEST CATEGORY BURIALS
▲ EARLY
● MIDDLE
○ LATE

0   50miles
0   50kms

between material culture patterning and stress conditions are accepted (Blackmore *et al.* 1979), one might perhaps go as far as to posit a predatory relationship, with slave procurement the primary objective, between these areas and the south-eastern core, a social alternative to the suggestion of economic competition advanced by these authors.

Interpretation

It is the later first century BC which sees the opening up of major trading possibilities between south-east England and the Roman empire. According to the model we would predict competition between the existing weakly hierarchical polities[12] to attract imports from this new source. The most successful of these seems to have been one based on Hertfordshire, which eventually reached a position of dominance over the territories surrounding it, as reflected in the coinage of Tasciovanus, the cluster of high-category burials with Roman imports, and the major settlements of Verulamium and Braughing, which has produced clear evidence of industrial activity as well as yielding the earliest major imported ceramic assemblages (Partridge, forthcoming). Less wealthy contemporary burials with imports are known in the poten-

tially subordinate territories, for example, at Aylesford in Kent.

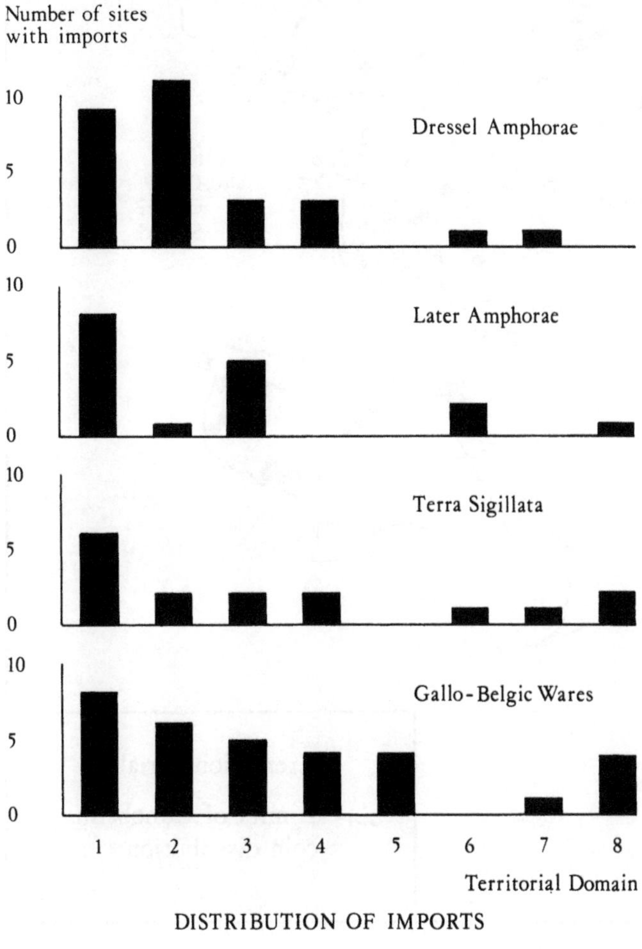

The first century AD, however, sees the clear eclipse of this polity in favour of one based on Essex. The reason for this contraction seems to have been the establishment of a trade monopoly based on Camulodunum, owing primarily to its geographical position at a time when the Roman army had just occupied the Rhineland and the Low Countries, and the Gallo-Belgic pottery industries had been established there, in support of the proposed conquest of Germany. Gradually this Essex polity, under the rule of Cunobelin, seems to have established.control over all those previously subordinate to the old Hertfordshire polity, and over east Kent and the Berkshire downs as well (Allen 1944), both areas being characterised by the circulation of late coinages issued by individuals, who were possibly genuine relations of Cunobelin — brother, son; the practice of supplanting ranking individuals in peripheral areas with members of the ruling lineage being one that has been noted historically elsewhere.

Conclusions

In terms of the very limited range of artefact and contextual categories analysed, and bearing in mind the range of untested assumptions it has been necessary to make, it can thus be argued that the dynamics apparent in the archaeological record for south-east England in the period preceding the Roman conquest accord with the kind of outcome we would predict from the general model of a prestige good system becoming incorporated at the periphery of an expansive empire-state. However, further progress will be difficult without a great deal of work into the problems of establishing the social meaning of artefact categories and the development of reliable techniques with which to monitor changing levels of production and consumption, especially for perishable materials.

While the research of anthropologists such as Meillassoux (1960) has provided us with considerable insight into the nature of the social relations which dominate the reproduction of the prestige good system, it is also true that our knowledge of the potential variants of its underlying structure is relatively poorly developed theoretically and empirically. Our formulations also need to be systematically extended to embrace the role of consumption in relation to the structures of production and circulation. There is also the crucial question, not addressed here, of how the dominant lineage may establish and legitimate hereditary power, and whether, and under what conditions, such inherently unstable systems of political dependency and social stratification can be transformed into the institutionalised control apparatus and rigid system of stratification characteristic of state society, a development which might or might not have occurred in south-east England had the Roman conquest not intervened.

Whatever the validity of this particular application, archaeologists seeking understanding of past socio-economic

Fig. 10.5. Frequency distribution of sites yielding Roman imports in different territorial domains.

Number of sites
with imports

DISTRIBUTION OF IMPORTS

change must pay far more attention in the future to the construction of theory relating social action and process to its material content and physical consequences. It is too early to judge whether the currently fashionable structural-marxist approaches will enable us to transcend the traditional dichotomy between idealism and materialism that pervades western thought,[13] and, in unifying the social and the material, bring us closer to the formulation of multi-linear evolutionary theory capable of explaining particular past developments in their wider context. In the current state of archaeology it would seem likely, however, that these approaches are capable of offering us greater insight into the factors underlying social evolution than many of the others at our disposal: in this case, how exchange relations have properties — temporal, spatial, material and social (cf. Bourdieu 1977) — that might shape the course of development followed by a particular social formation when it was exposed to the demands of an organised, commercial economy.[14]

Fig. 10.6. Hypothesised relations between south-eastern core area and peripheral zones, C 1st AD.

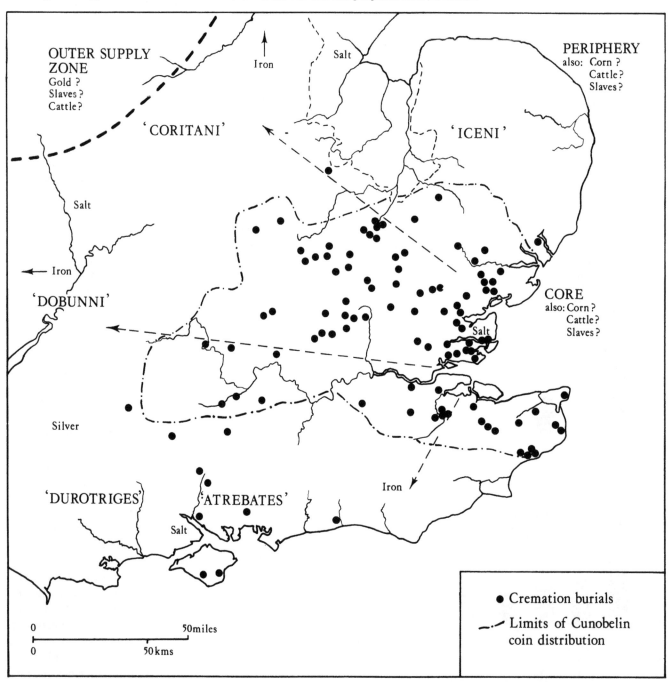

References

1 The term 'late pre-Roman iron age' covers the period from the first appearance in Britain of wheel-made pottery and metalwork with affinities to Continental late La Tène material to the Roman occupation of much of the island, i.e. from early first century BC to mid/later first century AD.
2 Essentially, the coastal areas on both sides of the Thames estuary, London and the home counties, together with parts of Cambridgeshire, Northamptonshire and Oxfordshire. Remarkably few later iron age sites in this region have been adequately investigated and published, so that one is forced to place excessive reliance on the few that have: for example Braughing (Partridge, forthcoming), Camulodunum – modern Colchester (Hawkes and Hull 1947), Verulamium – modern St Albans (Wheeler and Wheeler 1936) and Welwyn Garden City (Stead 1967).
3 From what we know of contemporary Roman needs, the procurement of slaves, almost impossible to monitor archaeologically, is likely to have been a major concern, with far-reaching demographic consequences.
4 For example, the uniformity of middle iron age ceramic design over large areas (Cunliffe 1978), the exchange of metalwork motifs and materials, and the existence of standardised units of iron and salt.
5 The principal differences being that whereas within the lineage the supply of prestige goods is merely used to regulate the advance of individuals to senior status, between groups it is used to maintain a *permanent* difference of status between lineages, which is nevertheless advantageous to the seniors of a dependent lineage in that they receive the prestige goods they require to regulate the reproduction of their own group.
6 And, hence, will continue to be precarious, even allowing for the constant manipulation of ideological constructs by individuals or groups to maintain and legitimate their positions in the hierarchy.
7 In this respect, it is noteworthy that sites like Camulodunum or Verulamium appear to consist of a series of settlement clusters – albeit with a degree of functional differentiation and zoning – separated by their fields, and are no more than spatially extensive versions of existing settlement types.
8 Using material collected in Whimster (1979).
9 For amphorae, see Peacock (1971) updated by Rodwell (1976). For imported finewares, see Rodwell (1976) and Rigby (1973).
10 It has, of course, been argued by a number of authors (e.g. Collis 1971) that such commodities were in fact distributed through a system of major and minor market sites, rather than by social networks. As Renfrew (1975) has indicated, it is not possible to distinguish between these alternatives from distributional information alone, as redistribution and market exchange are spatially homologous processes. The presence of bronze coinage on many of these sites cannot on its own be taken as evidence for the existence of a commercial economy (Haselgrove 1979); indeed with the demonstration that local exchange relations seem to have remained 'embedded' until well into the Roman period (Hodder 1979), the burden of proof rests firmly with those who would seek to claim otherwise for pre-Roman Britain.
11 Cremation burials plotted after Whimster (1979); coins of Cunobelin after Cunliffe (1978).
12 It could be argued that many of the assumptions about the nature of the preexisting social structure made here for southeast England are inappropriate or anachronistic – for example, lineage-organisation and collective ownership of the land or means of production. This will always be partly a matter of

judgement, particularly for regions such as this where our knowledge of the archaeological sequence prior to the developments under review is worse than inadequate. However, the existence of similar features of social organisation can be inferred from the ethno-historical surveys of authors such as Caesar or Tacitus for contemporary communities elsewhere in north-western Europe, particularly the Germanic zone (although their status as generalisations must be suspect). In this context, the settlement of the 'maritime part' of Britain some time before the middle of the first century BC by immigrants from 'Belgic Gaul' attested by Caesar (*De Bello Gallico* V, 12) may well be relevant, given the trans-Rhenine roots of the latter population (*ibid.* II, 3).
13 As well as bridging the unfortunate gulf which has begun to develop in archaeology between general theory and so-called 'middle range theory', concerned with the formation processes of the archaeological record and giving meaning to our observations on it. The static material patterning we observe is at least partly the outcome of the very social processes we are trying to explain at a higher level of abstraction – and to separate them in this way is to indulge in a dangerously circular exercise.
14 I am very grateful to Virginia Allon, Susanne Haselgrove and Stephen Shennan for their helpful comments on earlier drafts of this paper, while in more general terms, my debt to ideas developed by Michael Rowlands and his co-authors in various publications will be apparent; however, the responsibility for errors and the opinions expressed remains entirely my own. I should also like to thank the University of Durham for a grant enabling me to attend the SAA meeting in Philadelphia.

References

Allen, D.F. 1944. The Belgic dynasties of Britain and their coins. *Archaeologia* 90: 1–46.
Blackmore, C., Braithwaite, M. and Hodder, I.R. 1979. Social and cultural patterning in the late Iron Age of southern Britain, in B.C. Burnham and J. Kingsbury (eds.), *Space, Hierarchy and Society*. Oxford, British Archaeological Reports, 93–112.
Bourdieu, P. 1977. *Outline of a Theory of Practice*. Cambridge, University Press.
Bradley, R. 1978. *The Prehistoric Settlement of Britain*. London, Routledge and Kegan Paul.
Caldwell, J.R. 1964. Interaction spheres in prehistory, in J.R. Caldwell and R.L. Hall (eds.), *Hopewellian Studies* (Illinois State Museum, Scientific Papers 12, no. 6), 133–43.
Clifford, E.M. 1961. *Bagendon: a Belgic Oppidum*. Cambridge, University Press.
Collis, J.R. 1971. A functional and theoretical interpretation of British coinage. *World Archaeology* 3: 71–84.
Cunliffe, B.W. 1978. *Iron Age Communities in Britain*. London, Routledge and Kegan Paul.
Dupré, G. and Rey, P.P. 1973. Reflections on the pertinence of a theory of the history of exchange. *Economy and Society* 2: 131–63.
Ekholm, K. 1972. *Power and Prestige: the rise and fall of the Kongo Kingdom*. Uppsala, Skriv Service AB.
Frankenstein, S. and Rowlands, M.J. 1978. The internal structure and regional context of early iron age society in south-western Germany. *Bulletin of the Institute of Archaeology, University of London* 15: 73–112.
Friedman, J. and Rowlands, M.J. 1977. Notes towards an epigenetic model of the evolution of civilisation, in J. Friedman and M.J. Rowlands (eds.), *The Evolution of Social Systems*. London, Duckworth, 201–76.

Haselgrove, C.C. 1976. External trade as a stimulus to urbanisation, in B.W. Cunliffe and T. Rowley (eds.), *Oppida: the beginnings of urbanisation in Barbarian Europe*. Oxford, British Archaeological Reports, 25–49.

Haselgrove, C.C. 1979. The significance of coinage in pre-conquest Britain, in B.C. Burnham and H. Johnston (eds.), *Invasion and Response: the case of Roman Britain*. Oxford, British Archaeological Reports, 197–209.

Haselgrove, C.C., forthcoming. The archaeological context of Celtic coinage in Britain: a quantitative approach. Ph.D. dissertation, University of Cambridge.

Hawkes, C.F.C. and Hull, M.R. 1947. *Camulodunum* (Society of Antiquaries Research Report 14). London.

Hedeager, L. 1977. Processes towards state formation in early iron age Denmark. *New Directions in Scandinavian Archaeology*. Copenhagen, Nationalmuseet, 217–23.

Hodder, I. 1977. How are we to study distributions of Iron Age material?, in J.R. Collis (ed.), *The Iron Age in Britain: a review*. Sheffield, University Press, 8–16.

Hodder, I. 1979. Pre-Roman and Romano-British tribal economies, in B.C. Burnham and H. Johnson (eds.), *Invasion and Response: the case of Roman Britain*. Oxford, British Archaeological Reports, 189–96.

Hodder, I. and Orton, C. 1976. *Spatial Analysis in Archaeology*. Cambridge, University Press.

Hogg, A.H.A. 1971. Some applications of surface fieldwork, in M. Jesson and D. Hill (eds.), *The Iron Age and its Hillforts*. Southampton, University Press, 105–25.

MacCormack, C. n.d. Exchange and hierarchy. Unpublished manuscript, Cambridge.

Manning, W. 1979. The native and Roman contribution to the development of metal industries in Britain, in B.C. Burnham and H. Johnson (eds.), *Invasion and Response: the case of Roman Britain*. Oxford, British Archaeological Reports, 111–22.

Marshall, A. 1978. Environment and agriculture during the iron age: a statistical analysis of changing settlement ecology. *World Archaeology* 9: 347–56.

Mauss, M. 1954. *The Gift*. London, Routledge and Kegan Paul.

Meillassoux, C. 1960. Essai d'interprétation du phénomène économique dans les sociétés traditionelles d'auto-subsistance. *Cahiers d'Études Africaines* 1(4): 38–67.

Partridge, C., forthcoming. *Excavations at Skeleton Green, Puckeridge, 1971–2*. London.

Peacock, D.P.S. 1971. Roman amphorae in pre-Roman Britain, in M. Jesson and D. Hill (eds.), *The Iron Age and its Hillforts*. Southampton, University Press, 161–88.

Renfrew, C. 1975. Trade as action at a distance, in J.A. Sabloff and C.C. Lamberg-Karlovsky (eds.), *Ancient Civilisation and Trade*. Albuquerque, University of New Mexico Press, 3–59.

Rigby, V. 1973. Potters' stamps on TN and TR found in Britain, in A. Detsicas (ed.), *Current Research in Romano-British Coarse Pottery* (CBA Research Report 10), 7–24. London.

Rodwell, W.J. 1976. Coinage, oppida and the rise of Belgic power in southern Britain, in B.W. Cunliffe and T. Rowley (eds.), *Oppida: the beginnings of urbanisation in Barbarian Europe*. Oxford, British Archaeological Reports, 181–367.

Stead, I.M. 1967. A La Tène III burial at Welwyn Garden City. *Archaeologia* 101: 1–62.

Wheeler, R.E.M. and Wheeler, T.G. 1936. *Verulamium* (Society of Antiquaries Research Report 11). London.

Whimster, R.P. 1979. Burial practices in iron age Britain. Ph.D. dissertation, University of Durham.

PART III

The resource base
of early state
societies: the Aegean

The formation of the state is widely seen today as one of the major transformations in human existence, associated in many cases with what Gordon Childe called the 'urban revolution'. From the perspective of Mesopotamia, where that term was first applied, the transformation indeed seems revolutionary, with a quantum leap in population accompanying the irrigation-based urban development of the plains. But even in Mesopotamia the changes in question, however fundamental, now appear rather more gradual, in the light of longer chronologies for the Ubaid and Uruk periods, and of the demonstration that irrigation was in use at Chogha Mami in Iraq in the sixth millennium BC (Oates 1972). There can however be little doubt that the urban centres of the Mesopotamian Early Dynastic period had populations of many thousands and even tens of thousands.

Developments in Europe were of a different order. For although food production was well established in south-east Europe prior to 6000 BC, the first centres of what are generally regarded as small-scale state societies – the 'palaces' of Minoan Crete – did not emerge until around 2000 BC, and their equivalent on the mainland of Mycenaean Greece some six centuries later. For some centuries these remained the only urban (or near-urban) centres in Europe. Following their collapse, urban life did not reappear until the seventh century BC, where it is seen both in Greece and Italy. One of the most interesting features of European prehistory is thus the great range of ranked societies of very different kinds which developed in various areas during the four to six millennia which elapsed between the inception of farming and the imposition over most of Europe of Roman imperial rule. Some of these societies have been discussed in the previous section.

The urban centres of Europe, when they did emerge, were initially very small in size. John Cherry (Wagstaff and Cherry 1981) has estimated that the population of the 'urban' site at Phylakopi in Melos in its heyday around 1300 BC was no more than two or three thousand, and this may not have been untypical, even if just a few of the major palaces of Crete, particularly Knossos, were much larger. Indeed, the city states of classical Greece in the fifth century BC were often little greater in scale: a population of five thousand was perfectly usual. On the basis of some current definitions (e.g. Wright and Johnson 1975), the city states of ancient Greece would hardly qualify at all as state societies, lacking as they did any highly developed settlement hierarchy. In many of them the population was effectively concentrated within a single city. Yet to deny the status of state to the Greek *polis*, from which most of our ideas of political life derive, would seem a very arbitrary piece of definition.

The relatively late date of state formation in the Aegean (as compared with the Near East), and the small scale of the palace polities when they did emerge, have both contributed to their relative neglect by many students of the formation of complex societies. In the days when the distinction between 'primary' and 'secondary' states was rigidly applied, the Aegean examples clearly fell in the latter category, and broadly diffusionist models of Near Eastern economic dominance were applied. Such models are of course very appropriate to many instances of state formation, and are still generally accepted for the formation of the Etruscan and Roman civilisations in Italy in the early first millennium BC, and for the development of the highly ranked societies of southern France and Germany a few centuries later (Frankenstein and Rowlands 1978), as reviewed in the previous section. For the Aegean, however, this model of economic dominance no longer holds – the volume of prestige goods reaching Crete or Mycenae from Egypt and the Near East was small in the formative periods, and there is no evidence for a flow of raw materials from the Aegean to the supposed centres of 'higher' civilisation as the economic dominance model would require. Recent attempts to resuscitate this model by defining the Aegean as part of a larger Near Eastern 'world system' in the sense of Wallerstein (1974) founder upon the hard data.

There has of late been an awakening of interest in the problems of Aegean state formation. Initial approaches (e.g. Renfrew 1969) stressed the importance of trade in the key formative period in the centuries around 2500 BC, when many of the social and economic foundations of the subsequent palace civilisation were laid. This trade was conceived as largely internal to the Aegean as a whole, and stress was laid upon the importance of high-status goods, particularly of metal. At first sight the analogy here is with the models often put forward to explain the emergence of Mesoamerican civilisation. Both for the Olmec (Flannery 1968) and for the Maya (Tourtellot and Sabloff 1972; Rathje 1971), emphasis has been laid upon the importance of inter-regional trade, notably in prestige goods which were effectively manipulated by the emerging elite in a process which increasingly enhanced their status. These are not, of course, diffusionist models, for no 'higher' civilisation is involved as a diffusing centre. There is, however, no such broad inter-regional diversity involved in the Aegean as in Mesoamerica, and such long-distance links may have been much less influential than interactions with polities very much nearer home. An increasing level of interaction between local polities does indeed seem an important feature of the formative period. And since the participating centres were of approximately equal scale and status, a peer polity interaction model has been put forward (Renfrew 1981) to encapsulate the essential features of this process. There is no single external (or indeed internal) dominant centre, and no major ecological inter-regional diversity. Different centres had varying access to local resources, including metals, and different specialist outputs. The model holds that the increasing intensity of interaction was influential in promoting both the formation of elite groups in the different participating areas, and the

intensification of production, including agricultural production, to support both specialists and elite. The importance of the trading links is seen in the high level of interactions *within* the Aegean region. The development of an ideological unity (in religion, in political outlook and perhaps in language) may be seen as its most significant outcome, even though there was no political unification at this stage. Such interactions awakened aspirations, both spiritual and material, which could only be satisfied by further intensification of production. So that while the palaces of Minoan Crete and Mycenaean Greece and the early city states of the Greek world were politically autonomous, they were participating in a larger system without which they could not have come into being.

If such interactions played an essential role in all these small societies in awakening a demand, both for material goods and for a more complex social, political and religious life, the crucial process which allowed the fulfilment of this demand was the intensification of production, and especially of agricultural production. This is one of the central themes of each of the three contributions which follow. It has, of course, been a major theme of many treatments of the formation of complex society. The Aegean differs however from the Mesopotamian and Mesoamerican cases in that there is no single major technology – such as irrigation – which can be used as an explanation. Aegean societies were in no way 'hydraulic' – only in a very few areas did irrigation have any significant role at all at any period – and from the environmental standpoint this was no 'Asiatic mode of production'. On the other hand the economic control of the palace bureaucracies, documented in the clay tablets inscribed in the Minoan/Mycenaean Linear B script, resembles more the Near Eastern economic system than that of the Greek city states of nearly a millennium later (Finley 1957). The intensification process in the Aegean cannot then be linked with a single, dominant technological or organisational factor. More sophisticated approaches are needed, and it may well be that those now being developed for the Aegean will be found useful in other areas also.

One important focus of research in the Aegean over the past fifteen years has been the careful examination of food residues and other organic material from settlement sites. Gamble's paper demonstrates the contribution which these can make to a broader understanding of the mechanisms of intensification. The increased use of cattle, a species at first sight not well adapted to the island environment of Melos, correlates with the spatially inefficient nucleated settlement which accompanies other indications of complex society on the island. Gamble brings out the functional relationships, showing both to be features of the intensification of production of the period.

Intensification brings risks. The accompanying increase of population makes the system vulnerable to periodic shortfalls in production, due to climatic or other local factors. Halstead and O'Shea, in developing the concept of social storage, bring out the importance of social links working across the diversity of the landscape, which may be called on in times of stress. As they indicate, the southern Aegean is a region of high local diversity, and they imply that it was this diversity in the south which favoured the establishment of such links, culminating in the formation of the palaces, seen as institutions efficient in coping with localised shortfalls in production.

The social correlates of intensification are not readily elucidated for prehistoric societies, and it is sometimes easier to document the intensification of agricultural production than to specify the social structures which developed with it. Bintliff persuasively indicates in his paper the importance of the ownership and control of the land, and breaks new ground with his model of the evolving property relations in early Aegean society. This question has been recognised as a fundamental one since the time of Marx, and has been the subject of much discussion for Mesopotamian society, where relevant records are available. Chadwick (Ventris and Chadwick 1973) has lucidly set out the available evidence from the Linear B records, both for Crete and for Mycenaean Pylos. But Bintliff's is the first attempt to integrate this evidence with the available archaeological data on settlement and on production. Clearly there are problems which remain to be investigated in the testing of statements about property relations in prehistoric societies. Yet the techniques are available now for investigating land use and subsistence at the very local level as well as at the palace centres, so that it is no longer a constructive response to dismiss such matters as unknowable.

Each of these papers relates, in the data discussed, to the prehistoric Aegean. But, as I have tried to bring out, the problems of intensification and of ownership which they raise are of wider, indeed universal relevance.

A.C.R.

References

Finley, M.I. 1957. The Mycenaean tablets and economic history. *Economic History Review* 10: 128–41.

Flannery, K.V. 1968. The Olmec and the valley of Oaxaca: a model for interregional interaction in formative times, in E.P. Benson (ed.), *Dumbarton Oaks Conference on the Olmec*. Washington, DC, Dumbarton Oaks, 79–110.

Frankenstein, S. and Rowlands, M.J. 1978. The internal structure and regional context of early iron age society in south-western Europe. *Bulletin of the Institute of Archaeology, University of London* 15: 73–112.

Oates, J. 1972. Prehistoric settlement patterns in Mesopotamia, in P.J. Ucko, R. Tringham and G.W. Dimbleby (eds.), *Man, Settlement and Urbanism*. London, Duckworth, 299–310.

Rathje, W.L. 1971. The origin and development of Lowland Classic Maya civilisation. *American Antiquity* 36: 275–85.

Renfrew, C. 1969. Trade and culture process in European prehistory. *Current Anthropology* 10: 151–69.

Renfrew, C. 1981. Polity and power: interaction, intensification and exploitation, in C. Renfrew and J.M. Wagstaff (eds.), *An Island Polity, the Archaeology of Exploitation in Melos*. Cambridge, University Press, 264–90.

Tourtellot, G. and Sabloff, J.A. 1972. Exchange systems among the ancient Maya. *American Antiquity* 37: 126–35.

Wagstaff, J.M. and Cherry, J.F. 1981. Settlement and population change, in C. Renfrew and J.M. Wagstaff (eds.), *An Island Polity, the Archaeology of Exploitation on Melos*. Cambridge, University Press, 136–55.

Wallerstein, I. 1974. *The Modern World System*. New York, Academic Press.

Wright, H.T. and Johnson, G.A. 1975. Population exchange and early state formation in south-western Iran. *American Anthropologist* 79: 267–89.

Ventris, M. and Chadwick, J. 1973. *Documents in Mycenaean Greek* (2nd edn). Cambridge, University Press.

Chapter 11

**A friend in need is
a friend indeed:
social storage and
the origins of
social ranking**
Paul Halstead and
John O'Shea[1]

*Human communities have to cope with periodic
failures in food supply. Sedentary communities generally do
so by storing surplus from good years, but storage is no safeguard against sustained famine. In areas of ecological
diversity, inter-communal exchanges which balance out local
shortage and surplus commonly serve as an additional
defence. Such transactions, in which food is often exchanged
for more durable tokens of value, may be termed 'social
storage'. Durable tokens also provide a suitable vehicle for
the development of institutionalised inequality. Thus, short-
term attempts to stabilise economies through social storage
are seen as a recurrent stimulus to the emergence of complex
societies. A study of the redistributive economy of bronze
age Crete exemplifies this model.*

Introduction

This paper addresses two fundamental and related
aspects of complexity in human social organisation: (1) scale
(how many people are integrated within a given society) and
(2) differentiation (to what extent is there institutionalised
ranking among those people). The costs of both aspects are
self-evident (cf. Rubenstein 1978). Large-scale societies
either entail increased competition for resources, because of
the aggregation of population, or necessitate the expenditure
of considerable effort in maintaining far-flung social
relations; for low ranking individuals, vertical differentiation
may mean reduced access to resources, often coupled with
additional demands on their labour. Yet a trend towards
larger and more complex social groupings seems to be a
nearly universal phenomenon in human prehistory, suggesting that there are other factors whose benefits outweigh
these costs.

A variety of possible factors has been proposed (see
Cherry 1978), including long-distance trade (e.g. Sabloff and
Lamberg-Karlovsky 1975) and warfare (Carneiro 1970). But
such factors, which rely on the interaction between groups,
seem more appropriate for explaining the contagious spread
of complexity than its independent evolution. Ecological
diversity, with consequent local economic specialisation for
exchange, has also been suggested as the cause of early
regional integration and social complexity (Service 1962,
144–7). Only rarely can the products of local specialisation
be shown to be essential, however, and it seems that a prehistoric 'Acquisitive Society' must be assumed to account for
the expansion of such specialisation and exchange (Renfrew
1972, 497–9).

The present paper also discusses the relationship
between ecological diversity and exchange. In this case, however, emphasis is laid on the constant tension between inter-
annual environmental variability and relatively inflexible

human subsistence requirements. This tension is seen as a recurrent stimulus to social and economic adaptations which may, in certain circumstances, favour the independent development of social complexity.

Coping with uncertainty

Few societies lead the dire 'hand-to-mouth' existence which has traditionally been seen as the plight of all but the most advanced civilisations. Indeed, recent studies have reversed this proposition, identifying the simplest gatherer–hunters as the original affluent societies (Sahlins 1974, 1). Yet, neither the stark view of tradition nor the idyllic image of Sahlins portrays the true nature of primitive subsistence. Temporal variation in the abundance of food resources is a universal fact of life (Ricklefs 1979, 159); but whereas variation from season to season is predictable, that from one year to the next is not. Thus, for most groups, the procurement of food is relatively unproblematic in good years, but mortal deficiencies may be faced in the occasional bad year.

The causes of these fluctuations, be they drought, frost or predation, are often local in scope and often affect some species more than others. Modern gatherer–hunters commonly exploit both these tendencies, using diversification and mobility as safeguards against periodic scarcity (Lee and De Vore 1968). Low levels of population and of environmental exploitation allow such groups to weather out local scarcity by switching to less desirable, secondary resources or by moving out of a stricken area.

A third alternative is to store present abundance for use in the event of future scarcity. This strategy is the basis of sedentary economies and is particularly effective as a buffer against short-term, predictable shortage. With primitive storage techniques, however, it is an insufficient safeguard against prolonged, unpredictable famine. Again, diversification, through the cultivation of a range of different crops in a variety of scattered microenvironments (e.g. Lottinville 1973, 335), may dampen the effects of fluctuations but will be insufficient to cope with large-scale failure. Furthermore, available wild resources are generally inadequate to support large agglomerations of population.

Food may also be stored indirectly. Indirect storage involves the transformation of foodstuffs into a more stable, alternative form, from which food may later be recovered. A particularly elegant form of indirect storage is the use of agriculture and animal husbandry in tandem, whereby surplus plant food is converted into a more stable animal form which can be consumed in time of need (Flannery 1969, 87). Apart from animal husbandry, the transformations characteristic of indirect storage are cultural and involve the equivalencing of foodstuffs and non-food items through exchange transactions (Flannery 1968). In such transactions, food is exchanged for non-food tokens with at least the implicit understanding that such tokens can later

be re-exchanged for food. This type of exchange transaction will be termed *social storage*.

Social storage

Objections are often raised to this kind of equivalencing in simple societies on two grounds (Dalton 1967, 68; Nash 1967, 6–7; Sahlins 1974, 218): (1) that food is ultimately inconvertible for other materials; and (2) that status goods which have been 'purchased' through the exchange of foodstuffs may not be reconverted for food value. Both reflect a normative bias in the ethnographic observation of simple economies: such equivalencing does occur and prestige goods are exchanged for food (Downs 1972, 118; Gould 1966, 77; Suttles 1968, 60). In such instances, the active exchange of foodstuffs for valuable tokens is usually ascribed to some manner of social breakdown produced by scarcity (Dalton 1977, 198; Ford 1972, 43–5). The crucial factor is inter-annual variation. In good years, little food is exchanged and most transactions are limited to prestige goods or other valuables. These are the times which are observed by most anthropologists and which are the basis of the normative view of primitive economies (cf. Colson 1979, 18). Yet, in lean years, the story is different. We would argue, rather, that the persistent and high value placed on inter-community exchange in good years reflects the importance of such trade links as a safeguard against shortage: the channels must continue to be used and reinforced in good years, so that obligations will be sufficiently strong to be honoured in time of shortage. Thus, we see not the sudden shift in food exchange rules in lean years which is suggested by ethnographic sources, but rather the logical extension of a single adaptive system.

This convertibility of non-food tokens has some major implications for the study of social ranking. Firstly, tokens permit the development of far more ramified systems of social storage than can be maintained purely on the basis of direct reciprocity: such networks are, by virtue of their complexity, predisposed to simplification through centralisation – often under the aegis of a managerial elite (cf. Service 1962, 143–4). Secondly, wherever some social groups regularly produce a surplus and others regularly consume it, an even distribution of food can only be achieved at the expense of an uneven distribution of tokens. The stability of tokens then permits the sustained, unequal accumulation of wealth and its transmission across generations within a corporate group. This in turn makes possible the symbolic and active manipulation of wealth by such groups and so provides the critical preconditions for the emergence of institutionalised social differentiation.

However, the very stability which allows tokens to be accumulated also threatens to destroy their value. Clearly, the food which can be obtained through the reconversion of valuables is strictly limited by the system's ability to produce and mobilise surplus. If too many valuables exist relative to the potential of the system, the value of such tokens will decline; in other words, indirect storage networks may be faced with an inflationary problem. In general terms, there are two possibilities for curbing this inflationary tendency. The first is the removal of tokens from the local exchange system, by actively destroying them (as in the rivalry pot-latch), by placing them out of reach in burials, hoards or river offerings, or by exchanging them through long-distance trade (Downs 1972, 118–19; Piddocke 1968, 299). The second possibility is the formation of a hierarchy of increasingly scarce items, wherein a quantity of lower-level goods may be exchanged for a more highly valued item (Vayda 1961, 622). Again, the objective is to tie up valuable tokens and limit their downward conversion for food. Such a hierarchy tends to produce a constant upward conversion of wealth, with each successive level being less likely to be reconverted into food – although all levels still retain this potential (Bohannan 1955; Gould 1966). Hierarchies of valuable tokens are most typically encountered in association with societies organised at a high level of complexity. In such situations, the basic economic motivation for exchange at these higher levels may be overshadowed by the manipulation of prestige goods for social or political ends (Dalton 1977). Social storage systems may then 'take off', with the focus shifting from the redistribution of food to the upward mobilisation of resources and manpower for consumption by an elite.

This discussion also has very direct relevance to the specifically archaeological problem of formation processes. Tokens are often durable and so survive archaeologically, while they tend to be highly visible by virtue of their raw material or workmanship. Their provenance can frequently be determined by composition analysis, and, because of their role in social storage, they may, up to a point, stand proxy for the movement of foodstuffs which do not survive archaeologically. Moreover, the deflationary measures discussed above allow us, in large measure, to predict the disposal pathways through which such tokens were discarded and so incorporated in the archaeological record (cf. Clarke 1973). This model may, therefore, enable us to assess the significance of some of the richest bodies of data available to archaeologists.[2]

The character of a social storage network can, in large part, be predicted from consideration of its environmental context. The biotic community of a region limits the range of subsistence strategies which can be pursued and, in conjunction with local climate, determines the frequency and severity of shortages. Topography exerts a major influence on the ease of transportation between communities and likewise on the scale of failure and the homogeneity of its effects. Thus figure 11.1 shows inter-annual variation in wheat yields for Cyprus (area 9,000 sq. km), Greece (area 130,000 sq. km), W. Germany (area 250,000 sq. km) and finally for Europe as a whole. Essentially, large areas encom-

pass greater environmental diversity, which serves to dampen fluctuations in food supply. Similarly, the greater the diversity of the regional environment, the more likely it is that shortages can be evened out over the short distances imposed by a primitive transport technology. In other words, given knowledge of the biotic community, of local topography and of climatic variability, it is possible to predict the minimum size and likely intensity of an effective social storage system, together with the probable costs and benefits of centralisation of the system. Such independently derived expectations can then be tested against the archaeological evidence for the size, formality and complexity of the exchange system.

Social storage in the prehistoric Aegean

In the second half of this paper, the model just described is examined in a case study from the prehistoric Aegean (fig. 11.2). Farming spread over Greece from the seventh millennium BC: a range of crops was grown and domestic livestock would have served both as an additional source of diversity and as a form of mobile bank. In the central lowlands, where farming was established early on, soils are good and rainfall is moderately reliable (cf. Renfrew 1972, 272). In consequence, small-scale losses afflicting individual households – such as when a garden was raided by deer or a farmer misjudged the timing of his sowing – will have accounted for a large proportion of shortages (cf.

Fig. 11.1. Inter-annual variability in wheat yields (data from FAO 1946–74).

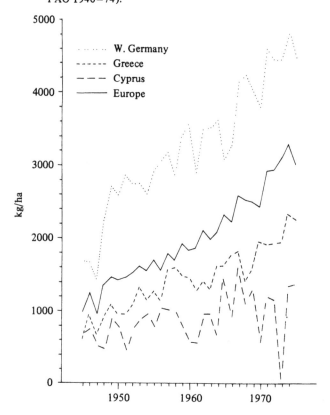

Ricklefs 1979, 850–2). Such shortages could be made up by local exchange between households, which may have been a factor in the emergence of the village rather than the household as the typical form of early settlement (Renfrew 1972, 238–9; Halstead 1981b, 312–13). In the more arid, less fertile areas of the south-eastern Aegean which were colonised rather later, more general losses due to drought will have been the greatest problem. In consequence, exchange between households within the same village would not have been effective. At the same time, settlement in villages, rather than in individual households, would have both increased the labour costs of agricultural production (Gamble 1981) and lessened the viability of sparse wild resources as an emergency food supply (Halstead 1981a).

Here, farmsteads or hamlets were the normal form of early settlement (Bintliff 1977, 83–4; Cherry 1979, 37–43). Among early farmers in both the central and the south-eastern Aegean, storage apparently took place at the level of the individual household (e.g. Hourmouziadis 1979; Whitelaw 1979) and contact between communities is most apparent in very general similarities of material culture (e.g. French 1972; Theocharis 1973).

Between the fourth and second millennia BC, large nucleated villages became the normal form of settlement in both zones (Branigan 1972; Renfrew 1972, 238–9; Cherry 1979, 43–6; Halstead 1981b, 313). This trend towards nucleation may have been at least partly due to the centralisation of growing networks of social storage, but in any

Fig. 11.2. Topographic map of Greece and the Aegean.

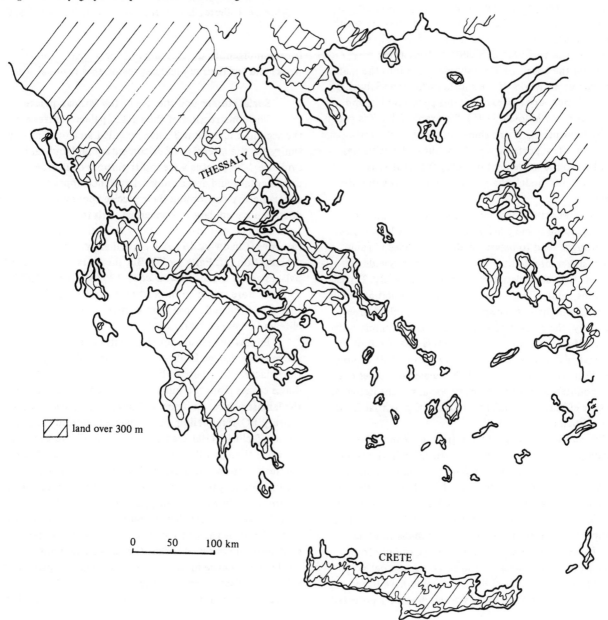

THESSALY

land over 300 m

0   50   100 km

CRETE

case these larger settlements were, by virtue of their size, committed to more active participation in regional social storage networks. In fact there is evidence for just this development: centrally located storage facilities now appear on some settlements (e.g. Heath 1958), while there is growing evidence for the exchange of durable craft items between communities (Renfrew 1972; 1973).

Exchange in the prehistoric Aegean has been discussed at some length by Renfrew (1972), who saw its amplification through the 'multiplier effect' as one of the key factors in the development of the Minoan and Mycenaean civilisations of second-millennium BC Crete and Greece. However, this is clearly only part of the story, because these palace-centred civilisations developed only in the southern Aegean; in Thessaly, in northern Greece, nucleation of settlements, centralised storage and the growth of inter-communal exchange all developed perhaps a thousand years earlier than in the south — but from then on bronze age Thessaly seems to have been less a case of multiplication than of long division, and the area became a cultural backwater.

In fact the coasts of Thessaly were tied into the maritime exchange networks of the southern Aegean (Schachermeyr 1976), but very few exotic items penetrated inland (Hanschmann and Milojčić 1976). This rapid fall-off is perhaps a little surprising if one thinks in terms of the movement of just a few portable valuables, but if the valuables were linked to the movement of bulky foodstuffs, as suggested by our model, the phenomenon is more understandable.

The most critical feature of the Thessalian plains is their topographic homogeneity, as a result of which losses due to drought tend to be very widespread indeed. Table 11.1a considers inter-annual variation in wheat yields in each of the four administrative districts of Thessaly. Partial correlations, controlling for time, reveal that fluctuations in the three inland districts covary to a considerable degree. Significantly, the more heterogeneous coastal administrative district of Magnisia is an exception to this rule. Each of the administrative districts covers about two and a half thousand square kilometres, so it is evident that major shortages could only be countered by very extensive social storage networks — and that effectively limits the indigenous potential for the growth of such networks.

The southern Aegean, by contrast, is of very diverse topography and there is much less covariation in the timing of fluctuations, for example between the four administrative districts of the island of Crete (table 11.1b). These districts still cover about two thousand square kilometres each, but in Crete good and bad years may balance each other out to a significant degree even within a single sub-district (fig. 11.3a). These sub-districts cover an average of only four hundred square kilometres, and so social storage networks extending over quite modest distances could have been viable. In Crete, therefore, there was much greater potential

Table 11.1. *Inter-annual variation in wheat yields, 1961–76: partial correlations between departments, controlling for time**

(a) *Thessaly*

	Trikala	Karditsa	Larisa	Magnisia
Trikala	–	.6266	.4715	.2576
Karditsa	.6266	–	.3644	.1419
Larisa	.4715	.3644	–	.7613
Magnisia	.2576	.1419	.7613	–

(b) *Crete*

	Chania	Rethymnon	Heraklion	Lasithi
Chania	–	.4235	.1706	.3293
Rethymnon	.4235	–	.4562	.2933
Heraklion	.1706	.4562	–	.1109
Lasithi	.3293	.2933	.1109	–

*High values indicate a high level of correlation; data from NSSG 1961–76.

for the indigenous development of local social storage networks and for their gradual expansion to a regional scale.

Social storage and the rise of the Minoan palace

The construction of the Cretan palace centres early in the second millennium BC has provided an excellent opportunity for the interplay of documentary and archaeological evidence. The palaces were multi-purpose centres, but the documentary and archaeological evidence appear to be contradictory concerning their precise economic role. The documents seem largely concerned with the collection of food and raw materials for use by the palace and its functionaries (Chadwick 1976) — superficially, a classic case of mobilisation (cf. Earle 1977). But the storage facilities of the palaces are of a size (Dewolf *et al.* 1963; Renfrew 1972, 291–6) more suited to the sort of bad year redistributive function discussed above than to merely provisioning the elite and its dependents.

In part the reason for this contradiction may be that the massive storage facilities were built at the beginning of the palaces' life, whereas the bulk of the documentary evidence comes from the fourteenth-century BC destruction of the largest palace, Knossos. In between, in the sixteenth century BC, remodelling of the palaces reduced their food storage facilities (Halstead 1981a), while the appearance at the same time of villas and minor palaces implies that this storage function was decentralised (fig. 11.3b). The documents support this interpretation: for example, the grain returns from just one locality, Dawo (Chadwick 1976, 118), would have been sufficient to bury the entire central court of the Knossos palace to more than one metre in depth, and so it seems inconceivable that the palace could have stored all the grain whose production it recorded. The palaces themselves in this later period concentrated on the production and storage of craft goods (Olivier 1967a; Graham 1979). Perhaps the two most important commodities were perfumed olive oil and woollen textiles, which take advantage of the enormous flexibility of the olive and the sheep in their ability to provide either food, in times of scarcity, or the raw materials for craft goods, in times of plenty.

The documentary evidence is richest for textile production (Killen 1963; 1964; forthcoming; Olivier 1967b). The palace at Knossos controlled one hundred thousand sheep in central Crete, and consideration of local livestock carrying capacity suggests that this was a majority if not all of the regional sheep population (Halstead 1980a). The use of sheep as a vehicle for social storage involves a constant tension between the interests of the individual, which will often favour the use of surplus grain to fatten sheep for slaughter, and the interests of the community, which will favour the retention of both sheep and surplus grain for exchange purposes. The exceptional level of palace interference in sheep-raising may have served to resolve this tension. This control would have enabled the palace both to maximise the number of sheep available as an emergency food supply and to regulate the production of more stable woollen textiles. The documents contain more detailed evidence for the dynamics of this process. Enormous variation in wool yields from one flock to another probably reflects differences in nutritional status, with some flocks being fed local grain surpluses and others subsisting on poor-quality graze. The wool flocks consisted primarily of wethers and of a few females drafted in to make up deficiencies in numbers. However, the substitute females were heavily concentrated in just a handful of flocks: it is suggested that certain flocks had been slaughtered wholesale in response to local crop failure and that they were only gradually being built back up to full strength.

What happened to the finished textiles? Some of the better pieces were apparently used in gift exchanges with other elites (Killen, forthcoming). The bulk were unaccounted for in the documents, but may have been exchanged out to clothe the populace. The foodstuffs in the palace magazines included produce which had arrived there without being recorded (Halstead 1981b, 332) so it seems likely that there was another undocumented level of exchange between the palace and the hinterland. Unlike the annual obligatory levies, which are recorded in the tablets, these transactions appear to have been of an opportunistic nature, with the palace perhaps employing cloth and other manufactured goods either to tap further resources from its territory or to acquire exotic raw materials and goods through long-distance trade.

Fig. 11.3. Crete (a) modern administrative regions
(b) prehistoric palaces and villas (after Cadogan 1976) in relation to modern land use (after Allbaugh 1953).

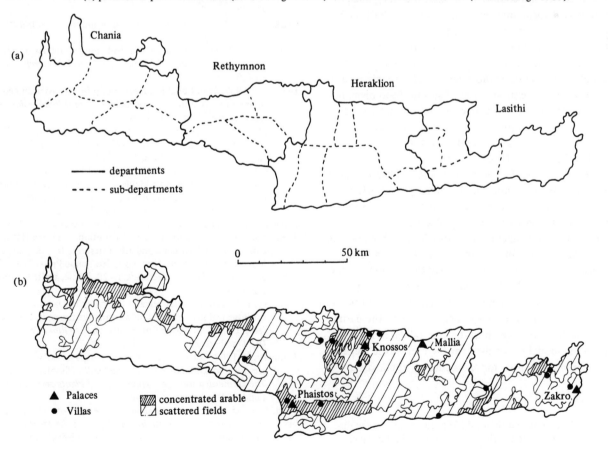

By the time of the final destruction, the palace's involvement in this opportunistic sphere had expanded to the point that a large army of artisans was maintained on a permanent basis (Chadwick 1976, 151). This drive to increase the stability of palace resources is seen in an even more marked form in the late thirteenth-century BC Mycenaean palace at Pylos (Chadwick 1976, 152), in mainland Greece, and signals the transition from social storage to true mobilisation. Such a shift, however, had the effect of tying up a large proportion of palace food resources, thus reducing the palace's ability to respond to periodic shortage and so perhaps sowing the seeds of its destruction.

Conclusion

This paper has stressed uncertainty in resource availability as a crucial factor for understanding past economies and the emergence of social ranking. It has argued that 'social storage' was an important buffer against periodic food shortage among early farmers in the Aegean and became increasingly vital and increasingly intensive with the appearance of large, nucleated settlements. Early social storage networks will have had the greatest potential for expansion in areas of topographic diversity, such as the island of Crete. It was further predicted that the durable and convertible nature of the tokens used in social storage transactions would have permitted the sustained accumulation and manipulation of wealth and power and so have facilitated the emergence of institutionalised social inequality. Certainly, in the Cretan palace civilisation, a complex, regional system of social storage was organised by, and at the same time served to maintain, an institutionalised elite. It is suggested that this elite directed the labour of those who received redistributive assistance towards the production of surplus food or manufacture of craft tokens. These tokens could then be used opportunistically to acquire food resources, labour, raw materials or other craft goods, and they were, of course, more stable than actual foodstuffs. During the later history of the Cretan palaces, there was a growing emphasis on such craft production and opportunistic exchange, doubtless in an attempt to regulate the inevitable fluctuations in the incoming and outgoing of resources. The transition from local, reciprocal exchanges of foodstuffs, through a regional social storage system administered by an elite, to a highly inegalitarian mobilisation economy may thus be seen as the product of repeated, short-term attempts by sedentary societies to stabilise an inherently unstable resource base. For any given region, the severity of uncertainty and the nature of viable solutions to it can both be ascertained independently, so the model tested here for the prehistoric Aegean has considerable potential for cross-cultural application.

Notes

1 See O'Shea 1981 and Halstead 1981a for more detailed discussion of many of the arguments advanced in this paper.

2 Similar ideas have been developed in a recent unpublished paper by Gordon Bronitsky of the Department of Anthropology, University of Texas of the Permian Basin.

References

Allbaugh, L.G. 1953. *Crete: a Case Study of an Underdeveloped Area.* Princeton, University Press.

Bintliff, J.L. 1977. The number of burials in the Mesara tholoi, in D. Blackman and K. Branigan (eds.), An archaeological survey of the Ayiofarango valley, *Annual of the British School at Athens* 72: 24–30.

Bohannan, P. 1955. Some principles of exchange and investment among the Tiv. *American Anthropologist* 57: 60–9.

Branigan, K. 1972. Minoan settlements in east Crete, in P.J. Ucko, R. Tringham and G.W. Dimbleby (eds.), *Man, Settlement and Urbanism.* London, Duckworth, 751–9.

Bronitsky, G. ms. Banking at Arroyo Hondo.

Cadogan, G. 1976. *Palaces of Minoan Crete.* London, Barrie and Jenkins.

Carneiro, R. 1970. A theory of the origin of the state. *Science* 160: 1187–92.

Chadwick, J. 1976. *The Mycenaean World.* Cambridge, University Press.

Cherry, J.F. 1978. Generalization and the archaeology of the state, in D. Green, C. Haselgrove and M. Spriggs (eds.), *Social Organisation and Settlement.* Oxford, British Archaeological Reports, 411–37.

Cherry, J.F. 1979. Four problems in Cycladic prehistory, in J.L. Davis and J.F. Cherry (eds.), *Papers in Cycladic Prehistory.* Los Angeles, Institute of Archaeology, University of California, 22–47.

Clarke, D.L. 1973. Archaeology: the loss of innocence. *Antiquity* 47: 6–18.

Colson, E. 1979. In good years and in bad: food strategies of self-reliant societies. *Journal of Anthropological Research* 35(1): 18–29.

Dalton, G. 1967. Traditional production in primitive African economies, in G. Dalton (ed.), *Tribal and Peasant Economies.* New York, Natural History Press, 61–80.

Dalton, G. 1977. Aboriginal economies in stateless societies, in T.K. Earle and J.E. Ericson (eds.), *Exchange Systems in Prehistory.* New York, Academic Press, 191–212.

Dewolf, Y., Postel, F. and van Effenterre, H. 1963. Géographie préhistorique de la région de Mallia, in H. and M. van Effenterre (eds.), *Fouilles Exécutées à Mallia: Site et Nécropoles 2* (Etudes crétoises 13). Paris, Paul Geuthner, 28–53.

Downs, J. 1972. *The Navajo.* New York, Holt, Rinehart and Winston.

Earle, T.K. 1977. A reappraisal of redistribution: complex Hawaiian chiefdoms, in T.K. Earle and J.E. Ericson (eds.), *Exchange Systems in Prehistory.* New York, Academic Press, 213–29.

FAO 1946–74. *Production Yearbook* 1–28. Rome, United Nations Food and Agriculture Organisation.

Flannery, K.V. 1968. The Olmec and the valley of Oaxaca: a model for inter-regional interaction in formative times, in E.P. Benson (ed.), *Dumbarton Oaks Conference on the Olmec.* Washington, DC, Dumbarton Oaks, 79–110.

Flannery, K. 1969. Origins and ecological effects of early Near Eastern domestication, in P.J. Ucko and G.W. Dimbleby (eds.), *The Domestication and Exploitation of Plants and Animals.* London, Duckworth, 73–100.

Ford, R. 1972. Barter, gift or violence: an analysis of Tewa inter-tribal exchange. *Anthropological Papers of the Museum of Anthropology* 46: 21–45. Ann Arbor, University of Michigan.

French, D.H. 1972. Notes on prehistoric pottery groups from central Greece. Athens, privately circulated.

Gamble, C.S. 1981. Animal husbandry, population and urbanisation, in C. Renfrew and J.M. Wagstaff (eds.), *An Island Polity: the archaeology of exploitation in Melos*. Cambridge, University Press, 161–71.

Gould, R. 1966. The wealth quest among the Tolowa Indians of northwestern California. *Proceedings of the American Philosophical Society* 110(1): 67–89.

Graham, J.W. 1979. Further notes on Minoan palace architecture, 1: west magazines and upper halls at Knossos and Mallia. *American Journal of Archaeology* 83: 49–63.

Halstead, P. 1981a. From determinism to uncertainty: social storage and the rise of the Minoan palace, in A. Sheridan and G. Bailey (eds.), *Economic Archaeology: Towards an Integrated Approach*. Oxford, British Archaeological Reports, 187–213.

Halstead, P. 1981b. Counting sheep in neolithic and bronze age Greece, in I. Hodder, G. Isaac and N. Hammond (eds.), *Pattern of the Past: Studies in honour of David Clarke*. Cambridge, University Press, 307–39.

Hanschmann, E. and Milojčić, V. 1976. *Die Deutschen Ausgrabungen auf der Argissa-Magula in Thessalien, 3: Die Frühe und Beginnende Mittlere Bronzezeit*. Bonn, Rudolf Habelt.

Heath, M.C. 1958. Early Helladic clay sealings from the House of Tiles at Lerna. *Hesperia* 27: 81–121.

Hourmouziadis, G. 1979. *To Neolithiko Dhimini*. Volos, Society for Thessalian Studies.

Killen, J.T. 1963. Some adjuncts to the SHEEP ideogram on Knossos tablets. *Eranos* 61: 69–93.

Killen, J.T. 1964. The wool industry of Crete in the late bronze age. *Annual of the British School at Athens* 59: 1–15.

Killen, J.T., forthcoming. *A Mycenaean Industry*.

Lee, R.B. and De Vore, I. (eds.) 1968. *Man the Hunter*. Chicago, Aldine.

Lottinville, S. (ed.) 1973. *Paul Wilhelm, Duke of Wurttemberg Travels in North America 1822–1824*. Norman, University of Oklahoma Press.

Nash, M. 1967. The organization of economic life, in G. Dalton (ed.), *Tribal and Peasant Economies*. New York, Natural History Press, 3–11.

NSSG 1961–76. *Agricultural Statistics of Greece*. Athens, National Statistical Service of Greece.

Olivier, J.-P. 1967a. *Les Scribes de Cnossos* (Incunabula Graeca 17). Rome, Edizioni dell' Ateneo.

Olivier, J.-P. 1967b. La série Dn de Cnossos. *Studi Micenei ed Egeo-Anatolici* 2 (Incunabula Graeca 18). Rome, Edizioni dell' Ateneo, 71–93.

O'Shea, J.M. 1981. Coping with scarcity: exchange and social storage, in A. Sheridan and G. Bailey (eds.), *Economic Archaeology: Towards an Integrated Approach*. Oxford, British Archaeological Reports, 167–83.

Piddocke, S. 1968. The potlatch system of the southern Kwakiutl: a new perspective, in E.E. LeClair and H.K. Schneider (eds.), *Economic Anthropology: Readings in Theory and Analysis*. London, Holt, Rinehart and Winston, 283–99.

Renfrew, C. 1972. *The Emergence of Civilisation: the Cyclades and the Aegean in the Third Millennium B.C.* London, Methuen.

Renfrew, C. 1973. Trade and craft specialisation, in D.R. Theocharis, *Neolithic Greece*. Athens, National Bank of Greece, 179–91. 179–91.

Ricklefs, R.E. 1979. *Ecology* (2nd edn). New York, Chiron.

Rubenstein, D.I. 1978. On predation, competition, and the advantages of group living, in P.P.G. Bateson and P.H. Klopfer (eds.), *Perspectives in Ethology* 3. London, Plenum Press, 205–31.

Sabloff, J.A. and Lamberg-Karlovsky, C.C. (eds.) 1975. *Ancient Civilisation and Trade*. Albuquerque, University of New Mexico Press.

Sahlins, M. 1974. *Stone Age Economics*. London, Tavistock Publications.

Schachermeyr, F. 1976. *Die Ägäische Frühzeit, I: die Vormykenische Perioden*. Vienna, Austrian Academy of Sciences.

Service, E.R. 1962. *Primitive Social Organization: An Evolutionary Perspective*. New York, Random House.

Suttles, W. 1968. Coping with abundance: subsistence on the northwest coast, in R.B. Lee and I. De Vore (eds.), *Man the Hunter*. Chicago, Aldine, 56–68.

Theocharis, D.R. 1973. *Neolithic Greece*. Athens, National Bank of Greece.

Vayda, A. 1961. A re-examination of Northwest Coast economic systems. *Transactions of the New York Academy of Sciences, Series II* 23: 618–24.

Whitelaw, T.M. 1979. Community structure and social organisation at Fournou Korifi, Myrtos. M.A. dissertation, Department of Archaeology, University of Southampton.

Chapter 12

**Leadership and
'surplus' production**
Clive Gamble

*The emergence of leadership and the early state in the
Aegean bronze age is discussed from the perspective of subsistence organisation. The consequences of intensification of
production above the level of community self-sufficiency are
examined, together with the contribution that a surplus
made to the establishment of larger effective political units.
An explanation for the integration of potentially self-
sufficient village communities into a wider polity is proposed
that acknowledges the importance of dependent ties based
upon necessary subsistence goods.*

A number of consequences have been drawn from the
potential of prehistoric subsistence strategies to provide a
surplus above basic requirements. As envisaged by Childe,

> Chiefs cannot rule over a community unless that com-
> munity can produce a social surplus above the needs
> of domestic consumption, sufficient to support the
> chieftain in idleness — i.e. as a full-time ruler. He is not
> likely to be tolerated unless his rule can confer tangible
> benefits that the previous system of government, or
> lack of government, failed to provide. (1951, 47)

The concept of absolute surplus used by Childe and others
was obtained by subtracting calorific needs from calorific
yields and converting the balance into extra people, such as
specialised craftsmen, merchants, priests, officials and clerks

(Childe 1954, 31), who were now free from the drudgery of
working the land. The production of such a surplus was
regarded as the critical variable in the emergence of more
complex social and economic institutions as represented by
the appearance of urban centres.

This view has been widely criticised. The substantivist
economists, and Pearson in particular (1957, 339) have
pointed out that:

> There are always and everywhere potential surpluses
> available. What counts is the institutional means for
> bringing them to life.

Sahlins has argued that:

> Too frequently and mechanically anthropologists
> attribute the appearance of chieftainship to the pro-
> duction of surplus. In the historic process, however,
> the relation has been at least mutual, and in the func-
> tioning of primitive society it is rather the other way
> around. Leadership continually generates domestic
> surplus. The development of rank and chieftainship
> becomes . . . development of the productive forces.
> (1974, 140)

The 'embedded' view of the economy points to complementary developments in society and the production required to
support and reproduce it. Polanyi's analyses of the circulation of goods and primitive valuables (Dalton 1977) have

formed the basis for many archaeological studies (e.g. Earle and Ericson 1977) that have investigated the appearance of ranking.

Agricultural production has not however received the same attention. Certainly, when they occur, the relation of large irrigation works to the development of society has been commented upon (e.g. Adams 1966). But in many parts of prehistoric Europe such spectacular modifications to the landscape are lacking, and yet ranking occurred. Consequently exchange studies, and in an earlier phase diffusionist arguments, have supplied the major explanatory framework. One aspect of the European radiocarbon revolution, with its implications for independent social evolution, that still needs investigation is the relationship between the local development of ranking and the agricultural base of such societies.

The present case study comes from the Greek bronze age, which on chronological grounds cannot be considered a pristine area of ranking. The evidence does suggest however that the Aegean civilisations enjoyed a considerable degree of independence in their emergence (Renfrew 1972). One important element in the process of social transformation was the diversity of Mediterranean polyculture – wheat, olives, grapes and animal products. Evidence of subsistence management is also found in the linear tablet archives and in the storage facilities associated with settlements. These crops and animals formed the resources that were available for social mobilisation by the emergent elites. We should expect, therefore, changes in the use and management of these resources to correspond with developments in leadership as new demands were put on the productive system. In this paper I will only deal with animal resources (see Whitelaw 1979; Gamble 1980; Halstead and O'Shea, this volume; Bintliff 1977, for a further discussion).

Melos

The case-study comes from the small Aegean island of Melos which lies almost midway between the major middle bronze age polities of palatial Crete and the late bronze age centres of the Greek mainland. A recent reinvestigation of the important coastal town of Phylakopi by Colin Renfrew has confirmed continuous occupation in five major phases from early to late bronze age. Exchange materials found at the site point to a change from Knossos to Mycenae as the dominant centre of political power in the Aegean between the middle and late bronze age.

A site survey of the island was organised (Cherry 1979, 1982) in order to place Phylakopi within its prehistoric settlement pattern and to derive population estimates for the bounded community (fig. 12.1). The survey results showed that during the early bronze age there was a pattern of small, dispersed farmsteads and settlements of which the contemporary phase at Phylakopi formed an example. This was followed by a significant settlement shift. In the middle and late bronze age, a period of some nine hundred years,

Phylakopi was the only settlement on the island. The size of the site increased as the formerly dispersed population began to aggregate. John Cherry's (1979) estimates for population size on Melos in the bronze age point to a slow growth during the entire period; of the order of 100 to 800 persons in two thousand years.

One consequence of this nucleation of settlement and aggregation of population would have been increased labour costs in subsistence agriculture. More than fifty per cent of Phylakopi's immediate catchment lies in the sea, and the ecofact evidence from the site does not indicate that marine resources were used to compensate for this loss of agricultural land (Gamble 1979). In particular an increase in travel time to agricultural plots and a possible fragmentation in land holding would require greater labour inputs if households were to maintain the same subsistence returns. We might expect therefore a change in the management of agricultural resources in order to cope with this circumstance and ensure the strategic goal of household and community self-sufficiency in food items.

The analysis of the animal bones from Phylakopi (Gamble 1982) points to one possible solution that was adopted by the prehistoric community. Melos, and the arid Aegean islands in general, are best adapted to the keeping of small ruminants such as sheep and goats. The secondary products – wool, hair and milk – from these animals are important resources both for household economies and for wider exchange networks. In the early bronze age, when Phylakopi was a small settlement within a dispersed pattern of island occupation, the animal bone residues were dominated by sheep/goat remains (fig. 12.2). Cattle and pig were present in small numbers. With the change in settlement pattern in the middle bronze age there is also a corresponding shift in the proportions of identified faunal remains. In particular cattle increases at the expense of sheep/goat, while pig continues at its former level. In the final late bronze age phase of the site, when Phylakopi is still the only site on the island, there is a decline in the proportion of cattle remains. One explanation for this change in the middle bronze age to an animal that is unsuited to the Melian environment recognises the secondary products of cattle and their importance in solving the higher exploitation costs that resulted from the aggregation of population. The importance of cattle as beasts of burden, their role in plough traction and in manuring the fields, was a solution, through a form of intensification, to the problems of distance/cost in the agricultural strategy. It should not however be interpreted as a maintenance of previous labour inputs. The keeping of cattle no doubt required labour input, and the decision would have been balanced against the alternative costs involved with distance factors. From the final phase of the late bronze age, when cattle remains decline, the first occurrence of donkey on the site has been identified. The suitability of this animal to the terrain and environment of Melos, and its competitive advantage over cattle for short-distance porterage, underscore the interpretation offered here for faunal changes, which acknowledges what Andrew Sherratt has designated the secondary products of domestication (1981).

Regional developments

Sahlins has written that 'maximum dispersion is the settlement pattern of the state of nature' (1974, 97).

Nucleation may bring certain social benefits but it invariably results in a greater labour input into subsistence. As was pointed out by Peebles and Kus (1977) and Brumfiel (1976), the size of sites, representing population aggregation, may correlate with higher potential productivity in the catchments around those sites, thereby providing some communities with a head start in the race towards chieftainship. This does not explain, however, why aggregation took place or

Fig. 12.1. Changing settlement patterns in Melos (after Cherry 1979).

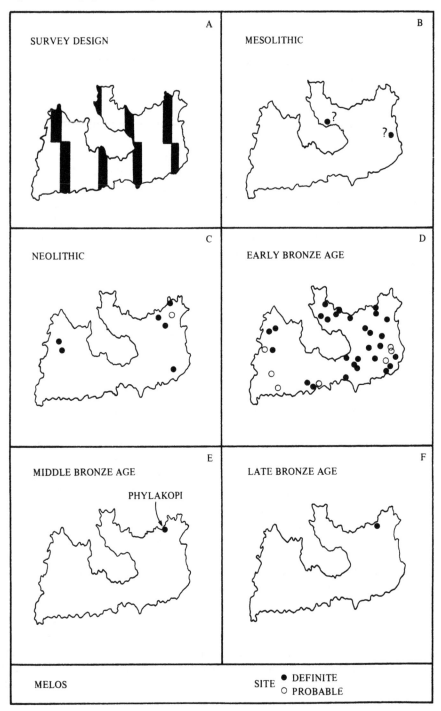

why the options provided by potentially higher productivity in such locations were taken up. So far the Melian example presented here has also only described change in agricultural decisions associated with the level of site organisation. What is needed is an explanation for settlement nucleation and population aggregation, and to do this Melos must be placed in its context within the wider Aegean world of which it formed a part.

At this regional scale it is possible to see the settlement shift on Melos in relation to the political formation on Crete, and later on the mainland, of what Colin Renfrew has termed Early State Modules (1975). The palaces and stronghold/citadels of these small polities (fig. 12.3) formed a redistributive focus that is attested in their storage facilities and in the evidence from the deciphered Linear B archives. John Killen (1964) has demonstrated for the wool tablets from late bronze age Knossos how target quotas of fleece production were set by the central administration for the shepherds who managed the palace flocks. Further observations based upon the archive material have suggested area specialisation in such labour-intensive crops as flax (Hutchinson 1977). The indication from these observations is that some inroads were being made into the autonomy of households and local communities over their own agricultural decisions. While it is difficult to establish the extent of such central demands on local production (Carothers and MacDonald 1979), it can be

Fig. 12.2. Faunal remains from the five city phases at Phylakopi.

Phylakopi City Phases

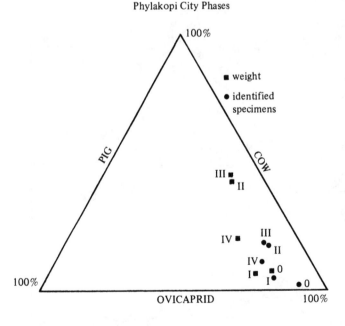

0, I = EARLY BRONZE AGE
II, III = MIDDLE BRONZE AGE
IV = LATE BRONZE AGE

weight in grams

suggested that one function of the palace centres was to make up any shortfalls in local subsistence budgets that resulted from specialisation upon particular commodities.

I have argued elsewhere that one consequence of this involvement of leadership with production would be the creation of dependent links that were derived from a practical, subsistence basis (1979; 1980). In other words, as Harner has implied (1975), intensification leading to surplus can result in scarcity in factors of production, such as available land, labour and the means of subsistence. Thus a basis for competition and the possibility of change and social developments is presented. In particular a strand in the web of effective authority of these early states was created through the demands of leadership on production, which resulted in social control. The size and the relative strength of the power base of these polities depends on their ability to prevent the accumulation of surplus in peripheral areas (Friedman and Rowlands 1977, 220), thereby forcing local communities and households to look to the centre for the means of social reproduction.

How might a small unit such as Melos have been linked into a wider political network? I would suggest that the shift in settlement pattern that led to an aggregated population reflected a dependent relationship between a minor and major partner in a system of alliances. The nature of this alliance changed during the course of the Aegean bronze age and led to a transformation of Melian society. Urbanisation, or more correctly the aggregation of population into a single settlement, was therefore a result of factors external to the local Melian system. It led for example to an intensification in agricultural production around the site of Phylakopi. It might also have resulted in use being made of the uninhabited parts of the island for the extensive management of sheep for wool, thus providing a commodity for external exchange. This speculative suggestion is offered as a hint of how we might tackle the problem of archaeologically invisible exports in agricultural production and some of the conditions we would need to establish in order to argue that surpluses of this form were indeed produced.

The impact that political growth and the development of leadership had upon systems of agricultural production also has a spatial dimension. This can most clearly be seen in what has been described as Systems Collapse among Early State Modules such as those represented by Minoan and Mycenaean Greece (Renfrew 1979). This failure to sustain growth may result from the inability of these Early State Modules to concentrate production within small spatial territories that could be easily managed from a centre. Earle (1976, 221) in dealing with polities of similar spatial size among the Olmec has noted that the central places of these Early State Modules lie some 20 km from their territorial boundaries, while centres in the Late Formative of the Valley of Mexico are only 4 km away from their boundaries. He suggests that

this may be a partial answer to a perennial archaeological dilemma concerning the apparent inability of the Olmec to develop an urban state organisation. Development of the primary state may require a much more compact population perhaps in a more nearly continual condition of interaction. (1976, 221)

The Greek examples briefly discussed here suggest that this is not just a feature of primary state formation but rather a more general problem associated with the emergence of more complex polities. The trajectory towards statehood involves a shrinkage in the spatial size of polities in order that production comes under the control of the centre. Once this is achieved the ambitions of empire that accompany the full emergence of the state can be realised, and spatial growth is both extensive and often spectacular in terms of the shortness of time in which it was achieved. This is possible as the new forms of sanction and control which were developed at the centre are applied over much wider areas. An essential component of this is the dominant role that the leadership

now plays in the organisation of agricultural production. It is on this basis that formal institutions with effective power emerge. By contrast the control and exchange of 'primitive valuables' is of limited importance in accounting for the effective power of such developing institutions.[1]

Note

1 I should like to thank the University of Southampton for financial support that made it possible to attend the 45th SAA meeting, and Dr Randy Helm for all his hospitality while I was staying in Philadelphia.

References

Adams, R. 1966. *The Evolution of Urban Society.* Chicago, Aldine.
Bintliff, J.L. 1977. *Natural environment and human settlement in prehistoric Greece.* Oxford, British Archaeological Reports.
Brumfiel, E. 1976. Regional growth in the Eastern Valley of Mexico: a test of the 'population pressure' hypothesis, in K.V. Flannery

Fig. 12.3. Suggested early state modules.

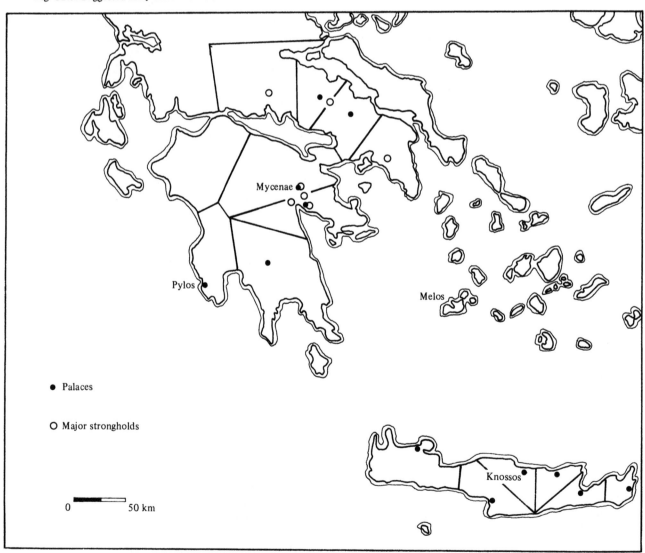

(ed.), *The Early Mesoamerican Village.* New York, Academic Press, 234–49.

Carothers, J. and McDonald, W.A. 1979. Size and distribution of the population in late bronze age Messenia: some statistical approaches. *Journal of Field Archaeology* 6: 433–54.

Cherry, J.F. 1979. Four problems in Cycladic prehistory, in J.L. Davis and J.F. Cherry (eds.), *Papers in Cycladic Prehistory.* Los Angeles, Institute of Archaeology, University of California, 22–47.

Cherry, J.F. 1982. A preliminary definition of site distribution on Melos, in C. Renfrew and J.M. Wagstaff (eds.), *An Island Polity: The Archaeology of Exploitation in Melos.* Cambridge, University Press, 10–23.

Childe, V.G. 1951. *Social Evolution.* London, Watts.

Childe, V.G. 1954. *What happened in History.* Harmondsworth, Penguin.

Dalton, G. 1977. Aboriginal economies in stateless societies, in T.K. Earle and J.E. Ericson (eds.), *Exchange Systems in Prehistory.* New York, Academic Press, 191–212.

Earle, T.K. 1976. A nearest-neighbour analysis of two formative settlement systems, in K.V. Flannery (ed.), *The Early Mesoamerican Village.* New York, Academic Press, 196–223.

Earle, T.K. and Ericson, J.E. (eds.) 1977. *Exchange Systems in Prehistory.* New York, Academic Press.

Friedman, J. and Rowlands, M.J. 1977. Notes towards an epigenetic model of the evolution of 'civilisation', in J. Friedman and M.J. Rowlands (eds.), *The Evolution of Social Systems.* London, Duckworth, 201–76.

Gamble, C.S. 1979. Surplus and self-sufficiency in the Cycladic subsistence economy, in J.L. Davis and J.F. Cherry (eds.), *Papers in Cycladic Prehistory.* Los Angeles, Institute of Archaeology, University of California, 122–34.

Gamble, C.S. 1981. Social control and the economy, in A. Sheridan and G. Bailey (eds.), *Economic Archaeology.* British Archaeological Reports, 215–29.

Gamble, C.S. 1982. Animal husbandry, population and urbanisation, in C. Renfrew and J.M. Wagstaff (eds.), *An Island Polity: The Archaeology of Exploitation in Melos.* Cambridge, University Press, 161–71.

Harner, M.J. 1975. Scarcity, the factors of production, and social evolution, in S. Polgar (ed.), *Population, Ecology and Social Evolution.* The Hague, Mouton, 123–38.

Hutchinson, J.S. 1977. Mycenaean kingdoms and medieval estates. *Historia* 26: 1–23.

Killen, J.T. 1964. The wool industry of Crete in the late bronze age. *Annual of the British School at Athens* 59: 1–15.

Pearson, H.W. 1957. The economy has no surplus: critique of a theory of development, in K. Polanyi, C.M. Arensberg and H.W. Pearson (eds.), *Trade and Markets in the Early Empires.* Glencoe, Free Press, 320–41.

Peebles, C.S. and Kus, S.M. 1977. Some archaeological correlates of ranked societies. *American Antiquity* 42: 421–48.

Renfrew, C. 1972. *The Emergence of Civilisation.* London, Methuen.

Renfrew, C. 1975. Trade as action at a distance: a question of integration and communication, in J.A. Sabloff and C.C. Lamberg-Karlovsky (eds.), *Ancient Civilisation and Trade.* Albuquerque, University of New Mexico Press, 3–59.

Renfrew, C. 1979. Systems collapse as social transformation: catastrophe and anastrophe in early state societies, in C. Renfrew and K.L. Cooke (eds.), *Transformations: Mathematical Approaches to Culture Change.* New York, Academic Press, 481–506.

Sahlins, M. 1974. *Stone Age Economics.* London, Tavistock Publications.

Sherratt, A.G. 1981. Plough and pastoralism: aspects of the secondary products revolution, in I. Hodder, G. Isaac and N. Hammond

(eds.), *Pattern of the Past: Studies in honour of David Clarke.* Cambridge, University Press, 261–305.

Whitelaw, T.M. 1979. Community structure and social organisation at Fournou Korifi, Myrtos. M.A. dissertation, Department of Archaeology, University of Southampton.

Chapter 13

**Settlement patterns,
land tenure and
social structure:
a diachronic model[1]**
John Bintliff

*Changes over time in settlement behaviour and land-use
strategies in prehistoric and early historic Greece are linked
to parallel socio-economic developments, in particular to the
rise and elaboration of ranking, via known and inferred
patterns of land tenure. In situations of population pressure,
'achieved' statuses based on landed wealth are converted to
'ascribed' formal rank, through such mechanisms as the
'client' system and 'cargo' redistributive system, typical for
recent peasant societies. Parallels with Roman and Saxon
society are drawn, and lead to a reinterpretation of Celtic
society in the pre-Roman period.*

I began this area of research with a set of archaeological observations on settlement numbers for the prehistoric and ancient periods in south-central mainland Greece,
considered (as in the pioneering study by Colin Renfrew,
1972a) to relate to population fluctuations (fig. 13.1). The
peaks are periods of high culture or civilisation (fig. 13.2),
early bronze age, late bronze age or Mycenaean, and classical
Greece. This is not a surprising finding in itself. But seen in
the field over several hundred sites, more archaeological and
geographical detail can be added,[2] taking modules of 2½–
5 km radius (fig. 13.3): a patterning not just in number but
in size of sites appears. In neolithic times our archaeological

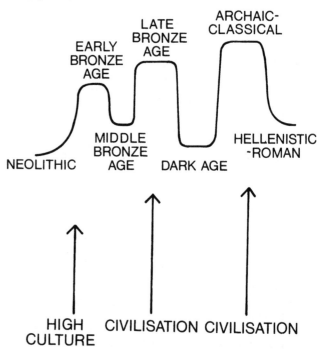

Fig. 13.1 and 13.2. Population fluctuations during the prehistoric and ancient periods in south-central mainland Greece
(fig. 13.1); periods of high culture/civilisation during the prehistoric and ancient periods in south-central mainland Greece
(fig. 13.2).

palimpsest suggests a loose scatter of hamlets, and low population, leading to the high culture of the early bronze age with a very dense scatter of farms and hamlets together with some district foci — a simple settlement hierarchy, high population; followed by a decline of population in the middle bronze age associated with nucleation into hamlets and villages; then by mature Mycenaean times a vigorous expansion of population, with the nucleated settlements blossoming into regional centres, surrounded by a network of lower settlement levels; another serious decline in the Dark Ages, low population and a loose scatter of nucleated hamlets, until the Late Geometric/Archaic revival of population leading into the Classical civilisation, with central places surrounded by a network of villages, hamlets and dispersed farms; finally a decline in the Hellenistic and Roman periods. Again, this is not a very surprising picture of the complex spatial organisation of civilisations, and its contrary in periods of less complex or vigorous local culture.[3]

The impetus behind these *population* expansions is variously interpreted — new cultigens such as the olive, the effect of novel iron tools, or the simple stimulus to produce more surplus by a burgeoning elite. But consider the orthodox explanations of these cyclical periods of complex and rudimentary *social* and *settlement* structure: they stress internal and external trade and exchange, and regional servicing, while surpluses for these purposes are obtained via the often unclearly stated allegiance of the peasant to the elite. Perhaps we are offered a kinship obligation, a social pyramid surmounted by a paramount chief, and from this leadership a further supportive following is attracted by the provision of redistributed prestige objects or raw materials, or regular feasts.[4]

Let us approach this issue in an entirely different fashion, by turning to ancient Greek and Roman civilisation, and in particular their social systems and their economy as admirably analysed by Finley (1973), Jones (1964), Hopkins (1978) and Andrewes (1977). The dominant theme of their writings is that the central source of wealth, status and political power in the ancient world lay in control of agricultural produce, and in the most direct way via the ownership of large private estates. Private land and the control over dependent labour or sharecropping tenants provide for the maintenance of the dominant ruling elite, together with its luxuries, and by definition landholding controls the right to power and decision-making: government offices are conditional upon high property qualifications.

Might we envisage a similar society, at least for Mycenaean and Archaic times, in which the ruling elites, betrayed archaeologically and historically, arose and were maintained by private dominance of land? Could we hypothesise that most peasants were tenants or labourers for these landowners, and that the supply of food surplus that fed the elite and its followers, supported their craft sectors and exchange relationships, came from the private wealth of a landed elite? Finally, were such a structure to be argued for

Mycenaean and Archaic society, could we find any archaeological trace of it? Let us return to our model Greek landscape. I believe the populations of these modules were supported predominantly by local food production. Therefore, the cyclical alternation of population seen here must reflect *intensification* and *deintensification* of land use. In periods of low population, large areas of the module went out of permanent cultivation (fig. 13.4). So the contrasted nucleation and dispersion of population must relate to a cyclical shift from, on the one hand, small infield round the low population centres, surrounded by extensive outfield, to, on the other hand, a vigorous pushing back of outfield to minimal proportions and a massive intake into intensive cultivation of the outer lands. Could this very conversion of the outfield be a major force in the rise of very complex stratified society? Let me suggest that middle bronze age and Dark Age hamlets communally controlled the infield land, with chieftains and 'big men' making more effective use of the outfield (perhaps notably with stock) and with larger than average infield holdings. Some of this wealthier peasantry stimulated the intake of the outfield into intensive use, by economic support for poorer peasants who became

Fig. 13.3. Model modules representing changing settlement patterns in prehistoric and ancient Greece.
● Village/hamlet/small district focus
■ Regional centre
X Farm

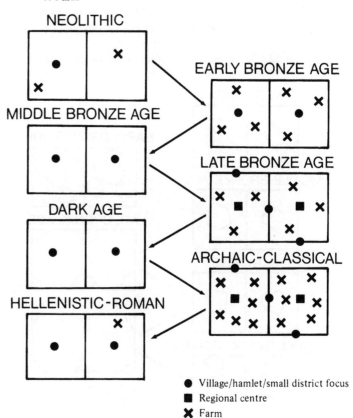

● Village/hamlet/small district focus
■ Regional centre
X Farm

sharecroppers in the new intake. Thereby some of the chiefs/ 'big men' became major landholders, with a large and growing body of peasant tenants.[5]

But how does this *economic* elite rise to *political* authority? In Roman government, we see the virtual restriction of official roles to those able to cover the expenses of the job, the costs of public feasts, assistance to the needy of the community and to the maintenance of community facilities. An excellent parallel can be found amongst Latin American peasant societies, in the Cargo System.[6] In any case, the dependence of a major part of the populace on the landowners in a patron—client relationship would be a powerful factor in concentrating community authority into the hands of the few. With communal dues being amalgamated with private wealth, the politico-economic nexus would be complete. Historically, such a transition as is here postulated, from wealthy peasant class to district political elite with hereditary privileges, has been eloquently documented for medieval communities in the Pyrenees by Lefebvre (1963). In a further stage of development, our local ruling families integrate with those of adjacent districts, from whence regional dynasties arise, higher levels of central people living in equivalent central places; finally, regional networks interconnect via nodal royal families in supra-regional central places: nascent palaces and cities.[7]

This is the controversial interpretation proposed: is there support in the historical evidence? For the archaic prologue to classical civilisation in Greece, the historical sources are unanimous in offering a picture of city-state societies for the most part ruled by aristocratic elites, whose means of support and control are argued to be their dominance in

ownership of productive land. The importance of trade, warfare and industry for archaic Greece, as for the ancient Greco-Roman world in general, is minimal in comparison to this fundamental connection between class, power and the land.[8]

What of Mycenaean civilisation? That expert on the Mycenaean archives, John Chadwick, offers this interpretation (fig. 13.5) of Mycenaean landholding: apart from large estates assigned to the King and his chief ministers, the land is split fairly equally, at least in one district for which we have a total record, between private and state land. The private land is owned by a numerous class of local nobles, comparable to a squirearchy, and from their ranks it seems provincial governors are chosen. Half of them sublet to a yeoman peasant class, who are believed to be men of substantial incomes. The importance of local estate owners in running local government and regional troop contingents could well reflect, in Chadwick's view, a preceding period in which each region was far more independent and run by the chief landowners as petty chiefdoms. Public land is assigned to a number of people, often high-ranking, under some obligation, probably for fulfilment of official duties. But most of it, in our one complete district, is tenanted out to a group called 'slaves of the deity' who are apparently the majority of the population of that region.[9] Two things are striking: firstly, virtually all the land is owned by the nobility, either by private inheritance or by virtue of their role as officials. Secondly, what about the poorer peasantry, a class that on calculations from the archives and estimates from archaeology of population density, should have been in the majority? There are grounds for seeing it as a serf population, possibly represented by the term used for the majority of state tenants — 'slaves'.

In conclusion, in the archaeological survey data for late prehistoric and early historic Greece, we are possibly witnessing the spatial correlates of socio-economic and political changes of vital importance to the rise and maintenance of highly stratified societies.

To what extent can this process be seen elsewhere, if

Fig. 13.4. Model modules representing changing land use in prehistoric and ancient Greece.

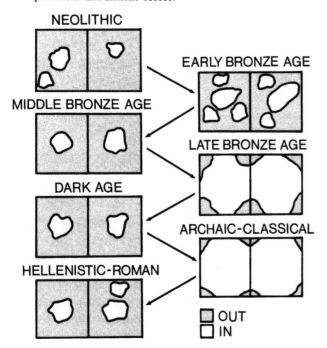

Fig. 13.5. Mycenaean landholding (after J. Chadwick).

MYCENAEAN LANDHOLDING

TEMENOS	:	KING'S ESTATE
		CHIEF MINISTER'S ESTATE
KEKEMENA	:	PUBLIC LAND
KTIMENA	:	PRIVATE LAND

we question orthodox explanations for the inception of pronounced political strata in complex societies?

The development of the Roman republic, then that of the empire, represents the story of a society in which power and decision-making remained in the hands of an elite defined by landholding qualifications (fig. 13.6).[10] This oligarchy pursued single-mindedly its own interests, military prestige and booty, in a succession of wars of conquest, by manipulating the majority of the populace, who were excluded from effective power by landowning inequalities. This land-based power was consolidated through the late republic by the virtual swallowing up of the landscape into large private estates, at the expense of the independent peasant smallholder. He was removed from the land by compulsory service in the wars of conquest, where he went as cannon-fodder to distant colonies, or, returning, became a tenant on the estates or swelled the urban poor. He was most frequently replaced in the countryside by slaves from the wars. The local land-based power was exported with the growth of empire to form new, but regionally rooted, provincial power strata along similar lines. In the late Roman period landholdings revert to an Archaic pattern, with the tying of peasantry to great estates and the corresponding decline of agricultural slave labour. Under this 'colonate' system the bulk of the peasantry were reduced both in law and achieved fact to the status of serfs. The continuity of

this social pattern in the eastern empire over the Dark Ages, and the suspected continuity in parts of the west such as Gaul and the Rhineland, are fundamental to the origins of mediaeval feudal societies in many regions of Europe. But further north and west we must assume virtually a complete discontinuity for the early Dark Ages, for example, in England. However, by mature Saxon times there seems to have occurred in these regions a rebirth of the process of gross landowning differentiation: for the sources, but only imperfectly the archaeology, indicate once again a highly stratified society founded on large estates and defined by a pyramid of landownership. From these two strands, one of continuity, the other of renewal, the mediaeval economy and its dependent socio-political system of land feudalism arose.[11] Professor Postan (1972) quotes with approval the words of Maitland: 'The estate became the state.'

In the light of the evidence presented hitherto for the primacy of landholding in late prehistoric and ancient Greece, and subsequently over most of Europe throughout the historical period till the high Middle Ages, are there other opportunities for application of the model? What of Celtic civilisation and its distinctive aristocratic society? In current views of the origins and development of this society, in particular specific studies of the social system such as that of Crumley (1974), or of Frankenstein and Rowlands (1978), the emphasis is on the role of external trade from the more advanced Mediterranean civilisations as a stimulus to *increased* internal political differentiation. Controlled access to external manufactures and prestige items, as the prime factor in this process, is seen to succeed the earlier operation of internal redistribution to their followers by aspiring nobles of regional craft products and raw materials. Food production is seen as a minor consideration, in some traditional way available as a surplus to the nobles, usually via a kinship network. Could we turn the tables on this approach, and look for evidence that food surplus and the allegiance of primarily subsistence peasants are the fundamental source of wealth and status for the social hierarchy? Let us hypothesise once more that private landownership is crucial, and that we are at a social and economic stage well beyond mere kinship obligations. An argument might now be put forward to the effect that an elite thus established utilises its regional power for obtaining prestige objects and raw materials, but that such goods are not vital to the power of the elite, its grip on the peasantry or the support of lesser nobles; indeed, much is merely a symbol of conspicuous consumption.

The most detailed study of pre-Roman Celtic social structure is by Daphne Nash: The Celts of Central Gaul (1975). She analyses exhaustively all available data from historical sources, the later sagas and law books, and indications from the archaeological record. That evidence points to a society built on local agriculture, in which social status and political power stem from landholding qualifications, and in which the ruling nobility live primarily off large estates manned by tenants, tied labour and slaves, together

Fig. 13.6. The growth of slavery in Roman Italy (after Hopkins 1978).

THE GROWTH OF SLAVERY IN ROMAN ITALY
- a scheme of interdependence

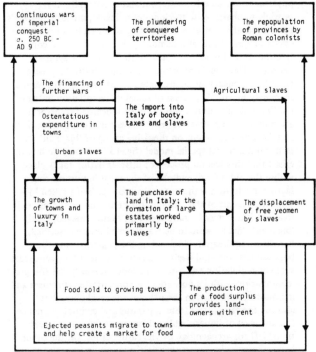

with a share of the crops produced by their free client farmers. The lower classes are only semi-free; the wealthier peasant or yeoman class has a minimal say in political power. Real power resides within the nobility proper, and rests upon the labour and physical support of private armies of free, semi-free and unfree client and slave cultivators.

The whole system was at an extreme point of stress by the Roman conquest: the peasant majority lay under a crushing weight of obligations to the elite. Nash finds Caesar's *Commentary* to this effect totally in harmony with the evidence from all other sources, and, significantly, they argue for such a system being in operation as far back as early La Tène times. The origin of this peasant oppression she places securely within an indigenous process of gross differentiation in landholding, as I would. If this model is highly plausible for La Tène times, with a high level of Mediterranean influence, surely it is even more relevant for Hallstatt Celtic society with its lower levels of external contact? So might we look once more at the neglected importance of the indigenous rather than the over-emphasised exogenous factors creating striking social stratification in Celtic Europe?

Finally, one further insight can be added to the overall analysis offered in this paper (returning to fig. 13.4). Is there any significance to an intensification of land use followed so systematically by a reversion to a different order of use? Let me suggest, following recent discussions on demography and carrying capacity, that the level of totally secure food extraction, or population carried, relative to the total conceivable carrying capacity (a ratio which ethno-historic analogues are beginning to indicate at around 30%), is reflected in our 'low' population periods, whilst the massive land intake of our climax civilisations pushes far beyond this. Preliminary analyses for classical Greece[12] suggest that the level of actual population to potential carrying capacity was as high as 80%, arguably a dangerous over-exploitation seen in the long-term. Mycenaean analyses are being processed. Are the seeds of decline for both civilisations perhaps already visible here, creating a marginal situation merely precipitated by internal conflict, external pressures, or climatic fluctuations? Precisely this sequence *can* be demonstrated for mediaeval western Europe, where expansion into the outfield and marginal lands under the feudal aristocracy brought economic ruin, and was largely responsible for the collapse of feudal society itself.

Notes

1 This essay is a brief summary of a much longer and more detailed study on the same theme, shortly to be published. It can therefore only suggest the nature of the evidence available to support these wide-ranging and, I hope, provocative statements and hypotheses.

2 Some relevant basic data can be found in the publication of my Ph.D. thesis (1977a), and the volume I edited entitled *Mycenaean Geography* (1977b), but much is still in preparation; see also Snodgrass 1977.

3 The indications of a serious decline in settlement numbers and overall population in southern Greece, on the basis of archaeological survey results for the Hellenistic and early Roman periods, are very much as expected from a study of contemporary sources. Amongst these, Strabo, and most especially Pausanias, offer a depressing catalogue of abandoned lands and run-down towns. Of course both periods were dominated by civilisations within which southern Greece formed a provincial limb. But archaeology and history combine to show us that with the decline of the vigorous regional states of the fifth to fourth centuries BC, the area in general undergoes a rapid economic and political regression, to reach a new nadir by the early imperial period.

4 To take the prehistoric fluctuations, for example, this list is representative of the chief factors held to explain cultural and population take-off in standard textbooks by Vermeule (1964), Renfrew (1972b; 1973) and Warren (1975).

5 Clearly by later middle bronze age and early Mycenaean times elites are indicated by tumuli, shaft graves and mansions, and even if the archaeological evidence for Geometric/Archaic times seems to reflect a more abrupt rise of elites coinciding with the population expansion towards the end of that period, semi-historical legends agree on the earlier importance of kings and hence at least a strong individual status distinction. So for both Mycenaean and Classical civilisational origins a degree of differentiation existed prior to the explosion of settlement and massive conversion of the outfield. I would like to offer two distinct and complementary explanations for these early examples of social distinctions: firstly, to suggest that middle bronze age mainland Greece and dark age southern Greece were primarily composed of numerous tribal groupings of small independent, and uncentralised communities, each recognising for limited purposes a tribal leader or 'king'. Such a figure had his prime function as war-leader and possibly as key performer of tribal ritual. Here might be sought the origin or such precocious phenomena as the Mycenae Shaft Graves, or the semi-historic kings of the Dark Ages, all before the tangible evidence for civilisational take-off in terms of settlement numbers and the rise of the palaces and towns that were to form the physical power base for emergent states. Secondly, it is possible to characterise the long-term development of Europe's pre-industrial societies as conforming to a pattern of recurrent cycles of agricultural and demographic expansion and contraction. If, at the lowest points in the cycle, low agrarian densities offer equal opportunities to each cultivator, there nonetheless ensues, as an intimate part of cultural recovery, a seemingly inevitable process of social differentiation in landholding and agricultural wealth. In this localised transformation numerous cultivators grow increasingly impoverished and may become dependent on the rising group of 'big men'. In terms of our initial spatial model (fig. 13.3), it may be hypothesised that this second process of differentiation takes place within the old infield, and one of the most important single factors in addition is the unequal advantage being taken by some individuals of the outfield, for herds and temporary cultivation. But it may be suggested that these achieved, chief/ 'big man' statuses were to be transformed into an ascribed, hereditary squirearchy dominating the peasantry and the possession of the land itself, as a result of the subsequent great surge of population and associated land intake. It was this great 'colonisation' with its potential for concentrated surpluses and manpower, nourished in the palm of the local elite, that allowed the take-off of state apparatus and civilisation; hence the low level of imperishable achievement (with rare exceptions) left for archaeology by the earlier elites. On the other hand, these earlier, 'pre-expansion' elite groups do raise the argument that the social inequalities of these two civilisations

are merely developments from the claimed establishment over
Greece of an alien and superior race, respectively in early
middle bronze age and early dark age times, over indigenous
peoples. There is a growing tendency, to which this author
subscribes, to doubt the arrival of a conquering elite in the
first case quoted. With the Dark Age, on the other hand, there
is little doubt that there *was* a major population incursion into
Greece, of the Dorians, and by historic times it is quite clear in
a number of states that the economy is run on a master race–
serf race, Dorian–Indigene basis (e.g. Sparta, Thessaly). But
the same general pattern of aristocratic–serf society is equally
widespread amongst states where the arrivals were wholly or
partially integrated with the indigenes, or states where the
arrivals made no recorded impact (e.g. Athens, Arcadia). All in
all, then, there would seem to be a much broader process in
action, involving the internal differentiation of social groups on
the basis of the dynamics of landholding. The established
existence of an elite may indeed be a result of ethnic dominance, though more commonly its origin should be sought in
earlier, less pronounced landholding differences; but in any
case the *crucial* element is the manipulation by that elite of the
process of colonisation of the outfield.

6 Cf. Vogt 1969. However, R.M. Adams has kindly pointed out
(pers. comm., August 1980) that a complicating factor with
the historical Mesoamerican Cargo System is its additional
function of preventing external, non-native, individuals from
assuming local government roles.

7 The rise of a landed elite, and its internal differentiation into a
graded hierarchy of regional and finally inter-regional interdependence, will, in this model, have resulted in the breakdown
or replacement of the simpler preexisting tribal structure of
villages and war-leader/ritual leader. A socio-political transformation of this nature has indeed often been claimed for
dark age/archaic Greece on the highly fragmentary indications gleaned from the critical study of myth, epic and later
historical tradition (cf. now Snodgrass 1980). It is tempting to
speculate on an application of this model to the inferred contrast between the socio-political structure of later neolithic and
early bronze age southern Britain, where Colin Renfrew has
argued plausibly for a transformation from 'group centred' to
'self centred' chieftain societies (cf. Renfrew 1979).

8 In addition to the references for Greco-Roman civilisation
cited earlier, cf. Finley 1971; Andrewes 1965; Snodgrass 1979,
1980.

9 The groundwork is in Chadwick 1976, whilst a brief summary
of this recent research appears in the minutes of the
Mycenaean Seminar (London Institute of Classical Studies) for
February 1979. However most of this new work is as yet
unpublished and is presented, with great gratitude, as pers.
comm. from Dr Chadwick.

10 Finley 1973; Garnsey 1976; Hopkins 1978; Jones 1964.

11 For a brilliant analysis see Postan 1972.

12 Data from Bintliff 1977a, and the ongoing Boeotia Survey
project in Central Greece under the joint direction of the
author and Anthony Snodgrass.

References

Andrewes, A. 1965. The growth of the city state, in H. Lloyd-Jones
    (ed.), *The Greek World.* London, Allen Lane, 22–65.
Andrewes, A. 1977. *Greek Society.* London, Allen Lane.
Bintliff, J.L. 1977a. *Natural Environment and Human Settlement in
    Prehistoric Greece.* Oxford, British Archaeological Reports.
Bintliff, J.L. (ed.) 1977b. *Mycenaean Geography.* Cambridge, British
    Association for Mycenaean Studies.
Chadwick, J. 1976. *The Mycenaean World.* Cambridge, University
    Press.
Crumley, C.L. 1974. Celtic social structure. *Anthropological Papers
    of the Museum of Anthropology* 54. Ann Arbor, University
    of Michigan.
Finley, M.I. 1971. *The Ancient Greeks.* London, Allen Lane.
Finley, M.I. 1973. *The Ancient Economy.* London, Chatto and
    Windus.
Frankenstein, S. and Rowlands, M.J. 1978. The internal structure and
    regional context of early iron age society in south-western
    Germany. *Bulletin of the Institute of Archaeology, University
    of London* 15: 73–112.
Garnsey, P. 1976. Peasants in ancient Roman Society. *Journal of
    Peasant Studies* 3: 221–35.
Hopkins, K. 1978. *Conquerors and Slaves.* Cambridge, University
    Press.
Jones, A.H.M. 1964. *The Later Roman Empire 284–602* (3 vols.).
    Oxford, University Press.
Lefebvre, H. 1963. *La Vallée de Campan.* Paris, Presses universitaires
    de France.
Nash, D. 1975. The Celts of Central Gaul: some aspects of social and
    economic development. D.Phil. dissertation, University of
    Oxford.
Postan, M.M. 1972. *The Medieval Economy and Society.* London,
    Weidenfeld and Nicolson.
Renfrew, C. 1972a. Patterns of population growth in the prehistoric
    Aegean, in P.J. Ucko, R. Tringham and G.W. Dimbleby (eds.),
    Man, Settlement and Urbanism. London, Duckworth, 383–99.
Renfrew, C. 1972b. *The Emergence of Civilisation.* London, Methuen.
Renfrew, C. 1973. *Before Civilisation.* New York, Alfred Knopf.
Renfrew, C. 1979. *Investigations in Orkney.* London, Society of
    Antiquaries.
Snodgrass, A.M. 1977. *Archaeology and the Rise of the Greek State –
    An Inaugural Lecture.* Cambridge, University Press.
Snodgrass, A.M. 1979. The problem of scale: heavy freight and
    archaic Greek trade. Unpublished paper presented to the
    'Economic Archaeology' Conference, January 1979, New Hall,
    Cambridge.
Snodgrass, A.M. 1980. *Archaic Greece.* London, Dent.
Vermeule, E. 1964. *Greece in the Bronze Age.* Chicago, University
    Press.
Vogt, E.Z. 1969. *The Zinacantan.* Cambridge, Mass., Harvard Uni-
    versity Press.
Warren, P. 1975. *The Aegean Civilisations.* Oxford, Elsevier–Phaidon.

PART IV

Post-collapse resurgence: culture process in the Dark Ages

Splendid this rampart is, though fate destroyed it,
The city buildings fell apart, the works
Of giants crumble. Tumbled are the towers,
Ruined the roofs, and broken the barred gate,
Frost in the plaster, all the ceilings gape,
Torn and collapsed and eaten up by age.
And grit holds in its grip, the hard embrace
Of earth, the dead departed master-builders . . .
The public halls were bright, with lofty gables,
Bath-houses many; great the cheerful noise,
And many mead-halls filled with human pleasure.
Till mighty fate brought change upon it all.
Slaughter was widespread, pestilence was rife,
And death took all those valiant men away.
The martial halls became deserted places,
The city crumbled, its repairers fell,
Its armies to the earth. And so these halls
Are empty, and this red curved roof now sheds
Its tiles, decay has brought it to the ground,
Smashed it to piles of rubble, where long since
A host of heroes, glorious, gold-adorned,
Gleaming in splendour, proud and flushed with wine,
Shone in their armour, gazed on gems and treasure,
On silver, riches, wealth and jewellery,
On this bright city with its wide domains . . .

The Ruin (translated Hamer 1970, 27)

With these words a Saxon writer, perhaps of the eighth century AD, described the relics of a vanished urban civilisation, separated from him by some three 'dark' centuries. The Roman conquest of west and north-western Europe during the first century BC and the first century AD had brought the various chiefdoms of the area, some of them discussed in Part Two, within the ambit of an efficient imperial administration. For nearly four centuries England was part of a complex urban society. However, with the decline of the Roman empire, towards the end of the fourth century AD, in outlying areas such as England urban society collapsed. The Dark Age had begun.

In this section the archaeology of that Dark Age period, and of the renaissance of complex society which emerged from it, is discussed. A processual or 'anthropological' approach to the problems of this period is new, and holds enormous potential. For although the investigation of Saxon settlements has been prosecuted vigorously for some fifteen years (see Biddle 1976), explanation and discussion has remained very much in the culture historical mould. Emphasis has traditionally been placed upon the written evidence for migrations, and the documentation for the early origins of Anglo-Saxon kingship. The three papers which follow in some senses pioneer new approaches to this material. Its potential relevance to a whole range of processual questions in altogether different contexts and periods is considerable.

Although the case has never been set out systematically, the rise of the Anglo-Saxon kingdoms may reasonably be seen as a classic instance of the reemergence of complex society following a major system collapse. The structure of the empire weakened and collapsed, and just as in comparable cases at Teotihuacan in Mexico around AD 700, or Huari in Peru around AD 800, the hierarchy of urban settlement in England disappeared, to be replaced at first by an archaeologically less obvious population, with a dispersed settlement pattern. And as in these American cases, ranked and then stratified societies developed again, focussed first upon a number of regional centres. Later (as with the Toltec of Mexico, and ultimately with the Inca of Peru), further unification took place and new and more complex polities emerged which were as large or larger than those which preceded them.

In an article which took as its starting point the collapse around 1100 BC of the Mycenaean states discussed in Part Three, I listed some of the common features of this phenomenon of resurgence during the 'Dark Age' aftermath of a system collapse (Renfrew 1979, 483):

Transition to lower (cf. 'earlier') level of socio-political integration:

(a) Emergence of segmentary societies showing analogies with those seen centuries or millennia earlier in the 'formative' level in the same area. (Only later do these reach a chiefdom or 'florescent' level of development.)

(b) Fission of realm to smaller territories, whose boundaries may relate to those of earlier polities.

(c) Possible peripheral survival of some highly organised communities still retaining several organisational features of the collapsed state.

(d) Survival of religious elements as 'folk' cults and beliefs.

(e) Craft production at local level, with 'peasant' imitations of former specialist products (e.g. in pottery).

(f) Local movements of small population groups resulting from the breakdown in order at the collapse of the central administration (either with or without some language change), leading to destruction of many settlements.

(g) Rapid subsequent regeneration of chiefdom or even state society, partly influenced by the remains of its predecessor.

All of these features apply to some extent to the aftermath of the Aegean palace civilisation of Crete and Mycenaean Greece, where following the Mycenaean collapse the city states of the Classical Greek world emerged some three or four centuries later. They apply also to the Mexican case of Teotihuacan. It is widely accepted now (cf. Culbert 1973) that the Classic Maya collapse, and probably that of Teotihuacan also, was essentially the result of internal factors. Population displacements, such as that of the Toltec, were as much the consequence as the cause of the collapse in organisation from which they ultimately benefited.

Each of these points can be illustrated in turn by the Anglo-Saxon case, in the aftermath of the collapse of Roman rule in the province of Britannia around 400 AD:

(a) Evidence for settlements in Britain in the fifth and sixth centuries AD is so scanty that information about social structure must come from the cemetery material, studied by Arnold, and (for Denmark) by Randsborg. There are clear indications of increasing ranking, culminating in the very rich Sutton Hoo burial, which is generally interpreted as the finery of an East Anglian king. There are evident analogies here with the pre-Roman iron age, although it is necessary to travel south to Germany and France, to the rich burials mentioned in Part Two, to find grave goods of the iron age of comparable wealth.

(b) The political units in Britain which emerged during the sixth and seventh centuries, although ruled by kings, are comparable in size and in some cases in actual territory to the polities of the first century BC. Maps based upon the seventh- or eighth-century Tribal Hidage (Loyn 1962, 307; Sawyer 1978, 112) show polities of analogous scale to those in the first century BC and the early first century AD as inferred from the distribution of the coins of the Celtic tribes (Cunliffe 1974, 105).

(c) No truly complex societies survived the Roman collapse in Britain itself, although the chiefdoms of Ireland (Niocaill 1972), largely uninfluenced by the Roman rule of England while it lasted, were not radically transformed by its demise. It was in Rome herself, and through much of Italy and in other areas of south Europe, that state society survived. Rome, although sacked in AD 410 by the armies of Alaric the Visigoth, was never abandoned as Teotihuacan was. From the European standpoint as a whole the events of the fifth century AD were less of a collapse than a transformation, and it was only in the northern and eastern provinces of the former Western Empire that urban society for a while disappeared.

(d) There is some evidence for the survival of Christianity in Britain after the Roman withdrawal (Biddle 1976, 110–11). It was however the mission of St Augustine to the Kingdom of Kent in AD 597 which introduced it as the religion of Saxon authority.

(e) Craft production indeed operated now at the local level for most commodities, until the trading developments of the seventh century, discussed by Hodges, brought more numerous imports. Prestige items were, however, as in many chiefdom societies (such as those of the later bronze age and iron age) made and exchanged on a regional basis.

(f) The arrival of overseas tribes in England is attested from the historical sources, which are to some extent supported by the finds from the early cemeteries. Indeed it was to be predicted that with the withdrawal of Roman rule the pressures, which had led during the late third and early fourth centuries to the construction of the forts of the Saxon shore, would result in local displacements of small groups across the English Channel or North Sea to take advantage of the new vulnerability of the land. The elements of continuity in the life of the country should not however be underrated (cf. Biddle 1974).

(g) The development of Anglo-Saxon society is the subject of the papers here by Arnold and Hodges. The influence of the Roman background was felt in the road system, and perhaps in the establishment of towns in such important Roman centres as London, York, Canterbury and Winchester. It was of course renewed with the reintroduction of Christianity.

These points document some of the elements which the resurgence of complex society in England may have in common with analogous processes in other areas. The thrust of Arnold's explanation is upon the consequences of population increase, and he therefore lays emphasis mainly upon endogenous factors. Hodges, on the other hand, stresses the increase in mercantile activity in the seventh century and subsequently; the very concept of a gateway city implies exogenous activities. The trade is seen as taking place primarily with other ports on the North Sea, rather than with the undoubtedly more complex Merovingian and then Carolingian Empire to the south. In the terms discussed in the introduction to Part Three, the dominant process here would thus be one of peer polity interaction taking place among the communities of northern Europe, rather than a relationship based upon commercial or cultural dominance by the larger polities to the south.

The climate of scholarship until recently prevailing in Anglo-Saxon studies has favoured the terminology of 'kings' and 'kingdoms' to describe the social system, so that the use of terms deriving from an anthropological tradition such as 'chiefdom' and 'state' (Service 1966) has only recently been introduced. It is notable but not altogether surprising therefore that the question as to precisely *when* the Anglo-Saxon state emerged as a stratified society has never been very clearly framed. This is, of course, a matter of definition. Yet it is important to note that, in the conventional terminology relating to early complex societies, King Ine of Wessex, the supposed founder of the port of Hamwih, or indeed Raedwald, King of the East Angles and putative subject of

the Sutton Hoo ship burial, would on current evidence be regarded as the rulers of chiefdoms rather than of states. It could well be argued that the organisational institutions of a state society are not effectively seen in England until the time of Offa in the later eighth century and again under King Alfred the Great in the later ninth century. The earlier kingdoms would, in these terms, be regarded as chiefdom societies.

Since the publication of Randsborg's original and clearminded study (Randsborg 1980), these objections no longer hold for the Viking state of Denmark. Indeed in his paper he discusses the inception of some of the features which lead one to think in terms of a state society. The Danish case is of course fundamentally different from the English one, since Scandinavia was never at any time brought under Roman rule. There was in fact no early state society in Denmark prior to around AD 1000, and hence no state collapse, although Randsborg traces the developments and apparent recessions of the ranked societies of the previous millennium. Indeed he lays no great stress on the position of Denmark, during the empire, lying on the periphery of the Roman world, nor on the effects of the collapse of Roman power in north-western Europe upon that periphery. In his paper, as in Arnold's, the emphasis is upon factors internal to the region under study.

These are pioneering papers, paving the way to a study of the first millennium AD in Europe in the same processual terms which are now usual in discussion of state formation in Mesopotamia (Adams 1966; Wright and Johnson 1975) in Mesoamerica (Flannery 1968; Tourtellot and Sabloff 1972) and elsewhere. The material is splendidly rich: the evidence of the chroniclers and from charters is increasingly being augmented by the results of urban and rural settlement archaeology, and by the skilful use of the extensive coin evidence. In the long term, through the continuing application of such approaches, it may be possible to understand the processes at work in north-western Europe during the first millennium AD more comprehensively than in these hitherto more widely familiar cases of early state formation.

A.C.R.

References

Adams, R.M. 1966. *The Evolution of Urban Society*. Chicago, Aldine.
Biddle, M. 1974. The development of the Anglo-Saxon town. *Settimane di studio del Centro italiano di studi sull'alto medioevo* (Spoleto) 21: 203–312.
Biddle, M. 1976. Towns, in D.M. Wilson (ed.), *The Archaeology of Anglo-Saxon England*. London, Methuen, 99–150.
Culbert, T.P. (ed.) 1973. *The Classic Maya Collapse*. Albuquerque, University of New Mexico Press.
Cunliffe, B. 1974. *Iron Age Communities in Britain*. London, Routledge and Kegan Paul.
Flannery, K.V. 1968. The Olmec and the valley of Oaxaca, a model for interregional interaction in formative times, in E.P. Benson

(ed.), *Dumbarton Oaks Conference on the Olmec*, Washington, D.C., 79–110.

Hamer, R. 1970. *A Choice of Anglo-Saxon Verse.* London, Faber.

Loyn, H.R. 1962. *Anglo-Saxon England and the Norman Conquest.* London, Longman.

Niocaill, G.M. 1972. *Ireland before the Vikings.* Dublin, Gill and Macmillan.

Randsborg, K. 1980. *The Viking Age in Denmark.* London, Duckworth.

Renfrew, C. 1979. Systems collapse as social transformation: catastrophe and anastrophe in early state societies, in C. Renfrew and K.L. Cooke (eds.), *Transformations: Mathematical Approaches to Culture Change.* New York, Academic Press, 481–506.

Sawyer, P.H. 1978. *From Roman Britain to Norman England.* London, Methuen.

Service, E.R. 1966. *Primitive Social Organization.* New York, Random House.

Tourtellot, G. and Sabloff, J.A. 1972. Exchange systems among the ancient Maya. *American Antiquity* 37: 126–35.

Wright, H.T. and Johnson, G.A. 1975. Population exchange and early state formation in south-western Iran. *American Anthropologist* 79: 267–89.

Chapter 14

**The evolution of
gateway communities:
their socio-economic
implications**
Richard Hodges

This paper discusses the concept of the gateway community and its implications for political power. Several examples are cited from early mediaeval history and archaeology, and the evolution of these communities is described and discussed. In particular, it has been possible to identify three major stages of development as a result of extensive excavations of emporia around the North and Baltic Seas. A notable feature of these sites is the planned character of their second stage; this suggests centrally controlled maximisation of trading in these pre-market contexts.

The nature of exchange in ranked societies is increasingly being demonstrated to be more complex than either Service (1962) or Fried (1967), for example, envisaged. In particular, the concept known as redistribution, whereby energy flows into a central agency and is then partly or wholly returned in some other form, has been the subject of considerable reappraisal (Earle 1977; Renfrew 1977). Earle (1977, 226) has proposed the case that redistribution is more significant as a control function for the acquisition of resources to maintain an elite than as a means of sustaining ecologically varied zones within a single political system, as Service, in particular, has argued. Yet the fact remains that as archaeologists we must still investigate the movements of resources, and the patterns of centres to which these resources are related, within a regional framework. It is essentially our perspective of the mechanisms governing these movements which has been altered. Therefore, it still holds that investigations of redistributive centres should enable us to chart economic trajectories as well as to study the development of social systems. Indeed, it is possible that such centres might be used to predict the extent of polities controlled from these points (cf. Renfrew and Level 1979). However, not all ranked societies are administered from finite centres or capitals; in a recent paper Blanton (1976) has shown that a considerable variety of administrative centres is known for complex societies. In particular, it is evident from European mediaeval history that 'capitals' as such were largely the result of state formation processes (Hodges 1982). Previous to this the administration of most of the multitude of post-Roman territories was organised from the particular royal estate at which the king or chief of that territory happened to be.[1]

The reasons for peripatetic kingship and its historical and archaeological character are not well understood. It has been contended that kingship of this kind was intended to preclude the rise of a dominant primate centre(s) and that it was a means of efficiently exploiting the resources of an ecologically varied territory. Equally it may be the product of a community in which there is a comparatively moderate degree of social stratification requiring kingship to be integrally involved with its people at village level (Hodges 1982). The excavated examples of such sites are few: three recently published examples would at least seem to demonstrate their size and complexity. Yeavering in Northumberland was the short-lived seventh-century palace of King Edwin; excavations there have revealed a series of timber long-halls as well as a small timber theatre which might have accommodated as many as three hundred persons. It was here that Bishop Paulinus at Edwin's request preached christianity to the assembled Northumbrian population (Hope-Taylor 1977). The West Saxon kings' palaces at Cheddar (Somerset) have also been extensively excavated to reveal the more modest settlement which witnessed the 941 *witan*, the 'parliament' of lay lords and bishops[2] drawn from the recently unified kingdoms of England. The small cluster of well-built long-halls effectively illustrates the modest size of this parliament (Rahtz 1979) (fig. 14.1). Thirdly, the imperial villa at Ingelheim near Mainz in the Rhineland provides an example of a political centre used by the Carolingian kings (and emperors) (Rauch and Jacobi 1976). This large stone-built enclosure contained several modest monumental buildings but was scarcely more extensive than a late mediaeval castle. In it was housed the administration for a political system that at one point stretched from Bordeaux to Bavaria, and from Hamburg to Cassino.[3]

Peripatetic kingship complicates any spatial analysis of ranked societies since the location of the settlements is usually difficult to determine. Instead, in post-Roman Europe either it is necessary to attempt some ranking of burials, if these occur, in order to obtain some socio-

economic perspective of individual territories, or it is possible to take a different regional perspective using the nodes in the long-distance trading networks. As a rule it is the latter sites which are the most readily distinguishable for the archaeologist, although they tend to be only scantily documented historically as they were not the seats of power.

Primate centres commanding long-distance trade through 'natural corridors of communication and at the critical passages between areas of high mineral, agricultural, or craft productivity' have been termed gateway communities by Hirth in a recent paper (1978, 37). These occur at the interface of different technologies or at the boundaries dividing different levels of socio-political complexity (fig. 14.2). Gateway communities are initially designed by the elite to reinforce their position through the acquisition of resources unavailable in their own territories. However, the passage of goods through these centres and the design of these communities provides us with a perspective of energy flow which would be virtually impossible to detect if we were to study the movement of the elite from estate to estate. Moreover, the evolution of these early mediaeval gateway communities, which must have had populations in the order of two to five thousand persons (Randsborg 1980, 80–1; Hodges 1982, ch. 3) will more accurately reflect social and economic change in the archaeological record than will, for example, structural developments at a small royal site.

Gateway communities first appeared in post-Roman Europe when the seventh-century kingdoms embracing France, West Germany and the Low Countries sought to trade with the smaller, less complex territories beyond their borders. Thus, for example, they traded with certain of the (seven) Anglo-Saxon kingdoms; with some of the multitude of Irish kingdoms, and with some of the Scandinavian kingdoms (see Hodges 1982). The gateway communities on the borders of the more complex primary area, the late Merovingian and Carolingian kingdoms, functioned as stations from which traders set off to trade their manufactured (mass-produced) goods to the less complex territories where production was primarily based at village level. At the gateway communities located on the borders of these secondary territories the traders paused for various periods of time before exchanging their goods for the products of the secondary kingdoms. Carolingian wine, pots, glasses and jewellery, for example, were exchanged for wool, metals and slaves. A few surviving royal letters from this period clearly demonstrate that this trade was cautiously agreed by the kings of the territories involved, and also that it was always monitored directly or indirectly by either kings or their agents.

It is clear that within the secondary areas the manufactured goods were passed on from one hierarchical level to the next, giving the spatial appearance of a dendritic exchange system (cf. Smith 1976). There is slight documentary evidence suggesting that these manufactured goods were given as gifts or receipts as the kings amassed their taxes (foodstuffs, wool, metals), part of which, we assume, was later exchanged at the gateway centre. To what extent this exchange network is truly a dendritic one remains to be tested, especially as the roving palatial administration provides a complicating economic network overlying the tree of networks stemming from the gateway community located on the borders of the territory. In these early mediaeval instances, however, the trading systems appear less exploitative than those examined by Smith in modern contexts (1976). The low level of social organisation required a modest tax burden at this time, and it can be demonstrated from the surviving laws of the period that the peasant farmers were far more affluent than their successors who were subordinated to state legislature (Hodges 1982). Nevertheless, it is apparent that the primary area was gaining raw materials from secondary, satellite areas, and that the elites

of these secondary areas used the relationship to reinforce their own status.

Historians and archaeologists have tended to aggregate the emergence, development and decline of these emporia, assuming their growth to take a linear path. This is often the result of 'before' and 'after' views of these sites, which have not been considered comparatively. In fact, studies of individual emporia in post-Roman Europe have shown them to possess periods of extreme activity and periods of virtual abandonment (Hodges 1982). It is these periods of growth and change, with special reference to the less complex stages, that I wish to discuss here. In particular, I wish simply to draw attention to the sequence of stages through which about a dozen of these sites appear to pass and to comment on the socio-economic implications of these observed stages (fig. 14.3).

The gateway communities in both the primary and the

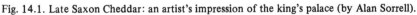

Fig. 14.1. Late Saxon Cheddar: an artist's impression of the king's palace (by Alan Sorrell).

secondary areas can be seen to pass through three major stages which I shall refer to as A, B and C, before in all circumstances there is the emergence of competitive mediaeval markets.

Stage A The first neutral trading sites appear to be the result of more regular long-distance trading systems which probably replaced irregular directional trade to the king, wherever he happened to be. The creation of these gateway communities meant that a king was prepared to chance an alien foothold on his borders once control of his community was stabilised.

Excavations of Stage A sites show them to be little more than impermanent camping-sites similar to the later mediaeval fairgrounds, which operated for short seasons. Only the debris of alien utensils marks out these settlements as a rule. However, at Löddeköpinge in south Sweden sunken huts have been found purporting to show intermittent use then disuse, indicated by the interleaving of drifted sand and occupation layers (Ohlsson 1975–6). In fact, there appears to be no marked rank–size difference between Stage A sites and, for example, the royal, religious or village settlements.

Fig. 14.2. Central place and gateway community hierarchies (after Kenneth Hirth).

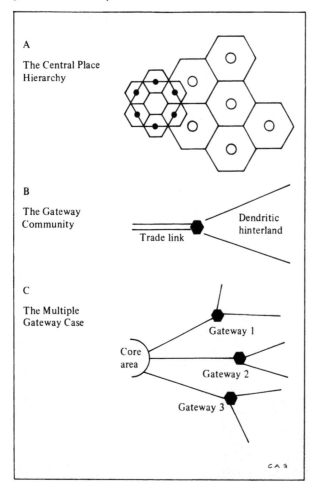

A

The Central Place Hierarchy

B

The Gateway Community

Trade link

Dendritic hinterland

C

The Multiple Gateway Case

Core area

Gateway 1

Gateway 2

Gateway 3

These initial gateway communities were modest responses to newly formalised alliances.

Stage B sites mark an ambitious maximising of the trade between the Carolingian kingdoms and the secondary territories. Indeed, these sites would appear to be the result of new levels of socio-political integration, especially within the secondary territories, as the kings or chiefs attained greater authority. The most extensively examined sites are those at Dorestad, at the mouth of the Rhine, Hamwih (Saxon Southampton), Ipswich in East Anglia, and Haithabu in north Germany (fig. 14.3). Each of these sites has a complex pattern of streets which in the latter three cases appears to have been laid out on a grid. Within the grid pattern lay dwellings and warehouses which were used by alien traders as well as by native craftsmen (fig. 14.4).

The development of these communities appears to reflect the increased needs of the Carolingian system, successfully allying itself with the expansionist goals of the newly formed polities in the secondary areas. Clearly, the interesting feature of these Stage B gateway communities is their origin, and I shall discuss this below.

Stage B sites are clearly primate centres, being five to ten times more extensive in area than any other settlements of the period. Consonant with this, the dendritic flow of goods out of these centres is readily apparent, with imported objects, for example, occurring on all categories of site, sometimes at great distances from the place of importation.

Stage C sites may be more accurately termed solar central places (Smith 1976). These function very differently from the previous two stages, since the community operates primarily as an administrative node within a regional framework where there is less emphasis on peripatetic kingship, and only modestly continues to be a centre for long-distance exchange. Strictly, therefore, these sites are no longer gateway communities, for despite the continuity of settlement, the function of the centre has altered. It is, however, a characteristic of many of these post-Roman emporia that they become administrative nodes in the transition from ranked societies to the formation of the state, maintaining only their localised economic interactions.

Gateway communities of stages A and B are the most appropriate to the study of change within the ranked societies of the post-Roman world. By contrast, the evolution of stage C communities and the emergence of competitive markets would appear to be a concomitant of the formation of the mediaeval states (cf. Hodges 1982; Randsborg 1980). Yet it is quite clear that we are not concerned with a linear evolution of settlements such as Doran (1979) predicts using a simulation model (fig. 14.5), or such as we might expect cultural ecologists to predict (cf. Blanton 1980). In fact, historical archaeology shows that sudden and decisive actions were required, first, to found the trading-places, and then to develop them with civic amenities, including native craftsmen to provide houses, household goods and foodstuffs for the assembled traders. This second

Fig. 14.3. Map indicating the major gateway communities of the seventh to tenth centuries AD in western Europe.

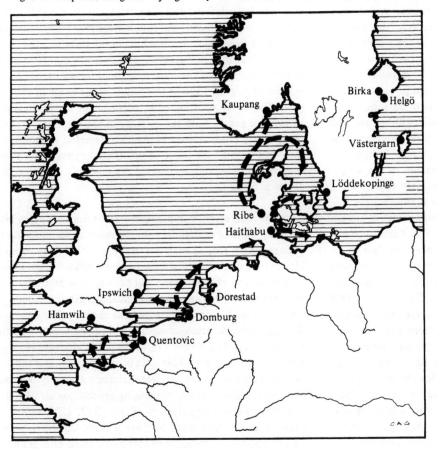

Fig. 14.4. A schematic plan of the street grid at Haithabu, near Schleswig, West Germany (after K. Schietzel).

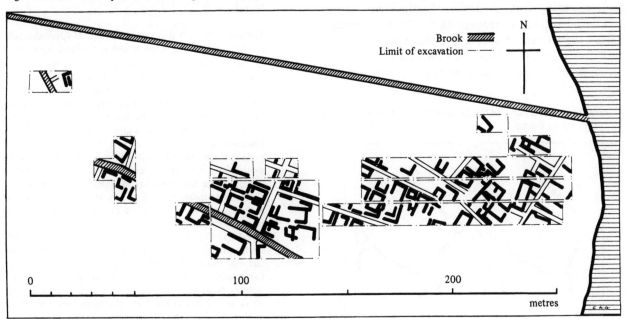

stage, in particular, shows a conscious intention to maximise the flow of goods both within the primary area, and, less predictably, within the secondary areas as well. This evolution illustrates a significant switch from strictly controlled long-distance trade to circumstances where the trade is maximised, with the result that it cannot be rigorously administered. Indeed, at stage B sites exchange can only be monitored at a distance, since the number of persons involved in it is decisively larger. The result will be that craft products of stage B gateway communities are likely to filter out to a localised population, circumventing the hitherto rigorous control of these products maintained by the kings.

Such decisive economic actions not only reflect the expansive aspirations of the Carolingians as they sought to establish an empire, but in the less complex societies beyond their borders it meant a shift from one social horizon to a more complex one *before* there was an increased flow of goods. To some degree the kings of the secondary areas were seeking to emulate the Carolingians, and this might account for their ambitious building programmes. Yet it seems likely that King Ina of Wessex, for example, had established a firm political base encompassing most of southern England before he or his son was able to found the fifty-hectare site at Hamwih, Saxon Southampton. This may have been envisaged as a means of securing long-term power for the dynasty. Similarly, King Godfred of Denmark created the emporium at Haithabu after he had won leadership over a confederacy of chiefdoms. The control of incoming prestige goods will have proved a valuable contributory factor in the consolidation of power within these secondary areas. Historians of the early mediaeval period now stress more than ever the significance of gift-giving as a means of political control and assert the importance of traded goods for this purpose (e.g. Grierson 1959; Charles-Edwards 1976; Sawyer 1977). Equally, we must not underestimate the internal socio-political prestige arising from contacts with foreign courts

through trade (cf. Wallace-Hadrill 1971, 98–123, who discusses Offa's relations with Charlemagne). In the event, the political goals of these two leaders were short-lived although continued Carolingian commercial input sustained the emporia that they had created. The critical point next arose with the collapse of the trading systems for a number of reasons (Hodges 1982); at this juncture the kings of the secondary areas were forced to adapt to the sudden cessation of prestige goods. With the collapse of the trading systems the gateway communities were either deserted or, because they had become the focus of substantial native populations, they began to assume a different regional role, that described above as Stage C.

In conclusion, comparative studies drawing upon historically defined spatial data should assist us to understand change within ranked societies in some detail. They should also permit us to formulate alternative archaeological models of growth and change which will have greater precision than the sometimes vague notions of linear growth (cf. Adams 1975). Gateway communities are the most readily detected sites and offer an archaeologically unique perspective of the passage of goods between two socio-political areas. Moreover, the evolution of these sites is one of the major indications available to use for demonstrating the early mediaeval shift from a subsistence, minimising production strategy to a politically maximising strategy (Earle 1977, 227). The creation and development of these centres, therefore, provide an opportunity to monitor the long-run social changes leading to the birth of the mediaeval European states.[4]

Notes

1 The period described in this essay extends approximately from AD 600–1000. This is the period of the Dark Ages which followed two hundred years of migrations that had in the early fifth century contributed to the collapse of the Roman Empire. After about AD 550 many small stable territories emerged across western Europe; these are usually referred to as the Merovingian kingdoms of France, West Germany and the Low Countries; the Middle Saxon kingdoms of England; the Early Christian kingdoms of Ireland and the pre-Viking (Vendel period) kingdoms of Scandinavia. Some historical sources are available for the Merovingian and later Carolingian (post-700) kingdoms; for the Anglo-Saxon kingdoms and, less fully, for the Early Christian Irish kingdoms. However, there are few historical references to the Scandinavian kingdoms before the later tenth century.

2 The Anglo-Saxon *witan* was an assembly of lay lords and clerics who probably numbered no more than fifty persons, and who aided the king in drawing up sets of laws and in formulating land charters. It was an altogether more modest meeting than, for example, the later mediaeval parliaments which were based in London and included representatives from most parts of England.

3 In this essay the primary area referred to in the text is composed of the Merovingian kingdoms which were to form the core of the Carolingian Empire. There were two principal Merovingian kingdoms: Neustria, covering northern France,

Fig. 14.5. Simulations of the location of gateway communities (after James Doran).

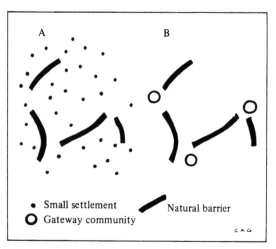

● Small settlement   ▬ Natural barrier
○ Gateway community

and Austrasia, covering the Rhineland and the Ardennes. As the Merovingian dynasty was replaced by the Carolingian so the ambitions of respective kings grew, and by 800 Charles the Great had conquered an area extending from Bordeaux to Bavaria, from the Danish border to Cassino in central Italy. This empire lasted only until the 830s when internal fissioning and external forces contributed to its fragmentation. By about AD 900 many of the later mediaeval states had reached at last embryo form. The secondary areas discussed include the seven major Anglo-Saxon kingdoms which were formed into short-term polities in the seventh, eighth and ninth centuries, but were only unified following the Viking raids of the ninth century; the patchwork of Early Christian kingdoms in Ireland which were often formed into short-lived polities but were only unified by the Anglo-Normans who conquered the island in the later twelfth century, and lastly the pre-Viking (Vendel period) kingdoms of Scandinavia as well as the Viking chiefdoms which were forged into the states of Denmark, Sweden and Norway between the later tenth and twelfth centuries.

4 I am grateful to Colin Renfrew for the invitation to attend the SAA symposium at Philadelphia, and to the University of Sheffield Research Fund which provided a travel grant that made the trip possible. I should also like to thank the editors, Graeme Barker, Klavs Randsborg and Ezra Zubrow for useful comments on the original paper. Philip Rahtz kindly supplied fig. 14.1.

References

Adams, R.M. 1975. The emerging place of trade in civilizational studies, in J. Sabloff and C.C. Lamberg-Karlovsky (eds.), *Ancient Civilization and Trade*. Albuquerque, University of New Mexico Press, 451–65.

Blanton, R.E. 1976. Anthropological studies of cities. *Annual Review of Anthropology* 5: 249–64.

Blanton, R.E. 1980. Cultural ecology reconsidered. *American Antiquity* 45: 145–51.

Charles-Edwards, T.M. 1976. The distinction between land and moveable wealth in Anglo-Saxon England, in P. Sawyer (ed.), *Medieval Settlement*. London, Edward Arnold, 180–7.

Doran, J. 1979. Fitting models and studying process: some comments on the role of computer simulation in archaeology. *Bulletin of the Institute of Archaeology, University of London* 16: 81–94.

Earle, T.K. 1977. A reappraisal of redistribution: complex Hawaiian chiefdoms, in T.K. Earle and J.E. Ericson (eds.), *Exchange Systems in Prehistory*. New York, Academic Press, 213–29.

Fried, M.H. 1967. *The Evolution of Political Society*. New York, Random House.

Grierson, P. 1959. Commerce in the Dark Ages: a critique of the evidence. *Transactions of the Royal Historical Society* 9: 123–40.

Hirth, K.G. 1978. Interregional trade and the formation of prehistoric gateway communities. *American Antiquity* 43: 35–45.

Hodges, R. 1982. *Dark Age Economics*. London, Duckworth.

Hope-Taylor, B. 1977. *Yeavering*. London, HMSO.

Ohlsson, T. 1975–7. The Löddeköpinge investigation: 1. The settlements at Vikhögsvagen. *Papers of the Lund Institute of Archaeology*, n.s. 1: 59–161.

Rahz, P. 1979. *The Saxon Palaces at Cheddar*. Oxford, British Archaeological Reports.

Randsborg, K. 1980. *The Viking Age in Denmark*. London, Duckworth.

Rauch, C.H.R. and Jacobi, H.J. 1976. *Die Ausgrabungen in der Konigspfalz Ingelheim, 1909–1914*. Mainz, Römisch-Germanische Kommission.

Renfrew, C. 1977. Alternative models for exchange and spatial distribution, in T.K. Earle and J.E. Ericson (eds.), *Exchange Systems in Prehistory*. New York, Academic Press, 71–90.

Renfrew, C. and Level, E.V. 1979. Exploring dominance: predicting polities from centres, in C. Renfrew and K.L. Cooke (eds.), *Transformations: Mathematical Approaches to Culture Change*. New York, Academic Press, 145–68.

Sawyer, P.H. 1977. Kings and merchants, in P.H. Sawyer and I.N. Wood (eds.), *Early Medieval Kingship*. Leeds, School of History, University of Leeds, 139–58.

Service, E. 1962. *Primitive Social Organisation*. New York, Random House.

Smith, C.A. 1976. Exchange systems and the spatial distribution of elites: the organization of stratification in agrarian societies, in C.A. Smith (ed.), *Regional Analysis* (vol. 2). New York, Academic Press, 309–74.

Wallace-Hadrill, J.M. 1971. *Early Germanic Kingship in England and on the Continent*. Oxford, University Press.

Chapter 15

**Stress as a stimulus
for socio-economic
change: Anglo-Saxon
England in the
seventh century**[1]
C.J. Arnold

*The paper considers a potential factor in the develop-
ment of complex societies. Stress on a viable, developing,
human society, caused by both internal and external stimuli,
may give rise to a series of discontinuities and cause a
restructuring of the system to maintain its existence. Anglo-
Saxon England in the seventh century, a period of marked
change, is considered as an example. Population density, the
economy, religion, social structure, settlement pattern and
subsistence are examined for the periods preceding, during
and succeeding the seventh century, and apparent discontinuities are isolated.*

Models for the increasing complexity in societies have
laid a great deal of emphasis on a number of interrelated
processes, both internal and external. As a result of such
processes the form, structure and organisation of a society
deviate to satisfy new demands, or tensions. Discussion of
such change has often been concerned with the concept of
the central place, population agglomeration and such social
and economic factors as craft specialisation, redistribution,
inter-regional diversity, imposition and emulation (for
example, Renfrew 1977). What has been most often observed
is the result of change, and an understanding of the forces
(the cause of feedback or the multiplier effect between subsystems) which produce the energy-giving catalyst is often
lost in descriptions of the accumulated deviations.

We are most concerned, here, with deviation amplify-
ing positive feedback processes, often referred to as the
vicious circle or spiral. Change in past societies has been
viewed as continuous systemic change or as discontinuities,
and even as continuous change giving rise to discontinuous
jumps. Inevitably, attention has been focussed on sudden
discontinuities.

The result of deviation in past human societies may be
viewed as the result of a series of interrelated discontinuities,[2] which may not be catastrophic, where sudden
change is produced as the result of a system approaching its
maximum potential. Beyond this there will be stress, an
impelling force producing a sudden increase in minor discontinuities. In other words, the greater mobilisation of
normal tension under conditions of more than usual block-
age. Within a human system one of the most significant
parameters is population density (Clarke 1978, 42–83).
Given a change in population density, the system must adapt
to the change. It is assumed that any one system has a
limited potential and that man is always trying to improve
his position. As Thelen put it, man is always trying to live
beyond his means, and life is a sequence of reactions to stress.
More significantly, man is continually meeting situations
with which he cannot quite cope (Thelen 1956, 184–6).
Interchange among the components of the system may result
in significant changes in the nature of the components them-

selves, with important consequences for the system as a whole. The system's structure may change or become elaborated as a condition of survival or viability. Sudden pressure from external human or environmental forces may be catastrophic. But given a gradual growth of population, often difficult to demonstrate archaeologically, with a response in other areas of the system, gradual change may give way to a series of discontinuities. With the lack of chronological precision in archaeology such a series may seem very sudden. But such peaks of tension may give rise to increasing complexity, a more complex structure almost satisfying the more complex demands (cf. Ashby's law of requisite variety (1956)).

In a viable non-urban society in which the acquisition and distribution of raw materials, production and the movement of products within and without is carried out by specialists and rigidly controlled by a minority in the hierarchy, there may be a climate for growth. A condition for the maintenance of a viable adaptive system may be change in its particular structure, but if the tensions are never completely relieved the system's maximum potential will ultimately be reached. At such a point the system is very fragile. The slightest imbalance from either internal or external forces may at worst cause its collapse, or, more importantly here, produce an environment in which a series of discontinuities must take place for the members' survival. Thus a restructuring takes place to absorb the areas of stress and allow further growth.

The seventh century AD in England is a period of dramatic, if underestimated, change. It is preceded and succeeded by at least two centuries of growth with no marked discontinuities except as the result of external forces. Certain changes are well documented: a change in religion, from paganism to Christianity;[3] the development of ports of trade and urban centres (Biddle 1976, 99–150); a change in pottery production from hand- to wheel-made vessels (Hurst 1976; Evison 1979, 50–7). Other changes are also becoming apparent and can be demonstrated from archaeological evidence: changes in social structure, burial rite, the economy (both as the result of internal practices and external pressures), settlement patterns and subsistence.

Anglo-Saxon England in the seventh century
The initial conditions
Following the migrations of the historical Angles, Saxons and Jutes into England in the fifth century, Anglo-Saxon society underwent a rapid development and period of stabilisation. By AD 600 population, as suggested by the distribution of cemeteries, was located in distinct agglomerated groups largely reflecting the documented kingdoms.[4] Their degree of social and economic development appears to be dependent to a large extent on geographical location. Coastal kingdoms like Kent reveal a more rapid development than landlocked groups like Wessex and Mercia.[5] This greatly

affected the method and success of obtaining semi-precious and precious raw materials such as gold, amber and garnet from the Continent.[6] There is very little evidence for the local exploitation of base metal resources. Settlements were located predominantly on light, fertile but badly drained soils, particularly in riverine locations.[7] Craft specialisation is apparent in the metal and unmechanised ceramic industries,[8] and the evidence for textile manufacture on settlement sites suggests that this may have been more than a craft industry for local consumption (Wilson 1976, 270–4). The import and distribution of prestige raw materials from the Continent and between groups were closely controlled – for instance, amber imported for use on bead necklaces, or gold coin used in the manufacture of jewellery.[9] The organisation of commerce was such that a standardised unit of weight was employed in those areas concerned with direct trade with the Continent.[10] Redistribution, in the institutional sense employed by Earle (1977), may have formed a major bond in the social structure; references to the lord in Old English literature as the 'giver of rings' and 'distributor of treasure' suggests 'the recruitment of goods and services for the benefit of a group not coterminous with the contributing members'.[11]

The structure of these societies is manifested in the disproportionate distribution of wealth represented in the pagan graves, with their accompanying grave goods, in communal cemeteries (fig. 15.1).[12] Such a practice, while a necessary activity within the societies' belief system, is also very wasteful of raw materials. The ends of the spectrum are represented by a group with large membership and no grave goods, and a group with very small membership with large quantities of grave goods, the various rankings having specific ranges of grave goods.[13] Females have a greater average and overall wealth.[14]

The areas with high population agglomeration and the greatest overall wealth, and which display the greatest involvement with international trade, are the first to exhibit discontinuities, documented both in historical records and archaeologically. Thus commercial success may be an important factor here in the speed with which such societies changed. For example, the most extreme case, Kent, displays a high level of overall wealth,[15] extensive international trade,[16] control of intermediate trade with other groups,[17] and the earliest evidence of a formal administration.[18] There are indications of a similar process of development taking place in all areas, although with differing speeds and methods of achievement, for instance the aggression of landlocked groups against coastal communities (see below, p. 127). Thus the slower rate of change in such groups becomes a relevant factor, speeding the discontinuities in others.

It is assumed that such societies continued to expand and change gradually through the early part of the seventh century until, at various times, they achieved what is here termed their maximum potential. This is the point at which tension within the system outweighs the effectiveness of the gradual changes taking place to maintain the system's viability.

Causes of stress

At this stage such societies were under stress; as a result of the assumed growth in population their inadequate systems were responsible for high levels of tension enhanced by external pressures. Significant changes can be observed in the various components. Males now display almost equal overall wealth with females in grave goods.[19] Greater quantities of prestige goods are found in the hands of elite groups; these are no longer buried in communal cemeteries, as was the norm during the sixth century, but are interred under large burial mounds[20] or accorded the exclusive privilege of burial within a church after the initial conversion to Christianity had taken place (fig. 15.2).[21] This class's appetite for ostentatious display, and possibly also the initial diversion of resources and manpower to the church, perhaps find a reflex in the graves of the remainder of the population. Their structure remains the same, but these graves also reveal a marked reduction in the value and quantity of grave goods, perhaps demonstrating a stress on resources (fig. 15.2). There is an inevitable danger of confusing this development with the effects of Christianity on the quantities of grave goods interred with the dead. However, this did not affect the elite graves under mounds, nor is there any evidence in England of any such restriction being imposed by the church.[22]

The availability of raw materials, whose control and distribution provided a powerful cohesive force in the social

Fig. 15.1. Schematic graphs illustrating the distribution of grave-goods in male (above) and female (below) graves in sixth-century Anglo-Saxon England.

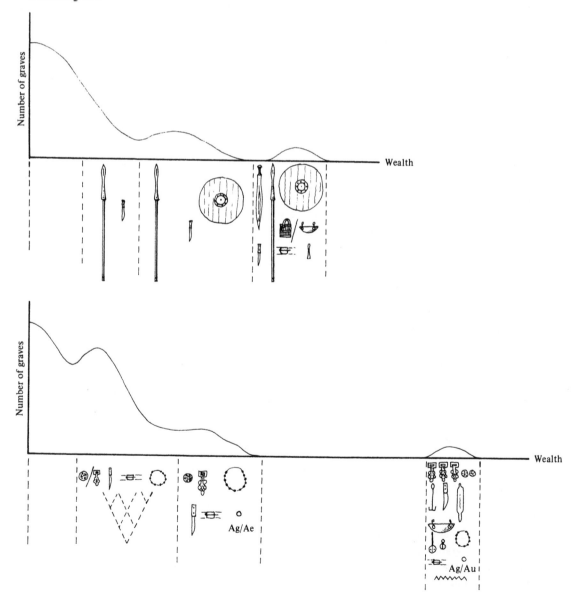

and economic structure, was also under severe pressure. The quality and quantity of imported gold, for instance, was seriously reduced, and exotic forms of metalwork become increasingly rare (fig. 15.3).[23] Attempts to instigate a gold coinage in England towards the middle of the seventh century, for whatever purpose, were unsuccessful.[24]

Under such unstable conditions, with stress in both the economic and the social structure, the decreasing supply and growing demand by at least one class of society invited an imbalance within society as a whole. Such an imbalance could be rectified only by new sources, or methods, of supply of raw materials, or by a marked reorganisation of the bonds in society and the means of wealth acquisition.

Related, or in addition, to such problems were three serious epidemics of plague, between AD 640 and 670,[25] and an increase in aggression against groups who were the earliest to be subjected, and responded to such stresses. The Anglo-Saxon Chronicle relates the various confrontations in the seventh century, the main antagonists being the kingdoms of Wessex and Mercia. Their aggression was either directed towards each other or against the coastal kingdoms (fig.

15.4).[26] The pressures caused by these various sources of stress may have found a temporary release in the new ideology, reflected in the increasing ease with which Christian missionaries found converts.[27]

The final conditions
Aggression, recorded by chronicles and, less directly, in the archaeological record, was directed towards the most developed groups, who, it is argued, had been constrained into responding to stress the earliest. Society became more rigidly organised under royal control, with law codes in the vernacular language which not only stipulate punishment for crimes, but also rank society on the basis of the degrees and nature of landholding.[28] Transference of property and land is also now recorded.[29] International exchange becomes centralised at ports of trade, which develop as centres of intense industrial activity (cf. Hodges, this volume), including the production of slow-wheel-thrown pottery partly replacing the handmade wares of the sixth and early seventh centuries (Hurst 1976; Evison 1979, 50–7). Gold gradually disappears from use in metalwork, and its place is taken by an increasing

Fig. 15.2. Schematic graphs illustrating the distribution of grave-goods in male (above) and female (below) graves in seventh-century Anglo-Saxon England.

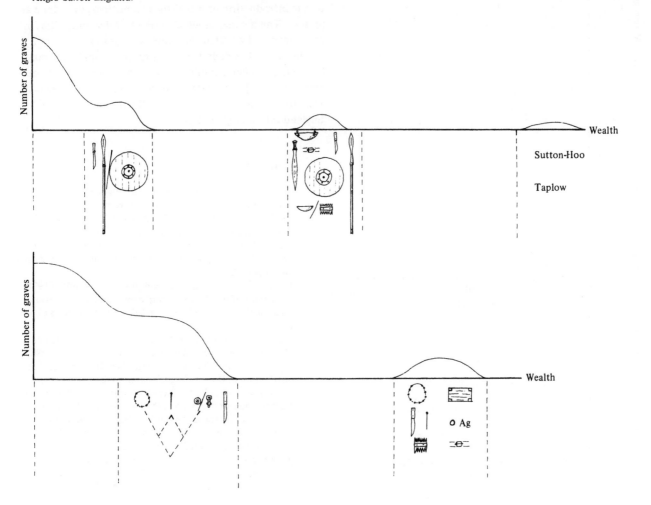

utilisation of imported (?) silver.[30] Silver coinage was minted towards the end of the century.[31] About ninety per cent of the known rural settlements are totally abandoned c. AD 700, and 'Middle Saxon' sites have not been found on rendzinas, shallow calcareous soils over chalk or limestone. This may suggest a shift away from the shallow, light soils favoured in the early period to heavier soils which are more fertile and produce a greater yield per acre.[32] Such a change in settlement location may reflect a reorganisation of the rural economy. Seed remains from excavated settlements indicate a change from hulled to naked varieties of wheat, the former favouring light soils, the latter heavy (D. Hinton, pers. comm.). The laying out of a totally new system of open fields for arable agriculture during the seventh century has been demonstrated in at least one area of England, and may

Fig. 15.3. Graphs comparing various methods of assessing quantities of gold in Anglo-Saxon England, AD 600–700.

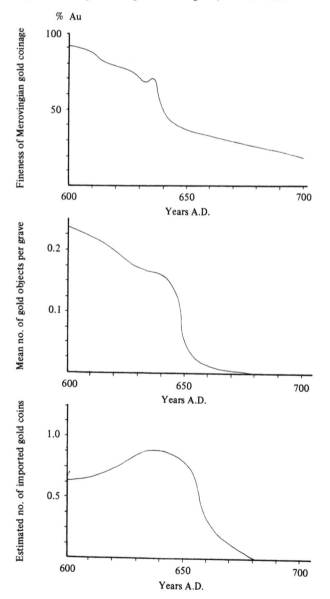

have necessitated a revision of the system of landholding.[33] Individual wealth is no longer displayed in the form of grave goods, although it may be argued that the early churches are not only a cause of stress by diverting resources, but also an expression of power and prestige, an investment in an alternative belief system (fig. 15.4). Major ecclesiastical centres developed in close association with early centres of power and ports of trade.[34]

Discussion

The evidence under discussion consists of changes which at this distance appear important. While some are better documented than others, the seventh century remains a period of innovation. We have sought to provide an explanatory model for such change, but chronological precision is inadequate for a less generalised analysis at present. The model attempts to explain a phase of interesting discontinuities as being the result of stress caused by both internal and external pressures on the system when it had reached its maximum potential, the point at which there had to be far-reaching changes. This phase of discontinuities takes Anglo-Saxon England over the boundary between its 'early' and 'middle' phases, and it is preferable to attempt to explain such changes rather than merely to characterise the boundary by the introduction of wheel-thrown pottery, as is done at present. The manner in which a series of discontinuities in components of a system promotes changes in other components and ultimately leads to a greater complexity may have a more general applicability to the emergence of complex societies. In this case-study the observed changes make a significant contribution to the ultimate unification of England into a single nation.

Notes

1   Anglo-Saxon England conventionally spans the period AD 400–1066, and is subdivided into three phases, early, middle and late, dated 400–650, 650–850 and 850–1066 (or the Saxo-Norman period 850–1150) respectively, on the basis of changes in pottery technology. The seventh century, therefore, bridges the boundary between the 'early' and 'middle' Anglo-Saxon periods.
2   For a recent discussion of discontinuity, see Renfrew 1978.
3   For details of the Anglo-Saxons' conversion to Christianity, see Stenton 1971, 96–176; Sawyer 1978, 91–8; Barley and Hanson 1968.
4   The distribution of pagan Anglo-Saxon graves (see Arnold 1980, fig. 1) reveals well-defined clusters of varying density in Sussex, Kent and the Isle of Wight. There is a more dispersed distribution in Dorset, Wiltshire, Hampshire and the upper Thames Valley. In Essex, there is another dense cluster, with further concentrations along the East Anglian Ridge through Cambridgeshire, spreading out into Norfolk and Suffolk. Further peaks occur in the East Midlands, Lincolnshire, and north of the River Humber on the Yorkshire Wolds. A dispersed pattern is found from the Severn estuary to Northumberland. Attempts have been made to reconcile the archaeological with the historical evidence (Davies and Vierck

1974). For the historical development of the Anglo-Saxon kingdoms, see Stenton 1971, 32–94; Sawyer 1978, 99–131.

5   For an analysis of the relationship between the emerging Anglo-Saxon kingdoms on the basis of archaeological evidence, see Arnold 1980.

6   Amber, either from the east coast or from the Baltic, was utilised in a variety of shapes and sizes as beads worn on necklaces (Jessup 1974, 26). Gold, imported Merovingian and Byzantine coin, appears to have been predominantly reworked into jewellery (Hawkes, Merrick and Metcalf 1966; Brown and Schweizer 1973), normally mercury-gilded on bronze or silver (Oddy 1977). The source of the mercury is unknown, but Spain remains Europe's principal source, which has interesting ramifications if this were the case during the sixth and seventh centuries. Some gold coin was mounted into pendants worn on necklaces. The remainder are found in graves or as stray finds (Metcalf 1974; Rigold 1974). Garnet, cut and polished, was an important element of polychrome gold and garnet encrusted jewellery (Jessup 1974, 25; Arrhenius 1971).

7   116 early Anglo-Saxon settlements are located on the following soil types; stagnogleys 26%; brown earth 15%; rendzinas 12%; argillic brown earth 8%; brown sands 6%; brown calcareous earth 6%.

8   For evidence of pottery specialists, see Myres 1977, 68–83.

The replication of designs of early Anglo-Saxon brooches strongly suggests specialist craftsmen: although not discussed here, see Avent 1975.

9   The unequal distribution of particular raw materials is most apparent from distribution maps. For gold coin, see Rigold 1975, figs. 423–5. For an analysis of the ratio of amber beads per grave in southern England, see Arnold 1980. Kent has a ratio of 16–20 per grave per sq. km for the early Anglo-Saxon period. This may be compared with 6–10 in Wiltshire.

10 Sets of weights and balances have been found in six graves in Kent. Six other balances are known from South Humberside, Cambridgeshire, Northamptonshire, Berkshire and Oxfordshire. The unit of weight is c. 3.1 g (Arnold, forthcoming). For a discussion of the distribution of balances in early Anglo-Saxon England, see Arnold 1980.

11 Earle 1977, 215. For the relevance of rings and ring-giving in Old English literature, see Magoun 1949.

12 For a more detailed analysis of the distribution of wealth in early Anglo-Saxon cemeteries, see Arnold 1980.

13 The generalised groupings of grave goods belonging to particular ranks in figure 15.1 are based on the analysis of a number of cemeteries in southern England (see n. 12). The degree of standardisation is proportional to the quantity of grave goods.

14 In seven sixth-century cemeteries in southern England the

Fig. 15.4. Diagram illustrating the incidence of warfare (closed symbols = aggressor) and church building in Anglo-Saxon England, AD 600–700.

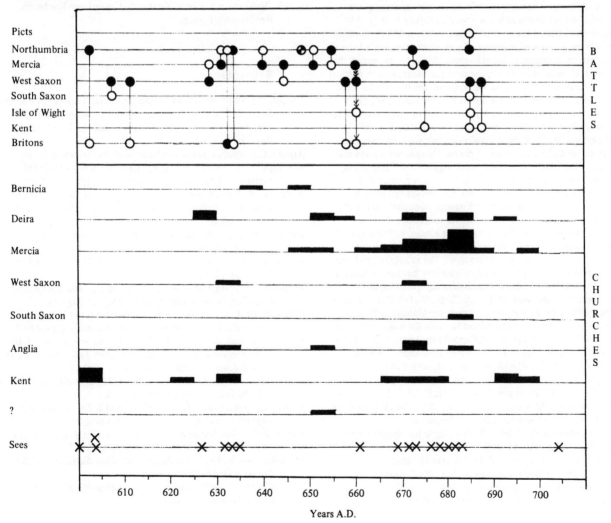

Years A.D.

average for male and female wealth, based on scores ascribed to grave goods, are 21.0 and 54.5 respectively (figures from Arnold 1980, table 4.6).

15   The average wealth score (see n. 14) for sixth-century graves (irrespective of the sex of the individual), in Kent is 30.8 (from sample of 333 graves). This may be compared with Wiltshire and Hampshire where the average score is 28.6 (from sample of 374 graves) (figures from Arnold 1980, table 4.6).

16   For a discussion of the commercial links of Kent with the Continent, see Hawkes 1969, 191; Grierson 1959; Bakka 1958, 59.

17   See n. 19.

18   See n. 28.

19   The average wealth scores for seventh-century graves in southern England are: male 123, female 126. Male graves reveal 5.8 types of object per grave, females 4.4. The figures are higher than for the sixth century due to the inclusion of rich barrow burials. Seventh-century communal cemeteries produce figures of: male 15.5, female 29.7 (figures from Arnold 1980).

20   e.g. Coombe, Kent (Davidson and Webster 1967); Ford, Wiltshire (Musty 1969); Sutton Hoo, Suffolk (Bruce-Mitford 1975; 1979); Taplow, Buckinghamshire (Meaney 1964, 59); Broomfield, Essex (Read 1894); Gally Hills, Surrey (Barfoot and Williams 1976).

21   The kings of Kent were buried in the church of SS Peter and Paul, Canterbury (H.E. I, 34). Note that there are interesting links between early church burials and barrow burial. An early seventh-century hanging bowl was the only surviving grave good in a robbed burial in the seventh-century church of St Paul-in-the-Bail, Lincoln (Colyer and Gilmour 1978). Hanging bowls are a common attribute of seventh-century male barrow burials; most contain a bronze vessel. Morris has suggested that the royal mausoleum at Repton may represent an ecclesiastical continuation of the barrow burial form, 'for it could be seen, in effect, as a stone barrow' (Morris and Roxan 1980, 180).

22   There are no particular grave goods found in early Anglo-Saxon cemeteries which demonstrate that the individuals were Christians. Much of the discussion on this topic has been concerned with the orientation of graves. Hawkes has argued that the predominance of an east—west alignment at Finglesham, Kent 'reinforces the impression that the community had become Christian' (1976, 51). An east—west alignment, however, was common in southern England throughout the sixth century. Rahtz has expressed further scepticism (1978).

23   Finds of gold coin in England are rare after c. 675 and the serious debasement of the imported coin may have caused problems to the goldsmiths (see n. 6). The supply of gold and its effect upon the production of jewellery has been discussed by Avent (1975, 7–8), and the increasing use of silver in ornamental metalwork by Wilson (1964, 9–10). For changes in the supply of gold and silver coinage, see Metcalf 1974.

24   Gold coin was minted in England towards the end of the first half of the seventh century at Canterbury, London and, quite probably, in the upper Thames valley at or near Dorchester (Sutherland 1948, 41–52; Rigold 1975, 663, 676).

25   A great plague is recorded in c. 640 (H.E. III, 13). St Gedd died 'during a time of plague' in 659 (H.E. III, 23) and in 664 there was 'a sudden plague, which first decimated the southern parts of Britain and later spread to the province of the Northumbrians' (H.E. III, 27). The plague had spread amongst the East Saxons by 665 (H.E. III, 30). Bede records a plague in Lichfield in c. 669 (H.E. IV, 3). See also Rackham 1979.

26   For a more detailed examination of the distribution of weaponry in early Anglo-Saxon graves, and of the incidence of warfare in the seventh century, see Arnold 1980.

27   Bede records the first conversion of the various kingdoms in the following years: Kent 597; East Saxons 604; Northumbria 625–7; East Anglia 627; Lindsey 628; West Saxons 635; Middle Anglia 653; Mercia 655; South Saxons c. 681; Isle of Wight 686.

28   Laws were first issued in Kent between 602 and 603?, and in Wessex between 688 and 694 (Whitelock 1979, 391–407; Attenborough 1922, 2–5).

29   The earliest charter preserved in a contemporary text is dated 679 and supports the authenticity of several slightly earlier documents with similar formulae. For details of charters, see Sawyer 1968.

30   See n. 23.

31   The earliest silver coinage was minted in the last quarter of the seventh century, although the actual date remains uncertain. For a discussion of coinage during the seventh century, see Metcalf 1974.

32   Nineteen Middle Saxon settlements are located on the following soil types: brown earth 32%; calcareous pelosols 15%; brown calcareous earths 15%; alluvial gley 10%. See Arnold and Wardle 1981.

33   For the reorganisation of field layout, see Hall 1979; and for changes in the concept of land ownership, see Sawyer 1978, 155.

34   The relationship of Winchester and Hamwih (see Hodges, this volume) and the history of other Saxon ports is discussed by Biddle (1976, 112–20). Similar relationships may have existed elsewhere, e.g. Eastry/Sandwich; Canterbury/Fordwich; Rendelsham/Ipswich.

References

Arnold, C.J. 1980. Wealth and social structure: a matter of life and death, in P. Rahtz, T. Dickinson and L. Watts (eds.), *Anglo-Saxon Cemeteries 1979*. Oxford, British Archaeological Reports, 81–142.

Arnold, C.J., forthcoming. The balance of Anglo-Saxon Trade.

Arnold, C.J. and Wardle, P.J. 1981. Early Medieval settlement patterns in England. *Medieval Archaeology* 25: 145–9.

Arrhenius, B. 1971. Granatschmuck und Gemmen aus Nordischen Funden des frühen Mittelalters. Ph.D. dissertation, University of Stockholm.

Ashby, W.R. 1956. *An Introduction to Cybernetics*. London, Chapman and Hall.

Attenborough, F.L. 1922. *The Laws of the Earliest English Kings*. Cambridge, University Press.

Avent, R. 1975. *Anglo-Saxon Garnet Inlaid Disc and Composite Brooches*. Oxford, British Archaeological Reports.

Bakka, E. 1958. On the beginnings of Salin's Style I in England. *Universitet I Bergen Arbok, Historisk-antikvarisk rekke* 3.

Barfoot, J.F. and Williams, D.P. 1976. The Saxon barrow at Gally Hills, Banstead Down, Surrey. *Research Volume of the Surrey Archaeological Society* 3: 59–76.

Barley, M.W. and Hanson, R.P.C. (eds.) 1968. *Christianity in Britain 300–700*. Leicester, University Press.

Biddle, M. 1976. Towns, in D.M. Wilson (ed.), *The Archaeology of Anglo-Saxon England*. London, Methuen, 99–150.

Brown, P.D.C. and Schweizer, F. 1973. X-ray fluorescent analysis of Anglo-Saxon jewellery. *Archaeometry* 15: 175–92.

Bruce-Mitford, R. 1975. *The Sutton Hoo Ship Burial, I.* London, British Museum Publications.

Bruce-Mitford, R. 1979. *The Sutton Hoo Ship Burial, II.* London, British Museum Publications.

Clarke, D.L. 1978. *Analytical Archaeology* (2nd edn). London, Methuen.

Colgrave, B. and Mynors, R.A.B. (eds. and Trans.) 1969. *Bede's Ecclesiastical History of the English People.* Oxford, Clarendon Press.

Colyer, C. and Gilmour, B. 1978. St Paul-in-the-Bail, Lincoln. *Current Archaeology* 63: 102–5.

Davidson, H.R.E. and Webster, L. 1967. The Anglo-Saxon burial at Coombe (Woodnesborough), Kent. *Medieval Archaeology* 11: 1–41.

Davies, W. and Vierck, H. 1974. The contexts of Tribal Hidage: social aggregates and settlement patterns. *Frühmittelalterliche Studien* 8: 223–93.

Earle, T.K. 1977. A reappraisal of redistribution: complex Hawaiian chiefdoms, in T.K. Earle and J.E. Ericson (eds.), *Exchange Systems in Prehistory.* New York, Academic Press, 213–32.

Evison, V.I. 1979. *A Corpus of Wheel-Thrown Pottery in Anglo-Saxon Graves.* London, Royal Archaeological Institute.

Grierson, P. 1959. Commerce in the Dark Ages: a critique of the evidence. *Transactions of the Royal Historical Society*, 5th series, 9: 123–40.

Hall, D.N. 1979. New evidence of modifications in open-field systems. *Antiquity* 53: 222–4.

Hawkes, S.C. 1969. Early Anglo-Saxon Kent. *Archaeological Journal* 126: 186–92.

Hawkes, S.C. 1976. Orientation at Finglesham: sunrise dating of death and burial in an Anglo-Saxon cemetery in East Kent. *Archaeologia Cantiana* 92: 33–51.

Hawkes, S.C., Merrick, J.M. and Metcalf, D.M. 1966. X-ray fluorescent analysis of some Dark Age coins and jewellery. *Archaeometry* 9: 98–138.

Hurst, J.G. 1976. The pottery, in D.M. Wilson (ed.), *The Archaeology of Anglo-Saxon England.* London, Methuen, 283–348.

Jessup, R.F. 1974. *Anglo-Saxon Jewellery.* Aylesbury, Shire Archaeology.

Magoun, F.P. 1949. On the Old-Germanic altar- or oath-ring (stallah-ringer). *Acta Philologica Scandinavica* 20: 277–93.

Meaney, A. 1964. *A Gazetteer of Early Anglo-Saxon Burial Sites.* London, George Allen and Unwin.

Metcalf, D.M. 1974. Monetary expansion and recession: interpreting the distribution patterns of seventh- and eighth-century coins, in J. Casey and R. Reece (eds.), *Coins for the Archaeologist.* Oxford, British Archaeological Reports, 206–23.

Morris, R. and Roxan, J. 1980. Churches on Roman buildings, in W. Rodwell (ed.), *Temples, Churches and Religion: Recent Research in Roman Britain.* Oxford, British Archaeological Reports, 175–209.

Musty, J. 1969. The excavation of two barrows, one of Saxon date, at Ford, Laverstock, near Salisbury, Wiltshire. *Antiquaries Journal* 49: 98–117.

Myres, J.N.L. 1977. *A Corpus of Anglo-Saxon Pottery of the Pagan Period.* Oxford, University Press.

Oddy, W.A. 1977. Gilding and tinning in Anglo-Saxon England, in W.A. Oddy (ed.), *Aspects of Early Metallurgy.* London, Historical Metallurgy Society, 129–34.

Rackham, J. 1979. *Rattus rattus*: the introduction of the black rat into Britain. *Antiquity* 53: 112–20.

Rahtz, P. 1978. Grave orientation. *Archaeological Journal* 135: 1–14.

Read, C.H. 1894. Account of the exploration of a Saxon grave at Broomfield, Essex. *Proceedings of the Society of Antiquaries* 15: 250–5.

Renfrew, C. 1977. Trade as action at a distance: questions of integration and communication, in J.A. Sabloff and C.C. Lamberg-Karlovsky (eds.), *Ancient Civilisation and Trade.* Albuquerque, University of New Mexico Press, 3–60.

Renfrew, C. 1978. Trajectory discontinuity and morphogenesis: the implications of catastrophe theory for archaeology. *American Antiquity* 43: 203–22.

Rigold, S. 1974. Coins in Anglo-Saxon burials, in J. Casey and R. Reece (eds.), *Coins and the Archaeologist.* Oxford, British Archaeological Reports, 201–15.

Rigold, S. 1975. The Sutton Hoo coins in the light of the contemporary background of coinage in England, in R. Bruce-Mitford, *The Sutton Hoo Ship Burial, I.* London, British Museum Publications, 653–77.

Sawyer, P.H. 1968. *Anglo-Saxon Charters. An annotated list and bibliography.* London, Royal Historical Society.

Sawyer, P.H. 1978. *From Roman Britain to Norman England.* London, Methuen.

Stenton, F.M. 1971. *Anglo-Saxon England* (3rd edn). Oxford, Clarendon Press.

Sutherland, C.H.V. 1948. *Anglo-Saxon gold coinage in the light of the Crondall Hoard.* Oxford, University Press.

Thelen, H.A. 1956. Emotionality and work in groups, in L.D. White (ed.), *The State of the Social Sciences.* Chicago, University Press, 184–6.

Whitelock, D. (ed.) 1979. *English Historical Documents, I, c. 500–1042* (2nd edn). London, Eyre and Spottiswoode.

Wilson, D.M. 1964. *Anglo-Saxon Ornamental Metalwork 700–1100 in the British Museum.* London, British Museum.

Wilson, D.M. 1976. Craft and industry, in D.M. Wilson (ed.), *The Archaeology of Anglo-Saxon England.* London, Methuen, 253–82.

Chapter 16

Rank, rights and resources — an archaeological perspective from Denmark
Klavs Randsborg

In the study of ranked societies too little attention has been paid to the importance of differential access to resources. The later prehistory of Denmark is surveyed with regard to evidence of changes in control of land, cattle, etc. Periods of expansion of settlement, and optimal climate, demonstrably saw less strict norms of inheritance of mobile wealth, as is evident from the richness of burial goods signalling status rivalry. Periods of contraction of settlement, such as the beginning of the first millennia BC and AD, see some intensification of production and new forms of settlement sites: for instance, in the phase around 300 AD the coming of very big regular farmsteads sitting on large 'private' crofts. This system is accompanied by poor graves in spite of the existence of a clear social stratification. Other aspects briefly discussed of the rank–resource linkage and its archaeological manifestations are, besides long-distance trade and warfare, the growing social complexity in the mentioned area, culminating in the Viking Age state at 1000 AD, with diminishing feud but significant expansion of private rights of land.

Ranked societies have gradually won a status as an intermediate form between unstratified societies and states. This was clearly demonstrated, for instance, by Service (1971), whose ideas have often been adopted by archaeologists.[1] In the studies of the structure of ranked societies the focus has often been on the chief and his supposed socio-economic role in the redistribution of the products and services of the society (e.g. Renfrew 1973). Support for this notion was found, for instance, in Sahlins's Polynesian studies (1958), where the degree of social stratification seemed to vary with the level of diversity of the environment; the chiefs were collecting and redistributing the products of the various sub-environments of the chiefdom. Lately this perspective has been somewhat challenged by stressing the point that the single household usually is relatively independent of the chief in terms of provisions (Peebles and Kus 1977). We ought to consider whether or not chiefly redistribution of subsistence and other basic goods is only associated with communities where the population belongs to the same or a related kin-group: in other words, where the kinship structure is 'elementary' (Lévi-Strauss 1969). The old Germanic societies, for instance, had an open kinship-structure which did not correspond to the political groupings in society, and redistribution of basic goods seems to have played a minor role in the social economy.[2] The position of the chiefs would therefore be dependent on other abilities, like organisation of internal markets and external exchanges, support for or heading of religious activities and war-parties, in addition to general leadership in political and judicial affairs. Within such a framework the chiefs function in a rather *ad hoc* way and are much dependent on their own economic resources, not only to perform the mentioned 'services', but also to sustain their households, their followers and, very important, the specialist craftsmen. Therefore, we cannot discuss chiefdoms without considering the resources of the chief and, for that matter, of the whole elite. Tribute and gifts to the chief are significant, but what really matters are his own economic prerogatives in the society. In this context the development and changes in the rights of property of an individual or 'private' character are very important, especially with regard to cattle, land and other basic resources (cf. Fried 1967; Randsborg 1980). In societies with a high degree of local autonomy in subsistence production, the emergence of differences in household size, or simply in the numbers of various classes of households, may bring about significant economic distinctions in the population. These are of special importance combined with and sustained by differences in social, political and ritual rank. A petty class of economically favoured groups in this respect rather independent of chiefly regulation, would markedly affect the character of the production and distribution of goods, especially in more developed ranked or pre-state societies.

In fact, we expect the role of 'private' property to become more important with the emergence of more complex societies. We also expect this development to correlate with a general trend towards stricter patterns of inheritance. Such patterns should be detected in the social attitudes towards death, where discontinuity in the deposition of costly artefacts with the deceased may reflect changes in the attitude to property, or rather, the emergence of 'property' itself, together with stricter norms of inheritance. We may also be in the position to study the sphere of 'the private' in the plan of settlements, for instance in the fencing of the farmsteads, or in the size and inner structure of the buildings. Such variations should be examined in conjunction with the general changes in subsistence and with an open eye to the potential impact of foreign contacts on the social structure, especially through trade.

In Denmark, archaeological data seem to be quite suitable for a discussion of models of society which, as indicated above, take into account the control and social distribution of the basic resources, especially those of chief and elite. In addition, we have here a fine opportunity to demonstrate the importance of the external exchanges for the office of the chief. We are considering the so-called bronze and iron ages (second and first millennium BC and first millennium AD, the bronze age ending at about 500 BC) and we take our point of departure from the burial data which have demonstrated important facets of the social development in the region.

The early bronze age of the second millennium BC saw much differentiation in burial wealth (fig. 16.1), seemingly corresponding to variations in social rank, since the symbols of political offices such as stools, staves, certain badges etc. are only found in the wealthiest (male) interments (Randsborg 1975). The graves are, basically, inhumations in

mounds. Around 1000 BC cremation becomes the exclusive category of burial, often in the form of small cemeteries of poorly equipped secondary graves in the earlier mounds. In spite of the modest graves we still assume a ranked society, as demonstrated by the occurrence of costly artefacts of gold and of foreign imports in some of the cremations, and by the conspicuous ritual trumpets and shields, golden cups, sets of exclusive jewellery, weapons, helmets, bronze buckets etc. found, probably as offerings, in the bogs and in other places (Broholm 1946–9; Thrane 1975). (It should be added that gold, copper and tin do not occur naturally in Denmark, nor in its neighbouring regions.)

In the earliest iron age, immediately after 500 BC, the cemeteries grew in size and were now separate from the earlier mounds. Also in this period we have poorly equipped graves, but conspicuous artefacts from other finds (Becker 1961; Brøndsted 1960). Around the birth of Christ, however, burial wealth again became common, comprising lavish Roman luxuries (Eggers 1951; Hansen 1976) and occurring up to about AD 300 when a new phase started, with only poorly equipped graves. From the beginning of the Christian era onwards the burials were not infrequently inhumations, but cremations were very common too.

The burial data of the close of the iron age, the Viking period, starting about AD 800 and ending a couple of centuries later, are also modest, apart from an interesting series of wealthy graves from the tenth century AD (Randsborg, forthcoming). The tenth century sees the first formation of a state society in the Danish region; a state was founded in the west, and around the year AD 1000 all of Denmark was integrated (Randsborg 1980). The wealthy graves comprise a group of high-ranking cavalrymen with full military equip-

Fig. 16.1. Distribution of wealth in male graves of Period II of the early bronze age in Denmark (second half of the second millennium BC) as measured by the amount of bronze in the grave; gold, if present, is given the value 1:100 grammes bronze. (Redrawn after Randsborg 1975.)

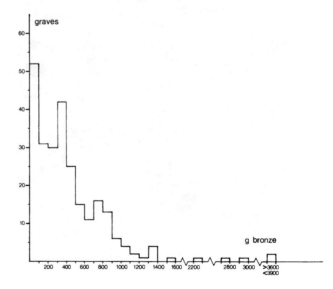

ment who were buried along the perimeter of the earliest state, and there only (fig. 16.2). Another type of interment, burial inside a carriage, often in exquisite garments, was a prerogative for women of the new ruling echelons.

The evidence from the Viking period points to a relation between the presence or absence of burial wealth, or even special types of graves, and the social position of the deceased. In a situation where this role is not a long-established one, as in the case of the cavalrymen, who owed their warrior position to the new state and not to the traditional system, the standing of the deceased might be emphasised at burial by various sumptuary rules. Other observations from the Viking age point in the same direction. The memory runestones, for instance, were only erected when and where the inheritance of status and property did not follow the traditional lines (Randsborg 1980, 25ff.).

It is tempting to extend these findings to the two earlier periods with wealthy graves: the early bronze age of the second millennium BC, and the iron age centuries around the birth of Christ. In those periods the societies were undoubtedly socially stratified, like the late Viking age state, but, of course, much smaller and simpler than this. For instance, in the Viking age the wealthy graves were of rather limited geographical distribution and belonged to only a few of the magnates. For the early bronze age, however, we have a sample suggesting that we are dealing with all the prominent personages, scattered throughout the region. The same holds true for the gradient of wealthy graves from the centuries around the birth of Christ, when, on the other hand, there are distinct geographical asymmetries in the distribution of Roman imports. This would indicate the coming of centres of exchange or of political mobilisation for export,

Fig. 16.2. Distribution of cavalrymen graves (small dots), royal fortresses and fortifications (large dots) and the royal burial ground and farmstead at Jelling in Jutland (Jylland) in the 10th century AD (late Viking Age). (Cf. Randsborg 1980, 126f.)

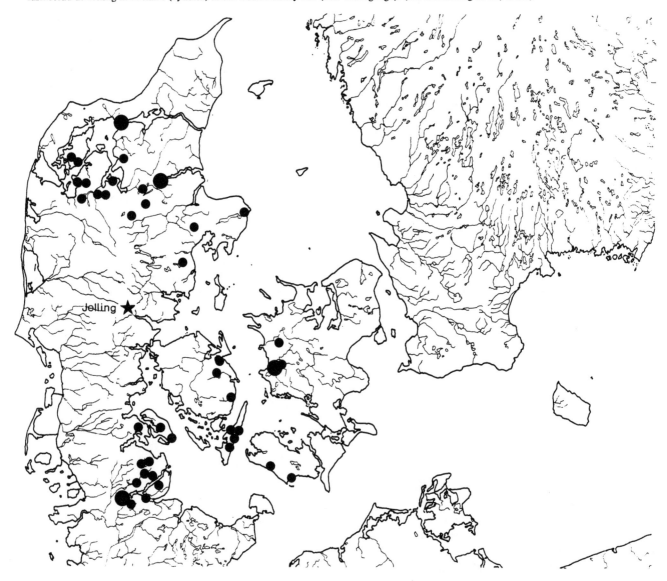

but not of a market economy, which would have produced a more even pattern of distribution.

It is difficult to know why the earlier periods of rivalry at burial started, but it is clear that the costly, traded goods played an important role as a medium for display. However, other periods of intensive trading – the late bronze age, the centuries around AD 400, and the early Viking age – have very few wealthy graves. Therefore, we should look for an explanation which takes the internal patterns of production and, especially, the social structure into account. In the following discussion we shall study the changes in subsistence and settlement during the bronze and iron ages, first and foremost with regard to distinctions in property.

The early bronze age was a period of expansion of the cleared land, or rather, the end of one. In the late bronze age, starting at the close of the second millennium BC, the areas of farming and pastures were reduced on marginal lands under the impact of harder weather conditions (fig. 16.3) (Randsborg 1980, 45ff., cf. LaMarche 1974; Hammer *et al.*, forthcoming). Before the birth of Christ the climate stabilised on a rather warm level and settlement again expanded. A new phase of deterioration of the climate started in the third century AD, leading to another period of interruption and

change in the settlement, accompanied by severe violence (Randsborg 1980, 48f.).[3] From this time onwards costly burial goods tended, as we have seen, to disappear from the record.

Altogether, the warm periods of expansion of settlement saw wealthy graves, while the intermittent phases of colder weather conditions and a contracting settlement had less conspicuous interments in spite of a continuation of the socio-political milieu. (This is not to ignore the fact that settlement was on a general track of expansion, nor that the society did become more complex and socio-economically differentiated over time.) There are no indications that the ranking systems broke down during the periods without wealthy graves. Seemingly, the phases of expansion saw less fixed norms of inheritance of costly mobile wealth, which was being interred in the graves to characterise the deceased and his social milieu. Thus, the standing of the high-ranking personages was continually demonstrated at death, and it is tempting to interpret this example of status rivalry in terms of less fixed, challenged, norms of succession to social position, cattle and land as well. A similar observation was inferred from the wealthy late Viking age interments. In fact, the late Viking age was also a period of optimum climate

Fig. 16.3. Correlations of climate, natural environment and settlement, major forms of subsistence, and relative population sizes for the period about 1500 BC to 1500 AD (1500 BC = early bronze age, 750 BC = late bronze age, 0 AD = early iron age, 500 AD = late iron age, 1000 AD = (late) Viking Age, 1500 AD = latest middle ages).

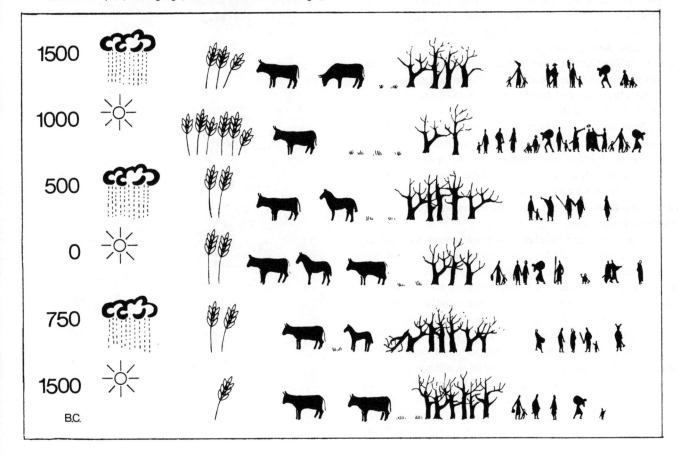

with a marked expansion of settlement, but, as mentioned above, the wealthy graves related to special cases, and we have no general revival of the earlier practices. In this period the social system of inheritance was rigorous (and had, no doubt, long been so). It was not altered, only shaken, by the emergence of the state. The formation of the state was, however, accompanied by a marked development in the private control of resources, as is very evident from the settlement data, where large magnate estates, for instance, are emerging during the late Viking age, around AD 1000.

In the Danish case the privately controlled basic resources are considered the foundation of the position of chiefs and elites, as was outlined at the beginning of this paper. We would therefore expect the development of society to correlate with changes in this sector, which can also be well studied from the settlement sites. It is of special interest to contrast the developments in settlement sites with the above notion of expansions and contractions of the settled area, possible intensification periods of production, and discontinuities in burial practices with regard to grave goods.

The settlement finds from the early bronze age are, unfortunately, very few, and it would be premature to generalise from these data; however, the house structures seem to be relatively modest in size. In the late bronze age and the earlier iron age we have an open settlement pattern where the hamlets were moving around on their domain at longer intervals of time (Becker 1965, 1968a, 1968b, 1971, 1972; Hvass 1975). In the late bronze age the houses were large, perhaps built for extended families, while the farmsteads from the beginning of the iron age, the latter half of the first millennium BC, were smaller and often with a stable. In this period the basic social unit of production seems to have been the nucleated family with direct control over its livestock. In spite of the obvious distinctions in the wealth of cattle from farmstead to farmstead, the villages are often surrounded by a common fence which may radiate from the largest farm, probably the headman's. In the period around the birth of Christ, which saw much status rivalry at burial, the farmsteads were also surrounded by 'private' fences close to the structures. However, the private area was still a relatively limited one.

More important changes took place around AD 300, or at the same time as wealthy graves disappeared again and harsher climatic conditions called for an intensification of production and a retreat from more marginal lands. The villages were totally reorganised and became rather permanent (Hvass 1978, 1979). The layout was regular, with extensive fences around the farmsteads, which were built on large rectangular crofts, but there was no longer any common fence (fig. 16.4). The constructions were also larger than before, and the main buildings now held several rooms including big stables (fig. 16.5). This would indicate a complex pattern of activities and probably also the addition of a number of servants, or family members, to the core-family of

the owner. The expansion of the private space and sphere was most probably accompanied by more concrete patterns of inheritance, like the ones predicted from the synchronous change in burial rites, since not every family could aspire to a farmstead. These observations would indicate that the wealthy strata and the 'chiefs' were now in command of larger personal resources than ever before.

The next step in this direction was taken in the late Viking age which, as mentioned above, saw the formation of the Danish state (Randsborg 1980). We observe a connection between the development of the state and a major change in settlement, with its economic rationale in the subsistence sphere, where cultivation of cereals, favoured by certain types of soil, was becoming very important due to a rapid population growth. In the present case the emergence of magnate estates in the villages is significant (Hvass 1979). The estates have very large, fenced crofts and a total separ-

Fig. 16.4. Part of the fourth-century AD iron age village at Vorbasse in Mid-Jutland (Jylland); cf. fig. 16.5. (After Hvass 1978.)

ation of the owner's fine dwelling (matched only by the halls of the royal fortresses) from the other farm buildings. The estates indicate, first of all, a social difference in access to land which was not seen on the village level in any earlier period. Secondly, they point to the emergence of important distinctions in living standards among the rural population. In short, we see another example of the relation between social development and 'private' rights to the resources.

However, this is only part of the story. Other important economic institutions of the state, like the petty townships, directed at international trade and craft production, regulated and taxed by the Danish kings, were first estab-

lished two hundred or more years before the late Viking age of around AD 1000. The same holds true for the beginning of a kind of incipient bureaucracy and for permanent royal command of larger military forces (Randsborg 1980, 11ff.). In fact, the early Viking age also illustrates several of the characteristics of an 'heroic', stratified society, between a simpler chiefdom and the true state. Some of these characteristics are important for our discussion of the roles of chiefs and 'kings' and of their economic position and prerogatives.

For instance, international trade was of very great significance to the royalty and other magnates. The kings

Fig. 16.5. Farmstead (black outline) from the fourth-century AD iron age village at Vorbasse in Mid-Jutland (Jylland); cf. fig. 16.4 (middle, left). (Note iron ovens outside the south-west corner of the fence.) (After Hvass 1978.)

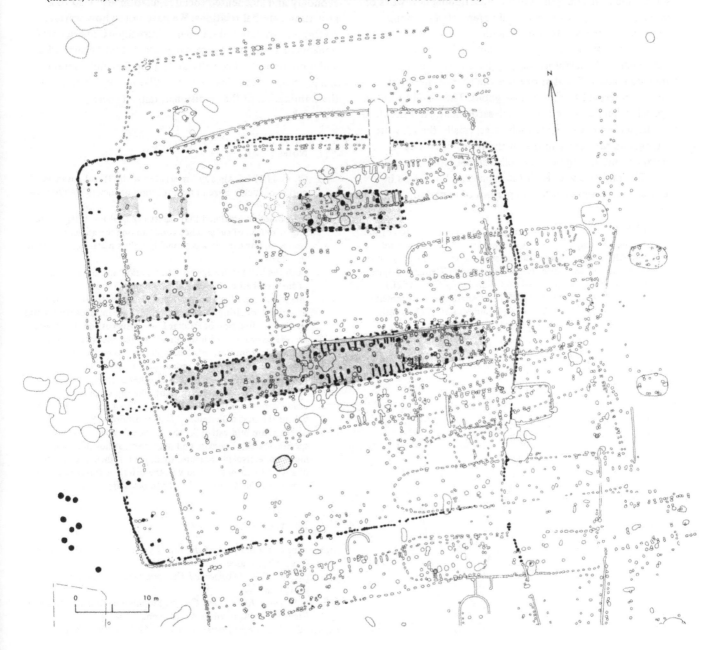

K. Randsborg 138

received personal revenues from trade, and in return protected the ports (where also their first minting of coins took place) (Randsborg 1980, 149f.). In the middle of the ninth century AD, international trade suddenly declined, and the Danish kings, heading a stratified society where the elite was greatly dependent on the taxation of trade, and on the trade itself, launched overwhelming attacks on Western Europe to relieve the pressures (fig. 16.6). However, c. AD 900 international trade revived for another fifty years, and the raids ceased. This was the culmination and end of the traditional stratified society with its unregulated militarism and status rivalry. A second decline in trade at about AD 950 was not accompanied by raiding. During exactly these decades the country was undergoing an inner, social development that was to make it the State of Denmark (cf. fig. 16.2). The establishment, heading the process, was finding new ways of employing its interests in economic prerogatives, among others in wider access to private lands.

To sum up the discussion of rank and resources, a few final remarks. Archaeologically, we have been considering three main areas. The first one was the changes in burial ritual with respect to costly grave goods. The second was the expansions and contractions of the settlement. And the third was the settlement sites themselves, especially their layout, fencing, and the type and size of the farmsteads. The descriptive modelling gave the following outcome.

The ranked societies of the bronze and iron ages in Denmark underwent successive periods of expansion and

Fig. 16.6. Distribution of foreign coins (b) in the burials of the Viking Age emporium of Birka (Sweden), declining around 950 AD, and the years with Danish raids on England (E), and on the Continent, basically on the Frankish(/German) empire (F). Data from Arbman 1943 (cf. Randsborg 1980, 152f.) (coins); Whitelock 1955, 135ff. (The Anglo-Saxon Chronicle); and Albrectsen 1976, Lauer 1905, and Musset 1971 (Continental written historical sources).

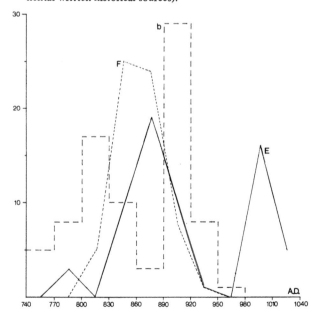

contraction of the settlement. During the periods of expansion – and optimal weather conditions – status rivalry was common in connection with burial, especially towards the end of such periods when stress might have built up. The graves of the high echelons held many grave goods, including exotic imports. These periods are normally thought of as especially active in trade. However, golden artefacts, from both graves, offerings and treasure hoards (see Albrectsen 1960) are, in fact, more common in the recession periods, which see harder weather conditions but also some intensification of the subsistence that enabled the population to survive, although under stricter patterns of control and inheritance of resources. The social development is accompanied by a rise in 'private' rights which were the basis of the position of the high-ranking lineages. Intensification of the economy and augmented social regulation also lead to a growth in external relations. We have noted how warfare, raiding and trading were, in part, mutually exclusive components in a system of external contacts that became more and more important socially during the first millennium AD. These activities culminated in the Viking age, which marks the termination of the traditional, ranked society in Denmark.

Notes

1 Cf. Fried 1967. Already Engels (1884, ch. 9) had advanced the notion of such a stage in the evolution of society ('*Militärische Demokratie*').
2 It is sometimes claimed that Tacitus (AD 98) was describing redistribution of subsistence goods among the ancient Germans; however, it was probably only a matter of tribute to the chiefs.
3 Both the late bronze age recession period and the iron age one of the first half of the first millennium AD show signs of an intensification of subsistence production, possibly in the form of cereal agriculture. An economic interest in fields would also lead in the direction of stricter lines of succession. However, the whole problem of intensification, and the social stress emanating from this, is too complicated to be incorporated here. Also, field systems, agricultural methods, etc. are still relatively poorly understood. Yet other problems have also been left more or less out of sight, like the squandering of costly goods in offerings, which comes to a halt too in the first half of the first millennium AD (Randsborg 1980, 49). The offerings are interesting for their lack of direction towards a specific (earthly) person, and may seem, although falsely, to be more 'collective' in character than, for instance, the interment of a wealthy magnate. And yet, the offerings too required the support of the wealthy echelons to be carried out.

References

Albrectsen, E. 1960. *Fynske guldfund* (Fynske studier III). Odense, Odense bys museer.
Albrectsen, E. 1976. *Vikingerne i Franken*. Odense, Odense Universitetsforlag.
Arbman, H. 1943. *Birka I, Die Gräber*. Stockholm, Kungl. Vitterhets Historie och Antikvitets Akademien.
Becker, C.J. 1961. *Førromersk jernalder i Syd- og Midtjylland*

(Nationalmuseets skrifter, større beretninger 6). København, Nationalmuseet.

Becker, C.J. 1965. Ein früheisenzeitliches Dorf bei Grøntoft, Westjütland. *Acta Archaeologica* 36: 209–22.

Becker, C.J. 1968a. Bronzealderhuse i Vestjylland. *Nationalmuseets Arbejdsmark*: 79–88.

Becker, C.J. 1968b. Das zweite früheisenzeitliche Dorf bei Grøntoft, Westjütland. *Acta Archaeologica* 39: 235–55.

Becker, C.J. 1971. Früheisenzeitliche Dörfer bei Grøntoft, Westjütland. *Acta Archaeologica* 42: 79–110.

Becker, C.J. 1972. Hal og hus i yngre bronzealder. *Nationalmuseets Arbejdsmark*: 5–16.

Broholm, H.C. 1946–9. *Danmarks Bronzealder*. København, Nyt Nordisk Forlag.

Brøndsted, J. 1960. *Danmarks Oltid* III (2nd edn), København, Gyldendal.

Eggers, H.J. 1951. *Der römische Import im freien Germanien* (Atlas der Urgeschichte 1). Hamburg, Hamburgisches Museum für Völkerkunde und Vorgeschichte.

Engels, F. 1884. *Der Ursprung der Familie, des Privateigentums und des Staats* (1st edn) (later editions, especially 1892, and numerous later printings). Hoffingen–Zürich, Schweizerische Genossenschaftbuchdruckerei.

Fried, M. 1967. *The Evolution of Political Society*. New York, Random House.

Hammer, C.U., Clausen, H.B. and Dansgaard, W., forthcoming. Past volcanism and climate revealed by Greenland ice cores, *Proceedings of the Symposium on Volcanism and Climate, I.U.G.G. Conference, Canberra, Australia, Dec. 1979*.

Hansen, U.L. 1976. Das Gräberfeld bei Harpelev, Seeland. *Acta Archaeologica* 47: 91–160.

Hvass, S. 1975. Das eisenzeitliche Dorf bei Hodde, Westjütland. *Acta Archaeologica* 46: 142–58.

Hvass, S. 1978. Die völkerwanderungszeitliche Siedlung Vorbasse, Mitteljütland. *Acta Archaeologica* 49: 61–111.

Hvass, S. 1979. Jernalderlandsbyerne ved Vorbasse. *Nationalmuseets Arbejdsmark*: 105–12.

LaMarche, V.C., Jr. 1974. Paleoclimatic inferences from long tree-ring records. *Science* 183 (no. 4129): 1043–8.

Lauer, P. (ed.) 1905. *Les Annales de Flodoard*. Paris, A. Picard.

Lévi-Strauss, C. 1969 (first published 1949). *The Elementary Structures of Kinship*. London, Eyre and Spottiswoode.

Musset, L. 1971. *Les Invasions: le second assaut contre l'Europe chrétienne (VIIᵉ–XIᵉ siècles)* (Nouvelle Clio 12 bis) (2nd edn). Paris, Presses Universitaires de France.

Peebles, C.S. and Kus, S.M. 1977. Some archaeological correlates of ranked societies. *American Antiquity* 42(3): 421–48.

Randsborg, K. 1975. Population and social variation in early bronze age Denmark: a systemic approach, in S. Polgar (ed.), *Population, Ecology, and Social Evolution*. The Hague, Mouton, 139–66.

Randsborg, K. 1980. *The Viking Age in Denmark*. London and New York, Duckworth and St Martin's Press.

Randsborg, K. 1981. Burial, succession and early state formation in Denmark, in R. Chapman, I. Kinnes and K. Randsborg (eds.), *The Archaeology of Death*. Cambridge, University Press, 105–21.

Renfrew, C. 1973. Monuments, mobilisation and social organisation in neolithic Wessex, in C. Renfrew (ed.), *The Explanation of Culture Change*. London, Duckworth, 539–58.

Sahlins, M. 1958. *Social Stratification in Polynesia*. Seattle, University of Washington Press.

Sahlins, M. 1965. On the sociology of primitive exchange, in M. Banton (ed.), *The Relevance of Models for Social Anthropology* (ASA Monographs 1). London, Tavistock Publications, 139–236.

Service, E.R. 1971. *Primitive Social Organization: an evolutionary perspective* (2nd edn). New York, Random House.

Tacitus, P.C. AD 98. *De origine et situ Germanorum* (often quoted as 'Germania'). Numerous later editions.

Thrane, H. 1975. *Europaeiske Forbindelser* (Nationalmuseets skrifter, Arkaeologisk–historick raekke 16). København.

Whitelock, D. (ed.) 1955. *English Historical Documents I, c. 500–1042*. London, Eyre and Spottiswoode.

PART V

Discussion:
contrasting paradigms

The development of archaeology over the past two decades has followed very different courses in Britain and in the United States. In America the impact of processual archaeology was considerable. Lewis Binford's important paper 'Archaeology as anthropology' was published in 1962, and *New Perspectives in Archaeology*, with papers by many of the first generation of apostles of the New Archaeology, appeared in 1968 (Binford and Binford 1968). With all the fervour of the recent convert, the senior and much respected south-western archaeologist Paul Martin described the radical nature of his own shift to a new 'revolution-inciting paradigm' as a consequence of contact with Binford and his students: 'As a result I have substantially altered the bearing, emphasis and procedures of my research. Thus a conceptual transformation, a revolution, has taken place for me' (Martin 1971, 1). The change in direction was a very widespread one, so that one reviewer of *New Perspectives* could write: 'If anyone thinks a revolution did occur, the same must now think the revolution is over. Suddenly the new archaeology is everybody's archaeology. The rhetorical scene is quiet' (Leone 1971).

In Britain, despite the energetic advocacy of David Clarke (e.g. Clarke 1968) and the quantitative sophistication of Doran and Hodson (1975) the shift to a new 'revolution-inciting paradigm' has been much less obvious. Discussions at many meetings in London, for instance, continue to focus

upon matters of fact — that is to say upon scholarly assessments of accumulated data. Theoretical or processual issues are rarely discussed at such meetings, and never in a general or cross-cultural way. Of course there are many archaeologists whose aspirations are indeed primarily processual, as papers in the present volume reflect. But their aspirations are not shared by the existing archaeological establishment. In Britain, if 'the rhetorical scene is quiet', it is not because the revolution has come, bringing peace in its triumphant aftermath, but because many of the most senior and established figures are scarcely aware that anything has changed significantly in the nature of archaeological thought.

This state of affairs is not as depressing as might at first appear. In the first place, some of the more admirable qualities of the traditional 'scholarly' approach have been retained, including a commendable aspiration to record competently a wide range of data from an excavation and to publish it adequately. I have suggested elsewhere (Renfrew 1980) that the New Archaeology is not always seen at its strongest in these matters. And secondly, there has been no slavish conformity to a single explanatory mode in formulating project design, and very little production of those somewhat spurious 'laws of culture process' that have characterised the more aggressively positivist tendency in American archaeology (Watson, LeBlanc and Redman 1971). The excesses of the 'Law and Order' school of thought have led, as Flannery (1973) points out, to a reaction in America by the 'young fogeys', who look wistfully back to the intellectually less taxing days of the pre-processual era. These recidivists are thus not very different in their intellectual outlook from the 'old fogeys' in Britain who contribute so resolutely to the quietness of the rhetorical scene. Flannery's third group, to which I infer he himself belongs, he characterises as the 'Serutan' (or 'Ex-Lax') school. British readers, being unaccustomed to the brand names for American medicinal products, will find this culturally encapsulated laxative terminology obscure. It may be more intelligible to refer to the 'natural regularity' group, which seeks cross-cultural regularities in the working of culture process, often within a systems framework, rather than laws of nature. Probably the majority of processualist workers in the United States and Britain would subscribe to some broadly systemic view in this way.

My point here is to indicate that the British response to the New Archaeology has been much more diverse than that in the United States, so that several schools of thought have been developing. Perhaps for this reason the intellectual scene, as far as archaeology is concerned, seems in some ways more lively than in America. Two of the most interesting of these directions are exemplified in the papers which follow, while Whallon adds an admirably firm recapitulation of the nature of explanation which springs from the mainstream of new archaeological thinking.

The paper by Gledhill and Rowlands represents a contribution towards an approach avowedly inspired by the writings of Marx, and influenced by the work of the French neo-Marxist and structuralist-Marxist school. There are several points of difference between its adherents and most processual archaeologists in Britain. Here it is pertinent to stress how the authors have succeeded in raising many important issues which are sometimes overlooked. In particular, the emphasis which they lay upon the socio-economic structure at a given time as determining, or at least influencing, the future trajectory of the society brings attention back, in a useful way, to specific structural features of the society in question. Their holistic approach, with its emphasis upon models of total systems, is a useful one. In leading them on to a discussion of larger 'global' or 'world' systems, it raises some interesting questions of archaeological methodology. The sceptic may ask whether the find of a few traded items in an area remote from the manufacturing centre automatically conjures up for us another 'world system', with core and periphery (Shaffer, forthcoming)? Can a 'peripheral' area simultaneously belong to two world systems? There may indeed be difficulties here which have yet to be fully explored, but the approach is undoubtedly a coherent one, and offers a refreshing alternative to some of the now rather familiar thought-clichés of the established processual outlook.

A third approach, to set alongside both the mainstream processual view of Whallon and the neo-Marxist

analysis of Gledhill and Rowlands, is offered by Hodder. Once again the influence of French structuralist-Marxism may be discerned, but here the direction is primarily an idealist one, with emphasis upon what Rappaport (1968, 237) would term the 'cognised' as much as the 'operational' aspects of society — upon the 'rules and concepts which order and give meaning to the social system' (and which constitute Hodder's 'social structure'). It remains to be seen how much further in practice this initiative will take us beyond the 'social ecology' enunciated by Flannery (1976). But clearly, with its emphasis upon the ideational and symbolic, it offers an alternative to the strictly operational, and perhaps rather narrowly materialist, nature of much recent work. Once again one may anticipate difficulties at the operational level: it may not always be easy, for instance, to identify archaeologically such concepts as purity and pollution without recourse to ethnographic analogy of a rather special kind. But we should not be too quick to ascribe supposed methodological inadequacies to a new theoretical framework whose methodology has not yet been fully worked out. Once again the ambitious aspirations of this contextual perspective serve to underline some of the limitations of current processual archaeology.

Our volume thus ends with three programmatic statements of world views which are to some extent mutually exclusive in their assumptions and in their conclusions. At present it would seem that one cannot be an enthusiastic member of one of these camps without rejecting, or at least questioning, the philosophical and methodological foundations of the others. Such diversity, so long as there is a real and continuous flow of ideas among the groups, is surely a valuable alternative to the habit-forming orthodoxy of 'normal' science. There is always the danger, it should however be remembered, of mistaking paradigms for theories. We should not forget that it is the purpose of scientific 'world views' to contribute to the solution of real problems: they cannot be justified from first principles alone on the basis of some *a priori* assertions about the nature of the world or of society (Binford 1981).

On one important point, it is interesting to note, these four commentators are agreed. As Gledhill and Rowlands put it: 'Theory cannot be built successfully by reifying categories of archaeological data.' Hodder similarly urges us to 'develop usable models and analogies for studies of the integration of beliefs and practices'. And Whallon likewise concludes with the reminder that: 'history may be built from data, but theory is built by theorising'. Most of the contributors to this volume would subscribe to these views. They are, however, confronted with the wealth of archaeological data from early Europe, and with the desire to construct theories and models which have a relevance to this material. But from what, and on what basis? Good theories (that is to say theories which have some application in the real world) are rarely formulated completely apart from those data which they may one day help to explain. With the current enthusiasm for new paradigms, a taste by no means restricted to contemporary archaeology (see Bird 1977), the impression is sometimes given that the theoretical has some supreme priority over the factual. To exaggerate this viewpoint is as potentially dangerous as to downgrade the significance of theory altogether, with that exaggerated esteem for unadulterated 'facts' which sometimes passes for scholarship.

The old relationship between theory and data should not be forgotten:

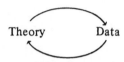

Theory   Data

The hypothetico-deductive approach rightly lays stress on the passage from theory to data, by means of deduced hypotheses and of hypothesis testing. And all four of our commentators agree that there is no convenient mechanical procedure for proceeding from Data to Theory. They agree that an 'inductive' approach, where theory is conceived as simply a generalisation from accumulated data – a 'reification' as Gledhill and Rowlands term it – is no way to proceed. Theories are created in the mind of the researcher – 'theory is built by theorising', as Whallon reminds us. But to say this should not be to imply that the researcher should distance himself too far from the data to which this theory will ultimately be applied. To do this carries with it the danger of constructing elaborate theoretical systems, internally coherent in themselves and perhaps intellectually satisfying in an ultimately rather circular manner, but yet incapable of interacting with the data through testing against existing material or by a quest for new finds.

Each of these final papers carries with it the admirable exhortation to *build theory*, and to build it not through some supposed inductive process but as a deliberate intellectual act. That is altogether commendable. But let us remember that our ultimate goal is not so much theories which conform to our own *a priori* view of the world, but theories which actually *work* – theories which help us to order the data which we have and to predict those which we don't.

A.C.R.

References

Binford, L.R. 1962. Archaeology as anthropology. *American Antiquity* 28: 217–25.

Binford, L.R. 1981. *Bones: Ancient Man and Modern Myths.* New York, Academic Press.

Binford, L.R. and S.R. (eds.) 1968. *New Perspectives in Archaeology.* Chicago, Aldine.

Bird, J.H. 1977. Methodology and philosophy. *Progress in Human Geography* 1: 104–10.

Clarke, D.L. 1968. *Analytical Archaeology.* London, Methuen.

Doran, J.E. and Hodson, F.R. 1975. *Mathematics and Computers in Archaeology.* Edinburgh, University Press.

Flannery, K.V. 1973. Archaeology with a capital S, in C.L. Redman (ed.), *Research and Theory in Current Archaeology.* New York, John Wiley, 47–58.

Flannery, K.V. 1976. Contextual analysis of ritual paraphernalia from Formative Oaxaca, in K.V. Flannery (ed.), *The Early Mesoamerican Village.* New York, Academic Press, 329–44.

Leone, M. 1971. Review of Binford, L.R. and S.R. (eds.), *New Perspectives in Archaeology. American Antiquity* 36: 220–2.

Martin, P.S. 1971. The revolution in archaeology. *American Antiquity* 36: 1–8.

Rappaport, R. 1968. *Pigs for the Ancestors.* New Haven, Yale University Press.

Renfrew, C. 1980. The Great Tradition versus the Great Divide: archaeology as anthropology? *American Journal of Archaeology* 84: 287–298.

Shaffer, J.G., forthcoming. Harappan commerce, an alternative perspective, in L. Flam and S. Paspner (eds.), *Current Anthropology in Pakistan: Archaeology and Cultural Anthropology.* Ithaca, Cornell University Press.

Watson, P.J., LeBlanc, S.A. and Redman, C.L. 1971. *Explanation in Archaeology, an Explicitly Scientific Approach.* New York, Columbia University Press.

Chapter 17

**Materialism and
socio-economic process
in multi-linear
evolution**
John Gledhill and M.J. Rowlands

This paper discusses the implications for archaeological theory of recent debates in anthropology concerning the nature of pre-capitalist social formations. We maintain that what is at issue is an adequate conceptualisation of the social totality and, implicitly, of social structure, one which avoids the traditional 'ethnocentrism' of extending concepts from the study of capitalist to pre-capitalist societies. We make some suggestions concerning ways out of this logical impasse, and present an attempt to reformulate a materialist explanation of long-term socio-economic change. A central issue, of long-standing significance in the study of social evolution, is reviewed in a discussion of the benefits of a 'world system' approach in defining the appropriate unit of social analysis. In conclusion, we argue that archaeology has a number of crucial advantages over the other social sciences for studying macro-social change but that these will not be realised until advances have been made in the conceptualisation of the issues involved.

Over the past few years a growing number of archaeologists have begun to move away from explanations derived from functional ecology, systems theory and the more naive forms of cultural materialism towards a focus on specific social and political processes and their economic functioning within defined historical circumstances. In questioning the kind of materialism that has formed the theory of the various neo-evolutionary schools, prehistorians can derive considerable encouragement from recent successes in social and economic history, in particular from the work of the French *Annales* school,[1] whose analyses of historical processes of 'long duration' have enjoyed a widening and potentially integrative influence in history and other social sciences. The dawn of a true 'social archaeology' may now be possible.[2] But in its way stands what some already see as a polarised wrangling over what should be considered 'determinant' in economic versus socio-political processes. This has already led to the creation of the new 'ism' of social determinism to characterise positions critical of the older forms of materialism.[3]

Our purpose in this paper is to demonstrate that such a position is theoretically misconceived and that any future archaeological theorising needs to take into account issues raised in recent debates in anthropology as to the nature of pre-capitalist social formations.[4] Self-styled 'Marxist theories' have had considerable impact in anthropology. But they have raised many more problems than they are capable of resolving in their attempts to universalise a body of Marxist concepts outside of the historical materialist hypothesis for nineteenth-century capitalism. Anthropological debates have now raged for a decade on whether concepts such as class, exploitation and mode of production can be extended (as universal categories) from the study of capitalist to that of pre-capitalist societies. At the heart of these debates lies a very basic question: what could it mean to say that the economy determines social form and historical process universally? On this fundamental issue, French Marxist anthropology is simply one stream, or, more accurately, one group of tendencies, in post-war Marxism in Europe.

The real question entailed by the historical materialist hypothesis is how one defines and conceptualises the 'social totality'. The most influential version in Europe, deriving from Althusser (for example, Althusser and Balibar 1970), sees it as a layer cake of 'relatively autonomous' structural levels, distributed between infrastructure (forces and relations of production) and superstructure (politico-juridical and ideological structures). In contrast to the cruder versions of cultural materialism, it is not argued that the superstructures are a product of the infrastructure, and, in the case of pre-capitalist formations, it is recognised that the 'economic' is, in fact, organised by what Althusserians see as 'superstructures', 'non-economic' social relations such as kinship, religion or bonds of personal dependence. This raises the issue of how this 'dominance of superstructural instances' can be squared with what is assumed to be the historical materialist hypothesis: 'determination by the economy in the last instance' of the structure of the social totality. It also poses the question of what determines the particular form of 'superstructure' which will be 'inserted into the economic base' in a particular case. The Althusserian response to these questions is a form of teleological functionalist argument which fails to provide any coherent account of the mechanisms of historical transformation which lead to changes in dominant structures, and suffers the general logical ills of explanations of this type (Friedman 1975; Hindess and Hirst 1977).

Godelier's brand of 'structural Marxism' differs somewhat from this, in denying any rigid distinction between base and superstructure, although Godelier himself offers little advance on Althusser on the question of what determines the form and nature of the dominant structure.[5] For Godelier, religion, for example, can be infrastructural if it functions as 'relations of production'. He would therefore deny the separation of religion from the economic to explain theocratic relations in early states. It cannot act as some kind of 'after the fact' ideological legitimation, because 'religion' constitutes the cultural form within which hierarchic economic relations were experienced and lived. Unfortunately, the initial assumption is still made that somehow the economic and the religious are distinguishable entities, differing simply in their relations of functioning with each other in given historical circumstances (cf. Kahn 1978).

In contrast to the Althusserian and structural Marxist positions, an alternative conceptualisation of the macrostructure of social totalities exists which is not identified with any hypothesis of determination by the economy at all, but by its holistic and dialectical view of social totalities and reality as a social process. In place of a 'layer-cake' model of

base and superstructure, Lukács (1968) proposed an organic model of social totalities in which the elements of economic, ideological, political and juridical relations cannot be separated from each other at the level of social practice. 'Vertical determination' is therefore denied in favour of the dialectical interplay of, say, economic and political processes within a diachronic frame of reference.

Since we are not concerned with defending the eternal truth of Marxist discourse, we see no need to preserve any particular conceptualisation of the social totality because of its genealogical purity. However, these debates have considerable implications for our conceptualisation of the nature of the pre-capitalist societies that we study in prehistory. The primary error to be exposed is the assumption that 'economics' (and indeed materialism) can be universally reduced to the categories of material production, technology, work processes and the form in which labour is exploited. The 'economy' in this sense clearly cannot even define the dynamics of 'modes of production' in Marx's general historical sense (cf. Banaji 1977). If we look at Marx's treatment of the 'ancient' mode in *Grundrisse*, for example, we find that slavery as a mode of exploitation does not define the driving contradiction of Roman society, whilst his account of European feudalism anticipates Weber in stressing the particular *political* characteristics of this system. The point here is not that 'Marx was right' – his analyses of these phenomena are far too schematic to deserve this accolade – but that from the outset Marx was forced to reject the kind of economic conceptualisation which has dominated much of subsequent historical materialist analysis. The lesson to be learnt from this would appear to be that we cannot understand the dynamics of social formations as historical totalities either by examining technology or work organisation or by inspecting the way in which surplus is extracted from direct producers. Economic and socio-political conditions cannot therefore be separated, and both are equally 'material': we cannot understand economic processes in the narrowest sense in isolation, but neither can we argue that real development trajectories are determined by purely 'cultural' or 'political' processes. What this perspective does imply is that theorising about long-term socio-economic change in prehistory involves us in the construction of models of total social systems in which ideological, political and economic processes are linked to each other in a dialectical interplay rather than as determinate levels in a social formation. In turn, it serves to emphasise that where social anthropology and a 'Marxist anthropology' have failed fundamentally is in their implicit acceptance that a static analysis is required prior to diachronic analysis; in both we have the absence of a genuine theory of history centred on social dynamics and transformation processes.

How then should we approach the materialist explanation of long-term socio-economic change? Let us consider the development of more complex stratified societies. Much of the discussion of this issue has been totally obfuscated by neo-evolutionist emphasis on the 'origin of the state', defined as an abstract configuration of institutions with universalisable properties. Let us suppose that the question is really about the evolution of new forms of dominance mechanisms underlying the elaboration in scale and integration of territorial political units. Elsewhere, we have offered elaborated models of these processes which seek to establish the following principles.[6] The dynamic of the underlying transformation processes derives from contradictions at two levels. Firstly, we have long-term contradictions which arise in the arena of socio-political action as political hierarchies are reproduced over time. Secondly, because the reproduction of political hierarchisation as a social process is dependent on material flows in a quantitative sense, we have contradictions arising from the dependence of social reproduction on material flows which must be captured, acquired and ultimately produced under conditions which include both social and physical limits and possible disruptions to such material flows. For example, and oversimplifying for the sake of brevity, it can be argued, in the cases of Mesopotamia, Mesoamerica and north China, that a collapse of extended territorial polities into competitive city states of a more nucleated kind represents a loss of control by earlier centres over resources flowing through a larger intersocietal exchange network (cf. Ekholm and Friedman 1979). Whether these resources are used in the subsistence sphere or for producing palaces, manufactured goods used in status prestations, or whatever, does not affect the basic principle that their significance is that their acquisition has become a condition for the maintenance of forms of political hierarchisation. The competition for resources manifested in such contexts is therefore really a product of inter- and intra-societal political competition. The development of the inter-regional network of trade and productive specialisation is itself, in fact, a product of socio-political development, not a 'purely economic' phenomenon.

These observations are still, however, rather imprecise. To go further, we need to examine the nature of internal stratification and its contradictions, and how this relates to contradictions in the differential advantage that competing factions enjoy in the control of material resources. Very schematically, it can be argued that the pre-city-state systems experience a progressive separation of functions within the ruling group, linked to internal competition for status and succession to offices, and problems in maintaining political control over extended territories and in deepening the dependence of subordinate strata on their ruling groups. The contradictions generate the elaboration of new strategies for maintaining dominance relations which in turn change the configuration of the system. One outcome of this is a possibility that segments of the dominant stratum and aspirant groups may achieve a degree of autonomy from state-sector mechanisms of wealth appropriation and accumulation, via mercantile activities. Attempts by the centre to control the political periphery may also involve the

allocation of 'benefices' of various kinds to secure loyalty, which may in the longer run enhance the possibilities for the emergence of competitive centres on the periphery.

Hence, early forms of territorial states feature relatively weak mechanisms for centralised political–economic control, and create the conditions for their own demise by attempting to resolve problems by elaborating elements which further outstrip the capacity of these mechanisms. For recentralisation and larger territorial polities to emerge, new and more effective measures for political–economic centralisation must be created, and 'the state' which exercises control in such systems will appear to represent a more autonomous kind of political institutional complex, comprised of a set of differentiated fractions (priestly, administrative, military etc.), and increasingly disembedded from subordinate ascriptive status groups. Since each fraction appropriates surplus via different mechanisms, conflicting interests over material resources are generated, some of which may, under certain conditions, be antagonistic to political centralisation as such. In mediating and manipulating these antagonisms, as well as those between exploited and exploiting strata, the rulers maintain their own position by engaging in a generalised form of power politics. Obviously we have an historical variable in the extent to which both political centralisation and state control over the economy (in particular the mercantile economy) is maintained in time and space. Explaining this pattern of variation leads us back to the analysis of the social and material conditions underlying the power balances within and between social strata that obtain in particular historical cases (cf. Gledhill, forthcoming), which themselves are not given but are products of preceding historical processes.

The final issue which we wish to discuss has already been anticipated in our earlier remarks. What is the appropriate unit of analysis in the study of social evolutionary processes? The bulk of conventional social theory is premised on the notion that we base analysis on 'the society' as a socio-political unit. But this position becomes untenable if the society in question cannot reproduce itself in isolation from other societies, to the extent that it would have developed differently if it were independent of its articulation into a larger system. Wallerstein has, of course, argued that leaving aside isolated self-sufficient communities, the only true 'social systems' are 'world systems', multi-society units defined by the existence of an integrated division of labour (Wallerstein 1974; 1979), though as we will see, it is important to stress that this integration is brought about by the interaction of a series of interdependent but often heterogeneous dynamics characterising the system's different components. It is clear that local material production processes frequently cannot be reproduced without inter-societal exchange and that interdependency in this sense has increased in scale and intensity through history. But this is really an insignificant point in itself, not least because increasing economic interdependency of this kind is evi-

dently linked, as we have already argued, to the socially
determined 'needs' of various forms of expansionary politico-
economic systems. Even the study of relatively early periods
of prehistory raises the unit of analysis issue in the light of
the scope of some of the interactions uncovered by archaeology in recent years, once we recognise the significance of
transactions in non-subsistence goods for the reproduction
and transformation of social structures (Bender 1978;
forthcoming). But in the case of more complex and hierarchic social systems it is even more evident that 'development' cannot take place in a closed space but involves the
interdependent development of core and peripheral areas.

Here, however, we should be careful to avoid some
potentially disastrous misconceptions which can arise from
a focus on the larger 'global' or 'world systems' unit of
analysis. Firstly, we must recognise that the relationships
within such systems cannot be reduced simply to material
flows. To begin with, the social structure of society X may
be systematically linked to that of society Y primarily via the
articulation of socio-political structure. Let us consider, for
example, a phenomenon which is of considerable significance
in the prehistory of many areas: nomad–sedentary relations.
Few nomadic pastoralist societies in fact reproduce themselves economically independently of regularised transactions
with sedentary communities (Baxter 1975). In addition to
symbiotic food transfers, it is also possible to see that demographic exchanges between sedentary, pastoralist and
hunter–gatherer societies constitute important long-term
conditions for the reproduction of the different kinds of
social aggregates concerned (see, for example, Spencer 1973).
But even the further addition of non-food exchanges and tax
and tribute transfers does not exhaust the possible scope and
nature of the interdependency which characterises some
cases of nomad–sedentary interaction. In the case of the
Central Asian pastoral formations, for example, it seems clear
that the existence of a 'conical clan' form of 'internal' socio-
political organisation, with its potential for escalating stratification and political centralisation, cannot be regarded as
something independent of the long-term dynamic interaction
between the frontier nomads and the civilised core of China
(Lattimore 1951). Lattimore has argued that the balance of
material advantage in the tributary relationship notionally
'imposed' by the Chinese fell overwhelmingly to the nomads.
This observation reinforces the hypothesis that Mongol socio-
political structure took the form it did partly because it
resulted from the negotiation of socio-political strategies
which permitted a permanent articulation of the dominant
strata in Mongol society with the Chinese stratification
system, enabling the nomad elite to share in the fruits of the
exploitation of the Chinese peasantry. Whilst the existence of
resource transfers from the Chinese core region underpinned
the structures created, acting as a condition for the reproduction of internal social differentiation in the nomadic
communities, the form of socio-political organisation generated should be seen as determined by the specific social

characteristics of the two systems thereby integrated: on the
one hand, internal social conditions in the pastoral communities (which ruled out simple replication of the Chinese
pattern),[7] and on the other, the form of articulation
demanded by regularised relations at the political level with
a different kind of society.

In general terms, the material economic dimension of
global system linkages is determined by the social structures
which mediate the forms of incorporation of a society into
another's sphere of influence and determine the effect this
has on the incorporated society's development. In the case,
for example, of economic relationships of a 'colonial' type
which do not involve actual conquest, the economic subordination of the periphery occurs because local elites have
both the desire and the capacity to impose a particular kind
of economy on the rest of their society under specific and
variable local social conditions. As Islamoğlu and Keyder
have argued apropos the 'peripheralisation' of the Ottoman
Empire to western European centres, the significance of the
changing structure of international trade in this period lay in
the fact that it mobilised certain latent contradictions in the
Ottoman system, which we must understand fully in order
both to explain why peripheralisation occurred and to understand the specific social and political forms which evolved
subsequently in this area (Islamoğlu and Keyder 1977). Most
important of all is the implication of the principle that
quantitative material economic development is a function of
the qualitative characteristics of socio-economic and political
structures, given that we clearly could not predict, for
example, the kind of structures which characterised the
formations of Classical Antiquity from observing the material
contribution to their evolution made by commercial relations
with Near Eastern societies. And it is also clear that the
timing of incorporation relative to the former notionally
'autonomous' development of the incorporated society also
has significant effects in terms of the degree to which its
existing structures are in a state of crisis.

We must conclude that if a world systems perspective
leads simply to a focus on inter-regional trading networks
and abstract processes of wealth accumulation as deter-
minants of local social forms, then the problems already
encountered with the conceptualisation of social totalities
will be extended to a wider plane but scarcely resolved. This
brings us to a further major issue.

It is seldom satisfactory in principle to try to explain
the past in terms of the properties of the future. Capitalist
accumulation in world systems that have arisen since the
sixteenth century has achieved a different form to that of
earlier systems where it operated under different conditions.
Whilst it cannot be denied that local 'societies' were involved
in production for a larger system in earlier pre-capitalist contexts, the developments which took place cannot be predicted from later situations, nor can the links between the
social elements involved be assumed to be of the same kind.
Indeed, even within the context of the discussion of the

evolution of the modern world system,[8] it is clear that one of the major problems with 'world systems' theorising has been a lack of a truly analytical periodisation of the successive phases of that process. Mercantile capital and the forms of accumulation associated with it were dominant in the early periods (Kay 1975), and mercantile capital is a phenomenon of considerable antiquity. But the structural place of merchant capital in early modern western European society differed from that which it occupied in earlier or coaeval civilisations, whilst it could also be argued that the appearance of centres based on the new forms of accumulation associated with modern industrial capital represented a crucial historical transformation which generated qualitatively new types of core—periphery relations relative to those of earlier imperial systems, including the Spanish-American empire.

What we are trying to grasp, then, are dynamic processes which generate spatial and diachronic variation in individual socio-political units. Within global systems, individual societies move along a series of interdependent development paths: neither their social structures nor even geographical extension, demographic size and composition can ultimately be taken as 'givens', but must usually be regarded as effects continually produced by wider processes of interaction and incorporation.[9] The distinction between 'internal' and 'external' relationships is therefore only a viable one in a limited sense. At given moments of time, existing societies can be linked together in new ways, and the results of this linking are not predictable without understanding how this change in external conditions of reproduction bears on internal structures. On the other hand, since such phenomena as 'trade' actually do modify conditions of reproduction for local societies, the distinction between internal and external factors is itself undesirable as a dichotomy, since it disguises the true nature of social evolutionary processes. One of archaeology's advantages over other social sciences is that it offers us ready access to a macro-spatial picture over long periods of time. That this advantage has not been fully exploited theoretically is another demonstration of the fact that theory cannot be built successfully by reifying categories of archaeological data.

Notes

1 Out of the work of the more recent generation of *Annales* writers, two works which would particularly repay a reading by archaeologists for their general methodological interest would be Braudel 1972 and Ladurie 1974. For surveys and assessment of *Annales* as a whole, see the special issue of *Review*, vol. 3/4, 1978, and the introduction to Burke (ed.) 1972, which also contains an important essay by Braudel: 'History and the social sciences'.

2 It is perhaps worth emphasising that 'social archaeology' has thus far frequently failed to break effectively with existing explanatory paradigms such as ecological functionalism, despite real advances in conceptualisation, and in the issues posed for research and methodology. A number of the contri-

butions to, for example, Redman *et al.* 1978 would fall into this category.

3 'Social determinists' *stricto sensu* would presumably ignore physical-geographical, ecological and climatological factors. But such a stance in no way follows from the principle that the historical effects of these variables (and their unquestionable significance in evolutionary processes) are produced by the mediation of social processes in a way which is complex and which escapes analysis based on non-specific historical models and the crude forms of reductionism recently criticised by Sahlins (1976).

4 Fuller discussion of the general issues raised here is provided by Kahn and Llobera 1980, Gledhill 1981 and Gledhill, forthcoming.

5 For some analytical contrasts between the work of Godelier and Friedman (1975) and Friedman and Rowlands (1978), see Gledhill 1981.

6 See Friedman and Rowlands 1978, Rowlands 1979, and Gledhill, forthcoming. On the peripheries of more complex core areas and 'world systems' analysis, see also Frankenstein and Rowlands 1978, Gledhill 1978 and Rowlands 1980.

7 For a discussion of the limits of techno-ecological explanations for the characteristics of pastoral social organisation, see Burnham 1979.

8 For this debate see, for example, Frank 1978, Banaji 1977 and Brenner 1977.

9 Conventional materialist theories have generally attempted to correlate local variation in social structure with local techno-economic variation or resource endowments. Here we are arguing that the link to material economic aspects of social reproduction is generally much more indirect. Simple correlations between local resource base and degree of political complexity or regional dominance frequently fail to materialise because the capacity to accumulate goods and people within a political unit may depend on more complex sources of advantage in a wider system, such as the ability to adopt local labour processes/divisions of labour which secure higher rates of accumulation overall in circumstances which depend crucially on the place a society can occupy within the bigger network (see Rowlands 1979).

References

Althusser, L. and Balibar, E. 1970. *Reading Capital.* London, New Left Books.

Banaji, J. 1977. Modes of production in a materialist conception of history. *Capital and Class* 3 (Autumn): 1–40.

Baxter, P.T.W. 1975. Some consequences of sedentarisation for social relationships, in T. Monod (ed.), *Pastoralism in Tropical Africa.* Oxford, University Press, 206–28.

Bender, B. 1978. Gatherer—hunter to farmer: a social perspective. *World Archaeology* 10(2): 204–22.

Bender, B. 1981. Gatherer—hunter intensification, in A. Sheridan and G. Bailey (eds.), *Economic Archaeology.* Oxford, British Archaeological Reports, 149–57.

Braudel, F. 1972. *The Mediterranean and the Mediterranean World in the Age of Philip II* (2nd edn). London, Collins.

Brenner, R. 1977. The origins of capitalist development: a critique of neo-Smithian Marxism. *New Left Review* 104: 25–92.

Burke, P. (ed.) 1972. *Economy and Society in Early Modern Europe: Essays from 'Annales'.* London, Methuen.

Burnham, P. 1979. Spatial mobility and political centralisation in pastoral societies, in Equipe écologie et anthropologie des sociétés pastorales (ed.), *Pastoral Production and Society.*

Cambridge, Maison des Sciences de l'Homme and Cambridge University Press, 349–60.

Ekholm, K. and Friedman, J. 1979. 'Capital', imperialism and exploitation in ancient world-systems, in M.T. Larsen (ed.), *Power and Propaganda*. Copenhagen, 41–58.

Frank, A.G. 1978. *Dependent Accumulation and Underdevelopment*. London, Macmillan.

Frankenstein, S. and Rowlands, M.J. 1978. The internal structure and regional context of early iron age society in south-western Germany. *Bulletin of the Institute of Archaeology, University of London* 15: 73–112.

Friedman, J. 1975. Tribes, states and transformations, in M. Bloch (ed.), *Marxist Analyses and Social Anthropology*. London, Malaby Press, 161–202.

Friedman, J. and Rowlands, M.J. 1977. Notes towards an epigenetic model of the evolution of 'civilisation', in J. Friedman and M.J. Rowlands (eds.), *The Evolution of Social Systems*. London, Duckworth, 201–76.

Gledhill, J. 1978. Formative development in the North American southwest, in D. Green, C. Haselgrove and M. Spriggs (eds.), *Social Organisation and Settlement*. Oxford, British Archaeological Reports, 241–90.

Gledhill, J. 1981. Time's arrow: anthropology, history, social evolution and marxist theory. *Critique of Anthropology* 16: 3–30.

Gledhill, J., forthcoming. The transformation of asiatic formations: the case of later post-classic Mesoamerica, in M. Spriggs (ed.), *Marxist Perspectives in Archaeology*. Cambridge, University Press.

Hindess, B. and Hirst, P.Q. 1977. *Mode of Production and Social Formation*. London, Routledge and Kegan Paul.

Islamoğlu, H. and Keyder, C. 1977. Agenda for Ottoman history. *Review* 1(1): 31–55.

Kahn, J. 1978. Perspectives in Marxist Anthropology: a review article, *Journal of Peasant Studies* 5(4): 485–96.

Kahn, J. and Llobera, J.R. 1981. Towards a new anthropology or a new marxism?, in J. Kahn and J.R. Llobera (eds.), *The Anthropology of Pre-Capitalist Societies*. London, Macmillan, 263–329.

Kay, G. 1975. *Development and Underdevelopment: a Marxist analysis*. London, Macmillan.

Ladurie, E. Le Roy 1974. *The Peasants of Languedoc*. Urbana, University of Illinois Press.

Lattimore, O. 1951. *Inner Asian Frontiers of China*. Boston, Beacon Press.

Lukács, G. 1968. *History and Class Consciousness*. London, Merlin Press.

Redman, C., Berman, M., Curtis, K., Langhorne, W., Versaggi, N. and Wanser, J. (eds.) 1978. *Social Archaeology*. New York, Academic Press.

Rowlands, M.J. 1979. Local and long-distance trade and incipient state formation on the Bamenda plateau in the nineteenth century. *Paieduma* 25: 1–19.

Rowlands, M.J. 1980. Kinship, alliance and exchange in the European Bronze Age, in J. Barrett and R. Bradley (eds.), *Settlement and Society in the British Later Bronze Age*. Oxford, British Archaeological Reports, 15–55.

Sahlins, M. 1976. *Culture and Practical Reason*. Chicago, University Press.

Spencer, P. 1973. *Nomads in Alliance*. Oxford, University Press.

Wallerstein, I. 1974. *The Modern World System*. London, Academic Press.

Wallerstein, I. 1979. *The Capitalist World Economy*. Cambridge, University Press.

Chapter 18

**The identification
and interpretation
of ranking in
prehistory: a
contextual perspective**
Ian Hodder

A distinction is made between social systems (patterns of relationships and roles) and social structure (the rules and concepts which order and give meaning to the social system). Most archaeological studies of ranking have examined only functional relationships in social systems, and there is a need to examine how ranking is presented and accepted within the social structure. The dangers of the ecological functionalism rife in prehistoric archaeology are, first, that ranking in, for example, burial is seen as directly reflecting social hierarchy, whereas, in fact, burial patterns are meaningful transformations of social differentiation. Second, interpretation of changes in ranking must consider the cultural as well as the adaptive context within which evolution occurs.

The aim of this paper is to attract attention to a distinction between social system and social structure which has rarely been made in archaeology and which is absent from the articles in this volume. It will be suggested that the making of such a distinction leads to an awareness of the limitations of existing archaeological studies devoted to the identification and explanation of social hierarchisation or ranking.

Most archaeological work on hierarchisation has been concerned with *social systems*, by which is meant the patterns of relationships and roles, the communication and use of power, relations of dependence and authority, the movement of resources and trade. It is in discussions of social systems that archaeologists talk descriptively of degrees of complexity and of adaptation and homeostasis. Functional relationships are set up between trade, hierarchy, subsistence and so on — between the different subsystems of the total social system. This functional and utilitarian view of society has been the main concern of recent work, and is identifiable by reference to the following texts on ranking: Brumfiel 1976; Carneiro 1970; Cherry 1978; Crumley 1976; Earle 1977; Flannery 1972; Gall and Saxe 1977; Johnson 1973; Renfrew 1975; Wright 1977; Yoffee 1979.

By *social structure*, on the other hand, is meant the rules and concepts which order and give meaning to the social system. The framework of rules is built up from general principles which exist in all societies but which are manipulated and negotiated in particular ways specific to each context. These structural and symbolic principles by which interaction is organised include, for example, the rules of ideologies of domination and the symbolic principles of purity, hygiene, godliness, etc. All these various dimensions of meaning are organised and continually reorganised in relation to each other. The structures are continually being renegotiated and manipulated as part of the changing strategies and relations between groups with different powers.

Ranking in social systems: some problems

Existing studies of ranking within prehistoric social systems have been concerned with description and with functional relationships. Thus analysis proceeds by describing burial and settlement patterns, and by examining relationships with trade, subsistence and so on (Flannery 1972; Peebles and Kus 1977; Renfrew 1975; Wright 1977). Societies are classified into chiefdoms, stratified societies or states, or into degrees of complexity, with associated categories of exchange (reciprocal, redistributive, prestige etc.), and with associated typologies of evolutionary development (however multilinear – Sanders and Webster 1978). The functional relationships between the different categories and divisions of societies concern regulation and equilibrium within an ecological framework. For example, in Flannery's (1972) systems model for the growth of states, the job of self-regulation within the socio-cultural system 'is to keep all the variables in the subsystem within appropriate goal ranges – ranges which maintain homeostasis and do not threaten the survival of the system' (Flannery 1972, 409). 'Culture from a systemic perspective, is defined . . . as interacting behavioural systems. One asks questions concerning these systems, their interrelation, their adaptive significance' (Plog 1975, 208). Such an emphasis on functional relationships assumes that if ranking 'works' (i.e. if it functions to do something like coping with exchange or a very dry environment or just to keep itself going), then the 'working' is a sufficient explanation. There is a certain circularity in such arguments. By its very existence a society 'works'. To show that an institution functions in a certain way does not by itself constitute an explanation of that institution. Unless the analyst is willing to accept that human societies function just to keep themselves functioning within a social and physical environment, it must be acknowledged that broader questions must be asked. While an awareness of the circularity of such functional arguments is shown in the work of Flannery (1972), Flannery and Marcus (1976), Renfrew (1972), and Friedman and Rowlands (1977), the problems and limitations have yet to be fully laid bare.

It is not the concern of this paper to contest the view that the explanation of ranking involves functional relationships, but rather it is suggested that such explanations are insufficient and incomplete. The point can be further demonstrated by considering the emphasis on 'wholeness' in systems theory. The ecological and functional viewpoint explains one subsystem in terms of its connections to others. As one part of the system changes, the others regulate and adapt to regain homeostasis. One subsystem which has recently been seen as important is the ideational (Drennan 1976; Fritz 1978; Flannery and Marcus 1976). Flannery (1972, 409) accepts that the human population's 'cognised model' of the way the world is put together is not merely epiphenomenal but plays an essential part in controlling and regulating societies. Everything ideational is put in a separate subsystem and then the functional links between this and the other subsystems are examined in terms of regulation and management.

The idea of wholeness in archaeological systems theory thus concerns the functional relationships between separate subsystems. The structure of the whole derives from the functional links between the parts, and there is no real concept of wholeness itself except as a by-product of the relationships between parts. Few archaeologists have claimed that there are absolute one-to-one behavioural links between environments and human societies. So if one asks 'why does the system have the form it does?', 'what structures the whole?', the functional view inherent in systems theory can only provide partial answers.

On the other hand, it may be easier to answer such questions satisfactorily if archaeologists consider the symbolic principles which link the parts together. These principles permeate the functional relationships, and they form the whole. The whole does not come from the parts but from the underlying structures. It is not adequate to separate everything ideational into a separate subsystem. Rather, idea and belief are present, and are reproduced, in all action, however, economic or mundane. Structures of meaning are present in all the daily trivia of life and in the major adaptive decisions of human groups. Material culture patterning is formed as part of these meaningful actions and it helps to constitute changing frameworks of action and belief. The concept of wholeness from this structural point of view is more absolute and more far-reaching than in systems theory as used by archaeologists.

So beliefs are important in understanding the functional relationships between the different subsystems, and it is insufficient to place them in their own ideational subsystem. Renfrew (1972, 498) suggested that the 'symbolic', and 'constructs of the human mind', linked the functioning of the different subsystems together. Many archaeologists have made similar claims. For example, Childe (1949, 22) noted that the 'environments to which societies are adjusted are worlds of ideas, collective representations that differ not only in extent and content, but also in structure'. Thus the behavioural and adaptive interrelations, and the self-regulation, take place within a framework of ideas. The objects found by archaeologists are not just functional tools but must be treated 'always and exclusively as concrete expressions and embodiments of human thoughts and ideas' (Childe 1956, 1). But in such viewpoints there is a danger that societies, their beliefs, rules and norms, are set up as abstractions which have little relation either to practical action or to the individual. It becomes difficult to explain behavioural variability and adaptive intelligence. Such difficulties resulted, rightly, in the rejection of what was termed the 'normative' approach (Binford 1972; Willey and Sabloff 1974). If beliefs and ideas are once again to be given a central role in studies of past socio-cultural systems, theoretical consideration must be given to the individual and his daily practices in the lived world. Cultural patterning is not produced by a set of static fixed norms but is the framework within which action and adaptation have meaning; at the same time it is reproduced in those actions and in the adaptive responses that are made. There is no dichotomy between an interest in culture and meaning and a concern with adaptive variability.

Thus, in studies of ranking it *is* necessary to examine how hierarchisation works and functions, but it is also necessary to examine the meaningful context of that functioning. It is necessary to consider how the ranking is represented and presented to the individual, how beliefs are manipulated and negotiated in the changing relationships between and practices of groups within societies. There is a need to be concerned with aspects of legitimation which relate to the definition and justification of the social order. Examination must be made of forms of ideology whereby structures of signification are mobilised to legitimate specific instances of domination. While the debate over the nature of ideology in the writings of, for example, Habermas (1971) and Althusser (1969) cannot be described here, an attempt will be made to examine the implications of a concern with beliefs and ideologies for the analysis and interpretation of ranking.

A contextual approach

An archaeology in which an emphasis is placed on the particular way, in each spatial and historical context, that general symbolic and structural principles are assembled into coherent sets and integrated into social and ecological strategies can be called a 'contextual' archaeology. Such an approach incorporates at least two areas of interest. The first concerns the formal analysis of sets and the notion that culture is meaningfully constituted in the sense that each material trait is produced in relation to a set of symbolic schemes and has a meaning dependent on its place within those schemes. So the same material thing may have different meanings in different contexts. The second component of a contextual approach concerns the implementation and reconstitution of beliefs in practices, the ideological manipulation of beliefs as part of social and economic strategies, and the development of models concerning such interrelationships.

These two aspects of a contextual approach have a direct bearing on both the analytical identification of ranking in prehistory and the explanation of that ranking. Analyses of social hierarchisation, especially in its incipient stages, have been heavily dependent on burial data. From analyses of mortuary remains it is suggested that, for example, degrees of ranking in a particular society can be identified, and that the relative wealth and status of women and men can be assessed. But if it is accepted that artefacts have different meanings in different contexts, a number of difficulties emerge. For example, Pader (1980) has shown that different sections within the same Anglo-Saxon cemetery use the same artefacts in very different ways. A formal analysis of the placing of artefacts in the graves and on the bodies showed that in any one spatial segment of the cemetery an artefact type might be placed according to strict rules, but that these rules differed from area to area within the cemetery. The artefact types meant different things amongst different subgroups of the society buried within the cemetery, and any overall assessment of ranking which was based on artefact assemblages without reference to the local context and structure of use would be misleading. Similarly, things may have different meanings when associated with males as opposed to females, and it is difficult to see how the wealth or status of the one can be compared with that of the other without reference to context.

Additional problems derive from the facts that the burial context itself is different from non-burial activities and that the same material item may have a different meaning in each of the two contexts. Burial ritual may be used as part of an ideology which faithfully represents and mirrors aspects of a living society, but it is equally possible that the ideology may be concerned with distorting, obscuring, hiding or inverting particular forms of social relationships. The patterning of material remains in graves must be understood as specific to a burial and ritual context, while the relationship between patterns in life and patterns in death must itself be seen as specific to a wider cultural context. Models and generalisations about the nature of ritual activity must be examined (Turner 1969), and ethnographic studies of attitudes to death and their effects on mortuary remains must be studied and extended in ethnoarchaeology (Bloch 1971; Okely 1979; Hodder 1982). The degree of organisation and role differentiation in death does not relate directly to patterns in life. Rather there is a symbolic and ideological basis which must itself be understood. A lack of patterned role differentiation in death does not, as has been suggested by Rathje (1973) and others, necessarily imply a 'mobile' society or one that is relatively egalitarian, since in the context of the mortuary ritual distinct social differentiations may be denied or obscured (as in the case of modern Church of England burial: Parker Pearson, pers. comm.).

The general importance of examining beliefs and principles of meaning in studies of ranking in burial can be demonstrated by considering three ways in which domination might become accepted ideologically (Giddens 1979). (1) An ideology might be used to *deny* the conflict within society. It is normally in the interests of dominant groups if the existence of contradictions is denied or their real locus is obscured. (2) An ideology may represent the sectional interests of one group as the *universal interests* of the total society. So the ideas of the ruling class become the ruling ideas. (3) *Naturalisation* occurs in an ideology when the arbitrary existing system of relations appears immutable and fixed, as if they are natural laws.

Depending on the ideology, material symbols in burial could be used and could relate to ranking in different ways.

If there was an ideology of denial, we might find that the burial pattern denied the social differentiation. What goes in the graves and the associated ritual can be used as part of an ideology which makes domination acceptable by denying it. The same pattern might occur in burial when sectional interests are presented as universal – the second type of ideology. But with the third type, naturalisation, we might find that burial differentiation accurately reflects social differentiation. Indeed, *all* aspects of material culture under such an ideology might reinforce social differentiation and make it appear natural by endlessly repeating the same organisation in all spheres, down to the trivia of cooking pots, stools and hair combs. So how material culture relates to society depends on the ideological structures and symbolic codes. The archaeologist cannot disregard meaning and symbolism in analysing ranking, because behind the social system is *a structure of meaning which determines the relationship between material culture and society*.

It might be expected that the various archaeological studies of ranking which appear to be influenced, however slightly, by French structural-Marxism (Friedman and Rowlands 1977; Frankenstein and Rowlands 1978; Bender 1978: see also Haselgrove, and Gledhill and Rowlands in this volume) might give a more adequate consideration to ideologies and beliefs. Unfortunately there is so far in these writings little discussion of the specifically archaeological problems of the identification of ranking which are posed by the realisation of the importance of ideology and legitimation. In addition there is little emphasis on formal analyses and on the structure of ideas. Material culture items remain in their treatment largely utilitarian, and the emphasis is still on functional relationships.

If a contextual approach has implications for the analysis and identification of ranking, it also has significance for the explanation of changes in hierarchical differentiation. It has already been suggested that traditional explanations concern regulation and management. An evolutionary framework has been adopted in archaeology according to which it is suggested that the best adapted society is selected for survival, and survives. Some notion of 'progress' underlies all such studies in that the goal of increased ranking is to achieve some 'better' harmonisation or regulation of competing social demands and physical constraints. A contextual archaeology emphasises the importance of the historical context in that the meaning of an artefact is dependent on its history of use and in that a particular organisation of social relationships can be understood only in terms of a structural transformation from a previous phase, manipulated as part of social and ecological strategies. The nature of a change to or in ranking cannot, therefore, be predicted as a part of changing functional relationships, since it also depends on the particular cultural framework out of which the new phase is meaningfully transformed. So, while it is necessary to emphasise the particular historical context, the evolutionary analogy with the natural sciences is misleading.

The long prevalence of the evolutionary model in archaeology has allowed social change to be viewed as the empirical rearrangement of objective variables. But an adequate explanation of incipient ranking in prehistoric Europe must be concerned with more than regulation, adaptation and survival. The hierarchisation must also be seen as a development from a particular integration of actions and beliefs in a preexisting context. It is not a question of the survival of the fittest but of contextually appropriate manipulations of symbolism and conceptual schemes as part of social and ecological strategies.

Conclusion

Martins (1974, 246) describes the critique of functionalism as an initiation *rite de passage* into sociological adulthood, and I have elsewhere suggested (1981) that for archaeology to reach maturity the wider debate needs to be opened concerning the various critiques of and alternatives to the ecological functionalism which dominates prehistoric archaeology. In this paper I have indicated that any discussion of ranking should incorporate a broader perspective which includes not only functional relationships but also the structure of ideas, legitimation, beliefs and ideologies.

But there are many alternatives to a strict ecological functionalism, and it needs to be emphasised that the viewpoint put forward here is *not* structuralist. A contextual approach as defined above is not concerned with abstract formulations, with intuitive speculations about universals of the human mind, or with purely formal analyses. Rather, the aims are to examine analytical techniques and to develop usable models and analogies for studies of the integration of beliefs and practices. The concern is with particular historical contexts and with the meaningful production of material items within cultural 'wholes'. Ranking is one aspect of social systems which could benefit from studies concerned with social structure. But structure is part of a total context in which a cultural meaning is both given to ecological relationships and reproduced by them.

It has not been possible within the space of a short paper to provide numerous detailed examples of the type of analyses and models that might be involved in a contextual approach to ranking. It is apparent that any restriction of analyses to one class of data, such as mortuary remains, is to be avoided because the relationship between patterns in life and patterns in death depends on the cultural context. The rules used in generating burial practices must be analysed in relation to other spheres of activity; other 'ritual' sites, settlement organisation, types and distributions of artefacts, the organisation of prestige exchange, and so on. Transformations between the different spheres can be identified. An example of a model which might be used to interpret such transformational rules concerns societies which emphasise group purity and personal body boundaries. In certain cases, concepts of purity and pollution involve complex ritual at the life/death boundary and an emphasis on the material display of social roles in burial. In other societies without strong beliefs of this form, social differentiation at death may be less marked than in life. Models must be developed — and this will involve ethnoarchaeology to a great extent — about the way such aspects of belief are manipulated ideologically in social change and are at the same time the currency according to which such change occurs.

References

Althusser, L. 1969. *For Marx.* London, Allen Lane.

Bender, B. 1978. Gatherer–hunter to farmer. *World Archaeology* 10: 204–22.

Binford, L. 1972. *An Archaeological Perspective.* New York, Academic Press.

Bloch, M. 1971. *Placing the Dead.* London, Seminar Press.

Brumfiel, E. 1976. Regional growth in the eastern valley of Mexico: a test of the 'population pressure' hypothesis, in K.V. Flannery (ed.), *The Early Mesoamerican Village.* New York, Academic Press, 234–49.

Carneiro, R. 1970. A theory of the origin of the state. *Science* 169: 733–8.

Cherry, J. 1978. Generalisation and the archaeology of the state, in D. Green, C. Haselgrove and M. Spriggs (eds.), *Social Organisation and Settlement.* Oxford, British Archaeological Reports, 411–37.

Childe, V.G. 1949. *Social Worlds of Knowledge.* Oxford, University Press.

Childe, V.G. 1956. *Society and Knowledge.* London, George Allen and Unwin.

Crumley, C. 1976. Toward a locational definition of state systems of settlement. *American Anthropologist* 78: 59–73.

Drennan, R.D. 1976. Religion and social evolution in Formative Mesoamerica, in K.V. Flannery (ed.), *The Early Mesoamerican Village.* New York, Academic Press, 345–68.

Earle, T.K. 1977. A reappraisal of redistribution: complex Hawaiian chiefdoms, in T.K. Earle and J.E. Ericson (eds.), *Exchange Systems in Prehistory.* New York, Academic Press, 213–29.

Flannery, K.V. 1972. The cultural evolution of civilisations. *Annual Review of Ecology and Systematics* 3: 399–426.

Flannery, K.V. and Marcus, J. 1976. Formative Oaxaca and the Zapotek cosmos. *American Scientist* 64: 374–83.

Frankenstein, S. and Rowlands, M. 1978. The internal structure and regional context of early iron age society on south-western Germany. *Bulletin of the Institute of Archaeology, University of London* 15: 73–112.

Friedman, J. and Rowlands, M. (ed.) 1977. *The Evolution of Social Systems.* London, Duckworth.

Fritz, J.M. 1978. Paleopsychology today: ideational systems and human adaptation in prehistory, in C. Redman *et al.* (eds.), *Social Archaeology: Beyond Dating and Subsistence.* New York, Academic Press, 37–69.

Gall, P. and Saxe, A. 1977. The ecological evolution of culture: the state as predator in succession theory, in T.K. Earle and J.E. Ericson (eds.), *Exchange Systems in Prehistory.* New York, Academic Press, 255–68.

Giddens, A. 1979. *Central Problems in Social Theory.* London, MacMillan.

Habermas, J. 1971. *Knowledge and Human Interests.* London,, Heinemann.

Hodder, I. Towards a mature archaeology, in I. Hodder, G. Isaac and N. Hammond (eds.), *Pattern of the Past: Studies in honour of David Clarke,* Cambridge, University Press, 1–13.

Hammond (eds.), *Pattern of the Past: Studies in honour of David Clarke.* Cambridge, University Press, 67–95.

Hodder, I. 1982. *Symbols in Action.* Cambridge University Press.

Johnson, G. 1973. Local exchange and early state development in Iran. *Anthropological Papers of the Museum of Anthropology* 51. Ann Arbor, University of Michigan.

Martins, H. 1974. Time and theory in sociology, in J. Rex (ed.), *Approaches to Sociology.* London, Routledge and Kegan Paul, 246–94.

Okely, J. 1979. An anthropological contribution to the history and archaeology of an ethnic group, in B.C. Burnham and J. Kingsbury (eds.), *Space, Hierarchy and Society.* Oxford, British Archaeological Reports, 81–92.

Pader, E.J. 1980. The analysis of symbolism and social relations in mortuary remains. Unpublished manuscript, Department of Archaeology, University of Cambridge.

Peebles, C. and Kus, S. 1977. Some archaeological correlates of ranked societies. *American Antiquity* 42: 421–48.

Plog, F.T. 1975. Systems theory in archaeological research. *Annual Review of Anthropology* 4: 207–24.

Rathje, W.L. 1973. Models for mobile Maya: a variety of constraints, in C. Renfrew (ed.), *The Explanation of Culture Change.* London, Duckworth, 731–57.

Renfrew, C. 1972. *The Emergence of Civilisation.* London, Methuen.

Renfrew, C. 1975. Trade as action at a distance, in J. Sabloff and C.C. Lamberg-Karlovsky (eds.), *Ancient Civilisation and Trade.* Albuquerque, University of New Mexico Press, 3–59.

Sanders, W. and Webster, O. 1978. Unilinealism, multilinealism and the evolution of complex societies, in C. Redman *et al.* (eds.), *Social Archaeology: Beyond Dating and Subsistence.* New York, Academic Press, 249–302.

Turner, V.W. 1969. *The Ritual Process.* London, Routledge and Kegan Paul.

Willey, G.R. and Sabloff, J.A. 1974. *A History of American Archaeology.* London, Thames and Hudson.

Wright, H.T. 1977. Toward an explanation of the origin of the state, in J.N. Hill (ed.), *The Explanation of Prehistoric Change.* Albuquerque, University of New Mexico Press, 215–30.

Yoffee, N. 1979. The decline and rise of Mesopotamian civilisation. *American Antiquity* 44: 5–35.

Chapter 19

**Comments on
'explanation'**
Robert Whallon

*The papers comprising this symposium are reviewed as
a whole, and some disappointment is expressed with most of
the 'explanations' offered. It is suggested that this is largely
due to a general lack of clear and explicit understanding of
the nature of scientific explanation, and to a consequent lack
of any consistent and controlled methodology among the
papers. Most 'explanations' are characterised as inductive
generalisations, and it is suggested that little progress will be
made until this approach is altered fundamentally.*

As a discussant 'from the outside', that is, one whose
research interests and qualifications relate primarily to
societies on quite a different level of complexity, my concern
was to evaluate and comment on the papers from this symposium on general logical and methodological grounds.
Although there was much with which I was quite impressed,
I must admit a rather general disappointment, which was, I
am afraid, the stronger reaction.

On the one hand, I thoroughly applaud the considerable effort by all authors to reanalyse, reinterpret, and add
significantly to the data of European archaeology. These
data, for many periods, are very rich and consequently offer
great potential to archaeologists for the development and
testing of a multitude of models and theories. At the same
time, however, the data of European archaeology have been
analysed, synthesised, published, and taught repeatedly for

so many years that it often may require a major effort of will and conviction to initiate significant new approaches to its interpretation and understanding. Nevertheless, these papers show that this can be done, and is being done, at a gratifyingly accelerating pace.

On the other hand, I felt an equally clear disappointment with what passed for explanation, or explanatory models, in these papers, and this concern will be the focus of the rest of my comments. This is, of course, an unfairly disproportionate emphasis upon criticism, but it is by addressing such perceived problems that progress and improvement are perhaps most effectively made. These critical comments are offered, therefore, in a spirit of constructive suggestion of possible ways to improve, broaden, and put on a more rigorous footing the approaches to interpretation and explanation begun in these papers.

By way of preface, I must, of course, assume that the conscious intent or purpose of each paper was to present an *explanation* of the data discussed. The relevance and accuracy of any commentary is obviously conditional upon a correct understanding of goals and intent. In this instance, my remarks are predicated upon Renfrew's assertion that explanation was, indeed, the goal, and I therefore assume an explicit interest in explanation and explanatory models on the part of each author.

With this in mind, I find an almost overwhelming emphasis on *description* in these papers. The emphasis naturally varies, but pure description is prominent in virtually all papers, some consisting strictly of a narrative recitation of the patterns seen in some body of data over some delimited span of time. (In many cases today we may find these descriptions 'better' than earlier descriptions of the same or similar data because of a growing awareness of the importance and interest of many factors which frequently were ignored previously. This, however, does not alter their purely or essentially descriptive character.)

As 'explanations' we find a wide variety of 'models' offered. Some are nothing more than empirical generalisations from the data, but most go somewhat further and attempt to build an interpretive picture of the organisation and operation of the societies, economies, demographic processes, etc. of the places and times considered.

Most such interpretation and the building of such reconstructed pictures of former conditions, processes, and events are heavily tied to analogy. Analogy is, of course, fundamental to science as a whole, and archaeology, particularly, could not exist as a discipline without it. However, for reliable and replicable interpretation, it must be used with some care, and with explicit attention to its role and to its limitations. From this point of view, I found the use of analogy less than satisfying in the majority of these papers. Ethnographically, the analogies offered display an extremely limited familiarity with the range of organisational diversity of societies at the levels of complexity being considered. Certain apparently attractive phenomena, such as the 'big

man', have been blown into quasi-universal characteristics when, in fact, they are simply one of a number of alternative ways of organising economic flow and of maintaining different levels of social and economic control within such societies.

More pervasive and worrisome is an apparent tendency to reify the levels of organisational complexity identified by Service, Sahlins, and Fried, and to treat them as some sort of universal ethnographic description which provides definitive 'modal types' or universal analogues for all societies, past and present. Some of the papers in this present collection do indeed note this tendency and properly warn against it, but it is clearly a warning unheeded by the majority. Even the models of catastrophe theory are occasionally used, not to model, but as simple analogues to sudden changes seen in the data from the past. From all this, it is clear that there is some general misunderstanding (or at least a generally different understanding) of just what a *model* is, and exactly what *explanation* itself is.

Colloquially, 'to explain' can often mean to paint a convincing picture, one in which gaps in what actually is known may be filled by inferential reconstruction, or even by 'reasonable' conjecture. In my opinion, this is the kind of explanation we are offered in most of these papers; they give us a number of ingenious, stimulating, and frequently plausible interpretations ('explanations') of specific sets of archaeological or archaeological—historical data. But this is the point — these explanations are all specific, particularistic, and mostly *ad hoc*. A 'scientific' explanation is something more than this, something of more general significance and applicability. It covers the specific data at hand as a case in which certain general principles, processes, variables, and relationships are given particular form at a given time and place.

In other words, a scientific 'explanation' (of any given phenomenon or class of phenomena) specifies both:
(1)   the relevant and critical variables, and
(2)   the precise form of the relationships among these variables.

At the highest level, such an explanation involves variables of great generality and universal applicability and constitutes a theoretical statement. At a lower, more concrete and typically operational level, such an explanation constitutes a model. At this level, values or ranges of values may be assigned to the relevant variables, thereby determining the exact form of the model from the given relationships among these variables. The variables again are of general relevance and applicability; the model is tied explicitly to specific cases through the specification of definite values or ranges of values for these variables. At a lower level still, the specific forms taken by these variables in particular cases may be considered, and it is here that considerations other than 'scientific' explanation enter the discussion, with many, if not most, aspects of these specific forms being determined by history, geography, climate, geology, chance, etc.

Here, I think, is where the primary distinction lies between what is presented as explanation in most of these papers and what I sought as explanation in them. The distinction is between *abstraction*, in which variables and relationships of general relevance are considered, and a *particularism* in which consideration is limited to the specific variables and their given forms in individual cases. It is the latter that I find most commonly, and often exclusively, in these papers. For example, 'bronze' is not a variable, nor is 'engraved conch shell' a variable, but 'wealth', in the form of scarce goods requiring considerable investment of labour, *is* a variable.

This is not to say, of course, that the study of data and of specific forms in particular instances is not of value and often great interest. It is obviously immensely interesting to us as we investigate archaeological sequences around the world, and it is from this information that history is written. On the other hand, we are not interested simply in the facts that bronze weapons and ornaments are concentrated in a limited number of burials in the north European early bronze age, and that elaborately engraved conch shells were limited in occurrence to only a few burials in certain Mississippian mounds. We are interested also in the more general fact that 'wealth', whatever its specific form, has a restricted and highly patterned distribution in a large number of societies at many different times and places. It is this general fact that is comparable among societies and which can be tested for correlation with other aspects of these societies and their environments. Thus, it is from such general facts (variables and the relationships among them) that universal, explanatory models and, ultimately, theory must be built.

What I would like to suggest, then, is that the authors of most of these papers are tied too closely to their data. They are too immersed in the substantive details of these data and the problems of their description and synthesis to come to grips directly with the question of explanation. A few papers do refer to general variables, and one or two actually do broach the question of general, abstract model-building in which data are used explicitly to test the models in question. With these few exceptions, however, attempts at explanation in these papers are all made inductively, by generalisation from the specific cases and data at hand. Will this approach to the explanation of archaeological data, multiplied, refined, expanded, and so on, in fact bring us much further toward the emergence of general, explanatory models or toward theory, however? I would venture to predict not, and see this as a classic case of trying to build theory 'from the bottom up', that is, by inductive generalisation from the data, a procedure generally recognised by practitioners and philosophers of science alike as ultimately frustrating and ineffective.

On the contrary, theory is built by theorising, and explanatory models are built by model-building — both processes of abstract, logical reasoning and not of empirical research. Models and theory cannot be created 'from the bottom up', but require abstraction, or distance from any set of data. 'Explanation' thus takes place on two levels, the abstract level at which the general understanding of organisation and process is developed, and the particularistic level at which specific historical, geographical, etc. causes are sought for the specific forms in which this organisation and process are manifested in particular cases. Recognition of this distinction and of the existence of these two levels of discourse and explanation would be an important methodological step in our field. However, the important distinction between these two levels, and the different forms of argument and reasoning they require, are scarcely recognised, if at all, in the papers here.

A notable consequence of the lack of recognition of this distinction is the variety of ways in which 'explanations' are developed in the various papers. The pervasive use of analogies in inductive generalisation has been noted. However, the ways in which analogy is used, and the particular analogies selected, are remarkably diverse. There is a range from quite specific references to certain cultures or forms of organisation, and to certain mathematical models, on the one hand, to the Service—Sahlins—Fried levels of socio-cultural complexity on the other, and a frequent, implicit use of 'common sense' or simple opinion in some papers.

My worry here is not simply that little care is taken in the development of arguments by analogy. The point is, rather, that we find an uncontrolled mixing of particularistic and abstract, of specific and general, without recognition of the different levels or kinds of reasoning and argument necessary in either case. The consequence is a lack of any uniform principles of interpretation or argumentation. The examples here run the gamut from flat assertion of opinion to clearly developed testing of an abstract, general model, most falling indifferently somewhere in between these extremes. With no principles of interpretation and argumentation, we are assured that the likelihood is high that other archaeologists would make something quite different of the data in any one of these cases.

However, what is important and of concern to us if processual 'explanation' truly is our goal, is not that such interpretations would vary, but that we would have little or no idea as to *why* they would vary. Consequently, we would be unable rigorously and comparatively to evaluate the different interpretations, and we would have little or no control over the development of 'better' interpretations or explanation. Clearly, the development of better explanatory interpretations of archaeological data is not a function of more, or more detailed, examination of the data themselves, but of the development of new *ways* of examining the data. Yet these 'ways', that is, the principles behind examining the data, here being almost universally *implicit*, and often involving a mixture of approaches to different levels of phenomena, are, in fact, largely inaccessible. Such principles can be developed, in these circumstances, only in a 'hit-or-miss', trial-and-error fashion.

By way of example, I should like to mention briefly one area of research in our field, known particularly well to me, in which some distinct progress is being made both toward what I here have called theory, and in the derivation from this emergent explanatory theory of the more specific models which allow the theory to be tested against empirical data by evaluating the degree to which any relevant example may be predicted by, i.e., subsumed under, this theory as a particular case. I refer to the work of Jochim (1976) and Keene (1979; forthcoming) on hunter—gatherer subsistence systems. Simplifying greatly the extensive and detailed presentations and arguments of their research, Jochim developed the general, theoretical proposition that hunter—gatherer subsistence was structured according to two principles: the 'Simon satisficer' criterion for decision-making as modelled in game theory, and the 'law of least effort' (1976, ch. 1). These two theoretical propositions say nothing about the real world, however, until they are tied to specific situations through the development of models that specify both the particular criteria to be satisfied and the returns obtained per unit effort in the procurement of various alternative resources which might be exploited to satisfy these criteria. It was at the level of this specific model-building that Jochim had the greatest difficulty, and although a number of relatively effective measures were developed, both for the subsistence criteria to be satisfied and for returns for effort expended, he was forced in a few aspects of his work to rely on descriptive models inductively derived from ethnographic data (Jochim 1976, ch. 3). Keene's critical contribution to the explanation of hunter—gatherer subsistence patterns was to identify more accurately a set of theoretically specifiable subsistence criteria to be satisfied — essentially, a spectrum of human nutritional requirements that can be measured and predicted directly from our knowledge of human physiology and the climatic conditions in which a population lives (Keene, forthcoming; 1979, 375, table 16.4). Keene further refined the application of the law of least effort to the explanation of hunter—gatherer subsistence patterns by showing how a form of mathematical modelling applied to a series of resource 'costs', measured as functions of resource density, mobility, aggregation, and risk entailed in procurement, could predict optimal solutions to the problem of satisfying specified nutritional requirements.

Note that Jochim's and Keene's fundamental theoretical principles that 'explain' hunter—gatherer subsistence patterns, through identification of the critical variables to be considered and through the specification of their relations of effective 'satisfaction' and minimisation, are context-free. Their application to particular cases is effected through the measurement or estimation of the values of these variables in a given case and the application of the appropriate methods (mathematical in Jochim's and Keene's approach) for the derivation of the consequent predictions, or *model*, of subsistence patterns. The *explanatory theory* here is thus universal in applicability and can be used to model hunter—gatherer subsistence in any conceivable climatic situation with any conceivable array of available resources. I am sure that both Jochim and Keene would insist that innumerable points demand clarification, refinement, or revision in their work. Nonetheless, I believe that their work provides a good example of both explanation and modelling as I have referred to them here, and of an effective approach to theory-building in at least one small part of the range of variability in cultural systems, the explanation of which I take to be the ultimate goal of our discipline.

My conclusion, therefore, is an exhortation to those who profess explanation as their goal in this field to distinguish clearly between the particularistic work that is required for the reconstruction of culture history and the abstract business of model-building and theorising. Although 'history does not repeat itself', processes do (Pred 1973, 286). Thus, history may be built from data, but theory is built by theorising.[1]

Note

1 I would like to thank my wife, Barbara Segraves-Whallon, for her helpful comments, suggestions, and corrections. My perversity, however, in not heeding all her good advice must be held responsible for the flaws remaining in these 'comments'.

References

Jochim, M.A. 1976. *Hunter—Gatherer Subsistence and Settlement: A Predictive Model*. New York, Academic Press.

Keene, A.S. 1979. Economic optimization models and the study of hunter—gatherer subsistence settlement systems, in C. Renfrew and K. Cooke (eds.), *Transformations: Mathematical Approaches to Culture Change*. New York, Academic Press, 369—404.

Keene, A.S., forthcoming. Models for the study of prehistoric diet, in R.L. Gilbert and J.H. Mielke (eds.), *Techniques for the Analysis of Prehistoric Diets*. Oxford, Miss., University Press of Mississippi.

Pred, A.R. 1973. *Urban Growth and the Circulation of Information: The United States System of Cities, 1790—1840*. Cambridge, Mass., Harvard University Press.

PART VI

Epilogue

Chapter 20

**Meaning, inference and
the material record**
Lewis R. Binford

The papers assembled here represent a major shift in interests from what we might have heard from a similar group ten to fifteen years ago. Most of the papers address a body of data which the authors believe in one way or another reflects on the ideas they are using to 'understand' processes which operated to bring about transformations in ancient society. Emphasis is generally placed on the appearance of ranking and/or other institutional forms of social inequality.

These are, of course, interests in process, in dynamics, the active characteristics of living systems. Archaeologists dig up static mute things, mere arrangements of matter; how may such things realistically speak to such issues?

I tend to think of what archaeologists do when engaged in intellectual activity as largely understandable in terms of relatively few operations. I will present these conceptual guides to viewing archaeologists' activity and see how the papers tend to group when viewed from these perspectives.

The first major distinction I make is between *what the world is like and why it is that way*. When we are engaged in making statements as to what the world is like we are using a paradigm or an observational language to relate how the world appears to us. For us as archaeologists there is a kind of dual challenge since what the world is like takes two forms: one is an orientation toward the archaeological record which is contemporary and with us in the here-and-now. We fre-

quently wish to describe the characteristics of this 'world'. On the other hand, being archaeologists, we wish to talk about the world of the past, we wish to say what that world was like. Both of these are descriptive tasks but tasks which place very different intellectual demands upon us. In the former case we may use an observational language which appeals to general experiences with the world of everyday experience. We may talk of colour, size, shape, number of items, association, covariation, and all manner of other properties of the archaeological record. The utility of the descriptive devices which we use are evaluated through the interaction which occurs between the world of experience and the words we use to assimilate these experiences meaningfully. Things are not so simple when we face the task of describing the past. The observational language which we use quite literally falls on deaf ears as far as permitting us to interact with experience is concerned: the past is gone, mute and only recognisable as such through inference. We cannot use a 'direct' strategy of describing the past. All our experience is in the present and all the normal ways of evaluating our observational language or our cognitive devices for giving meaning to experience are also restricted to the present; the past cannot cry out and protest against our descriptions. It cannot intrude itself on our ways of thinking since it is passive and mute. Quite literally, our descriptions of the past are constructions. The accuracy of such inventions can only be evaluated by evaluating our 'observational language', our intellectual tools for inference – in short, our methods.

In addition to these descriptive interests we as archaeologists are interested in understanding, in seeking answers to the 'why' questions of why the world is the way it appears to be. When we ask such questions we are seeking explanations, we are seeking a kind of understanding which goes beyond an unweighted description of the world; we want to know what makes the world work the way it appears to. When we address such questions we are demanding of ourselves a different kind of intellectual endeavour. We are demanding the use of our creative powers to imagine the links of determinant interaction, the 'causal' links if you will, which glue together the dynamics of experience and render it both understandable and capable of being anticipated. This concern with causation, determinacy, is the context of *theory building*.

The reader will recognise that I have not yet used a word which is quite current in archaeology and other social sciences, that is, *Model*. In archaeology, this word refers to a wide variety of intellectual products. Much of its ambiguous usage derives from a failure to recognise some of the distinctions which I have suggested thus far. For instance in archaeology, a model is frequently 'built' of what the past was like. This is a speculative description of the past. This is frequently accomplished by using certain, largely implicit, assumptions as to how the world is in general. Such conceptualisations of the past are at least minimally based on some conditions in the present, some properties of experience which can be assumed also to have characterised the past. In a more technical sense these are frequently characterised as uniformitarian assumptions. That is, at least with respect to some properties, the past is considered to be similar to the present. (See Binford 1981 for a more detailed discussion of such assumptions.) I would suggest that the accuracy with which we can infer the past is directly related to the degree that our uniformitarian assumptions are justifiable. Concern with the justification of such assumptions and with the development of strongly warranted means for giving meaning to our contemporary observations made on the archaeological record is what I have called middle range research. I detect very little concern with this area of archaeological research in these papers. More are engaged in building models of the past which if 'true' would accommodate the particular 'facts' of each author's case as described. No methods for inferring past conditions independently of the nascent theories of dynamics are evident. In short no operational objectivity (see Binford 1982) seems to have been achieved.

This is not unique to those concerned with complex societies, nor to the British, but I find it interesting that there appears to be little recognition of the problems which are, strictly speaking, archaeological and revolve around our use of archaeological observations either for gaining a knowledge of the past or for rendering the past accessible for

testing ideas we might have regarding the way the world works.

As state-of-the-art type comments, many of these papers seek to build models of the past for accommodating certain 'cases' which are summarised as currently archaeologically described; yet there is little concern with the actual methods of inference which permit one to move from descriptive statements about the archaeological record to descriptive statements about the past. About the only hints of concern in this regard have to do with the 'interpretation' of mortuary data. The inference of ranking and various social inequalities is seemingly linked almost exclusively to mortuary arguments.

Most of these papers are models in the sense of 'pictures' of the past where the methods for 'viewing' have not yet been seriously addressed.

In situations where 'model' building is common, I have found that those building the model feel that the internal 'logic' of the presentation is compelling, and hence their position appears 'self-evident' and clear. Such a view is generally derived from having adopted a methodology, yet being totally innocent or unselfconscious relative to the assumptions inherent in the methods used in such situations.

I have found that one of the most revealing diagnostic tactics for looking at theories and models is to examine the character of the uniformitarian assumptions inherent in the arguments, in spite of the suggestions by some archaeologists that we must avoid such assumptions (Gould 1980). Avoidance is methodologically impossible in any situation of inference. We must have what A.N. Whitehead (1932, 188) has termed the 'eternal objects', the common points of reference between our experience and the 'past', if we are to reason to the past in any realistic sense.

From the perspective of the types of uniformitarian assumptions which are well represented in these papers I find them very 'historical' in character. When I use the term 'historical' I am not referring to their concern with the past nor to their emphasis on chronicle, nor even to the degree to which they are particularlistic or exhibit more generalising interests (see Carr 1961 for a debunking of such ideas). Such characteristics are not unique to history, for instance, as distinct from anthropology etc. In general what I find most common to historians is the character of their uniformitarian assumptions. Most often historians treat 'human' events and the 'human' past, and consequently they make the assumption of a common and constant human mentality. The uniformitarian assumptions which historians make most commonly are about the 'nature' of man.

> . . . the ordinary historian . . . according to him, all history properly so called is the history of human affairs . . . The archaeologist's use of his stratified relics depends on his conceiving them as artifacts serving human purposes and then expressing a particular way in which men have thought about their own life . . .
> (Collingwood 1956, 212)

Under this view the past is a 'human' past and the only way that we could make inferences to the past from the products of human behaviour would be through an understanding of 'human nature' itself.

> When a man thinks historically, he has before him certain documents or relics of the past. His business is to discover what the past was which has left these relics behind . . . this means discovering the thought (in the widest sense of that word . . .) which is expressed by them. To discover what this thought was, the historian must think it again for himself. (Collingwood 1956, 282–3)

This approach has been called the method of empathetic understanding, and it should be clear that the uniformitarian assumptions being made are about our own psychic propensities under differing conditions.

This seems to be the major methodology when giving meaning to many of the mortuary 'facts' cited in many of the papers in this volume. We hear appeals to prestige, rivalry, display, conspicuous consumption, etc., all of which in the long run postulate a kind of universalistic psychological response to social conditions. Similarly, there is a variety of arguments which range between strict 'formalist' and 'substantivist' views on economics, both of which rest in the final analysis on assumptions about the behavioural playing out of 'human' motives through economising decisions. On the more formalist side there are what appear as rather direct appeals to the 'profit motive' and the entrepreneurs' world view. These are all variously disguised statements about 'human nature' or what a 'reasonable man' might be expected to do under various conditions.

These approaches are in direct conflict with views commonly associated with the 'anthropological' position. Under arguments advanced which might be associated with a more traditional anthropological viewpoint was the view that our feelings, our ways of thinking, our ways of responding to the world were conditioned by *our cultural context*; therefore, we could not project *our* responses onto actors in different cultures at different times or under changes in cultural conditions. According to the anthropological view, the use of the methods of 'empathetic understanding' was an ethnocentric approach and not defensible. As I read Hodder's paper this seems to be his message. He appears to have noted the same thing that I have, namely that much of the discussion regarding the meaning to be given to the past as seen through the archaeological record is proceeding with a 'historian's' bias as rendered plausible through the use of the methods of empathetic understanding. He is insisting on the positions argued by Franz Boas (1940) and other leaders of the anthropological reaction against ethnocentrism and racism.

Hodder's version is of course 'culturally' updated and drips with Parsonian idealism. In fact, Hodder appears to adopt for archaeology a British view of social anthropology.

The anthropologist is concerned with a systematic

understanding of what he sees . . . He learns the culture, as he learns the language of the people . . . The first step is to find out . . . the meaning which people themselves attach to what they do . . . In short, the work of the social anthropologist may be regarded as an . . . act of translation in which the author and translator collaborate. (Pocock 1961, 85–8)

As Hodder realises, the 'authors' are long since gone, so the character of the 'translation' rests solely with the translator. This 'realisation' leads inevitably to his denial of objectivity, to the claim that we practise an art, and the assertion that all insight into the past is subjective.

This, of course, is not even logical unless one accepts the proposition that:

> All archaeological data are expressions of human thoughts and purposes and are valued only as revelations thereof. (Childe 1962, 10–11)

> It is the mediate agency of a mind that brings about the cultural relationships between cultural products. (Taylor 1948, 143)

Hodder's appeals for the consideration of cultural context are surprisingly reminiscent of Taylor's analogous appeals (see Taylor 1948, 1972). They both seem to derive from a complete acceptance of the Parsonian equations of culture with ideas (see Harris (1979, 279) for a discussion of this issue). Of course, once such a position is adopted, *no* methodology of inference appears possible which does not adopt the method of 'empathetic understanding'. If this is rejected all science also must be rejected.

While Hodder's criticism of much that is presented in contemporary archaeology is valid, since it is uncommonly lucid with respect to ethnographic analogy and empathetic assumptions, I should hope that no one would be misled into following Hodder's 'remedial' suggestion. *We do not have to try to study mental phenomena. In fact we study material phenomena.* We study material things, matter in various forms and arrangements. To equate these forms, distributions and patterns of association with an ideational 'system' seems to be strange at best. Systems of adaptation are material systems composed of matter and energy sources. Information may be important in organising and integrating a system, but it is not the system. Culturally organised systems of adaptation are no less concrete and materialistic. They are composed of things, places, persons, resources, communication channels, energy pipelines, etc. We do not find 'fossilised' ideas, we find the arrangements of material which derive from the operation of a system of adaptation culturally integrated at some level. I don't have to know how the participants thought about the system to investigate it as a system of adaptation in a knowable natural world. That is, I fully recognise that we are not observing a purely 'practical' system given in terms of some universalistic assumptions of reason or practicality deriving from a 'rational' human nature. Only when we can view culturally organised phenomena against a backdrop of phenomena not subject to culturally organised variability can we gain an appreciation for cultural properties themselves. I do not have to know how the participants thought about the system to investigate those very properties.

Only when you insist that the sole uniformitarian principle which can link the present and the past is 'human nature' do you get into the relativists' trap which Hodder is inviting archaeologists to enter (see Habermas 1971). On the other hand, most archaeologists have not shed the idealist baggage they inherited from the last century. The methods of empathetic understanding will not work in seeking explanations for cultural differences and similarities. I simply don't know what it was like to think like a Neanderthal man, in spite of Hodder's implied claim that he could perhaps achieve such contextual empathy. Fortunately this is not necessary. We can study properties of adaptation, properties of organisations involving energy demands for maintenance, reproduction and growth. The appearance of complex systems was among other things a growth process; it was a process of internal differentiation. We need to get down to the task of studying material systems.

While doing so we must become much more self-aware and face quite squarely the methodological problems of inference from which the silly equation of artefacts with fossilised ideas protected us in blissful naivety for so many years. Truly archaeologists must lose their 'innocence' (Clarke 1973).

I commented in Philadelphia after listening to these papers that this is a 'long way from Beaker Folk'. I have suggested here that clearly the concern with social evolution and a desire for explanations of major transformations, such as the appearance of ranking, are new domains of discourse for archaeologists. There is some indication, as in Hodder's appeals for a 'new' cultural relativism, and in some of the arguments which appear to be rather straightforward 'formalist' economic positions, that we need to do some catching up with events which have already been argued in anthropology and the social sciences in general. Fortunately, in our ontogeny we don't have to recapitulate phylogeny. We don't have to make all of those old mistakes with 'wide-eyed' enthusiasm. Clearly in moving away from discussions of the 'Beaker Folk' to considerations of why ranking or stratification came into being we have lost some innocence; we now need to lose much more if we are going to use the archaeological record to the fullest in furthering the evaluation of our explanatory ideas and in providing the only truly important body of relevant facts regarding long-term evolutionary processes. We need to abandon the idealist view, we need to stop trying to reconstruct the past largely by using historical methods of empathetic understanding.

These papers represent a kind of intellectual push—pull, where Hodder seeks to draw the field off into subjectivism and idealism, while Rowlands and Gledhill are beckoning with a very cautious materialistic call (see Friedman 1974).

In between these poles are almost all the intellectual legacies of western economics; we heard a full-blown Adam Smith approach to economics where land is viewed as the source of wealth and power. Similarly we saw the idea of sharing risk developed into a near Hobbesian contract in the 'social storage' argument. At the other end of the economic spectrum that old standby of the west, the 'free enterprise' system, was clearly on centre stage in many of the models presented. Most of these arguments lack the level of sophistication currently evident in debate in much of social science (Sahlins 1976; Harris 1979; Godelier 1977).

Nevertheless, there is no question but that we are now 'participating' in the discussions of central interest to social scientists. We need to 'clean up our act' so that the wealth of past experience can realistically be brought to bear in evaluating some of the ideas we heard used in these papers. Archaeology seems to be in the middle of a major set of changes in which 'learning to do science' is a painful process. I am of the opinion that the rewards will be well worth the struggle.

References

Binford, L.R. 1977. General introduction, in L.R. Binford (ed.), *For Theory Building in Archaeology*. New York, Academic Press, 1–10.

Binford, L.R. 1981. *Bones: Ancient Men and Modern Myths*. New York, Academic Press.

Binford, L.R. 1982. Objectivity, explanation, and archaeology 1980, in C. Renfrew, M.J. Rowlands and B. Segraves-Whallon (eds.), *Theory and Explanation in Archaeology*. New York, Academic Press.

Boas, F. 1940. *Race, Language and Culture*. New York, Free Press.

Carr, E.H. 1961. *What is History?* New York, Vintage Books–Random House.

Childe, V.G. 1962. *A Short Introduction to Archaeology*. New York, Collier Books, Macmillan Co.

Clarke, D.L. 1973. Archaeology: the loss of innocence. *Antiquity* 47: 6–18.

Collingwood, R G. 1956. *The Idea of History*. Oxford, University Press.

Friedman, J. 1974. Marxism, structuralism and vulgar materialism. *Man* 9: 444–69.

Godelier, M. 1977. *Perspectives in Marxist Anthropology*. Cambridge, University Press.

Gould, R.A. 1980. *Living Archaeology*. Cambridge, University Press.

Habermas, J. 1971. *Knowledge and Human Interests*. Boston, Beacon Press.

Harris, M. 1979. *Cultural Materialism*. New York, Random House.

Pocock, D.F. 1961. *Social Anthropology*. London, Sheed and Ward.

Sahlins, M. 1976. *Culture and Practical Reason*. Chicago, University Press.

Taylor, W.W. 1948. A study of archaeology. *American Anthropologist* 50(3), part 2, Memoir Number 69.

Taylor, W.W. 1972. Old wine and new skins: a contemporary parable, in M.P. Leone (ed.), *Contemporary Archaeology*. Carbondale, Southern Illinois University Press.

Whitehead, A.N. 1932. *Science and the Modern World*. Cambridge, University Press.

INDEX

For EU product safety concerns, contact us at Calle de José Abascal, 56–1°,
28003 Madrid, Spain or eugpsr@cambridge.org.

www.ingramcontent.com/pod-product-compliance
Ingram Content Group UK Ltd.
Pitfield, Milton Keynes, MK11 3LW, UK
UKHW030904150625
459647UK00025B/2883